BROKEN MUSIC

For Luzzi

Ursula Block
Michael Glasmeier

BROKEN MUSIC
ARTISTS' RECORDWORKS

Primary Information – daadgalerie Berlin – gelbe Musik

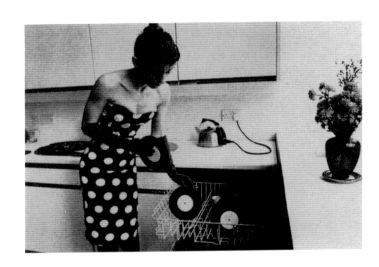

H e r m i n e   P e r f o r m s   t h e   W a s h i n g - u p

Vor wenigen Tagen erhielt ich eine Postkarte nach einer Fotografie, auf der Hermine
zu sehen ist, wie sie Schallplatten in eine
Geschirrspülmaschine einordnet. Diese
scheinbar absurde Handlung, die jeden
Musikfreund mit schierem Entsetzen erfüllen
muß, hat mich an die Zeit meiner ersten
Berührug mit diesen wunderbaren Objekten
erinnert. Ich war etwa dreizehn Jahre alt als
ich - ohne jedoch ein Abspielgerät zu besitzen - begann, die 1955 noch gebräuchli-
chen, leicht zerbrechlichen Schellackplatten
zu sammeln. Ich erhielt diese von einem

A few days ago I received a postcard, a
photograph on which Hermine stacks
records in a dishwashing machine. This
seemingly absurd act, which must horrify
every music lover, reminded me of my first
contact with these wonderful objects. I was
about thirteen years old when I - not owning
a record-player - started to collect the fragile
shellack discs which were still in use in
1955. I got these from a friend whose father
ran a cinema, they usually had no protective
cover and were scratched and dusty. So I
washed the records in warm soapy water

Il y a quelques jours j'ai reçu une carte postale, une photographie qui représente Hermine rangeant des disques dans un lave-
vaisselle. Cette acte en apparence absurde
et à la vue de duquel tout ami de la musique doit trembler d'effroi m'a rappelé
l'époque de mon premier contact avec ce
merveilleux objet. J'avais environ treize ans
lorsque je commençai - je n'avais pas de
tourne-disque - à collectionner ces disques
fragiles de gomme laque encore en usage
en 1955. Un ami dont le père possédait un
cinéma me les procurait; ils me parvenaient

Freund, dessen Vater ein Kino betrieb, in der Regel ohne Schutzhüllen und daher angekratzt und verstaubt. So wusch ich die Platten in warmer Seifenlauge und rieb sie anschließend kräftig trocken. Und, da dies für lange Zeit die einzige Möglichkeit war, meine Zuneigung zu der in den geheimnisvollen Rillen verborgenen Musik auszudrücken, wusch ich sie häufiger und häufiger.

Das erste "Abspielgerät" entstand etwas später aus einem Metallbaukasten, mit dessen Hilfe sich die Rotationsmechanik herstellen ließ. Der eigene Arm wurde zum "Tonarm", eine dünne Stricknadel in der Hand haltend. Und es bereitete unbeschreibliche Freude, diesen schwarzen Scheiben einen Ton oder gar eine Folge von Tönen zu entlocken. Es mußte absolut still im Raum sein, und nur, wenn man das Ohr sehr dicht an die Nadel hielt, war zu verstehen, daß der Musiktitel vorab angesagt wurde: "Sie hören jetzt das Ave Maria von Bach-Gounod aus dem gleichnamigen Gloria-Film". Zerbrach eine Platte bei der Prozedur, wurde sie wieder zusammengeklebt ...

Welch ein großes Vergnügen nach vielen Jahren zu entdecken, daß sich einige Komponisten und vor allem aber bildende Künstler auf ähnlich ungewöhnliche Weise mit Schallplatten beschäftigen: sie verfremden, zerstören, collagieren oder einfach anders benutzen.

Die von Ursula Block und Michael Glasmeier für die daadgalerie zusammengetragene Austellung *Broken Music* stellt in bisher einzigartiger Dichte und Ausführlichkeit Zeugnisse dieser Auseinandersetzung von Künstlern mit dem Medium vor, wie auch der hier vorliegende Katalog dieses Phänomen akribisch genau und zum ersten Mal umfassend beschreibt.

Dank gilt allen Leihgebern, die ihre Schallplatten und Objekte für die Ausstellung zur Verfügung stellten. Insbesondere sei Hanns Sohm gedankt, ohne dessen Informationen und rare Schätze das Projekt in dieser Vollständigkeit nicht hätte realisiert werden können. Einige der beteiligten Künstler installierten Arbeiten eigens für die Ausstellung.

In den Dank an die Organisatoren der Ausstellung und Herausgeber des Katalogs schließt das Berliner Künstlerprogramm alle Mitarbeiter an diesem Projekt ein, die ein mehr als sonst übliches Maß an Geduld und Liebe zur Sache aufbringen mußten. Dank gilt auch dem Kunstfond e.V., Bonn, für die initiale finanzielle Unterstützug und dem Senator für Kulturelle Angelegenheiten, der das Projekt im Rahmen des Festivals Neuer Musik Berlin INVENTIONEN '89 förderte.

Besonders freuen wir uns über das ungewöhnlich große Interesse der zahlreichen Galeriebesucher und die Absicht des Gemeentemuseums Den Haag und des Magasin Grenoble, Ausstellung und Katalog zu übernehmen.

Berlin, am letzten Tag der Ausstellung
René Block

and vigorously rubbed them dry. For a long time this was the only way to express my affection for the music hidden in those mysterious grooves, and I washed them over and over again.

The first "player" was created a little later with the help of a steel construction set which included the necessary parts to build the rotary mechanism. My arm was the tone arm; my hand, holding a knitting needle, was the pickup. I got an indescribable thrill whenever I could elicit a sound or even a sequence of sounds from the black discs. The room had to be absolutely quiet, and only when the ear was very close to the needle, could I decipher that the titles were announced: "You will now hear the Ave Maria by Bach-Gounod from the Gloria-Film with the same title". When a record broke during this procedure, it was glued together again.

What a great pleasure to discover after so many years, that some composers and most of all visual artists treat records in a similarly unusual way: to alienate, destroy, paste together or simply to use them differently.

The exhibition *Broken Music*, which has been collected for the daadgalerie by Ursula Block and Michael Glasmeier, testifies in a hitherto unique density and completeness to this relationship between the artists and the medium. The catalogue on hand describes this phenomena meticulously and for the first time comprehensively. Thanks to all lenders, who placed their records and objects at our disposal for the duration of the exhibition. Special acknowledgement to Hanns Sohm, without whose information and rare treasures this project in its completeness could not have been realized. Some of the participating artists installed works especially for the exhibition.

The Berliner Künstlerprogramm wants to express its gratitude to the organizers of the exhibition and publishers of the catalogue, including all who worked on this project and had to summon a great degree of patience and love for the cause, above and beyond the usual.

Thanks also to the Kunstfond e.V., Bonn, for their initial financial support and to the Senator für Kulturelle Angelegenheiten, who supported the project within the festival Neuer Musik Berlin INVENTIONEN '89.

We are especially happy about the unusual great interest of the numerous gallery visitors and about the intention of the Gemeentemuseum Den Haag and of the Magasin Grenoble to take over the exhibition and catalogue.

Berlin, the last day of the exhibition

normalement sans l'enveloppe et, il va de soi, rayés et empoussiérés. Je les lavais donc dans de l'eau chaude et savonneuse avant de les assécher vigoureusement. Et, étant donné que pendant longtemps cela fut la seule possibilité que j'avais d'exprimer mon penchant pour la musique que cachaient ces mystérieux sillons, je les lavais de plus en plus souvent.

Un peu plus tard vint le premier "tourne-disque" dont le mécanisme de rotation fut fabriqué à l'aide d'un jeu de construction en métal. Muni d'une fine aiguille à tricoter, un de mes membres supérieurs servait de "bras" à l'appareil. Et je ressentais une joie indescriptible à extraire de ces plaques noires un son, voire une séquence de sons. Un silence absolu devait régner dans la pièce et il n'était possible de percevoir ce que promettait l'étiquette qu'en tenant son oreille très près de l'aiguille: "Vous entendez maintenant l'Ave Maria de Bach-Gounod provenant du film Gloria du même nom". Si un disque se brisait lors de cet opération, il était tout simplement recollé...

Quelle bonheur de découvrir après plusieurs années que des compositeurs et surtout des peintres ou des sculpteurs s'intéressent aux disques d'une manière tout aussi inusitée: ils les transforment, les détériorent, en font des collages ou leur donnent une autre fonction.

L'exposition *Broken Music* préparée par Ursula Block et Michael Glasmeier pour la daadgalerie présente des documents témoignant de l'intérêt des artistes pour ce médium qu'est le disque; à l'exemple du catalogue qui l'accompagne elle décrit ce phénomène avec une grande minutie et pour la première fois dans toute son étendue. Nous remercions toutes les personnes qui ont bien voulu prêter des disques ou des objets pour l'exposition. Mention particulière doit être faite de Hanns Sohm dont les informations et les précieux trésors ont permis de donner plus d'ampleur au projet. Quelques-uns des artistes participants ont installé des travaux qu'ils ont spécialement adaptés à l'espace de la galerie.

Le Künstlerprogramm de la DAAD à Berlin tient à exprimer sa reconnaissance à plusieur personnes. D'abord aux organisateurs de l'exposition et éditeurs du catalogue, aux collaborateurs qui ont fait preuve d'une patience et d'un dévouement extraordinaires; au Deutscher Kunstfond e.V. de Bonn pour son aide financière initiale et au sénateur responsable des affaires culturelles qui a inscrit le projet dans le cadre des INVENTIONEN 89, le festival de nouvelle musique de Berlin.

Nous nous réjouissons particulièrement du grand intérêt qu'ont montré les nombreux visiteurs et de l'intention du Gemeentemuseum de la Hague et du Magasin de Grenoble de reprendre l'exposition et le catalogue.

Berlin, le dernier jour de l'exposition

Ursula Block

Broken Music
oder
His Master's Noise

Broken Music zeigt Arbeiten bildender Künstler, die mit dem und für das Medium Schallplatte entstanden sind: Schallplatten, Schallplattenhüllen, Schallplattenobjekte, Schallplatteninstallationen. Im Gegensatz zum Komponisten oder Musiker, der die Schallplatte zuallererst als ein seine musikalischen Ideen zu transportierendes Vehikel begreift, interessiert den bildenden Künstler besonders die sowohl optische wie auch akustische Präsenz der Schallplatte. Anfang der 60er Jahre nannte Milan Knížák seine Schallplattencollagen *Broken Music* - indem er Schallplatten zerstörte, bemalte, beklebte und zerbrach - brach er gleichzeitig mit den konventionellen Hörgewohnheiten. *Broken Music* steht für ein Brechen mit überkommenen Vorstellungen als Aufbruch zu etwas Neuem. Dieser Ansatz - etwas vereinfachend zwar, aber gerade deswegen schlüssig - schien überzeugend genug, um die ganze Ausstellung darunter zusammenzufassen.

Von konkretem musikalischen Material ausgehend versteht Knížák sich als Komponist. (Wie mit Schallplatten geht er auch mit Partituren um. Das Arditti String Quartet spielte nach einer seiner Partiturcollagen die dem Katalog beiliegende Flexidisc ein.)

"Ich war nicht interessiert an irgendeiner schon existierenden Musik - so mußte ich meine eigene machen", erklärte Jean Dubuffet. Er 'machte' diese mit den einfachsten technischen Hilfsmitteln. Auf eine später mögliche Perfektionierung verzichtete er ganz bewußt. Die ungeglätteten Klänge entsprachen eher seiner musikalischen Vision und standen in unmittelbarem Zusammenhang mit seinem bildnerischen Werk.

Neben Knížák und Dubuffet nehmen Künstler wie Laszlo Moholy-Nagy, Marcel Duchamp, John Cage, Nam June Paik und Lawrence Weiner und ebenso die jüngeren Christian Marclay und Piotr Nathan Schlüsselpositionen im kreativen Umgang mit der Schallplatte ein. Die Ausstellung versucht diese Positionen zu markieren und so weit wie möglich deren historische Wurzeln auszumachen.

Sie zeigt Beispiele einer originalen Schallplattenmusik u.a. von Knížák, Marclay und Boyd Rice, die Moholy-Nagy theoretisch wie auch praktisch vorbereitete. Er suchte nach Möglichkeiten, seine Kompositionen direkt auf die unbearbeitete Schallplatte zu gravieren. (Siehe auch seinen Aufsatz in diesem Katalog).

Viele der ausgestellten Schallplatten funktionieren einfach wie akustische Erinnerungen oder Dokumente, so bei Schwitters, Yves Klein, Karel Appel, Allan Kaprow, Wolf Vostell oder der *selten gehörten Musik*. Andere Schallplattenobjekte entstanden aus einem Spiel mit dem Wort Schall-Platte oder auch daraus, technische Begriffe wörtlich umzusetzen: *Aus einer LP ausgekoppelte Single* (Claus Böhmler) oder *Liszten!* (Stuart Sherman) einer Schallplatte, die sich halb aus der Partitur und halb aus der Schallplattenaufnahme einer Komposition von Franz Liszt zusammensetzt.

In einem Raum ist John Cages *33 1/3*, eine Komposition für 12 Plattenspieler und circa 100 Schallplatten, realisiert. Die Ausstellungsbesucher sind zu kompositorischem Spiel aufgefordert: aus konkretem Material, den 100 Schallplatten, jedes Mal wieder etwas Neues entstehen zu lassen.

Mit Nam June Paiks Klangskulptur *Random Access* (Schallplattenschaschlik) steht jedermann ähnliches 'Komponieren' frei, in diesem Fall sogar mit einem frei beweglichen Tonarm.

Zwischen Visuellem und Akustischem findet eine ständige Auseinandersetzung statt. Man spricht davon "to sculpt a noise / sound", was die Schallplatte auf greifbare Weise tut. Sie bringt Klang in eine plastische Form. Umgekehrt bietet sie wiederum die Möglichkeit, den geformten 'eingefrorenen' Klang als plastisches Material zu gebrauchen. Während Ben Vautier mit der Schallplatte als akustischem Versatzstück eine Skulptur komponiert, legt Christian Marclay den Fußboden eines Raumes mit Platten aus, was manchen Ausstellungsbesucher (der bei Cage und Paik noch begeistert mitgespielt hat) nun doch zögern läßt. Zu sehr ist er darauf festgelegt, möglichst keine Spuren auf der Platte zu hinterlassen. Mit Hunderten von aus Schallplatten ausgesägten *Snowflakes* bedeckt Piotr Nathan die Wände eines Raums.

Claus Böhmler führt uns sein Schallplattenarchiv auf dem Videorekorder in einer einzigen Kameraeinstellung vor, und dies in einem Medium, das normalerweise der Aktion vorbehalten ist. KP Brehmer wiederum - durch Tim Wilson inspiriert, der seine Schallplatten 'lesen' kann - stellt akustische Signale durch eine Zeichnung dar. Marcel Duchamp hingegen entwirft die *Optical Discs* und läßt sie auf dem Plattenteller rotieren.

Offensichtlich übt das Medium Schallplatte auch seine Faszination auf die sogenannte Volkskunst aus. Eine Vitrine in der Ausstellung mit allerlei Kuriosem gefüllt trägt dem Rechnung. Schallplattenhüllen als originale Kunstwerke und solche nach Entwürfen von bildenden Künstlern runden das Bild in entscheidender Weise ab. Nicht zuletzt durch diese ergibt sich eine stattliche Namensliste von an der Ausstellung beteiligten Künstlern, deren Aufzählung fast so etwas wie eine Geschichte der Kunst des 20. Jahrhunderts zeichnet.

"Die Platte hat einen Sprung" (W.C. Williams), und nicht die glatte reibungslose Wiedergabe, bedeutet Qualität und Konzept zugleich.

Broken Music
or
His Master's Noise

Broken Music shows works of visual artists created with and for the medium of the record: records, record-covers, record-objects, record-installations. In contrast to the composer or musician who perceives the record first and foremost as a vehicle transporting his musical ideas, the visual artist is especially interested in the optical as well as the acoustical presence. In the early 60's, Milan Knížák called his record-collages *Broken Music* - by destroying, painting, pasting, and breaking records - he also broke with the traditional habits of hearing. *Broken Music* stands for a break with conventional ideas, as a breakthrough into something new. This start - somewhat simple to be sure, but thereby all the more conclusive - seemed convincing enough to form the concept for the whole exhibition.

Working with concrete musical material, Knížák considers himself a composer. (He handles scores the same way as records. The Arditti String Quartet performed one of his score-collages that is included as a flexidisc in the catalogue.)

"I was not interested in any kind of music already existing - so I had to make my own", explains Jean Dubuffet. He "made" it with the simplest mechanical aids and he quite certainly dispensed with any possible perfection of realization coming later. The rough, uneven sounds suited his musical vision and stood in direct relationship with his visual work.

Besides Knížák and Dubuffet, artists such as Laszlo Moholy-Nagy, Marcel Duchamp, John Cage, Nam June Paik, and Lawrence Weiner and also the younger artists Christian Marclay and Piotr Nathan hold key positions in the creative use of records. The exhibition tries to define these positions and as far as possible, to determine their historical roots.

It shows examples of an original record music, a.o., by Knížák, Marclay, and Boyd Rice, which was prepared theoretically and practically by Moholy-Nagy. He sought possibilities to engrave his compositions directly onto the ungrooved record surface. (See also his essay in this catalogue.)

Many of the records exhibited function simply as acoustic memories or documents as by Schwitters, Yves Klein, Karel Appel, Allan Kaprow, Wolf Vostell or the *selten gehörte Musik*.

Other object-records come out of a play with the word

Sound-Disc (in German Schall-Platte) or from a literal translation of technical terms: *Single taken from LP* (Claus Böhmler) or *Liszten!* (Stuart Sherman), a record which consists partly of the score and partly of the recording of a composition by Franz Liszt.

John Cage's *33 1/3*, a composition for 12 record-players and about 100 records, is realized in one room. The visitors to the exhibition are directed to a compositional game: out of the concrete material, the 100 records, to let something new to be created every time.

Nam June Paik's sound-sculpture *Random Acess* (record-schaschlik) allows anyone to try similar "composing", in this case even with a moving tone arm.

A constant confrontation between the visual and the acoustic takes place. One talks about, "to sculpt a noise/sound", something the record does in a tangible way. It captures sound in a plastic form. On the other hand it offers the possibility to use the shaped "frozen" sound as plastic material.

Whereas Ben Vautier uses the record as an acoustic set piece to compose a sculpture, Christian Marclay covers the floor of a room with records, making some visitors of the exhibition (who still play along enthusiastically with Cage and Paik) hesitate after all; the conditioning to leave no traces on a record is too strong. Piotr Nathan covers the walls with hundreds of *Snowflakes* cut out of records.

Claus Böhmler shows us his record archive on Video in one single take and this in a medium that is normally reserved for moving action. KP Brehmer - inspired by Tim Wilson who can read his records - depicts acoustic signals in a drawing. On the other hand Marcel Duchamp devises the *Optical Discs* and lets them rotate on a turntable.

The medium record apparently fascinates the so-called folk art as well. A showcase filled with all kinds of curiosities accounts for that.

Record-covers as original art works, such as those designed by visual artists, round off the picture in a decisive way. They add to a considerable list of names of participating artists. A list that represents something like a history of art of the 20th century.

The "defective record" (W.C. Williams) and not the even, smooth reproduction means quality and concept at the same time.

Broken Music
ou
His Master's Noise

Broken Music exposition d'art plastique, présente des traveaux conçus pour et avec le médium qu'est le disque: disques, couvertures de disques, objets de disques, installations de disques. Contrairement au compositeur et au musicien pour lesquels le disque est avant tout un véhicule servant à transporter les idées musicales, l'artiste s'intéresse ici autant à l'aspect optique qu'à la présence acoustique du disque. Au début des années 60 Milan Knížák donna à ses collages de disques le nom de *Broken Music* - en détruisant les disques, en les peignant, en les cassant ou en y faisant des appliques à la colle, il rompit avec les habitudes d'écoute conventionnelles. *Broken Music* signifie une rupture avec les conceptions dépassées, une percée vers quelque chose de nouveau. Cette idée - quelque peu simplificatrice, mais non moins concluante - semble assez pertinente pour pouvoir servir de fil conducteur à l'exposition entière.
Knížák travaille avec du matériau musical concret et il se décrit lui-même comme un compositeur. (Il compose avec des partitions de la même manière qu'avec des disques. Le Arditti Quartet a enregistré suivant une de ses partitions-collages le flexidisc accompagnant le catalogue).
"Je n'étais pas attiré par une quelconque musique déjà existante - je dus donc faire ma propre musique", disait Jean Dubuffet. Et il la 'fit' en ayant recours aux moyens techniques les plus simples. Il renonça consciemment à la possibilité d'un perfectionnement ultérieur. Les sons âpres correspondaient mieux à sa vision musicale et ils étaient en relation directe avec son oeuvre picturale.
Outre Knížák et Dubuffet, Laszlo Moholy-Nagy, Marcel Duchamp, John Cage, Nam June Paik et Lawrence Weiner ou les artistes plus jeunes tels Christian Marclay et Piotr Nathan jouent un rôle décisif en ce qui a trait à la création à l'aide de disques. L'exposition tente de délimiter ces positions et de faire ressortir dans la mesure du possible leurs racines historiques.
Elle présente des exemples d'une musique originale pour disques des oeuvres de Knížák, Marclay, Boyd Rice pour lesquelles Moholy-Nagy posa les jalons théoriques et pratiques. Il voulait trouver des moyens lui permettant de graver directement ses oeuvres sur un disque non préparé (c.f. son article dans ce catalogue).
Plusieurs disques exposés sont tout simplement des souvenirs acoustiques ou des documents, comme chez Schwitters, Yves Klein, Karel Appel, Allan Kaprow, Wolf Vostell ou la *selten gehörte Musik*. D'autres ob-

jets de disques jouent sur le mot Schall-Platte [plaque-son] ou ils essaient de transposer littéralement des termes techniques: *Aus einer LP ausgekoppelte Single (Un single tiré d'un LP)* (Claus Böhmler) ou *Liszten!* (Stuart Sherman), un disque qui ultilise et la partition et l'enregistrement d'une composition de Franz Liszt.
Dans une pièce de la galerie on a réalisé *33 1/3* de John Cage, une composition pour 12 tourne-disques et environ 100 disques. Les visiteurs sont priés de prendre part au jeu de la composition: à partir du matériau concret, les 100 disques, de créer à chaque fois quelque chose de nouveau.
Avec *Random Access* (brochette de disques), une sculpture sonore de Nam June Paik chacun peut également 'composer librement', voire dans ce cas avec le bras transportable d'un tourne-disque.
Il existe entre le visuel et l'acoustique une constante relation réciproque. On parle de "to sculpt a noise / sound" (sculpter un son), ce que fait le disque de façon tangible en donnant au son une forme plastique; et inversément il offre la possibilité d'utiliser le son formé et "figé" en tant que matériau plastique. Ben Vautier compose une sculpture où le disque joue le rôle d'un élément acoustique, Christian Marclay recouvre le plancher d'une pièce avec des disques, ce qui fait hésiter certains visiteurs qui chez Cage ou Paik peuvent encore participer avec enthousiasme et qui maintenant s'efforcent - trop peut-être - de ne laisser aucune trace sur les disques. Piotr Nathan recouvre les murs d'une pièce avec des centaines de *Snowflakes* découpés dans des disques.
Claus Böhmler nous présente ses archives de disques sur l'appareil vidéo; la caméra garde toujours la même perspective, et ce dans un médium qui normalement est destiné à l'action. S'inspirant de Tim Wilson qui peut 'lire' ses disques, KP Brehmer crée des signaux acoustiques à l'aide d'un dessin.
Marcel Duchamp esquisse parcontre les *Optical Discs* et les laisse tourner sur l'appareil.
Il ne fait aucun doute que le disque fascine également ce que l'on nomme l'art populaire. Une vitrine remplie de toutes sortes de choses curieuses prend ce phénomène en considération.
Les couvertures de disque - soit des oeuvres d'art originales, soit des réalisations faites à partir des esquisses d'un artiste - complètent éloquemment le tableau.
Il en résulte une liste imposante des noms des artistes participants à l'exposition, une liste dont l'énumération constitue presque une histoire de l'art au vingtième siècle.
"Le disque est fêlé" (W.C. Williams) signifie qualité et concept, et non la reproduction impeccable.

18.2.1988 - 12.2.1989 *Broken Music*. daadgalerie, Berlin
p. 11 **Nam June Paik, Milan Knížák, Karl-Heinz Eckert, Piotr Nathan**
p. 12 **Nam June Paik, Tomas Schmit, Stefan Wewerka**
p. 13 **Ben Vautier**

John Cage. *33 1/3*. 1969. Installation for *Broken Music*. daadgalerie, Berlin, 1988/1989

Piotr Nathan. *Sowflakes*. Installation for *Broken Music*. daadgalerie, Berlin, 1988/89

TRADE MARK

"GRAMMOPHON"

Michael Glasmeier

Die Musik der Engel

*Die Schallplatte räumt auf mit dem Musik-
dilettantismus der Haustöchter, mit dem
unerträglichen Konzertbetrieb und befreit
den musikalischen Menschen, den Künstler von den Hemmungen des Tages durch
das Medium der Musik.*
Erich Mendelsohn[1]

Die Gründungsväter des Mediums Schallplatte faszi-
nierte die Wiedergabe der menschlichen Stimme, nicht
die Musik. Bezeichnenderweise stellte Edison, als er
1878 die zehn Anwendungsmöglichkeiten des Phonographen beschrieb, die Musik erst an die vierte Stelle
nach den Aufgaben des Apparats als Diktiergerät,
Buch für Blinde, Sprachunterrichter, gefolgt von den
Funktionen als Spielzeug, Uhr, die die Zeit ansagt, pä-
dagogisches Instrument und in Verbindung mit dem
Telefon als Aufzeichnungsgerät[2]. Deutlich wird, daß
der Freizeitaspekt, der heute das fast ausschließliche
Ziel der Schallplattenproduktion ist, dem gesellschaftlichen Nutzen untergeordnet war. Es ging also
primär um die Erweiterung der Schriftkultur im phoneti-
schen Bereich, während sich die Kunst in Form von
aufgenommenen Arien und Chansons sensationsbe-
wußt auf den Jahrmärkten vergnügte. Die eigentliche
Vermassung von Musik entwickelte sich mit den technischen Verfeinerungen, die es um 1900 erlaubten, die
Stimmen nicht nur einmalig aufzuzeichnen. Bis dahin
mußte jede Aufnahme für die Walze ständig repetiert
und auch die Schallplatte konnte nur in begrenzter
Auflagenhöhe gepreßt werden. Das Singen im Studio
war eine Tortur der gnadenlosen Wiederholung, die direkt an die zu erstellende Stückzahl der Schallplatten
gekoppelt war. Außerdem mußte jede Schallplatte als
Ganzes aufgenommen werden, da es bis zur Erfindung des Tonbandes keine Schnittmöglichkeiten gab.
Ein falscher Ton, und die Aufnahme war hinüber.
    Die anfänglich noch unmittelbare Verbindung von
Produktion und Reproduktion findet sich optisch umgesetzt in dem Firmensignet des Engels, der mit einer
Art Federkiel der Schallplatte Rillen einschreibt. Dieser

aktive, unmittelbare Vorgang beleuchtet das Wunder-
bare der Erfindung, gleichsam ein Unikat der unver-
wechselbaren Physiognomie einer individuellen Stimme
herzustellen, das vergleichbar wäre mit dem hand-
schriftlichen Dokument im Bereich der Schriftkultur.
Kaum zufällig wurde dieses Signet 1909 durch den
Hund Nipper abgelöst, der geduldig der mechanischen
Stimme seines Herrn lauscht. Die Schallplatte wird
Massenmedium, Diener der Musik, nicht Auslöser.
Rudolph Lothar 1924:

In seinem Buche *Die Grundlagen der Musik* schrieb
Felix Auerbach (1911): "Was das Reich der Musik
angeht, so kann man sich schwer entschließen, den
Grammophonen einen Platz unter den Musikinstrumenten einzuräumen, und es ist sogar recht zweifel-
haft, ob sie ihn sich je erobern werden. Heutzutage
jedenfalls gehören sie in das Kapitel der Verirrungen
des Kunstbetriebes, indem sie Zerrbilder gerade von
den besten Originalen entwerfen, und so den Geschmack breiter Massen, statt zu heben, hoffnungs-
los verderben." Seit dieser kategorischen und apo-
diktischen Verwerfung der Sprechmaschine haben
sich die Ansichten gründlich geändert. Heute sehen
die besten Musiker in der Sprechmaschine einen
Kulturfaktor allerersten Ranges, der für die Verbreitung und Popularisierung edler Musik mehr getan
hat, als irgendein Faktor im Musikleben aller Zeiten.
Die Sprechmaschine gibt keine Zerrbilder, sondern
ein ebenso genaues Tonbild, wie die Photographie
ein Lichtbild liefert. Ja ein weit genaueres und
besseres, denn die Photographie muß sich mit
schwarzweiß begnügen und auf die Farben des Originals verzichten, indes eine gute Platte die feinsten
Farbschattierungen und die zartesten Nuancen einer
Stimme oder eines Orchesterstückes fehlerlos wie-
dergibt. So hat denn auch die Sprechmaschine ihre
ursprünglichen Feinde längst bekehrt, und aus
manchem Saulus ist ein Paulus geworden.[3]

Produktion / Reproduktion

*... ich möchte betonen, daß ich überhaupt
keine Schallplatten zuhause habe ...*
John Cage[4]

Doch können sich die Künstler zu Beginn dieses Jahrhunderts nicht mit einer Paulusrolle einverstanden erklären. Die Angriffe der Futuristen, Dadaisten und Bau-
häusler gegen die Etablierung eines bürgerlichen
Kunstverständnisses bei gleichzeitiger Perfektionierung
der Massenmedien müssen gezwungenermaßen eben
diese neuen Medien wie Film, Photographie und
Schallplatte mit einschließen. Die Neuorientierung der
Künste wird in Experimenten erprobt, welche die rein
reproduzierende Funktion der Medien auflösen und für
neue Überraschungen sorgen. Der Film erzählt nicht
mehr, sondern zeigt rhythmische Strukturen[5]. Mit den
Photogrammen können Photographien ohne den Umweg durch die Außenwelt direkt in der Dunkelkammer

Self-portrait by **Enrico Caruso**, n.d.

Trademark with the dog *Nipper* of Emile Berliner's gramophones according to a painting by **Francis Barraud** (1895)

hergestellt werden[6]. Die bildende Kunst bringt den Alltag in das vornehme Museum.

Kennzeichen aller dieser Medienforschungen ist die Transformation der Reproduktionsmittel in Produktionsmittel. Laszlo Moholy-Nagy:

> Es liegt in der menschlichen Eigenart begründet, daß die Funktionsapparate nach jeder neuen Aufnahme zu *weiteren neuen Eindrücken drängen*. Das ist einer der Gründe für die immer bleibende Notwendigkeit neuer Gestaltungsversuche. *Unter diesem Gesichtspunkt sind die Gestaltungen nur dann wertvoll, wenn sie neue, bisher unbekannte Relationen produzieren.* Damit ist wiederum gesagt, daß die Reproduktion (Wiederholung bereits existierender Relationen) *ohne* bereichernde Gesichtspunkte aus dem besonderen Gesichtspunkt der schöpferischen Gestaltung im besten Falle nur als virtuose Angelegenheit zu betrachten ist.
> Da vor allem die Produktion (produktive Gestaltung) dem menschlichen Aufbau dient, müssen wir versuchen, die bisher nur für Reproduktionszwecke angewandten Apparate (Mittel) zu produktiven Zwecken zu erweitern.[7]

Im Bauhaus versucht Moholy-Nagy diese Erweiterung unter anderem auch am Beispiel der Schallplatte praktisch umzusetzen, indem er vorschlägt, die Rillen der Wachsplatten auf dem Umweg photographischer Vergrößerung und Verkleinerung direkt herzustellen, ohne das Dazwischen einer musikalischen Aufnahme, um so neue und ungeahnte Töne zu produzieren, eine wahre Engelsmusik[8].

Geräusche

> *Um zu einer mehr universalen Gestaltung zu gelangen, wird die neue Musik eine neue Ordnung der Töne und der Nichttöne (bestimmter Geräusche) wagen müssen.*
> Piet Mondrian[9]

Die Musiker interessieren die Überlegungen von Moholy-Nagy kaum. Sie reagieren auf die neue Dynamik des Großstadtlebens, die ja vor allem ein Produkt der Maschinenarbeit und der Medien ist, mit einer Erweiterung des Klangmaterials, Harmonieauflösung, synästhetischen Versuchen mit Farbklavieren oder Kompositionen für elektroakustische Instrumente[10]. Die wohl fruchtbarste Neuerung für die Musik ist jedoch die Besinnung auf das Geräusch und auf die Zeit. Das Geräuschkunst-Manifest, das der Futurist Luigi Russolo 1913 formulierte, hat bis heute Auswirkungen auf die Avantgarde-Musik bis zu Pop oder dem Neuen Hörspiel[11].

> Jede Äußerung unseres Lebens ist von Geräuschen begleitet. Das Geräusch ist folglich unserem Ohr vertraut und vermag uns unmittelbar in das Leben zu versetzen. Während der Ton, der nicht am Leben teilhat, der immer musikalisch eine Sache für sich und ein zufälliges, nicht notwendiges Element ist, bereits für unser Ohr das geworden ist, was für das Auge ein allzubekanntes Gesicht ist, offenbart sich hingegen das Geräusch, das verworren und unregelmäßig aus dem unregelmäßigen Gewirr des Lebens zu uns dringt, niemals ganz und hat zahllose Überraschungen für uns bereit. Wir sind deshalb sicher, daß wir durch Auswahl, Koordinierung und Beherrschung aller Geräusche die Menschen um eine neue, ungeahnte Wollust bereichern können. Obwohl die Eigenart des Geräusches darin besteht, uns brutal ins Leben zu versetzen, DARF SICH DIE GERÄUSCHKUNST NIE AUF EINE IMITATIVE WIEDERHOLUNG DES LEBENS BESCHRÄNKEN! Sie

Thomas Alva Edison at 5 A.M. on July 16, 1888 after a 72-hour-shift with the new phonograph. Drawing according to a photograph

Recording music for phonograph-cylinders (woodcut according to a painting by **Franz Thiel**, 1899)

wird ihre größte Emotionsfähigkeit aus dem akustischen Genuß selbst schöpfen, den die Inspiration des Künstlers aus den Geräuschkombinationen zu ziehen versteht.[12]

Um die Geräusche der technischen Zivilisation in die Musik einzuführen, konstruiert Russolo seine *intonarumori*, Vorläufer der Klangskulpturen und Instrumente, die so tönen, als ob die Maschinenwelt mit den Orchesterinstrumenten zusammen auftritt. Sie werden wie ein Grammophon angekurbelt[13]. Allerdings sind diese Geräuschmacher relativ zahm und eher für Kammermusik geeignet. Von einer gewalttätigen rhythmischen Maschinenmusik, wie sie heute beispielsweise von Vivenza oder den "Einstürzenden Neubauten" produziert wird, sind sie weit entfernt.

Auch Edgard Varèse, Erik Satie oder George Antheil komponieren mit Geräuschen, doch ohne sie zu imitieren. Sie führen sie real in die Musik ein, d.h. Schreibmaschine, Sirene, Flugzeugmotor und Amboß sind als Objekte des musikalischen Ausdrucks, als Instrumente auf der Bühne anwesend.

Erst mit den Möglichkeiten der technischen Reproduktion von Klängen kann sich das Geräusch etablieren. Es ist von nun an beliebig verfügbar, abrufbar. Es lagert in den Rundfunkarchiven und auf den Schallplatten und wartet auf seinen großen Einsatz. 1948 verwendet Pierre Schaeffer für seine *Musique Concrète* Schallplatten aus dem Schallarchiv und nennt eine der so entstandenen Kompositionen *Studie über Plattenteller*[14]. Den Vorgang der Komposition mit Schallplattengeräuschen schildert John Cage, der 1939 mit *Imaginary Landscape No. 1* mit Meßschallplatten zu Testzwecken operierte.

Frequenzaufnahmen und Aufnahmen vom Gejaul eines Generators wurden auf Plattentellern verwendet, deren Umlaufgeschwindigkeit sich variieren ließ, so daß man gleitende Töne erhielt. Um den Klang zu erzeugen, setzte man eine Nadel auf die Platte, obwohl daraus zuweilen ein unscharfer Einsatz resultierte. Dem war eine Anordnung von Knöpfen vorzuziehen, durch die es möglich war, die Nadel vor dem gewünschten Einsatz auf der Platte zu haben, wobei, je nach Stellung der Knöpfe, Klang und Stille erzeugt wurde. Auch hier konnte man die Lautstärke des Klangs wiederum sehr genau steuern. Ein Spieler kann mehrere Plattenteller bedienen und eine einzelne Stimme aufführen, die für Erdrutsch, Regen, Preßluft oder für irgendwelche anderen konkreten Klänge geschrieben ist. Ein kleines Kontaktmikrophon, wie es für die Marimbula benutzt worden war, wandelt sanfte Klänge in solche von aufdringlicher Qualität oder Charakter um.[15]

The first tin-foil phonograph, 1877

Zeit

Der musikalische Ton hat einen direkten Zugang zur Seele. Er findet da sofort einen Widerklang, da der Mensch "die Musik hat in sich selbst".
Wassily Kandinsky[16]

Die zeitlichen Dimensionen in der Musik zu verschieben, ist der andere Schwerpunkt der avantgardistischen Experimente zwischen den Polen der Mikrostücke von Anton Webern und des circa 18 Stunden dauernden, aus 840 Wiederholungen bestehenden *Vexations* von Erik Satie, das John Cage 1949 publizierte. John Cage:

> Wenn sie in Betracht ziehen, daß ein Ton durch seine Höhe, seine Lautstärke, seine Farbe und seine Dauer charakterisiert wird, und daß Stille, welche das Gegenteil und deshalb der notwendige Partner des Tons ist, nur durch ihre Dauer charakterisiert wird, dann kommt man zu dem Schluß, daß die Dauer, das heißt die Zeitlänge, die fundamentalste der vier Charakteristiken des musikalischen Materials ist. Stille kann nicht als Tonhöhe oder Harmonik gehört werden; sie wird als Zeitlänge gehört.[17]

Was diese Reflexion über die musikalische Zeit so bedeutsam macht, ist das Fehlen einer Begrenzung, und damit werden in letzter Konsequenz alle Töne gleichwertig, "die Summe aller Klänge ist grau"[18]. Musikalische Themen, Sätze, Leitmotive, Kodas verlieren ihren Sinn. Anfang und Ende eines Stückes müssen durch eine Situation bestimmt werden, die es ermöglicht zuzuhören, um das Stück als Komnposition wahrzunehmen; denn mit der Einführung des Geräusches kann alles Klang sein oder werden. Das Konzert ist der Rahmen, der bestimmt, was als Musik gehört werden soll. Damit steht die avantgardistische Musik der Zeit im stärksten Widerspruch zur Schallplatte, die zeitlich begrenzt ist und die allein schon durch das Wechseln der Seiten eine Zäsur in den kontinuierlichen Ablauf des musikalischen Ereignisses setzt. Mit *4'33* von John Cage wissen wir zudem, daß es nur einer einfachen Geste bedarf, um Musik zu entfachen, einer Geste, die sich im wesentlichen mit dem Optischen verbindet[19]. Dieser Vorgang kann als Theatralisierung der Musik begriffen werden, die nicht mehr zu dirigiert werden braucht, sondern im Raum stattfindet. Durch die Einführung des Zufalls in die Komposition wird das musikalische Werk vollends an seine Aufführung gebunden, die mit jeder Wiederholung sich verändert. Zeit, Raum und Zufall machen die Aufführung einmalig und unwiderruflich.

> Die Identität des Werks mit sich selbst ist ... nicht länger mit der Identität der Aufführungen untereinander auch nur entfernt identisch, sondern, wo sie nicht gänzlich aufgelöst ward, als Identität der Ver-

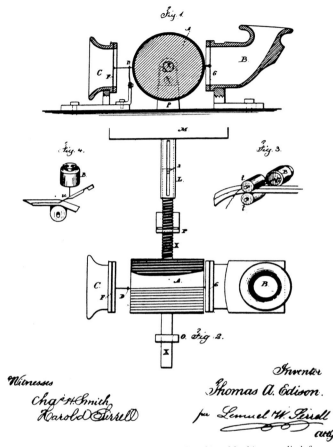

T A. EDISON.
Phonograph or Speaking Machine.
No. 200,521. Patented Feb. 19, 1878.

The patent for **Edison's** *Phonograph or Speaking Machine*, applied for on December 24, 1877

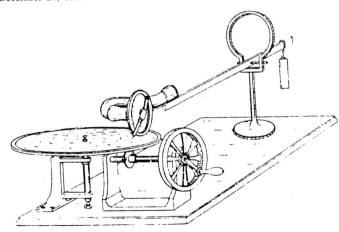

Emile Berliner's gramophone, 1888, technical drawing

Piano recording in the late 1880s, using a **Edison phonograph**

suchsanordnungen zu verstehen. Durch die Nicht-Identität der Aufführungen aber, durch die postulierte Unwiederholbarkeit einer jeden, wird es zu einem unmittelbar wider den Sinn solcher Musik gerichteten Unterfangen, eine von ihnen auf Tonband oder Schallplatte zu fixieren. Cage, und was namentlich in Amerika an kompositorischer Bewegung sich an ihn geschlossen hat ... verlangt nach leibhaftiger Aufführung durch gegenwärtige, in Präsenz hic et nunc agierende Musiker.[20]

Komponisten

Uebrigens glaube ich, daß unsere heutigen Komponisten oft schon bei ihrer Arbeit mit der Apparatur der Schallplatte rechnen, sich bei der Komposition darauf einrichten. Ich kann mir nicht helfen, die wertvolleren unter unseren modernen Schlagern klingen mir gerade mechanisch übermittelt, also etwa auf Elektrola, am besten, am echtesten!
Heinrich Mann[21]

Eigentlich sollte man annehmen, daß die solchermaßen befreiten Klänge und die damit verbundene Potenz, das Medium Schallplatte als Partner, Gegenspieler oder Produktionsmittel, wie es Moholy-Nagy vorschlägt, einzusetzen, den Komponisten reizen müßte. Doch sind hier nur Marginalien überliefert, die zudem meist von Komponisten stammen, die eine Erweiterung des musikalischen Materials propagieren (Darius Milhaud, Paul Hindemith, Ernst Toch) oder die im intermedialen Bereich arbeiten (Edgard Varèse, John Cage). Theodor W. Adorno spricht von dem "panischen Schreck, den vor dieser Erfindung manche Komponisten bekunden"[22], Igor Strawinsky von den Möglichkeiten, "spezifische Musik für die phonographische Wiedergabe zu schaffen, eine Musik, die erst ihr wahres Bild, den Orginalklang, durch die mechanische Wiedergabe erhielte"[23].
Ablehnung und Begeisterung polarisiert auch die Interpreten, personifiziert durch den Dirigenten Sergiu Celibidache, der allein im Live-Auftritt eine Sinfonie verwirklicht hört, und durch den Pianisten Glenn Gould, der das Husten und Schnupfen während des Konzerts

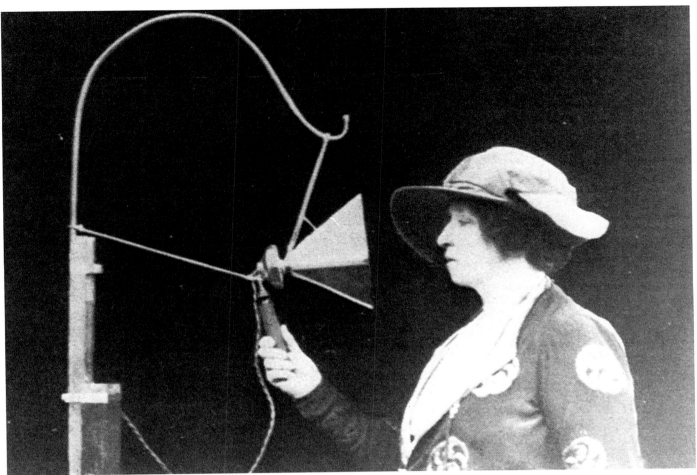

The singer **Nellie Melba** in front of a coal microphone during the session for her first electrically recorded disc, photograph, n.d.

nicht mehr ertragen konnte[24]. So bleibt es den bildenden Künstlern nach dem zweiten Weltkrieg überlassen, unbekümmert sowohl an die Pioniere der Schallplatte als auch an die Geräusch-, Zeit-, und Theatervorstellungen der musikalischen Avantgarde anzuknüpfen.

Die Kunst der Künste

> Wohl hat vor der Erfindung von Schallplatte und Tonband niemand gehört, was wir heute jederzeit hören können und oft hören: zweimal dieselbe Aufführung.
> Heinz-Klaus Metzger[25]

Mit dem Abschied vom Tafelbild hat sich die bildende Kunst sämtliche anderen künstlerischen Ausdrucksformen angeeignet: Film, Photographie, Theater, Architektur, Literatur und Musik. In dieser Aufzählung irritiert die Musik, da sie die einzige unsichtbare Kunst ist. Doch mit einer der ersten Kompositionen eines bildenden Künstlers, mit Marcel Duchamps *Erratum musical* von 1913 wird deutlich, daß hier einerseits die Partitur als Bild gelesen werden kann, andererseits sich eine Aufführung an die oben beschriebene Theatralisierung bindet. Die gleiche Konzeption findet man auch bei den Aufführungen von Fluxus-Konzerten, wenn beispielsweise Arthur Køpcke in *music while you work* die Funktion der Schallplatte als Lieferant für Hintergrundmusik umkehrt und sich von einer präparierten Schallplatte von seiner Hausarbeit auf der Bühne immer wieder unterbrechen läßt. Die Partitur oder die Anweisungen werden bildhaft, die Ausführung wird Aktion, die sich mit jeder Aufführung verändert, da die bildhafte Notation im wesentlichen nur ein Vorschlag ist und keine kompositorische Fixierung im klassischen Sinn. So ist es dem Aufführenden in *music while you work* freigestellt, welche Schallplatte er präparieren, welche Hausarbeit er machen, wie lange die Aufführung dauern soll[26].

Aus dieser Sicht sind Schallplatten von künstlerisch-musikalischen Aktionen Dokumente wie akustische Photographien, und hier wie dort muß die Phantasie arbeiten, um das Fehlende zu ergänzen, aber nicht im Sinne Rudolph Lothars, der emphatisch der Sprechmaschine sehende Qualitäten zuschreibt:

> Sie ist ein Spielzeug für den Unverständigen, ein Zeitvertreib der Banausen, ein Spektakelmacher für den Plebejer, aber eine Quelle reinsten, künstlerischen Genusses für den musikalisch empfindenden Menschen, der die Illusionskraft besitzt, die Nebengeräusche nicht zu hören, die Maschine nicht zu sehen, wohl aber in Bildern zu schwelgen, die ihm die Töne vorzaubern.[27]

Von einem "schwelgerischen" Sichgehenlassen kann man beim Hören der Schallplatten von Joseph Beuys, Henning Christiansen, Hermann Nitsch oder Dieter Roth schwerlich reden. Aber Bilder, Erinnerungen an Ausstellungsobjekte, an Personen sind vorhanden, die das Gesamtwerk eines Künstlers akustisch erweitern. Herr Edison hätte an ihnen seine helle Freude.
Helmut Heissenbüttel schreibt in seinem Aufsatz *Die Schallplatte als Mittel historisches Bewußtsein zu gewinnen*:

> Musik ist, und das kann tatsächlich die Schallplatte differenzierter zeigen als jede andere Möglichkeit, akustisch und nicht nur über die Notierung vermittelte Musik. Sie ist darüber hinaus der Ort, an dem sich intellektuelle Einsicht und sinnliche Wahrnehmung am meisten entgegenkommen, ja an dem sie zur Deckung zu bringen sind.[28]

Aus dieser Warte sind auch Aufnahmen von Klangskulpturen, Klanginstallationen oder Performances mehr als Dokumentationen. Gebunden an die Bewegung der Plastik, den Raum oder die Theatralisierung fehlt ihnen zwar die optische Präsenz, aber sie kann dennoch als unmittelbar musikalischer Ausdruck gehört werden und somit das eigene Heim mit den von der Optik abgekoppelten Klängen in einen magischen, rätselhaften Ort verwandeln wie auf dem Bild *L'assassin menacé* von René Magritte. Die Klänge verweisen zunächst auf nichts, sind unbekannt und erfordern daher eine erhöhte Aufmerksamkeit. Sie sind als Hintergrundmusik erst nach längerer Gewöhnung zu nutzen. Sie haben das Museum, die Galerie verlassen, und lagern an einem neuen Ort. Sie verwandeln sich und werden autark.
Auffällig oft reden Künstler auf Schallplatten über sich und ihre Arbeit, eine Haltung, die bei Alan Kaprow und Yves Klein nicht nur aufklärerisch ist. Es ist das ursprüngliche Interesse an der Physiognomie der Stimme, die mit der Sound Poetry seit der Erfindung der Schallplatte den ganzen Reichtum menschlicher und lyrischer Artikulationen verbreitet. Auf dem Weg der Sprache kann allerdings auch, wie es das Unternehmen *Art By Telephone* gezeigt hat, die Kunst in das Museum gelangen.
Überhaupt scheint der aufzeichnende Engel den Künstlern eher zu liegen als der lauschende Nipper, es sei

denn, er bellt. Die Künstler fragen nicht nach der Klangqualität. Sie bestehen auf dem ursprünglichen Charakter der Aufnahmen, wenn sie die Schallplatte als reproduzierendes Medium benutzen. Im Gegensatz zu den gewerkschaftlich organisierten Berufsmusikern, die auch schon mal einen Schönberg runtergeigen müssen, bekennen sich die Künstler zu einem kreativen Dilettantismus, der mit Musikinstrumenten oder Sprache experimentiert. Die Tonbandaufnahmen, die Jean Dubuffet, Dieter Roth oder André Thomkins zuhause produzieren und als Schallplatten in kleiner Auflage auf den Markt bringen, sind alles andere als Hausmusik. Sie sind Grenzverletzungen des sogenannten guten Geschmacks, dem schon Marcel Duchamp an die Kehle wollte, und Selbstversuche in, an und mit Musik und Sprache, deren Ausdrucksmöglichkeiten vom Bruitismus bis zum Schweigen reicht. Dieter Roth:

> Nach vielen Jahren des die gelernten, die sogenannten guten Musiker (verschiedener Musikarten oder Musikspielweisen) Beneidens und vielen Jahren des Selbergernkönnenwollens hatte ich mir eine sozusagen alkoholische Spielweise anerzogen (auf welchem Instrument immer), die gut (klassisch hochgebrachten Hörern) erschien, witzig, leicht süsslich, angenehm nicht zu gut seiend. Darunter - drunter aber wußte ich von meiner Ambition (ganz alleine - wenn ich jemanden von ihr und meiner Verzweiflung der Güte klassisch hoher Musik gegenüber sprach war Abneigung, Nichtglauben, Komplimentfischereiverdacht die Wirkung), und ich hatte die Idee, das wär doch was (was? was wär es?), das Nichtkönnenzeigen, die Scham, sie erleidend zeigen![29]

Die musikalische Sprengkraft, die hier von den Künstlern ausgeht, ist sicherlich ein Reflex auf die tägliche akustische Umwelt. Viele Künstler lassen sich von der Musik während ihrer Arbeit inspirieren oder sind mit Musikern befreundet. Was mit Piet Mondrian und seiner Liebe zum Jazz begonnen hatte, wird mit Franz Kline oder Tomas Schmit fortgesetzt. Andy Warhol besaß in Velvet Underground seine Hausband, und schließlich treten die Künstler selbst als Pop- und Jazz-Stars auf die Bühne. Laurie Anderson kam in die Hitparade und Martin Kippenberger, A.R. Penck, Salomé und viele andere produzieren ihre eigene Hintergrundmusik nach dem Motto von Kippenberger:

> Musik ist schön.
> Wie solls weitergehn?
> Umso lauter
> umso besser.[30]

Verpackung

Karl Valentin: So runde, dunkelschwarze Platten.
Verkäuferin: Ja, ich meine, wollen sie Schallplatten mit Musik oder mit Gesang?
Karl Valentin: Nein, nur mit Schall, billigem Schall.[31]

Auffällig ist die Liebe der bildenden Künstler zur improvisierten Musik. Hier existieren Wechselbeziehungen, innere Verwandtschaften nicht nur soziologischer Art. Besonders deutlich wird die gegenseitige Befruchtung beim Betrachten der Plattencover, die eine Art Subkunstgeschichte der Moderne schreiben. Sie sind, wenn sie von Künstlern gestaltet werden, keine Gebrauchsgraphik, d.h. nicht auf den ersten Blick produktbezogen. Sie verzichten daher auf ein Starportrait oder zitieren es ironisch. Nicht dem Produkt untergeordnet, liefern sie ein zusätzliches Produkt, eine zusätzliche bildnerische Aussage und originalisieren somit die Reproduktion. Ein eindringliches Beispiel für dieses Vorgehen finden wir in Richard Hamiltons Beatles-Platte. Starphotos und Texte werden von der Außenhülle, die sich in schlichtem, kühlem Weiß mit eingeprägtem Bandnamen präsentiert, verbannt. Ironischerweise ist jedes Cover trotz Millionenauflage einzeln numeriert, und es stellt sich die Frage, was soll dadurch zum leicht erschwinglichen Multiple gemacht werden: das Cover von Hamilton oder die Schallplatte der Beatles? Für eine ähnliche Verwirrung sorgt auch Andy Warhols Hosenschlitz-Ready-made für die Rolling Stones, das durchaus im Sinne von Campbells' Tomatensuppe als ein Warhol aufgefaßt werden kann, dem zufällig eine Stones-Platte beiliegt.

Wenn Künstler ihre eigenen Schallplatten produzieren, bieten sich die Platteninformationen im individuellen Stil dar. Die Cover sind zumeist exquisit gestaltet, handelt es sich doch oft nur um kleine Auflagen. Mit ihren Beilagen, Aktionsphotos, graphischen Ein- und Ausfällen, Numerierung und Signatur sind sie kleine, kostbare Objekte, den Künstlerbüchern vergleichbar, die ebenfalls Materialien, Informationen und Handgemachtes unter einem Konzept zusammenstellen, nur daß die Künstlerschallplatte kaum Möglichkeiten hat, ihre Größe beliebig zu verändern, sie muß sich an die Standards der Industrie halten. Christian Marclay vereint schließlich wieder das Cover mit der Schallplatte als *Record Without A Cover*. Gleichzeitig bietet er eine Schallplatte ohne Rillen in luxuriöser Verpackung als Multiple an. Punk, New Wave und polnische Musiker nehmen seit Mitte der 70er Jahre vor allem die handgemachten Verpackungsideen der Künstler auf, um sich bewußt von den Staralüren des Musikmarkts und seinen Normen, die scheinbar verbindlich sind, abzusetzen; denn ein Angriff auf die Verpackung trifft den Nerv des Inhalts.

Weißes Rauschen

Aus Kinos kommt eine Musik, das sind Platten, auf denen vererbt sich die Stimme von Menschen. Und alles singt.
Irmgard Keun[32]

Bildende Künstler als musikalische Dilettanten sind im Musikgeschäft nicht sonderlich gefragt. Trotzdem besitzen sie eine Vorreiterfunktion. Sie kennen im Gegensatz zu den etablierten E- und U-Musikern keine Vorbehalte, und kümmern sich bei ihren Experimenten nicht sonderlich um eine musikgeschichtliche Einordnung, die ja den Komponisten permanent im Nacken sitzt. Künstler sind Praktiker und Forscher wie der Eskimo Nanook, der in dem nach ihm benannten Film von Robert Flaherty aus Neugier in eine Schallplatte beißt, um so im körperlichen Zugriff die Gesetze mechanischer Musik zu begreifen.
Egon Friedell über den Dilettantismus:

Wir kommen heutzutage mit Gehirnen zur Welt, die gleichsam schon gefächert sind. Wir vermögen uns nicht vorzustellen, daß ein Mensch mehr als *eine* Sache kann. Wir kleben jedem eine bestimmte Etikette auf und sind erstaunt, mißtrauisch, beleidigt, wenn er sich nicht an diese Etikette hält. Wir bemerken jedoch in wirklich kultivierten Zeiten bei sämtlichen begabten Menschen die größte Vielseitigkeit. Sie beschäftigten sich mit allem und konnten auch alles. In Griechenland war ein Mensch, der für hervorragend gelten wollte, genötigt, in nahezu allem hervorzustechen: als Musiker und Rhetor ebensogut wie als Feldherr und Ringkämpfer. Der Spezialist wurde von den Hellenen geradezu verachtet: er galt als "Banause". Und vollends in der Renaissance war Begabung, virtu, einfach dasselbe wie Vielseitigkeit. Ein begabter Mensch war damals ein Mensch, der so ziemlich alle Gebiete beherrschte, auf denen sich Begabung zeigen läßt. Nur in entarteten Kulturen taucht der Spezialist auf.
Und schließlich muß man sich klar machen, daß "Dilettantismus" nahezu immer die Form ist, in der das Neue sich äußert.[33]

Die Abkehr vom Spezialistentum bringt der Moderne Kompositionen für Schallplatten, die in den 30er Jahren von den Musikern gefordert wurden, durch den bildenden Künstler. Die *Chöre & Soli* der "Tödlichen Doris" bieten dafür ein herausragendes Exempel. Auf den Spuren Edisons und Berliners konkretisieren sie im Medium selbst, was es heißt, Diskologe, praktischer Wissenschaftler zu sein. Ihr Produkt folgt dem Standard einer Wagnerkassette. Darin befinden sich acht kleine, bunte Platten, ein Romanfragment, und sogar das Abspielgerät wird mitgeliefert. Jeder Gesang dauert technisch bedingt 30 Sekunden, also fast die Zeit, die man zum Einlegen der Platten in den Apparat benötigt. Kaum gehört, ist es auch schon aus mit dem Musikgenuß. Mit dem Faktor Zeit setzt sich auch Marcel Duchamp auseinander. Seine *Rotoreliefs*, die er 1935 für den Plattenspieler konzipierte, sind sechs zweiseitig mit farbigen Motiven bedruckte Scheiben, die mit Hilfe eines viereckigen Sockels auf den Plattenspieler gelegt werden. Bei einer Umdrehung von 33 RPM vermitteln die zweidimensionalen Flächen einen räumlichen Eindruck[34]. Dieses künstlerisch-physikalische Experiment wurde von André Thomkins später malerisch weitergeführt und ist heute noch ein beliebter Effekt der Picture-Disc.

Die Auseinandersetzung mit der Zeit am Medium Schallplatte kann aber auch direkt geschehen; denn die Schallplatte ist eine Zeitmaschine, die es vermag, musikalische Sensationen durch einfache Manipulationen am Geschwindigkeitsregler des Apparates auszulösen. Durch diesen Trick, den Nam June Paik am Beispiel Schönberg selbst wieder auf einer Schallplatte festhält, auf die Dieter Roth mit einer Single kritisch antwortet, wird Musik zum Geräusch, Geräusch zur Musik und musikalische Zeit wieder zu einem unbestimmten Faktor. Gleichzeitig kann so auf relativ einfache Weise von Künstlern und von Herrn Jedermann mit vorgefundenem musikalischen Material komponiert werden.. Die Zeitverschiebung spitzt sich dramatisch zu, wenn man wie Boyd Rice mit Unendlichkeitsrillen arbeitet. Das hat den Vorteil, daß sehr viele Stücke, die ohne Ende klingen, auf eine Schallplatte passen, und es erlaubt dem Konsumenten eigene Kompositionen mit dem Tonarm.

Man kann aber auch die Platte selbst manipulieren, indem man ihr Kratzer zufügt, sie zerschneidet, wieder zusammensetzt, mit anderen Platten kreuzt und hört, was dabei herauskommt. Der Lärm, den Milan Knížák mit seinen Collagen auf diese Weise produziert, klingt wie eine archaische Musik, die den gesamten Kosmos der reproduzierten Klänge durcheinander wirbelt. Auf eine ähnliche Weise komponiert Christian Marclay live mit Bergen von unbearbeiteten und bearbeiteten Schallplatten auf vier Schallplattenspielern mittels Tonarm, Verstärker und Geschwindigkeitsveränderungen eine konzeptionelle, rhythmisch strukturierte laute Reise durch die Musikgeschichte, und die bekannten Ohrwürmer, Melodien und Eintagsfliegen vermischen sich miteinander, zerfetzen sich gegenseitig und lösen sich in ungeahnte Klänge auf. Schallplatte ade, Musik okay.

Knížák und Marclay sind es auch, die die skulpturalen Eigenschaften der Schallplatten hervorheben. Hat der Betrachter der Schallplattenskulptur von Nam June Paik noch die Möglichkeit Klänge zu produzieren, bietet Knížák eine andere Musik durch aufmontierte Kinderinstrumente an, so haben sich bei Marclay die Klänge endgültig zur Ruhe begeben. Die Schallplatten schweigen als Turm, oder sie müssen es sich gefallen lassen, als Boden zu dienen, auf dem man Spuren hinterläßt.

Auch die Schallplattenobjekte von Joseph Beuys, Henning Christiansen oder die Silhouetten von Piotr

Nathan schweigen. Aber dennoch sind sie nicht stumm, da es nur der erotischen Berührung einer Nadel bedarf, um ihnen zumindest ein Geräusch zu entlocken. Als Kunstobjekt haben sie ihr eigentliches Dasein verwirkt. Der Geist der Reproduktion ist aus diesen Objekten vollends gewichen. Sie symbolisieren eine konkrete Zeit, ohne zu dauern. Sie sind abgelagerte Zeit wie die Erinnerung. Zur Skulptur geronnen, dreht sich nichts mehr außer im Kopf des Betrachters, dessen Schädel möglicherweise, wie es Rainer Maria Rilke sich ausdachte, eines Tages auf der Suche nach dem "Ur-Geräusch" mit der Nadel Edisons in Berührung kommt.

> Die Kronen-Naht des Schädels (was nun zunächst zu untersuchen wäre) hat - nehmen wir's an - eine gewisse Ähnlichkeit mit der dicht gewundenen Linie, die der Stift eines Phonographen in den empfangenden rotierenden Cylinder des Apparates eingräbt. Wie nun, wenn man diesen Stift täuschte und ihn, wo er zurückzuleiten hat, über eine Spur lenkte, die nicht aus der graphischen Übersetzung eines Tones stammte, sondern ein an sich und natürlich Bestehendes -, gut: sprechen wir's nur aus: eben (z.B.) die Kronen-Naht wäre -: Was würde geschehen? Ein Ton müßte entstehen, eine Tonfolge, eine Musik ...[35]

Advertisement, 1904

nates the wonder surrounding invention: the creation of the unmistakable physiognomy of an individual's unique voice; a procedure quite similar to hand written documents produced in a culture centered around writing. It was hardly a coincidence that in 1909 this trademark was retired in favor of the dog Nipper listening patiently to the mechanical voice of his master. The record had become mass medium - music's servent, not its initiator. In 1924 Rudolph Lothar:

Music of the Angels

The record does away with the musical dilettantism of "Haustöchter" (daughters living at home), with the unbearable business of concerts; and it frees that musical individual, the artist, from the day's constraints, through the medium of music.
Erich Mendelsohn[1]

The founding fathers of the record medium were fascinated by the reproduction of the human voice, not by the reproduction of music. Characteristically, when in 1878 Edison described the ten applications of the phonograph, he placed music in the forth position: coming before it were its functions as a dictating machine, a book for the blind, and a language teacher; following it were its functions as a child's toy, a clock which announces the time, a pedagogical instrument, and, in connection with the telephone, a recording machine[2]. It becomes clear that its recreational aspect - which today is practically the exclusive goal of record production - was considered to be a far second behind its social benefit. Essentially, the record was seen as an instrument for expanding a writing oriented culture into the phonetic field, while its artistic use went, in the form of arias and chansons, to amuse itself at the fairs as the newest sensation. The real loss of music's individuality came in 1900 with those technical refinements which made it possible to record a voice more than once. Until this innovation, each recording for the cylinder had to be repeated, and the record could only be pressed in limited numbers. Studio singing was a torture of relentless repetitions, the number of which was directly related to how many records were to be produced. Moreover, since the ability to edit would not be possible until the invention of magnetic tape, each record had to be recorded as one piece from beginning to end. One wrong note and the entire recording was ruined.
This initial and immediate connection between production and reproduction is visually manifested in the trademark of an angel inscribing grooves on the record with a kind of quill. This active, direct procedure illumi-

In his book *The Fundamentals of Music* (1911), Felix Auerbach wrote: "Concerning the realm of music, it is difficult to decide whether to give the gramophone a place amoung musical instruments; indeed, it is quite dubious whether it will ever win such a status. Today at any rate, it belongs to the chapter on aberrations in the art-business, owing to the fact it sketches out distorted pictures from the best originals; thus, rather than improving the taste of the masses, it hopelessly destroys it." Opinions have changed considerably since this categorical and apodictic rejection of the "speaking machine". Today the best musicians view the speaking machine as cultural achievment of the highest order; something which has done more for the distribution and popularization of fine music than any other factor in the musical life of any other period. The speaking machine does not produce distorted pictures, but a sound picture which is just as exact as the picture created by photography. Yes, even a somewhat better and more exact picture since photography must remain content with black and white by dispencing with the original colors. A well recorded record, however, can reproduce the most subtle hues and colors, the most delicate nuances of a voice or an orchestral piece. Thus has the speaking machine converted its original enemies, and many a Saulus has become a Paulus.[3]

Production / Reproduction

...I should like to make it clear that I do not have any records in my home...
John Cage[4]

Yet at the beginning of this century, artists could not reconcile thelmselves to a Paulus role. The attacks of the Futurists, Dadaists and the Bauhaus against the establishment of a bourgeois comprehension of art and their simultaneous perfection of the mass media included, by necessity, the new media of film, photography, and recording. In the Arts the new orientation was to discover through experimentation: that what does away with the reproducing function of the media, in favor of providing new surprises. Film no longer tells stories but shows rhythmic structures[5]. With the help of the photogram, photos can be produced in the darkroom without having to make a detour to the outside world[6]. The fine arts brought everday life into the high-brow museum.
The distinguishing trait of all this media research is the transformation of the means of reproduction into the

Advertisement, 1937

Advertisement, 1904

means of production. Laszlo Moholy-Nagy:

> It lies in the peculiarity of human nature that after every new recording the functioning apparatus is pushed ahead to *further new impressions.* That is one of the reasons for the necessity to always continue experiments in *New Plasticism. From this standpoint, the configurations are only worthwhile when they produce new, previously unknown, relationships.* In other words, this means that reproduction (repetitions of already existing relations) *without* richer viewpoints from the special standpoint of creative production can, only in the best cases, be considered as a virtuosic opportunity.
> As production (productive creation) above all serves the human condition, we must attempt to further our purposes of creative production through the uses of those apparatuses (methods) which until now, have been used only for reproduction purposes.[7]

In the Bauhaus, Moholy-Nagy attempts, in effect, to convert this expansion by using, among other things, the record, insofar as he proposes directly processing the grooves of the wax-record with photographic enlarging and reduction but without the intervention of musical recording, thereby producing new and unexpected tones - truly an angel's music[8].

Sounds

> *To reach a more universal form, the new music must venture to reach a new order of tones and anti-tones (certain noises).*
> Piet Mondrian[9]

Musicians are hardly interested in Moholy-Nagy's reflections. They react to the new dynamics of city-life which are, above all, a product of machinery and media, thereby offering a greater range of sound-material, decomposition of harmony, experiments with synesthesia and the "Farbklavier" (color keyboard), and compositions for electro-acoustic instruments[10]. Probably the most fruitful innovation for music is the consideration of noise and time. The *Art of Noises* manifesto, formulated in 1913 by the fururist Luigi Russolo, today still has a bearing from avant-garde music to pop music, and finally to the radio play.[11]

> Every manifestation of our life is accompanied by noise. Noise, therefore, is familiar to our ear, and has the power to pull us into life itself. Sound is extraneous to life, always musical and a thing unto itself, an occasional but unnecessary element, and has become to our ears what an overfamiliar face is to our eyes. Noise, however, reaching us in a confused and irregular way from the irregular confusion of life, is never entirely complete, and promises innumerable surprises. We are therefore certain that by selecting, coordinating and commanding every noise we shall enrich mankind with a new and unexpected delight. Although it is characteristic of noise to recall us brutally to real life, THE ART OF NOISE MUST NOT BE LIMITED TO IMITATIVE REPRODUCTION! It will achieve its greatest emotive power in the sheer acoustic enjoyment that the artist will create from combined noises.[12]

To integrate the noises of technical civilization into music, Russolo constructed his *intonarumori*: a forerunner of sound-sculptures and those instruments which sound as if the world of machines were performing along with the orchestra's instruments. They cranked up like a gramophone[13]. Yet these noise makers are relatively tame and, consequently, better suited for chamber music. They are far from being the sort of violent, rhythmic, masculine music as is produced today by Vivenza or the "Einstürzenden Neubauten".
Edgard Varèse, Erik Satie, and George Antheil also created compositions utilizing - but without imitating - noises. They brought them virtually into the music: i.e. typewriter, siren, airplane-engine, and anvil are on the stage as instruments, as objects of musical expression. Noise can establish itself only through the possibility of

technical reproduction of sounds. From now on it is arbitrarily available and recallable. Stored in radio archives and on records, it stands ready for its great mission. In 1948 Pierre Schaeffer used records from the sound archive for his *Music Concrète*, calling one of these compositions *A Study of Turnable*[14]. The pioneering work for compositions using record noise was outlined by John Cage who, in his 1939 piece *Imaginary Landscape No. 1*, worked with test records for measuring purposes:

> Frequency records and the recording of the whine of a generator were used on turntables, the speed of which could be varied, thus making sliding tones available. To produce the sound, a needle was lowered to the record, although this sometimes resulted in a blurred attack. A button arrangement was preferred, whereby it was possible to have the needle on the record before a required entrance, sound or silence being produced by the position of the button. Here again, the loudness of the sound could be controlled very exactly. One player can operate several turntables and perform a single line written for the sound of a landslide, that of rain, of compressed air, or any other recorded sounds. A small contact microphone, such as was used with the marimbula, transforms slight sounds into ones that have an imposing quality and character.[15]

A.M. Cassandre. *Pathé*. 1932. Poster

Time

> *Musical sound has a direct entrance to the soul. There it immediately finds an echo; there man has "music in himself".*
> Wassily Kandinsky[16]

The dislocation of the time dimension in music is another of the main points of avant-garde experimentation, running from the micro-pieces of Anton Webern to Erik Satie's *Vexations* (published by John Cage in 1949) comprised of 840 repetitions lasting approximately 18 hours. John Cage:

> If you consider that sound is characterized by its pitch, its loudness, its timbre, and its duration, and that silence, which is the opposite and, therefore, the necessary partner of sound, is characterized only by its duration, you will be drawn to the conclusion that of the four characteristics of the material of music, duration, that is, time length, is the most fundamental. Silence cannot be heard in terms of pitch or harmony: It is heard in terms of time length.[17]

What makes this reflection on the time element in music so meaningful is the absence of any mention of a limitation; consequently all sounds eventually become equal: "the sum of all sounds is grey"[18]; musical themes, movements, leitmotives, and codas lose their meaning. The beginning and end of a piece must be determined by an ambiance that enables one to listen in such a way that one can perceive the

piece as a composition: for by means of the introduction of noise, everything can be sound, or be turned into sound. The concert is the framework which determines what should be heard as music. Thus contemporary, avant-garde music exists in stark contradiction to the record which by its very nature is temporally limited and which, by the mere changing of sides, creates a break in the continuity of the musical event. John Cage's piece *4'33* teaches us, additionally, that it only requires a simple gesture to bring music into being, a gesture that is essentially connected with something visual[19]. This event can be seen as a dramatization of a music which no longer needs to be conducted but which takes place in space. By the introduction of coincidence into composition, the status of the musical work is completely linked to its performance - something differing with every repetition. Time, space, and coincidence make the performance unique and irrevocable.

> The identity of the work with itself is [...] no longer even distantly identical to the identity of the performance; rather, where not totally resolved, it is to

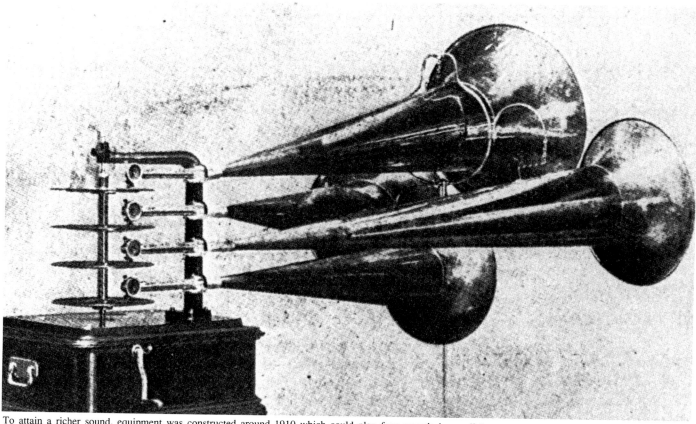

To attain a richer sound, equipment was constructed around 1910 which could play four records in parallel.

be understood as the identity of an experimental arrangement. However, through the non-identity of the performances and through the postulated irrevocability of each of these, it becomes an undertaking in total contradiction to the spirit of such music that it should be recorded on tape or disc. Cage, and those of the American compositional movement that side with him, [...] desire performances personified by the musicians being present, acting hic et nunc in presence.[20]

Composers

Incidentally, I believe that even during their preliminary work, contemporary composers frequently reckon with recording equipment, adapting their composition accordingly. I can't help myself; it is just when they are transmitted mechanically, on Electrola, *for instance, that the more worthwhile of our modern hits sound at their best - that is, the most authentic to me.*
Heinrich Mann[21]

Actually, one assumes that the composer would be attracted by sounds set free to such an extent and the resulting power to use the medium of the record as either a partner, opponent, or as the sort of means of production suggested by Moholy-Nagy. However, marginalia here only have been handed down steming, moreover, from composers who propagate an expansion of musical material (Darius Milhaud, Paul Hindemith, Ernst Toch) or those who work in the intermedial sphere (Edgard Varèse, John Cage). Theodor W. Adorno describes the "horrifying panic that some composers admit to in the face of this invention."[22] Igor Stravinsky considers the possibilities for "creating specific music for phonographic reproduction, music that would only get its true image, that of the original sound, through mechanical reproduction"[23]. Rejection and enthusiasm polarizes interpreters too: for example, the conductor Sergiu Celibidache can only hear the symphony become reality in a live performance, versus the pianist Glenn Glould who could no longer endure the coughing and sneezing during his concerts[24]. So it is left up to the post-war visual artists to blithely take up the baton both from the pioneers of the record and

Luigi Russolo and the painter **Ugo Piatti** in the studio in Milano with the *intonarumori*. 1914

from the musical avant-garde with their ideas of noise, time, and drama.

The art of the arts

> *No doubt, before the invention of the record and the tape, nobody ever heard what we can now listen to often and at any time: the same performance twice.*
> Heinz-Klaus Metzger[25]

In taking leave of the picture panel, the fine arts have appropriated all other artistic forms of expression: film, photography, theatre, architecture, literature, and music. Music is a source of irritation in this list, as it is the only invisible art. However, one of the first compositions by a visual artist, Marcel Duchamp's *Erratum Musical* (1913), makes it clear that, on the one hand, the score can be seen as a picture and, on the other hand, the performance is tied to the dramatization described above. The same concept can also be found in performances of Fluxus-concerts, as, for example, in

music while you work in which Arthur Køpcke inverts the function of the record as a supplier of background music and allows himself to be repeatedly interrupted from his housework on the stage by a prepared record. The score or directions become vivid; the implementation becomes an action that changes with every performance because the pictorial notation is basically only a suggestion and not a compositional specification in the classic sense. Therefore, the performer in *music while you work* is free to decide which record to prepare, what housework to do, and what the duration of the performance will be[26].

According to this, a record of artistic-musical events is a document, like an acoustic photograph, and so in a similar way one has to use one's imagination to supplement what is missing, but not in the way suggested by Rudolph Lothar when he emphatically ascribes the properties of vision to the speaking-machine:

> It is a plaything for the ignorant, a pastime for philistines, a showman for plebians; but a source of the purest artistic pleasure to the musically sensitive

person who possesses the power of illusion not to hear extraneous noises, not to see the machine, but to indulge himself in the images conjured up by the musical sounds.[27]

It is hardly possible to talk of "indulgently" letting oneself go when listening to records by Joseph Beuys, Henning Christiansen, Hermann Nitsch or Dieter Roth. However, pictures or recollections of exhibition pieces and of individuals that increase the acoustical dimension of an artist's work do exist. Mr. Edison would have experienced great joy in them. As Helmut Heissenbüttel writes in his essay *The Record as a Means of Gaining Historical Awareness*:

> Music is, and a record can, indeed, show this more distinctly than any other means, an acoustic phenomena and not something merely conveyed via notation. In addition, it is the place where intellectual insight and sensory perception approach one another, even to the point were they are made to coincide.[28]

From this standpoint, the recordings of sound sculptures, sound installations, or performances are also more than simply documentation. Attached to the movement of sculpture, space, or dramatization, they do lack visual presence; nevertheless, they may be heard as a direct musical articulation and consequently can, by means of the sounds unharnessed from visual effect, transform one's own home into a magical, mysterious place, as seen in René Magritte's painting *L'assassin menacé*. These sounds are initially both unassociated and unfamiliar thus requiring a higher level of concentration. Only through prolonged familiarity, can they be applied as background music. They have abandoned the museums and galleries and have settled down in a new place. They are metamorphosed and have become self-sufficient.

It is conspicuous how often artists talk about both themselves and their work on records: in the case of Alan Kaprow and Yves Klein, it is a stance that is not merely educational; rather it is the initial interest in the

physiognomy of the voice which, together with sound poetry, has increased the whole wealth of human and lyric expression since the invention of the record, although art can also reach museums along the avenues of speech, as the *Art by Telephone* enterprise has demonstrated.

In any case, artists seem to prefer the recording angel to a listening Nipper - unless he is barking. Artists do not expect high sound quality. When using the record as a reproductive medium, they demand that the recordings sound spontaneous. In contrast to unionized, professional musicians who on occasion are obliged to haphazardly throw off a work by Schoenberg, artists are comitted to a creative "dilettantism" that experiments with musical instruments or with speech. The tape recordings which Jean Dubuffet, Dieter Roth, or André Thomkins produced at home and put on to the market as limited edition LPs are far from being domestic music. They violate the frontiers of so-called good taste - something which Marcel Duchamp had already wanted to get rid of - and do-it-yourself experiments in, by, and with music and speech; their modes of expression range from Bruitism to silence. Dieter Roth:

> Nach vielen Jahren des die gelernten, die sogenannten guten Musiker (verschiedener Musikarten oder Musikspielweisen) Beneidens und vielen Jahren des Selbergernkönnenwollens hatte ich mir eine sozusagen alkoholische Spielweise anerzogen (auf welchem Instrument immer), die gut (klassisch hochgebrachten Hörern) erschien, witzig, leicht süsslich, angenehm nicht zu gut seiend. Darunter - drunter aber wußte ich von meiner Ambition (ganz alleine - wenn ich jemanden von ihr und meiner Verzweiflung der Güte klassisch hoher Musik gegenüber sprach war Abneigung, Nichtglauben, Komplimentfischereiverdacht die Wirkung), und ich hatte die Idee, das wär doch was (was? was waäres?), das Nichtkönnenzeigen, die Scham, sie erleidend zeigen![29]

The musically explosive force that radiates from these artists is certainly a reflection of their everyday acoustic environment. Many artists let themselves be inspired by music while working or they have friends who are musicians. What started with Piet Mondrian's love of jazz, was to continue with Franz Kline or Tomas Schmit. Andy Warhol had his own in-house band in the Velvet Underground, and finally artists themselves appear on stage as pop and jazz stars. Laurie Anderson made the charts and Martin Kippenberger, A.R. Penck, Salomé and many others are producing their own background music, following Kippenberger's motto:

> Music is beautiful.
> Where does it go from here?
> The louder
> the better.[30]

The Eskimo **Nanook** in **Robert Flaherty's** documentary film *Nanook of the North*. 1922

The comedian **Karl Valentin** from Munich in his film *Im Schallplattenladen*. 1934

Packaging

> *Karl Valentin: One of those round, dark black discs.*
> *Sales assistant: Fiñe, but do you want records with music or with singing?*
> *Karl Valentin: No, just with the sound of the record, cheap sound.*[31]

Visual artists have an obvious love of improvised music. This is where interrelations and internal relationships that are not purely sociological can be found. The cross-fertilization becomes particularly clear when contemplating record sleeves which by themselves form a sort of sub-history of Modern Art. When designed by artists, the sleeves are not commercial art; i.e., not at first glance product related. For this reason they can do without a photo of the star or just ironically cite it. Not subordinate to the product, they are an additional visual statement - bringing originality to the reproduction. A vivid example of this procedure can be found in Richard Hamilton's Beatles record. Texts and photos of the stars are banished from a sleeve which is smooth, cool, white, and embossed with the band's name. Ironically, despite the millions of copies printed, each sleeve is individually numbered, thus raising the question: what is intended to become the easily attainable multiple in this procedure: Hamilton's cover or the Beatles' record? A similar confusion is created by Andy Warhol's Zipper cover made for the Rolling Stones, which when seen in the spirit of the Campbell's Tomato Soup creation, can be taken as a Warhol which happen to have a Stones' LP enclosed.

When artists create their own records, the LP's information is presented in an individual style. The sleeves tend to be exquisitely designed, and they are often issued in limited editions. With their accompanying info, action photos, graphic inspirations and outcomes, numberings and signatures, they are small, exquisite objects, comparable to artists' books which similarly unite under a single concept materials, information, and craft, the only difference between the two objects being that arists' records scarcely have the opportunity to abruptly change format: they must follow set standards. Christian Marclay eventually re-unified cover with record as in *Record Without A Cover*, while at the same time going on to offer a grooveless record in luxury packaging as a multiple. Since the mid-seventies Punk, New Wave, and Polish musicians have absorbed in particular the artists' do-it-yourself packaging ideas, in an effort to consciously reject the apparently compulsory star mania and norms of the music business; an attack upon the packaging strikes at the heart of the contents.

White Noise

> *Music is coming out of cinemas; these are discs on which people's voices are transmitted. And all are singing.*
> Irmgard Keun[32]

Visual artists as musical "dilettantes" are not particularly sought after in the music business. Nevertheless, they serve a purpose as trail blazers. Unlike the musicians in the classical and light music establishment, they show no reservations and when experimenting are not particularly concerned about correct musical chronology, a problem which composers constantly have breathing down their necks. Artists are practicians and researchers like Nanook the Eskimo, who in Robert Flaherty's film of the same name, bites into a record out of curiosity in order to gain physical access to the laws of mechanical music.
Egon Friedell on dilettantism:

> Nowadays we come into the world with brains which are, as it were, already pigeon holed. We are not capable of imagining that a person can do more than *one* thing. We put everyone in a special category and are astonished, suspicious, or offended if they refuse to keep to our definition. Extreme versatility, however, can be observed in all gifted people of truly advanced times. They were interested in everything and could also master everything. In Ancient Greece, if a man wanted to be credited with excellence, he was obliged to distinguish himself in virtually all fields: in music and oratory as well as in military command and wrestling. The Ancient Greeks frankly despised specialists; they considered them "philistines". By the time of the Renaissance, talent, "virtu", was practically synonymous with versatility. A talented individual was an individual who mastered all the possible areas in which talent could be ex-

pressed. The specialist only surfaces in degenerate cultures. And finally it must be realized that innovations nearly always manifest themselves in the guise of "dilettantism".[33]

Visual artists made it possible to turn away from spezialization which brought about compositions for records to the Modern Age, something which had already been demanded by musicians in the 30's. The *Chöre and Soli* by the "Tödliche Doris" is an excellent example of this. Following in the footsteps of Edison and Berliner, they use the medium of recording itself to put into concrete terms what it means to be a discologist, a practical scientist. Their product follows the standard of a Wagner cassette. Inside are eight small, brightly colored discs and a booklet; even a tiny recordplayer is included. For technical reasons, each song lasts only 30 seconds: that is almost as long as it takes to insert the disc into the apparatus. No sooner is it heard that the musical pleasure is past. Marcel Duchamp also concerned himself with the problem of time. His *Rotoreliefs*, designed in 1935 for the record player, are six discs printed with color motives on both sides, and which are laid on the turntable with the help of a square plinth. At 33 RPM the two dimensional surfaces give an impression of being three dimensional[34]. This experiment in art and physics was subsequently continued pictorally by André Thomkins and is even today a popular effect in picture discs.

The problem of time in the medium of the record can, however, also be tackled directly since a record is a time machine which is capable of releasing musical sensations through a simple manipulation of the apparatus' speed selector. With this trick Nam June Paik took, for example, a piece by Schönberg and re-created it on his own record; he later received a critical reply from Dieter Roth via a single: music becomes noise, noise becomes music and musical time again becomes an indeterminate factor. At the same time, both the artist and the man in the street can use this relatively simple procedure in order to compose with found musical material. The displacement of time is dramatically intensified when locked grooves are used, as in the work of Boyd Rice. The advantage of this is that many of the pieces which have unending sounds, can fit on one record, thus enabling the consumer to make his own compositions using the pick-up arm.

However, the record itself can also be treated by scratching it, cutting it up, putting it together again with other records, and then listening to the result. The noise produced in this way by Milan Knížák's collages, sounds like an archaic music which throws the entire cosmos of reproduced sounds into confusion. Christian Marclay uses a similar method when composing live with mountains of treated and untreated records on four turntables with pick-up arms, amplifiers, and speed changesmus, thereby creating a conceptional,

rhythmically structured, plotted journey through the history of music which includes an intermingeling of familiar, catchy lines, melodies, and one-hit-wonders,- all of which rip each other to shreds and then dissolve into unsuspected sounds. Bye-bye records, hello music.

Knížák and Marclay are those who also bring out the sculptural qualities of records. While an observer of Nam June Paik's record sculpture still has the opportunity to produce sounds, Knížák presents another kind of music through his installations of children's instruments, and in Marclay's sculptures, sounds have finally been laid to rest. The records exist as a silent tower or have to suffer the fate of being used as a floor on which tracks are left behind.

The record objects of Joseph Beuys and Henning Christiansen, or the silhouettes of Piotr Nathan, also remain silent. Yet they are not dumb; the erotic touch of a needle suffices to coax at least a noise from them. As an object of art they have forfeited their real existence. The spirit of reproduction has completely abandoned them. They symbolize a concrete time, yet have no duration. They are, like memories, stored up time. They have coagulated into sculpture, and there is nothing revolving anymore except in the head of the observer whose skull, as Rainer Maria Rilke imagined, might one day, in search of the "archetypal sound", possibly come into contact with Edison's needle.

> The coronal seam of the skull (which should be examined next) has - let's assume - a certain similarity to the densely winding line which the stylus of the apparatus engraves in the receiving cylinder. And if, as now, the stylus were deceived and on its return journey guided along a track that did not originate from the graphic translation of a sound but from something existing naturally and in itself - good, let's just say it: it would simply be (e.g.) the coronal seam -: What would happen: A sound would be generated, a sequence of sounds, music...[35]

La Musique des anges

> *La disque fait table rase du dilettantisme musical des filles de bonne famille, de l'activité insupportable des salles de concert, et, par l'intermédiaire de la musique, il libère l'homme musical, l'artiste, des contraintes de la journée.*
> Erich Mendelsohn[1]

Les inventeurs du disque étaient fascinés par la reproduction de la voix humaine, non par celle de la musique. En 1878 dans son énumération des possibilités d'utilisation du phonographe Edison ne plaça la musique qu'en quatrième position: elle y apparaît après les fonctions de dictaphone, de livre pour aveugles, de professeur de langues et avant celles de jouet, d'horloge qui donne l'heure, d'instrument pédagogique et, en relation avec le téléphone, d'appareil enregistreur[2]. Il ressort que le temps libre, ce qui de nos jours constitue le but quasi exclusif de la production discographique, était moins important que l'utilité sociale. Il s'agissait avant tout de donner à la culture de l'écrit une expansion dans le domaine de la phonétique, tandis que l'art qui cherchait la sensation allait s'amuser dans les foires avec des arias et des chansons enregistrées. La popularisation proprement dite de la musique s'est développée grâce aux raffinements de la technique qui vers 1900 permirent l'enregistrement multiple des voix. Jusqu'alors chaque enregistrement sur cylindres devait être repris du début et l'on ne pouvait presser les disques qu'en petite quantité. Le chant en studio était synonyme de répétition incessante, une torture proportionnelle au nombre de disques à produire. De plus, chaque disque devait être enregistré intégralement, car avant la découverte de la bande magnétique, toute coupure était impossible. Une fausse note et c'en était fait de l'enregistrement.

Encore immédiate à ses débuts la relation entre production et reproduction trouve sa correspondance visuelle dans la vignette de l'ange qui grave les sillons du disque à l'aide d'une espèce de tuyau de plume. Ce procédé actif et direct met en lumière le

Revue-scene from the German film
Traummusik with **Lizzi Waldmüller**. 1940

merveilleux de cette découverte: produire un exemplaire unique de la physionomie de la voix d'un individu, un document qui serait comparable au manuscrit dans la tradition écrite. Ce n'est pas par hasard que l'ange fut remplacé en 1909 par le chien Nipper qui épie patiemment la voix mécanique de son maître. Le disque devient un mass media, un serviteur de la musique et non pas son déclencheur. Rudolph Lothar écrit en 1924:

> Dans son livre *Les Fondements de la musique* Felix Auerbach a écrit (1911): "En ce qui a trait au royaume de la musique, il est difficile de ranger les gramophones parmi les instruments de musique, et il est même douteux qu'ils acquièrent un jour une telle position. Aujourd'hui ils appartiennent de toute façon au chapitre des erreurs de l'activité artistique, et ce dans la mesure où ils esquissent des images déformantes des meilleurs originaux, images qui, au lieu de le cultiver, détériorent irrémédiablement le goût de la masse." Les opinions ont considérablement changé depuis ce rejet catégorique et apodictique de la machine parlante. Les meilleurs musiciens actuels la considèrent comme un facteur culturel de premier ordre qui, plus tout autre élément dans l'histoire de la vie musicale, a contribué à la diffusion et à la popularisation de la musique. La machine parlante ne déforme pas; elle produit au contraire une image sonore aussi précise qu'une photographie, voire encore plus précise et de meilleure qualité, car si la photographie doit se contenter du blanc et noir et renoncer aux couleurs de l'original, un bon disque reproduit infailliblement le coloris le plus fin, les nuances les plus douces d'une voix ou d'une pièce pour orchestre. Ainsi, la machine parlante a depuis longtemps converti son ennemi d'origine, et d'un Saül elle fait un Paul.[3]

Sounding postcard of the fifties

Production / Reproduction

> *...je tiens à préciser que je n'ai aucun disque chez moi...*
> John Cage[4]

Au début de ce siècle les artistes se déclarent toutefois insatisfaits du rôle de Paul. Les futuristes, Dada et Bauhaus qui s'en prennent à l'établissement d'une compréhension bourgeoise de l'art, laquelle s'associe à un perfectionnement des mass media, doivent nécessairement inclure dans leurs attaques ces nouveaux média que sont le film, la photographie et le disque. Cette nouvelle orientation des arts prend forme grâce à des expérimentations qui abolissent la fonction purement reproductrice des media et créent de nouvelles surprises. Le film ne raconnte plus, il met à jour des structures rythmiques[5]. Avec les photogrammes il est maintenant possible de faire des photographies directement en laboratoire, sans passer par l'extérieur[6]. Les arts plastiques font entrer le quotidien dans le noble musée.
La caractéristique de toutes ces recherches basées sur les media est la transformation des moyens de re-

Die ſprechende Poſtkarte
iſt jetzt im Pariſer Poſtverkehr eingeführt worden. Die Erfindung ſtammt aus Amerika. Um eine ſprechende Poſtkarte abſenden zu können, nimmt man ein gewöhnliches Poſtkartenformular, verſieht es mit der Adreſſe des Empfängers und klebt auf die Rückſeite ein auf der Walze des Phonographen beſprochenes Papier auf. Damit der Adreſſat nun hören kann, was ihm der andere mitteilen will, muß er ebenfalls die Karte auf die Walze eines Phonographen legen, und dann erſchallt die Stimme des Abſenders der Karte. Die ſprechende Poſtkarte, der man den Namen sonorine gegeben hat, wird vor allem dazu dienen, das Briefgeheimnis zu wahren, was bisher bei geſchriebenen, offenen Poſtkarten nicht möglich war. Natürlich kann auf dieſe neue Art und Weiſe nur zwiſchen Perſonen korreſpondiert werden, die ſich im Beſitze der dazu nötigen Apparate befinden. Die Pariſer Poſtverwaltung hat daher nach Art unſeres Telephon=Adreßbuches ein Verzeichnis der Bewohner von Paris herausgegeben, die Phonographen für die ſprechende Poſtkarte ihr eigen nennen.

Speyerer Zeitung, 2/12/1905

Sounding postcard of the fifties

Promotion-record, n.d.

production en moyens de production. Laszlo Moholy-Nagy:

> Il est dans la nature de l'homme de vouloir pousser après chaque nouvel enregistrement les appareils fonctionnels *vers de nouvelles impressions.* Voilà qui explique entre autres le constant besoin d'innovation au niveau de la forme. *De ce point de vue les formes ne sont valables que lorsqu'elles produisent de nouvelles relations jusqu'alors inconnues.* Cela implique que du point de vue spécifique de la forme créatrice - *abstraction faite* des points de vue irrélevants - la reproduction (la répétition de relations déjà existantes) ne peut être considérée dans le meilleur des cas que comme une affaire de virtuosité.
> Dans la mesure où la production (la réalisation productive) sert à l'évolution de l'homme, il devient indispensable d'essayer d'orienter les appareils (moyens) utilisés jusqu'à date à des fins de reproduction vers des fins de production.[7]

Au Bauhaus Moholy-Nagy tente de réaliser cette extension en utilisant entre autres le disque; il propose de graver les sillons des disques de cire au moyen de l'agrandissement et de la réduction photographiques, sans passer par un enregistrement musical; il en résulte des sons nouveaux et inusités, une vraie musique d'ange[8].

Bruits

> Pour obtenir une forme plus universelle la nouvelle musique devra oser un nouvel ordre des sons et non-sons (bruits spécifiques).
> Piet Mondrian[9]

Les musiciens s'intéressent à peine aux réflexions de Moholy-Nagy. Ils réagissent à une nouvelle dynamique de la vie dans les grandes villes, phénomène issu du travail de la machine et des media, et qui implique une extension du matériau sonore, une dissolution de l'harmonie, des essais synthétiques avec des orgues de couleur ou des compositions pour instruments électro-acoustiques[10]. Toutefois, l'innovation la plus décisive pour la musique est sans doute l'intérêt que suscitent les facteurs bruit et temps. Le manifeste de l'art du bruit formulé par le futuriste Luigi Russolo en 1933 a influencé jusqu'à notre époque la musique d'avant-garde, y compris le pop et les nouvelles pièces radiophoniques[11].

> Les bruits accompagnent chaque manifestation de notre vie. Le bruit est donc familier à notre oreille et il peut nous transposer directement dans la vie. Le son, qui ne participe pas de la vie et qui musicalement est toujours une chose pour soi et un élément aléatoire, non nécessaire, est devenu à notre oreille ce qu'un visage connu est à notre oeil; le bruit par

contre nous parvient dans la confusion et l'irrégularité du brouhaha de la vie: il ne se révèle jamais entièrement et il nous réserve d'innombrables surprises. Nous avons donc la certitude que grâce à la sélection, la coordination et le maîtrise de tous les bruits, nous pourrons enrichir l'humanité d'une nouvelle jouissance inespérée. Bien qu'il soit dans la nature du bruit de nous transposer brutalement dans la vie, L'ART DU BRUIT NE DOIT JAMAIS SE RÉSUMER À UNE RÉPÉTITION IMITATIVE DE LA VIE! De lui-même il atteindra sa force émotive optimale à partir du plaisir acoustique que l'inspiration de l'artiste sait tirer de la combinatoire des bruits.[12]

Voulant introduire les bruits de la civilisation technique dans la musique Russolo construit ses *intonarumori*, prédécesseurs des sculptures sonores et des instruments qui vibrent comme si le monde de la machine était en accord avec les instruments de l'orchestre[13]. Ils fonctionnent comme les gramophones à l'aide d'une manivelle. Mais ces faiseurs de bruit sont relativement timides et ils conviennent mieux à la musique de chambre. Nous sommes encore très loin d'une musique de machine violemment rythmique comme celle que produisent aujourd'hui Vivenza ou les "Einstürzenden Neubauten".

Edgard Varèse, Erik Satie ou George Antheil composent également avec des bruits, sans toutefois les imiter. Ils les incorporent réellement à la musique, c'est-à-dire que la machine à écrire, la sirène, le moteur d'avion et l'enclume sont présents sur la scène en tant qu'objets de l'expression musicale, en tant qu'instruments.

La reproduction technique des sons donne au bruit la possibilité de s'instaurer en un élément toujours accessible pouvant être retracé et réulitisé à souhait. Entreposé dans les archives des maisons de la radio et sur des disques, il attend de faire son entrée. En 1948 Pierre Schaeffer utilise pour sa *musique concrète* des disques d'archive[14]; John Cage, qui en 1939 fit appel à des disques-épreuves pour son *Imaginary Landscape No.1*, décrit le fonctionnement de la composition à base de bruits.

Des enregistrements de fréquences et du crissement d'un générateur furent placés sur des tourne-disques dont on pouvait varier la vitesse afin d'obtenir des glissandi. On produisait le son en déposant une aiguille sur le disque, même si parfois l'entrée était imprécise. Il était donc préférable d'avoir recours à une série de boutons permettant de placer l'aiguille sur le disque avant l'entrée en question et, dépendant de la position du bouton, de créer soit le son, soit le silence. Il était également possible de régler l'intensité sonore avec une extrême précision. Un participant peut utiliser plusieurs tourne-disques et produire une seule voix écrite pour tremblement de terre, pluie, air comprimé ou tout autre son concret. Un petit microphone de contact, tel que celui employé pour le marimbula, transforme les sons modérés en des sons d'une qualité ou d'un caractère plus percutant.[15]

Temps

Le son musical est en contact direct avec l'âme. Il y trouve immédiatement un écho, car l'homme a la musique en lui.
Wassily Kandinsky[16]

Le déplacement des dimensions temporelles constitue l'aspect fondamental des expérimentations avant-gardistes, des pièces microscopiques d'Anton Webern jusqu'aux *Vexations* d'Erik Satie, une oeuvre d'une durée de dix-huit heures qui est formée de 840 répétitions; John Cage la publia en 1949. John Cage:

Si l'on considère qu'un son est caractérisé par sa hauteur, son intensité, son timbre et sa durée, et que le silence, partenaire indispensable du son parce que son contraire, n'est caractérisé que par sa durée, il appert que la durée, c'est-à-dire l'étendue dans le temps, est le plus important des quatre paramètres du matériau musical. Le silence ne peut être perçu comme hauteur ou harmonie; il n'est perçu que comme durée.[17]

Cette réflexion sur le temps musical omet de manière significative toute délimation et les sons deviennent en conséquence équivalents, "die Summe aller Klänge ist grau"[18]. Les thèmes, phrases, leitmotive et codas perdent leur sens. Pour être perçus en tant que tels le début et la fin d'une pièce doivent être déterminés par un contexte nous permettant d'entendre la pièce comme une composition; car avec l'introduction du bruit, tout peut être ou devenir son. Ce contexte constitue le cadre de ce qui depuis Cage peut être entendu comme musique. Il existe de ce point de vue une forte contradiction entre la musique avant-gardiste de notre époque et le disque qui est limité dans le temps et qui de plus, lorsqu'on le retourne, interrompt le déroulement continu de l'événement musical. Depuis *4'33* de John Cage nous savons en outre qu'un seul geste suffit pour engendrer la musique, un geste essentiellement relié à l'aspect visuel[19]; car un concert a lieu sur la scène et il y a toujours quelque chose à voir sur la scène. Ce procédé implique une théâtralisation de la musique qui n'a plus besoin d'être dirigée mais qui prend place dans l'espace. Par l'introduction du hasard dans la composition l'oeuvre musicale devient complètement dépendante de son exécution, laquelle est différente à chaque répétition. Le temps, l'espace et le hasard font de l'exécution d'une pièce un événement unique et irrévocable.

L'identitié de l'oeuvre avec elle-même ne correspond plus du tout à l'identité des exécutions entre elles; et là où elle n'est pas entièrement dissolue, elle signifie l'identité des préraratifs de l'expérimentation. Toutefois, en raison de la non-identité des différentes exécutions et du postulat de leur irréproductibilité, il va à l'encontre du sens d'une telle musique de vouloir

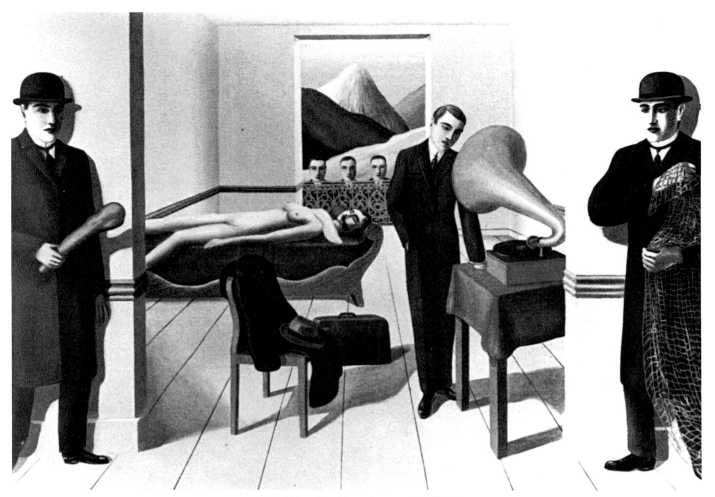

René Magritte. *L'assasin menacé*. 1926/27

12 ROTORELIEFS

These discs, turning at an approximate speed of 33 revolutions per minute, will give an impression of depth and the optical illusion should be more intense with one eye than with two.

The 12 drawings will be best seen kept in their black frame, the larger ones through the larger side of the frame.

In order to make use of the turnstile of the long playing record machines, see drawing showing how to place the pack of discs, above the pin, on white cardboard.

marcel duchamp

Marcel Duchamp. *12 Rotoreliefs*. 1953. Edition of 1000 unnumbered, unsigned sets

fixer sur bande ou sur disque une de ses exécutions. Cage et les compositeurs américains qui s'en inspirent exigent une éxécution vivante grâce à la présence hic et nunc de musiciens agissants.[20]

Compositeurs

> D'ailleurs je crois que nos compositeurs actuels pensent à l'appareillage du disque en travaillant et qu'ils l'intègrent dans leurs compositions. Je n'y peux rien, même les meilleurs succès modernes me semblent procéder d'une transmission mécanique; quelque chose comme: Elektrola, qualité et fidélité optimales!
> Heinrich Mann[21]

On pourrait donc supposer que les compositeurs auraient dû être séduits par l'idée d'utiliser, comme le propose Moholy-Nagy, les sons ainsi libérés et les possibilités offertes par le disque en tant que partenaire, antagoniste ou moyen de production. Les essais dans ce sens restent cependant marginaux et ils furent pour la plupart l'oeuvre de compositeurs qui élaborent une extension du matériau musical (Darius Milhaud, Paul Hindemith, Ernst Toch) ou qui travaillent dans des domaines interdisciplinaires (Edgard Varèse, John Cage). Theodor W. Adorno parle de la "peur panique"[22] que manifestent certains compositeurs devant cette découverte, Igor Stravinsky des possibilités "de créer une musique propre à la reproduction phonographique, une musique qui n'atteindrait son authencitité, la sonorité originale, que lors de la reproduction mécanique"[23].
Les interprètes se scindent également en deux clans distincts représentés d'une part par le chef d'orchestre Sergiu Celibidache et d'autre part par le pianiste Glenn Gould: le premier ne dit entendre réellement une sym-

phonie qu'en concert, tandis que le deuxième ne peut plus supporter la toux et les reniflements du public[24]. Après la Deuxième Guerre Mondiale il ne resta plus que les peintres et les sculpteurs pour reprendre en toute insouciance le sentier des pionniers du disque ou de l'avant-garde musicale influencée par les réflexions sur le théâtre, le bruit et le temps.

L'Art des arts

> Avant la découverte du disque et de la bande magnétique personne n'a jamais entendu ce qu'aujourd'hui nous pouvons entendre en tout temps et que nous entendons souvent: deux fois la même exécution.
> Heinz-Klaus Metzger[25]

En évacuant le tableau les arts plastiques se sont appropriés des autres formes d'expressions artistiques: le film, la photographie, le théâtre, l'architecture, la littérature et la musique. La musique irrite au sein de cette énumération, car elle est la seule manifestation invisible. La première composition d'un artiste non-musicien, l'*Erratum musical* de Marcel Duchamp (1913), témoigne présicément du fait que la partition peut ici être lue comme un tableau et que son exécution suppose le phénomène de la théâtralisation tel que décrit plus haut. On retrouve la même conception lors des concerts Fluxus, lorsque par exemple Arthur Køpcke inverse dans *music while you work* la fonction du disque en tant qu'émetteur de musique d'ambiance et qu'il utilise un disque préparé l'interrompant sans cesse dans les travaux ménagers qu'il effectue sur la scène. La partition ou les indications prennent un caractère métaphorique, l'exécution devient une action différente d'une fois à l'autre, puisque la notation métaphorique est une proposition et non une fixation de la composition au sens classique de terme. Ainsi, dans *music while you work* le participant détermine librement le choix du disque à préparer, les travaux ménagers qu'il veut effectuer ainsi que la durée de l'action dans son ensemble[26].
De ce point de vue les enregistrements d'actions artistiques et musicales sont des documents semblables à des photographies acoustiques: dans un cas comme dans l'autre la fantaisie doit travailler pour compléter ce qui manque, mais non pas comme le pense Rudolph Lothar qui prête à la machine parlante des qualités pouvant influencer la perception visuelle:

Piet Mondrian in his New York studio, n.d.

> C'est un jouet pour les cancres, un passe-temps pour les gens terre-à-terre, un faiseur de spectacle pour la plèbe, mais aussi une source du plus pur plaisir esthétique pour l'homme sensible à la musique, lequel réussit grâce à sa fantaisie à faire abstraction des bruits de fond et de la machine pour s'enivrer des images que les sons font apparaître comme par enchantement.[27]

Il est difficile de parler d'un "abandon grisant" à l'écoute des disques de Joseph Beuys, Henning Christiansen, Herman Nitsch ou Dieter Roth. Mais il existe des images, des souvenirs rappelant des objets d'exposition ou des personnes, des éléments susceptibles de servir de compléments acoustiques à l'oeuvre d'un artiste. Herr Edison y trouverait beaucoup de plaisir.

Helmut Heissenbüttel écrit dans son article *Mettre les disques au service de la conscience historique*:

> La musique est - et c'est le disque qui le montre de la manière la plus nuancée - acoustique et non pas seulement ce que la notation transmet. Elle en outre le lieu où se rencontrent le plus facilement la réflexion intellectuelle et la perception sensuelle, voire le lieu où elles s'équivalent.[28]

De ce point de vue les enregistrements de sculptures sonores, d'installations sonores ou de performances sont plus que des documents. Tributaires du mouvement de l'objet, de l'espace ou de la théâtralisation, la présence visuelle leur fait défaut; cette dernière peut cependant être perçue comme présence musicale immédiate et transformer ainsi le salon de l'auditeur qui se remplit des sons coupés de leur aspect visuel en un lieu magique et énigmatique, comme dans le tableau *L'assassin menacé* de René Magritte. Les sons ne renvoient premièrement à rien de particulier, ils sont inconnus et nécessitent de ce fait une attention accrue. Ils ne peuvent être utilisés comme musique d'ambiance qu'après une certaine période d'adaptation. Ils ont quitté le musée et la galerie pour prendre possession d'un lieu nouveau. Ils se transforment et deviennent autonomes.

Les artistes se racontent fréquemment sur leurs disques ou encore ils y parlent de leur travail, une attitude qui chez Alan Kaprow et Yves Klein n'est pas uniquement informative. Il s'agit du même intérêt porté à la physionomie de la voix et qui depuis l'invention du disque a enrichi grâce à la sound poetry les articulations humaines et lyriques. Mais, comme l'a démontré *Art by Telephone*, l'art peut également par l'intermédiaire du langage faire son entrée dans le musée.

D'ailleurs, sauf quand il jappe, le chien Nipper convient moins aux artistes que l'ange dessinateur. Ces derniers n'exigent pas la qualité sonore lorsqu'ils se servent du disque comme d'un moyen de reproduction. Contrairement aux musiciens organisés en syndicats qui doivent bien de temps à autre jouer un Schönberg, ils avouent un certain dilettantisme créateur qui expérimente avec les instruments de musique ou le langage. Les enregistrements sur bande magnétique que produisent chez eux Jean Dubuffet, Dieter Roth ou André Thomkins et qu'ils distribuent en petite quantité sur le marché n'ont rien de commun avec la musique d'amateurs. Ils empiètent sur les frontières de ce "bon goût" que Marcel Duchamp voulait étrangler; ce sont des auto-expérimentations sur et avec la musique ou le langage, des essais dont les possibilités d'expression vont du bruitisme au silence. Dieter Roth:

> Nach vielen Jahren des die gelernten, die sogenannten guten Musiker (verschiedener Musikarten oder Musikspielweisen) Beneidens und vielen Jahren des Selbergernkönnenwollens hatte ich mir eine sozusagen alkoholische Spielweise anerzogen (auf welchem Instrument immer), die gut (klassisch hochgebrachten Hörern) erschien, witzig, leicht süsslich, angenehm nicht zu gut seiend. Darunter - drunter aber wußte ich von meiner Ambition (ganz alleine - wenn ich jemanden von ihr und meiner Verzweiflung der Güte klassisch hoher Musik gegenüber sprach war Abneigung, Nichtglauben, Komplimentfischereiverdacht die Wirkung), und ich hatte die Idee, das wär doch was (was? was wääres?), das Nichtkönnenzeigen, die Scham, sie erleidend zeigen![29]

La force explosive de la musique se dégageant ici des artistes est certainement une réaction à l'environnement acoustique quotidien. Maints artistes se laissent inspirer par la musique en travaillant ou ils ont des amis musiciens. Franz Kline, Tomas Schmit poursuivent ce que Piet Mondrian avait entrepris avec son amour pour le jazz. Andy Warhol avait son propre orchestre dans sa maison du Velvet Underground et finalement les artistes se produisent sur la scène comme des vedettes de la musique pop ou du jazz. Laurie Anderson a été au hit-parade et Werner Kippenberger, A.R. Penck, Salomé et plusieurs autres font leur propre musique d'ambiance suivant la devise de Kippenberger:

> La musique est belle.
> Comment continuer?
> D'autant plus fort
> d'autant mieux.[30]

Emballage

> *Karl Valentin: des disques ronds, tout noirs.*
> *Vendeuse: Oui, mais, je veux dire, voulez-vous des disques avec de la musique ou du chant?*
> *Karl Valentin: non, seulement avec du son, du son pas cher.*[31]

On est frappé par l'amour que portent les artistes à la musique improvisée de l'underground. Il existe ici des réciprocités, des affinités qui ne sont pas seulement d'ordre sociologique. Les pochettes de disque qui nous racontent une sorte de sous-histoire de l'art moderne témoignent clairement de cette influence réciproque. Réalisées par des artistes elles sont plus que des oeuvres graphiques commerciales, c'est-à-dire qu'à première vue elles ne se rapportent pas directement au produit et qu'elles s'intéressent davantage au thème de l'emballage et au contenu. Elles renoncent en conséquence au portrait de la vedette ou elles se contentent de le citer avec ironie. Indépendantes du produit, elles présentent un produit supplémentaire, un énoncé pictural, faisant ainsi de la reproduction quelque chose d'original. Ce procédé est particulièrement marquant dans les réalisations de Richard Hamilton pour les disques des Beatles. Il élimine les photographies des vedettes et les textes de l'enveloppe sobre, froide avec son fond blanc duquel ne se détachent que les noms des vedettes. L'ironie veut cependant que chaque pochette soit numérotée, et l'on peut se poser la question à savoir quel est le multiple facilement accessible? Hamilton ou les Beatles? Andy

Warhol crée la même incertitude avec son ready made en forme de braguette pour les disques des Rolling Stones, un objet qui comme la soupe aux tomates Campbell peut être perçu comme un Warhol auquel aurait été ajouté par hasard un disque des Stones.
Lorsque les artistes réalisent leurs propres disques les informations prennent un caractère individuel. Les pochettes sont souvent très originales, car il s'agit de petits pressages. Les pièces jointes, les photos d'actions, les idées et attaques graphiques, la numérotation et la signature en font des petits objets précieux, comparables aux livres d'art qui réunissent à l'intérieur d'un concept des matières, des informations et du "fait main"; les disques faits par les artistes n'ont cependant pas la possibilité de changer les dimensions du produit et ils doivent s'en tenir aux normes imposées par l'industrie. Christian Marclay pour sa part conjugue la pochette et le disque: son *Record Without A Cover* présente un disque sans sillons dans un emballage luxurieux qui devient le multiple. Punk, New Wave et les musiciens polonais reprennent depuis le milieu de années 70 les idées de l'emballage fait main afin de se dissocier du marché musical standardisé ainsi que des allures de star, un phénomène qui n'a qu'en apparence un caractère obligatoire; car toute entorse à l'emballage touche le contenu en plein coeur.

Bruit blanc

Des cinémas vient une musique, ce sont les disques sur lesquels la voix des hommes se perpétue. Et tout chante.
Irmgard Keun[32]

Sur le marché musical les artistes dilettantes musiciens sont très peu en demande. Ils remplissent pourtant une fonction de précurseurs, puisque à l'inverse des musiciens établis dans les sphères de la musique

sérieuse ou de divertissement, ils n'ont pas de préjugés. Leurs expérimentations accordent peu d'importance au fil de l'histoire musicale qui opprime en permanence les compositeurs. Les artistes sont des praticiens et des chercheurs comme l'inuit Nanook qui dans le film de Robert Flaherty tente de croquer dans un disque afin de saisir physiquement les lois de la mécanique.
Egon Friedell à propos du dilettantisme:

Aujourd'hui nous venons au monde avec des cerveaux divisés dès le départ en compartiments. Nous sommes incapables de concevoir qu'un homme puisse faire plus d'une chose. On colle à chaque individu une étiquette précise et s'il en déroge nous réagissons avec stupeur, scepticisme, voire on crie à l'outrage. Pourtant nous savons que dans les époques de grande culture les hommes doués possédaient plusieurs talents. Ils s'intéressaient à tout et ils étaient capables de tout. En Grèce un homme devait, s'il voulait passer pour talentueux, exceller dans presque tous les domaines: la musique, la rhétorique tout comme l'armée ou la lutte. L'Hellène méprisait le spécialiste en tant qu'individu terre-à-terre. Et en pleine Renaissance le talent, la vertu étaient synonymes de talents multiples. Un homme talentueux était jadis un homme maîtrisant presque tous les domaines dans lesquels il est possible de faire preuve de sa valeur. Seules les cultures décadentes connaissent le spécialiste. Et finalement on doit comprendre que le dilettantisme est la forme à travers laquelle le nouveau s'exprime presque toujours.[33]

Ce refus de la spécialisation a contribué par l'intermédiaire des arts plastiques à l'avènement des compositions pour disques que les musiciens des années 30 avaient réclamé. Les *Chöre & Soli* des "Tödliche Doris" en sont un exemple frappant. Sur les traces d'Edison et de Berliner ils réalisent à l'intérieur du médium lui-même ce que signifie le fait d'être discologue, scientifique praticien. Leur produit répond au standard d'un coffret de Wagner: on y retrouve huit petits disques colorés, un livret, et même le tourne-disque est inclus dans l'emballage. Chaque chant a une durée techniquement déterminée de 20 secondes, exactement le temps qu'il faut pour placer le disque sur l'appareil. A peine l'a-t-on entendu que le plaisir de l'écoute s'est évanoui. Marcel Duchamp s'intéresse également au facteur temps. Ses *Rotoreliefs* conçus en 1935 pour le tourne-disque sont composés de six disques à deux faces imprimées, qui doivent être placés sur l'appareil à l'aide d'une boîte carrée. Lorsqu'elles sont reproduites à une vitesse de 33 tours-minute, il se dégage des surfaces bidimensionnelles un effet spacial[34]. Par la suite André Thomkins poussa plus loin cette expérimentation esthétique et physique qui constitue encore aujourd'hui un des effets préférés du picture-disc.
Appliquée au disque la réflexion sur le temps peut se produire directement, car il s'agit d'une machine temporelle apte à déclencher des sensations musicales à

l'aide de simples manipulations du régulateur de vitesse. Ce truc - que Nam June Paik fige sur un disque en se servant de Schönberg et auquel le single de Dieter Roth a répondu de manière critique - oriente la musique vers le bruit, le bruit sur de la musique, et le temps musical devient indéterminé. D'autre part il est relativement facile aux artistes ou à monsieur tout le monde de composer avec du matériau musical déjà existant. Le décalage du temps devient dramatique lorsque Boyd Rice joue avec des sillons infinis. Cela permet d'intégrer sur le même disque plusieurs pièces en apparence infinies et le consommateur peut également créer ses propres compositions en se servant du bras du tourne-disque.

On peut également manipuler les disques soi-même en leur ajoutant des rayures, en les découpant pour les recoler ensuite autrement, en les croisant avec d'autres disques et en écoutant ce qui en résulte. Le "tapage" résultant ainsi des collages de Milan Knížák ressemble à une musique archaïque qui mélange tout le cosmos des sons reproduits. Christian Marclay procède de façon similaire en composant avec des montagnes de disques travaillés, manipulés sur quatre

tourne-disques à l'aide d'un bras, d'un amplificateur et de changements de vitesse; on prend part à un voyage conceptuel à travers l'histoire de la musique, un voyage bruyant et rythmiquement structuré au cours duquel les rengaines connues, les mélodies et les succès éphémères s'entremêlent, se déchirent les uns les autres et se disolvent dans des sonorités inusitées. Adieu le disque, en avant la musique.

Knížák et Marclay mettent également en valeur les propriétés sculpturales des disques. La personne qui observe la sculpture de disques de Nam June Paik a encore la possibilité de produire des sons, et Knížák présente une autre musique, une musique faite à l'aide du montage d'instruments pour enfants; mais chez Marclay les sons se taisent définitivement. Les disques se taisent sous la forme d'une tour, et ils doivent accepter de servir de tapis.

Les objets de disques de Joseph Beuys, Henning Christiansen ou les silhouettes de Piotr Nathan se taisent également. Pourtant ils ne sont pas tout à fait muets, car il suffit du contact érotique d'une aiguille pour leur soutirer ne serait-ce qu'un bruit. Et en tant qu'objets esthétiques ils se créent une présence spéci-

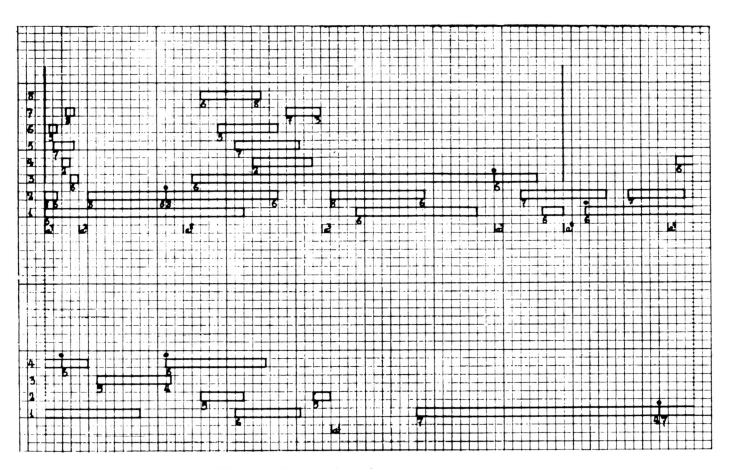

John Cage. *Imaginary Landscape No. 5*. 1952. For any 42 phonograph records, score

fique. L'esprit de la reproduction est complètement absent de ces objets qui, démunis de toute durée, symbolisent un temps concret; tel un souvenir, ils sont temps entreposé. Une fois transformés en sculpture, il ne se passe plus rien, si ce n'est dans la tête de l'observateur dont le crâne, dans sa quête du "bruit original", entrera peut-être un jour en contact avec l'aiguille d'Edison, comme le pensait Rainer Maria Rilke.

> La suture coronale du crâne (ce qu'il faudrait d'abord examiner de plus près) présente - supposons-le du moins - une certaine similitude avec cette ligne abondamment sinueuse que grave le burin du phonographe dans le cylindre en rotation de l'appareil. Que se passerait-il si l'on déviait le burin et que sur son chemin de retour on l'orientait vers une piste qui ne procède pas de la traduction graphique d'une note, mais qui serait quelque chose existant naturellement pour soi-même -, soit: disons-le seulement: ce serait précisément (par exemple) la suture coronale: que se produirait-il? Une note devrait se faire entendre, une séquence de sons, une musique...[35]

Notes

Titles which appear in the bibliography at the book's end will be given in abbreviated form in the following notes.

1 Quoted from: *50 Jahre Carl Lindström GmbH.* p.47

2 cf. Herbert Jüttemann: *Phonographen und Grammophone.* p.32

3 Rudolph Lothar: *Über Sprechmaschinen.* p.56 f.

4 John Cage: *Pour les oiseaux.* p.42. The German translation quoted from: *Für die Vögel. John Cage im Gespräch mit Daniel Charles.* Berlin 1984. p.49. The English translation quoted from: *For the Birds. John Cage in conversation with Daniel Charles.* p.50

5 cf. Hans Richter: *Filmgegner von heute - Filmfreunde von morgen.* Berlin 1929

6 cf. Floris M. Neusüss: *Fotogramme - die lichtreichen Schatten.* Kassel 1983

7 Laszlo Moholy-Nagy: *Malerei Fotografie Film.* p.28

8 cf. Laszlo Moholy-Nagy: *Neue Gestaltung in der Musik.*

9 Piet Mondrian: *Die neue Gestaltung in der Musik und die futuristischen italienischen Bruitisten.* In: De Stijl 2 (1923). p.22

10 cf. *Für Augen und Ohren.*

11 cf. et al. Klaus Schöning (ed.): *Hörspielmacher.* Königstein/Ts 1983

12 Luigi Russolo: *The Art of Noises.* In: *Futurismo & Futurismi.* p.561. The German translation quoted from: Umbro Appollonio: *Der Futurismus.* Köln 1972. p.107

13 cf. illus. in Russolo: *Die Geräuschkunst 1913 - 1931.*

14 cf. Fred K. Prieberg: *Musica ex machina.* p.82 ff.

15 John Cage: *For More New Sounds.* In: Richard Kostelanetz (ed.): *John Cage.* p.65 f. The German translation quoted from: Richard Kostelanetz: *John Cage.* Köln 1973. p.93

16 Kandinsky: *Über das Geistige in der Kunst.* Neuilly-sur-Seine 1952. Bern n.d.[10]. p.66

17 John Cage: *Defense of Satie.* In: Richard Kostelanetz (ed.): *John Cage.* p.81. The German translation quoted from: Richard Kostelanetz: *John Cage.* Köln 1973. p.111

18 René Block. In: *Für Augen und Ohren.* p.103 ff.

19 cf. Reinhard Josef Sacher: *Musik als Theater.* The piece *4'33* has also been recorded (Cramps Records).

20 Heinz-Klaus Metzger: *Über Schallquellen.* p.223

21 Quoted from: *50 Jahre Carl Lindström GmbH.* p.44

22 Theodor W. Adorno: *Die Form der Schallplatte.* p.533

23 Igor Strawinsky: *Meine Stellung zur Schallplatte.* p.65

24 cf. Matthias Fischer, Dietmar Holland, Bernhard Rzehulka: *Gehörgänge.*

25 Heinz-Klaus Metzger: *Über Schallquellen.* p.222 f.

26 cf. Arthur Køpcke: *Bilder und Stücke.* p.51

27 Rudolph Lothar: *Die Sprechmaschine.* p.60

28 Helmut Heissenbüttel: *Die Schallplatte als Mittel historisches Bewußtsein zu gewinnen.* p.592

29 Covertext of the record *Radio Sonate* by Dieter Roth

30 Kippenberger: *Durch die Pubertät zum Erfolg.* (cat.) Neue Gesellschaft für bildende Kunst. Berlin 1981. o.pag.

31 Karl Valentin: *Im Schallplattenladen.* p.521

32 Irmgard Keun: *Das kunstseidene Mädchen.* Düsseldorf 1979. p.95

33 Egon Friedell: *Über Dilettantismus.* In: E.F.: *Abschaffung des Genies.* Wien, München 1984[2]. p.269 f.

34 With these *Optical Discs* Marcel Duchamp wanted to create a completely accessible, publicly acceptable artwork and offered the discs in 1935 at an inventor's fair in Paris, without a great deal of success (cf. Herbert Molderings: *Marcel Duchamp.* Frankfurt a.M. 1987[2]. p.81 ff.). Only recently has this demand been fullfilled by its publication as a cutout in the French children's magazine *Diabolo.* (No. 12, 1988, pointed out by Margotow Archiv Wahlershausen).

35 Rainer Maria Rilke: *Ur-Geräusch.* p.180 f.

Theodor W. Adorno

Die Form der Schallplatte

Man möchte ihr keine andere Form zutrauen als sie selber zur Schau trägt: eine schwarze Scheibe, hergestellt aus einem Gemenge, das heutzutage so wenig mehr seinen ehrlichen Namen hat wie der Brennstoff der Autos Benzin heißt; zerbrechlich wie Tafeln, in der Mitte ein kreisrunder Zettel, der immer noch am echtesten aussieht, wenn darauf der Vorkriegs-Terrier die Stimme seines Herrn erlauscht; im Innersten darin ein kleines Loch, so eng zuweilen, daß man nachbohren muß, damit die Platte dem Teller sich auflegen läßt. Sie ist mit Kurven bedeckt; einer fein gekräuselten, gänzlich unleserlichen Schrift, die hie und da plastischere Figuren ausbildet, ohne daß der Laie ihr anhören könnte, warum; angeordnet als Spirale, endet sie irgendwo in der Nähe des Titel-Zettels, manchmal durch eine Querrinne mit diesem verbunden, damit die Nadel bequem auslaufen kann. Mehr will sie als >Form< nicht hergeben. Sie entstammt, vielleicht als erste der kunst-technischen Erfindungen, bereits jenem Zeitalter, das die Übermacht der Dinge über den Menschen zynisch bekennt, indem es die Technik von humanen Anforderungen und humanem Bedarf emanzipiert und Errungenschaften bereithält, ohne daß ihnen primär ein menschlicher Sinn zukäme; statt dessen wird der Bedarf erst durch die Reklame produziert, wenn das Ding vorliegt und nach eigener Bahn kreist. Eine eigene Form - wie sie noch die Frühzeit der Photographie kennt - ist nirgends mehr gewährt. Wie die Forderung >rundfunkeigener< Musik notwendig leer und unerfüllt blieb und nichts besseres zeitigte als einige Instrumentationsanweisungen, die praktisch sich nicht bewähren, so hat es grammophoneigene Musik nie gegeben, und es darf sogar als Vorzug der Schallplatten vermerkt sein, daß ihnen die kunstgewerbliche Verklärung künstlerischen Eigenseins im künstlerischen Eigenheim erspart blieb und sie von den phonographischen Ursprüngen bis zum elektrischen Verfahren (das dem photographischen der Vergrößerung zum Guten und Schlechten sehr verwandt sein mag) nichts waren, als eben die akustischen Photographien, welche der Hund so freudig wiedererkennt. Nicht umsonst wird der Ausdruck >Platte<, ohne Zusatz, in Photographie und Phonographie gleichsinnig gebraucht. Er bezeichnet das zweidimensionale Modell einer Wirklichkeit, die sich beliebig multiplizieren, nach Raum und Zeit versetzen und auf dem Markte tauschen läßt. Dafür hat sie das Opfer ihrer dritten Dimension zu bringen: ihrer Höhe und ihres Abgrunds.
Nach jeglichem Maße künstlerischer Selbstherrlichkeit wäre sonach die Form der Schallplatte schlechterdings ihre Nicht-Form; sie taugt zu wenig anderem, als die

Musik, um ihre beste Dimension geschmälert, abzubilden und aufzubewahren; eine Musik nämlich, die ohne die Schallplatte schon da war und von ihr nicht beträchtlich verändert wird. Schallplatten-Komponisten haben sich nicht gefunden; selbst Strawinsky, der es mit dem elektrischen Klavier gut meint, hat sich nicht daran versucht. Einzig die notwendige Kürze, nach dem Maß des Scheibentellers, mag die Schallplatten-Musik charakterisieren. Auch hier herrscht pure Identität zwischen der Platten-Form und der der Welt, in der sie spielt; die Stunden des häuslichen Daseins, die mit der Platte kreisen, sind zu karg, als daß der erste Satz der Eroica, ungeteilt, darin sich entfalten dürfte, und lieber sind ihnen Tänze, aus stumpfen Wiederholungen komponiert. Man kann mitten darin abstellen. Die Schallplatte ist ein Gegenstand jenes >täglichen Bedarfs<, der durchaus den Widerpart des menschlichen und künstlerischen ausmacht, denn dieser wäre nicht beliebig zu wiederholen und einzuschalten, sondern ist gebunden an seinen Ort und seine Stunde.
Dennoch, der Artikel Platte ist bereits zu alt, um nicht seine Rätsel zu präsentieren, verzichtet man erst einmal darauf, ihn als Kunst-Objekt zu sehen und forscht man lieber den Konturen seiner Dinglichkeit nach. Denn nicht im Grammophonspiel als einem Musiksurrogat: vielmehr in der Platte als Ding steckt, was sie etwa, auch ästhetisch, bedeutet. Sie ist, als künstlerisches Verfallsprodukt, die erste Darstellungsweise von Musik, die sich als Ding besitzen läßt. Nicht wie Ölbilder, die den Lebendigen von der Wand herab anschauen. So wenig diese mehr in die Wohnung passen, so wenig gibt es wahrhaft große Formate von Platten. Aber eben wie Photographien werden sie besessen; mit Grund hat das neunzehnte Jahrhundert samt den photographischen und den Briefmarken-auch die Schallplatten-Alben ersonnen, Herbarien künstlichen Lebens, gegenwärtig auf kleinstem Raum und bereit, jegliche Erinnerung zu beschwören, die sonst zwischen Hast und Einerlei des Privatlebens gnadenlos zerrieben wird. Mit den Schallplatten erobert sich die *Zeit* einen neuen Weg zur Musik. Es ist nicht die Zeit, in der Musik abläuft; nicht auch die, für welche sie, kraft ihres >Stiles<, als Denkmal einsteht. Es ist die Zeit als Vergängnis, dauernd in stummer Musik. Wenn die >Moderne< aller mechanischen Instrumente in der Starrheit ihrer Wiederholungen Musik uralt, von je gewesen erscheinen läßt und sie der trostlosen Ewigkeit des Uhrwerks unterstellt - dann ist Vergängnis und Erinnerung, wie sie den Drehorgeln als bloßer Klang zwangvoll, doch unbestimmt anhaftet, durch die Grammophonplatten handlich und offenbar geworden.
Den Schlüssel zum eigentlichen Verständnis der Schallplatten müßte die Kenntnis jener technischen Akte liefern, die einmal die Walzen der mechanischen Spielwerke und Orgeln in die phonographischen verwandelten. Wenn man späterhin, anstatt >Geistesgeschichte< zu treiben, den Stand des Geistes von

der Sonnenuhr menschlicher Technik ablesen sollte, dann kann die Vorgeschichte des Grammophons eine Wichtigkeit erlangen, welche die mancher berühmter Komponisten vergessen macht. Keinem Zweifel unterliegt: indem Musik durch die Schallplatte der lebendigen Produktion und dem Erfordernis der Kunstübung entzogen wird und erstarrt, nimmt sie, erstarrend, dies Leben in sich auf, das anders enteilt. Die tote rettet die >flüchtige< und vergehende Kunst als allein lebendige. Darin mag ihr tiefstes Recht gelegen sein, das von keinem ästhetischen Einspruch wider Verdinglichung zu beugen ist. Denn dieses Recht stellt, gerade durch Verdinglichung, ein uraltes, entsunkenes doch verbürgtes Verhältnis wieder her: das von Musik und *Schrift*.

Wer jemals den stetig wachsenden Zwang erkannte, den zumal in den letzten fünfzig Jahren Notenschrift und Notenbild auf die Kompositionen ausgeübt hat (das Schimpfwort >Papiermusik< verrät ihn drastisch), den kann es nicht wundernehmen, wenn eines Tages ein Umschlag von der Art erfolgte, daß die Musik, zuvor von der Schrift befördert, mit einem Male selber in Schrift sich verwandelt: um den Preis ihrer Unmittelbarkeit, doch mit der Hoffnung, daß sie, dergestalt fixiert, einmal als die >letzte Sprache aller Menschen nach dem Turmbau< lesbar wird, deren bestimmte, doch chiffrierte Aussagen jeder ihrer >Sätze< enthält. Waren aber die Noten noch ihre bloßen Zeichen, dann nähert sie durch die Nadelkurven der Schallplatten ihrem wahren Schriftcharakter entscheidend sich an. Entscheidend, weil diese Schrift als echte Sprache zu erkennen ist, indem sie ihres bloßen Zeichenwesens sich begibt: unablöslich verschworen dem Klang, der dieser und keiner anderen Schall-Rinne innewohnt. Ist in den Schallplatten die musikalische Produktivkraft erloschen; haben sie keine Form mehr mit ihrer Technik gestiftet, so verwandeln sie dafür den jüngsten Klang alter Gefühle in einen archaischen Text kommender Erkenntnis. Wenn aber der Theologe zur Konsequenz

sich gedrängt weiß, daß kein[e] Verstande >Leben< - als Ge[schöpfe - zugeschrieben werd[auch der Erwägung geneigt s[gehalt der Kunst erst aufsteigt Lebendigen sie verläßt: da[>wahr<, Bruchstücke der w[wenn Leben aus ihnen entw[vermöge ihres Unterganges u[Dann könnte, in einem schw[Form der Schallplatte sich be[die im Zentrum, der Öffnun[aber dafür dauert in der Zeit.

Daran hat die Physik ihren g[Chladnischen Klangfiguren, auf die bereits - nach de[Entdeckung eines der wichtigsten gegenwärtigen Ästhetiker - Johann Wilhelm Ritter als auf die schriftgemäßen Urbilder des Klanges hinwies. Die jüngste technische Entwicklung jedenfalls hat fortgeführt, was dort begann: die Möglichkeit, Musik, ohne daß sie je erklang, zu >zeichnen<, hat die Musik zugleich noch unmenschlicher verdinglicht und sie noch rätselhafter dem Schrift- und Sprachcharakter angenähert. Der panische Schreck, den vor dieser Erfindung manche Komponisten bekunden, trifft genau die ungeheure Gefahr, die dem Leben der Kunstwerke von dorther wie schon aus der sanfteren Barbarei der Schallplatten-Alben droht. Es mag in ihm jedoch auch die Erschütterung über jene Transfiguration aller Wahrheit der Kunstwerke sich anmelden, die im katastrophalen technischen Fortschritt flammend sich verheißt. Am Ende sind die Schallplatten - keine Kunstwerke - die schwarzen Siegel auf den Briefen, die im Verkehr mit der Technik allenthalben uns ereilen: Briefen, deren Formeln die Laute der Schöpfung verschließen, die ersten und letzten, Urteil übers Leben und Botschaft dessen, was danach sein kann.
1934

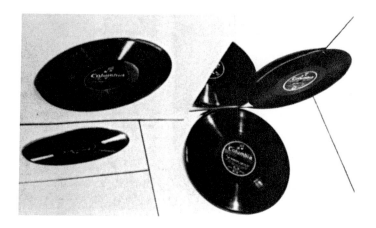

Florence Henri. 1931. Photo

The Form of the Record

One would not like to entrust it to any other form than that which it itself presents: a black slab created from a mixture which, these days, doesn't have a more decent name than what the combustible material in automobile gas is called; as brittle as slate, in the middle a circular piece of paper which always looks most genuine when upon it the pre-war terrier is listening to the voice of his master; in the very interior a small hole, at times so narrow that one must bore down again so the disc can be laid upon the turntable. It is covered with curves: a finely rippled, completely unreadable writing which now and again projects out even more vivid, three dimensional figures, without the layman being able to hear, why; disposed in a spiral, it ends somewhere in the proximity of the label paper, sometimes connected with this by a transverse furrow so that the needle can comfortably come to an end. As a >form<, it doesn't amount to much more. It originated as perhaps the first art-technological invention in an epoch which had already cynically avowed to the superiority of things over man, in that technology is emancipated from human demands and human needs and holds forth achievments without these ever being able to assume an essentially human meaning; instead of this, the need is produced only by advertisment, when the thing is present and spins around on its own track. Such a peculiar form - as the early epoch of photography is still familiar with - is nowhere else to be had. As the demand for 'radio-ready' music inevitably remained empty and unfulfilled and did not reveal anything better than a few orchestral hints which in practice prove to be a failure, so gramophone-ready music has never existed, and it might even be mentioned as a plus for the record that it has been saved the trouble of the handicraft transfiguration or artistic traits within its own artistic home; and from the phonographic origins down to the electrical procedures (which can be related both positively and negatively to the photographic process of enlargement) they were nothing more than exactly acoustical photographs, which the dog so happily recognizes again. Not in vain is the German expression >Platte< without addition, applied equally in both photography and phonography.[1] It signifies a two-dimensional model of a reality which can be arbitrarily multiplied, shifted about according to the laws of space and time, and then bartered in the market place. Yet for this it has had to offer the sacrifice of its third dimension: its tremendous heights and depths.

According to every measure of artistic arbitrariness, the form of the record would absolutely be its anti-form; it is fit for little else than to take music, reduced of its best dimension, and compact and conserve it; a music, namely, which was already there before the record and which has not been considerably changed by it. Composers for the record have not arisen; even Stravinsky, who had the best of intentions with the electric piano, has never made an attempt at it. Solely the unavoidable brevity, caused by the turntable's size, can characterize music for records. Yet also here rules a pure identity between the disc's form and that of the world in which it plays; the hours of domestic existence, turning about with the disc, are far too meager for the first movement of Eroica, in its entirety, to be able to blossom out; and anyway, dances, composed out of pointless repetition, are far more preferred. These can be turned off half way through. The record is an object of >everyday need<, which amounts to being the complete adversary of that which is human and artistic, for this cannot be arbitrarily repeated and turned on, but is rather bound to its place and time.

Nevertheless, the commodity of record is already too old for it to not reveal its puzzle, if one is first able to avoid seeing it as an art object and instead prefers to investigate the contours of its presence as a thing. For not in gramophone playing as a musical surrogate, but rather far more in the disc as a thing lies what it approximately, and also aesthetically, means. It is, as an artistic perishable product, the first presentation of music to be manifested as a thing. Not like oil murals which look down at the living from the wall. Just to the extent that these barely fit into an apartment, so to this same extent there cannot be truly large formats for records. Yet just like photographs, they become possessions; with good reason did the 19th century devise, along with the photographic and stamp album, the record album; artistic herbarium life, present in the smallest space and ready to conjure up every memory which otherwise would be mercilessly crushed between the haste and tedium of private life. With the record, *time* itself conquers a new pathway to music. It is not the time in which music flows; also not that for which music, by virtue of its >style<, stands as a monument. It is time as transitoriness, unending in muted music. When in the rigidity of their repeated music, all the mechanical instruments of the >Modern Spirit< appear ancient in the span of all that has been, and are made subordinate to the forlorn eternity of the clockwork - then are transitoriness and memory, as they are forcefully, yet uncertainly, inherent in the hurdy-gurdy as plain melody, made tangible and manifest in the gramophone.

The key to a proper understanding of the record would demand the knowledge of every technological file which at one time changed the mechanical music box's and organ's player rolls into the phonographic. When at a future time, instead of delving into >intellectual history<, one should decipher the postition of the intellect before the sundial of human technology, then can the early history of the gramophone acquire an importance which will make that of many famous composers forgotten. There is no doubt that by means of the record, music is robbed of living production and the requirement of practising art; and thus numbed, the record takes this life, benumbed, into itself, which otherwise would flee away. The dead art rescues >escaping< and ephemeral art as the only living one. It is here, perhaps, that its most fundemental right lies; that no aesthetic protest can be submitted against materialization. For this right again forwards, precisely by materialization, an ancient, submerged, yet authentic relationship: that of *music* and *writing*.

Whoever has recognized the steadily growing pressure which particularly in the last fifty years, musical notation and musical scores have exercised on composition (the curse word >papermusic< drastically gives this away), cannot be astounded by the fact that some day a transition of the sort will occur in that music, previously conveyed by writing, is, in a single stroke, itself changed into writing; at the price of its immediacy, yet with the hope, so fixed, it will finally be read as the >last language of mankind after building the Tower<, and in whose certain, yet cryptic statements is held every one of its >tenets<. However, if the notes were only their mere signs, then by the means of the needle's curving, they would clearly come closer to their true written character. Clearly, because this writing can be recognized as a genuine language, as it forgoes its plainly written character; inseperably united with the sound inherent in these and no other resonating channel. If music's productive strength is extinguished in records, and if with their technology they contribute nothing to artistic form, so to this extent they transform the youngest sound of old feelings into an archaic text of future understanding. When, however, the theologian knows he is forced to the consequence that in the strictest sense no art can be attributed to >Life< - considered as the birth and death of living beings - then perhaps he is also fit for the deliberation that the element of truth in art can only increase insofar as the appearance of that which is living departs from it; that the art work will only become >true<, fragments of the genuine language, when life vanishes from them; perhaps first even by virtue of its decline and that of art itself. Then it might be possible for the form of the record, in a seriousness difficult to access, to prove its worth; the etched spiral, to disappear down the center, the opening in the middle; yet for this it continues in time.

In this regard physics has a good portion; especially the Chladnien acoustical figures which - according to the discovery of Johann Wilhelm Ritter, one of the most important contemporary aestheticians - has already pointed out as being the written character of sound's archetype. The most recent technological development has, in any case, carried on what there began: the possibility that music, without ever having been sounded out, can be >depicted<; thus music has at the same time a still more inhuman materialization, and still more mysteriously approaches closer to written and verbal characteristics. The panicky fright which many composers testify to in view of this invention, equals exactly the enormous danger which from there, as already from the more gentle barbarousness of the record album, threatens the life of the artwork. It may, nevertheless, also make clear to him the shock of every transfiguration of truth in the artwork which burningly promises to be in the catastrophic progress of technology. In the end records - not artworks - are the black seals on the letters which in association with technology overtake us from everywhere; letters whose phrases close out the sounds of the creation, the first and the last, the judgement over life and the message of that which later can be.

1934

[1] That means, for the phonographic disc as well as for the photographic plate

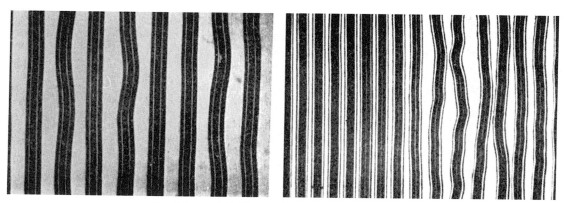

Schallplattenschrift "Nadelton" (record-writing), Photo, n.d.

La Forme du disque

On ne lui supposerait aucune autre forme que celle que lui-même il expose: une plaque noire, mince et ronde, fabriquée à partir d'un agrégat qui n'a guère de nos jours son nom honorable, pas plus que le carburant de l'auto ne s'appelle encore essence; fragile comme les tableaux noirs, une feuille circulaire en son milieu, qui semble encore plus vraie lorsque le fox-terrier d'avant-guerre y épie la voix de son maître; en plein centre un petit trou, quelquefois si étroit qu'il faut le repercer avant de placer le disque sur le plateau. Des lignes courbes le parcourent, une écriture finement ondulée tout à fait illisible, formant çà et là des figures plus plastiques néanmoins imperceptibles à l'oreille du profane, pourquoi; disposée en spirale elle s'évanouit quelque part à proximité de la feuille-titre à laquelle elle est parfois reliée grâce à un sillon perpendiculaire permettant à l'aiguille d'achever sa course sans effort. Voilà toute sa prétention en tant que >forme<. Il provient - peut-être la première invention de l'art technicisé - de cette époque qui déjà fait l'aveu cynique de la suprématie des choses sur les hommes, en affranchissant la technique des exigences et besoins humains et en présentant des acquisitions d'abord dépourvues de tout sens humain; au lieu de cela c'est la réclame qui crée le besoin, quand la chose est là et qu'elle suit son propre chemin. Une forme particulière - telle que la connurent encore les débuts de la photographie - n'existe plus. Comme le postulat d'une musique >spécifique à la radio< resta nécessairement vide et inaccompli, n'engendrant au mieux que quelques indications pour l'instrumentation jugées inaptes dans la pratique, il n'y a jamais eu non plus de musique spécifique au gramophone; et il convient de citer à l'avantage des disques qu'ils n'eurent pas à subir la transfiguration par les arts appliqués de l'originalité esthétique en intérieur présomptueusement artistique, et que, des origines phonographiques à l'électricité (laquelle peut se rapprocher en bien ou en mal du procédé photographique de l'agrandissement), ils ne furent que ces photographies acoustiques que le chien reconnaît en frétillant de joie. Ce n'est pas en vain que le mot [allemand] >Platte< a la même signification en photographie et en phonographie.[1] Il désigne le modèle bidimensionnel d'une réalité que l'on peut à loisir multiplier, déplacer dans le temps et l'espace, troquer sur les marchés. Voilà d'ailleurs pourquoi il lui faut sacrifier sa troisième dimension: sa hauteur et son abîme.

Selon les lois de la souveraineté de l'art la forme du disque ne serait purement et simplement que sa non-forme; elle n'est bonne à rien d'autre qu'à reproduire et conserver la musique amputée de sa meilleure dimension; c'est-à-dire une musique qui existait déjà et que le disque ne modifie pas de façon considérable. Il n'y a jamais eu de compositeurs de musique pour disques; même Stravinsky ne s'y essaya pas, et pourtant il avait eu une bonne intention avec son piano électrique. Seule la brièveté résultant des dimensions du plateau peut caractériser la musique pour disques. Entre la forme des disques et celle du monde dans lequel ils tournent s'instaure le règne de l'identité pure: les heures de >l'être-là< casanier, ces heures qui s'écoulent avec le disque, sont trop maigres pour que le premier mouvement de l'*Héroïque* puisse s'y épanouir sans coupure; aussi les disques préfèrent-ils les danses composées de fades répétitions. On peut arrêter en plein milieu. Objet >d'usage quotidien<, le disque s'oppose nettement au besoin humain et esthétique, lequel ne pourrait être répété ou interrompu à volonté, étant assujetti à son lieu et à son heure.

L'article disque est néanmoins déjà trop vieux pour ne pas présenter son énigme; afin que celle-ci se dévoile il faut d'abord renoncer à voir dans le disque un objet d'art et examiner enfin les contours de son caractère réifié. Car ce n'est pas dans le jeu du gramophone en tant que succédané de la musique, mais davantage dans le disque en tant que chose que se cache sa signification, même esthétique. Produit de la dégénérescence de l'art il est le premier mode de représentation musical qui se laisse posséder comme une chose. Non pas à la manière des tableaux à l'huile qui du mur jettent un regard sur les vivants. Si ces derniers ne conviennent guère au logis, il n'y a pas vraiment non plus de disques de grand format. Mais justement, on les possède comme on possède des photographies; après les collections de timbres et de photographies le dix-neuvième siècle inventa non sans raison les albums de disques, ces herbiers de vie artificielle qui dans un espace infime peuvent évoquer le souvenir qui sinon, coincé entre la hâte et l'uniformité de la vie privée, risque de s'effacer sans rémission. Avec les disques *le temps* s'empare d'une nouvelle voie vers la musique. Non pas le temps dans lequel la musique se déroule; non plus celui pour lequel, grâce à son >style<, elle s'érige en monument. C'est le temps en fuite qui perdure dans la musique muette. Quand, dans la rigidité de ses répétitions, le >moderne< des instruments mécaniques donne à la musique l'apparence d'exister depuis toujours et la soumet à l'éternité désolante de l'horloge - alors la fuite du temps, le souvenir, tels qu'ils s'attachent forcément mais indistinctement à la sonorité de l'orgue de barbarie acquièrent par le disque maniabilité et évidence.

La connaissance de ces actes techniques, qui jadis adaptèrent au phonographe les cylindres des orgues et des instruments mécaniques, devrait nous livrer la clé de la compréhension véritable des disques. Si l'on devait plus tard, au lieu de s'adonner à >l'histoire de l'esprit<, lire l'état de l'esprit à l'horloge solaire de la technique des hommes, la préhistoire du gramophone pourrait bien prendre l'importance qui nous fait oublier celle de certains compositeurs célèbres. Aucun doute: si tant est qu'à travers le disque la musique se voit exclue de la production vivante et de la pratique nécessaire de l'art, et qu'elle se fige, elle accueille en elle, en se figeant, cette vie qui sinon s'enfuit. L'art défunt sauve l'art >fuyant< et éphémère, alors le seul vivant. C'est en cela que réside peut-être son droit le plus profond: celui qui ne peut être abrogé par l'objection de la réification. Car ce droit réinstaure, précisément par la réification, une relation séculaire engloutie mais non moins authentique, celle de la *musique* et de l'*écriture*.

Qui a reconnu la contrainte toujours grandissante qu'exercent depuis les cinquante dernières années la notation et l'aspect graphique de la page musicale sur les compositions (l'expression péjorative >musique de papier< la dénonce énergiquement), ne s'étonnera pas de voir se produire un jour une transformation telle que la musique, autrefois déterminée par l'écriture, devienne soudainement elle-même écriture: au prix de son immédiateté, mais avec l'espoir que fixée de la sorte elle sera lisible en tant que >dernier langage de l'humanité entière après la construction de la Tour<, un langage dont les énoncés à la fois précis et énigmatiques habitent chaque >phrase<. Si les notes autrefois en étaient encore les signes, ce langage, en utilisant les circonvolutions de l'aiguille, se rapproche de façon décisive de son véritable caractère d'écriture. De façon décisive parce que, en s'abandonnant à sa nature de signe, cette écriture est identifiable en tant que langage authentique: liée indissociablement à la sonorité propre à ce sillon et à nul autre. Comme les disques anéantissent la force productive de la musique, comme ils ne créent plus la forme avec leur technique, ils transforment la sonorité la plus récente des sentiments nostalgiques en un texte archaïque de connaissance à venir. Mais si le théologue se voit dans l'obligation d'admettre qu'on ne peut imputer à aucune forme d'art, au sens le plus strict du terme, la >vie< comme naissance et mort des êtres; il sera peut-être alors tenté de dire que le contenu de vérité de l'art s'accroît seulement là où l'art abandonne l'apparence du vivant: que les oeuvres d'art ne deviennent de véritables fragments du langage authentique que lorsque la vie les quitte; peut-être même n'y parviendra que la destruction de l'oeuvre et celle de l'art lui-même. La forme du disque pourrait alors faire ses preuves avec un sérieux dont il est difficile de mesurer l'ampleur: la spirale de signes qui

disparaît en son centre, l'ouverture du milieu, pour perdurer dans le temps.

La physique joue ici un rôle important; surtout les figures de Chladni que - selon la découverte d'un des plus importants esthéticiens de notre époque - Johann Wilhelm Ritter considérait déjà comme des images sonores originales conformes aux lois de l'écriture. Quoi qu'il en soit les derniers développements de la technique ont poursuivi ce qui avait commencé là: la possibilité de >dessiner< la musique sans que jamais elle ne résonne, l'a réifiée d'une façon encore plus inhumaine et l'a rapprochée encore plus énigmatiquement du caractère du langage et de l'écriture. La peur panique, que certains compositeurs manifestent devant cette invention, exprime exactement l'énorme danger qui menace la vie des oeuvres d'art tant de ce point de vue que de celui de la douce barbarie des albums de disques d'autrefois. Ce danger pourrait également annoncer le choc devant la transfiguration de la vérité des oeuvres d'art, transfiguration dont le progrès catastrophique de la technique se fait la promesse enflammée. A la fin les disques sont - non des oeuvres d'art -, mais les cachets noirs des lettres qui nous rattrappent en tous lieux dans nos rapports avec la technique: lettres dont les formules renferment les sons de la création, les premiers et les derniers, jugement sur la vie et révélation de ce qui pourrait venir après.

1934

[1] C'est-à-dire: aussi bien la >plaque< photographique que le >disque< phonographique.

Laszlo Moholy-Nagy

Neue Gestaltung in der Musik
Möglichkeiten des Grammophons

Unter den heutigen musikalischen Versuchen spielen die Untersuchungen mit den Verstärkeröhren [!], welche einen neuen Weg in der Herstellung aller akustischen Erscheinungen ermöglichen, eine große Rolle. Die Bestrebungen der italienischen Bruitisten, neue Instrumente mit neuer Tonbildung zu konstruieren, sind durch die Versuche mit der Verstärkeröhre [!] als Einheitsinstrument, mit dem alle Arten akustischer Phänomene erzeugbar sind, im weitesten Masse erfüllt. Aber mit dieser Möglichkeit allein ist nicht alles erschöpft, was für die Umgestaltung der Musik zu erwarten wäre. Ich weise auf den ausgezeichneten Artikel von P. Mondrian: *Die neue Gestaltung in der Musik und die italienischen Bruitisten* (De Stijl) hin, worin er die Grundlagen zur Erneuerung der Tongestaltung analysiert.

Er sagt unter anderem: "Die Musik kann sich nicht entwickeln durch Bereicherung an Tönen oder Verfeinerung, noch durch Verstärkung der Töne, sondern durch die Aufhebung der Dualität zwischen dem Individuellen und dem Universalen, zwischen dem Natürlichen und dem Geistigen; das heißt, dass die Erreichung des Gleichgewichtes des Menschen das Ziel aller Gestaltung ist." Er sagt weiter: "Die Geräusche in der Natur ergeben sich aus einer gleichzeitigen und fortdauernden Verschmelzung. Die alte Musik hat, indem sie teilweise diese Verschmelzung und die Fortdauer zerstörte, aus dem Geräusch Töne abgeleitet und sie in einer bestimmten Harmonie geordnet. Um zu einer mehr universalen Gestaltung zu gelangen, wird die neue Musik eine neue Ordnung der Töne und Nichttöne (bestimmter Geräusche) wagen müssen. Das Wesentliche ist, uns in der Gestaltung von dem "Natürlichen", von dem "Animalischen" [zu] befreien, dessen charakteristische Merkmale Verschmelzung und Wiederholung sind. Will man die Verschmelzung und damit die Herrschaft des Individualistischen vermeiden, so müssen die Instrumente Töne derart bilden, dass sowohl Wellenlänge wie Schwingungszahl so gleichmäßig wie nur möglich bleiben. Demnach müssen die Instrumente derart gebaut sein, dass es möglich wird, jedes Nachschwingen mit plötzlichem Ruck abzubrechen. Man kann sich ohne eine andere Technik und ohne andere Instrumente diese Gestaltung nicht vorstellen."

Diese Forderungen, insofern sie durch technische Erfindungen *äusserlich* erreicht werden können, werden durch die Inanspruchnahme der Verstärkeröhre [!] erreicht.

Meine Bestrebung auf demselben Gebiet der Umgestaltungsversuche in der Musik ist eine andere und steht in enger Verbindung mit dem Gedankengang von Mondrian. Ich übergehe in den folgenden Ausführungen die Beweggründe zu der neuen Tongestaltung, ich zeige nur eine Möglichkeit zu ihrer Verwirklichung mit Hilfe eines neuen Ausdruckmittels.

Ich schlug vor, aus dem Grammophon als aus einem Reproduktionsinstrument ein produktives zu schaffen, so, dass auf der Platte ohne vorherige akustische Existenzen durch Einkratzen der dazu nötigen Ritzschriftreihen das akustische Phänomen selbst entsteht.

Da die Beschreibung dieses Vorgangs dort als Beispiel zu einem anderen Gedanken diente, habe ich nur kurz die Möglichkeiten, aber nicht die ausführlichen Beweise aufgezählt, die zu der Umgestaltung unserer bisherigen musikalischen Auffassung auf diesem Wege führen. Spekulativ ist klar:

1. Durch das Feststellen eines Ritzschrift-ABC ist das Generalinstrument geschaffen, das alle bisherigen Instrumente überflüssig macht.

2. Die graphischen Zeichen ermöglichen die Aufstellung einer neuen graphisch-mechanischen Tonleiter*), das heisst das Entstehen einer neuen mechanischen Harmonie, indem man die einzelnen graphischen Zeichen untersucht und ihre Verhältnisse in ein Gesetz bringt. (Hier ist die heute noch utopisch klingende Erwägung zu nennen: graphische Darstellungen auf Grund strenger Verhältnis-Gesetzmässigkeiten in die Musik zu übertragen.)

3. Der Komponist kann seine Komposition selbst schon auf der Platte reproduktionsbereit schaffen, also er ist nicht angewiesen auf das absolute Können des Interpretierenden. Dieser hat bis jetzt meistens seine eigenen Seelenerlebnisse in die in Noten aufgeschriebene Komposition hineinzuschmuggeln vermocht. Die neue Möglichkeit des Grammophons wird die heutige dilettantische Musikerziehung auf eine gesundere Basis stellen. Statt der vielen "Reproduktionstalente", die mit der *wirklichen* Tongestaltung weder aktiv noch passiv etwas zu tun haben, werden die Menschen zu *wirklich* Musikaufnehmenden oder Gestaltenden erzogen.

4. Die Einführung dieses Systems bei Musikaufführungen würde ebenfalls eine wesentliche Erleichterung geben: Unabhängigkeit von grossen Orchesterunternehmungen; ungeheure Verbreitung der schöpferischen Originale durch das einfache Mittel.

(Die Leistungsfähigkeit des Grammophons wurde in der letzten Zeit durch einige technische Verbesserungen vorzüglich gefördert. Es gibt unter anderem zwei wichtige Erfindungen auf diesem Gebiet. Die eine arbeitet mit elektrischem Betrieb und die andere mit einer neuen Membranerfindung und gibt schon fast vollkommen reibungslose Wiederholung hineingespielter Werke. Ich denke, wenn wir sie wirklich als Forderung haben, werden wir in kürzester Zeit technisch einwandfreie Apparate besitzen.)

Die praktischen Versuche mit dem Grammophon auf musikschöpferischem Gebiet glaube ich so zu beginnen:

1. Da die Ritzen in der auf mechanischem Wege entstandenen Platte mikroskopisch klein sind, muss zu allererst ein Mittel gefunden werden, von einer grossen Ritzschriftplatte, die mit der Hand bequem zu bearbeiten ist, auf technisch-mechanischem Wege Verkleinerungen im Format der heute üblichen Platten zu erzielen. Am besten, man lässt eine heutige Grammophon-(reproduktions)platte photographieren und von der Photographie ein Photo- oder Autotypie-Klischee auf zinkographischem, galvanoplastischem Wege herstellen. Wenn diese Platte nur annähernd spielbar wäre, ist die Grundlage für die Weiterarbeit auf diese Weise gesichert.

2. Studium der graphischen Zeichen der verschiedensten (gleichzeitig und isoliert. ertönenden) akustischen Phänomene. Inanspruchnahme von Projektionsapparaten. Film. (Darüber gibt es schon in physikalischen Spezialstudien eingehende Beschreibungen.)

3. Untersuchungen mechanisch-metallischer, mineralischer Klänge. Der Versuch, daraus - vorläufig graphisch - eine eigene Sprache zu bilden. Besondere Achtung auf die Zeichen, die durch die verschiedenen Klangfarben hervorgerufen werden.

4. Herstellung - graphisch - der grössten Kontrastverhältnisse. (Bevor man die Versuche auf der Wachsplatte anfängt, ist zu empfehlen, mit einer Nadel auf verschiedenen Grammophon(reproduktions)platten, den graphischen Wellenlinien der Musik, deren Gestaltungsfolge dem den Versuch Ausführenden bekannt ist, nachzugehen, um ein Gefühl für die graphische Darstellung zu bekommen.)

5. Dann kämen *Improvisationen* auf der Wachsplatte in Frage, deren klangliche Resultate theoretisch nicht abzusehen, von denen aber grosse Anregungen zu erwarten sind, da das Mittel uns ziemlich unbekannt ist.

---

*) Unsere heutige Tonleiter ist vielleicht tausend Jahre alt und ihrer Enge heute zu folgen nicht unbedingt notwendig.

In: Der Sturm, Heft 7 (1923).

New Plasticism in Music
Possibilities of the Gramophone

Among today's musical experiments, research with amplifying tubes - which offer new ways of producing sounds - plays an important role. The efforts of the Italian Bruitists to construct instruments that generate innovative sounds have been largely fulfilled by experiments with the amplifying tube as a standard instrument owing to its ability to produce all kinds of acoustic phenomena. Yet this ability does not exhaust all the possibilities that can be derived from the transformation of music. I refer to the outstanding article by *P. Mondrian: The New Plasticism in Music and the Italian Bruitists* (De Stijl), in which he analyzes the basis for the renewal of sound form.

Among other things, he says, "Music cannot develop through the enrichment or refinement of sound, nor through the amplification of sound, but by the abrogation of the duality between the individual and the universal and between the natural and the intellectual; in other words, the attainment of the balance of man is the goal of all form." He continues: "The noises in nature arise from a simultaneous and continuous fusion. The old music, by partially destroying this fusion and the continuity, has deduced sound from the noise and has arranged them in a certain harmony. To obtain a more universal form, the new music will have to make a new arrangement of sounds and non-sounds (certain noises). It is essential to free ourselves from the presence of the 'natural' and of the 'animal', for both of which fusion and repetition are characteristic signs. To avoid the fusion and thereby the domination of the individuality, the instruments must produce sounds in such a way that the wavelength, as well as the frequency of oscillations, remains as constant as possible. Accordingly, the instruments must be constructed in a way that makes a sudden interruption of the vibration possible. Without a new technology and without new instruments, this kind of New Plasticism is not conceivable."

These demands, as far as they can be achieved *physically* through technical inventions, are realized through the use of the amplifying tube.

My endeavor on the subject of transforming music is at once different and closely related to the reasoning of Mondrian. Without discussing the motives for new sound form, I will show one possibility for its realization with the help of a new means of expression.

I have suggested to change the gramophone from a reproductive instrument to a productive one, so that on

Grammofonplatte

Foto: **MOHOLY-NAGY**
bei von Löbbecke

a record without prior acoustic information, the acoustic phenomena itself originates by engraving the necessary "Ritzschriftreihen" (etched grooves).

The description of this process served as an example for another idea; therefore, I have only listed the possibilities and not the comprehensive proofs which lead to the transformation of our former concepts of music. Theoretically, the following points are clear:

1. By establishing a "Ritzschrift"(etching)-ABC, a generalized instrument, which renders all former instruments unnecessary, is created.

2. The graphic signs enable the arrangement of a new graphical-mechanical scale*): i.e, the development of a new mechanical harmony in which one can examine the graphic signs and relate their proportions to a rule. (The still utopian-sounding consideration of transferring diagrams to music on the basis of strict proportion-conformities should be considered here.)

3. The composer himself can create his composition, ready for reproduction, on the record; therefore, he is not dependent upon the absolute skill of the interpreter. Until now, the interpreter in most cases succeeded in smuggling his own heart and soul into the tone of the written composition. The new possibilities of the gramophone will provide a healthier basis for today's dilettante musical education. Instead of producing the many "reproduction-talents" who are neither actively nor passively involved in *real* sound form, people will be trained to be *true* music receivers or creators.

4. The introduction of this system during musical performances would be an essential advancement: allowing independence from large-scale orchestral enterprises; enormous distribution of the original creations by simple means.

(Indeed, the efficiency of the gramophone has recently been considerably advanced by technical improvements. Especially two important inventions exist in this field. One operates electrically, and the other employs the invention of a new membrane that reproduces recorded works virtually without friction. I think, with real demand, we shall have completely accurate equipment soon.)

A series of practical experiments with the gramophone in the field of creative music should begin like this:

1. Since the grooves on the mechanically produced record are microscopically small, we first have to invent a method of starting from a large engraved record, which can easily be worked on by hand, in order to reduce it by technical means to the size of conventional records. I suggest to have a gramophone(reproduction)-record photographed and to produce a photo- or half-tone engraving proof through zincographic

means or by galvanoplasty. Even if this record is only fairly exact and playable, we have at least established the basis from which to continue work in that direction.

2. Study of the graphic signs in the various (simultaneous and isolated sounding) acoustic phenomena. The use of projectors. Film. (Detailed descriptions exist in special physical studies.)

3. Examination of mechanical-metallic and mineral sounds. The attempt to construct - graphically, for the time being - a unique language. Special attention for the signs produced by the different timbres.

4. Production, graphically, of the highest contrasts. (Before experimenting on the waxplate, I suggest one uses a needle to trace the graphic wavelines on different gramophone-(reproduction)records of music, which is familiar to the one, who is undertaking the experiment, in order to develop a feeling for such diagrams.)

5. Finally, *improvisations* on waxplates could be made, from which the tonal results are not theoretically predictable, but great inspiration can be expected from these since the medium is quite unknown to us.

*) Our musical scale is approximately a thousand years old; to follow its confinement today is not absolutely necessary.

La nouvelle forme en musique
Les possibilités du phonographe

Parmi les expérimentations musicales actuelles, les essais avec les tubes amplificateurs, qui offrent une nouvelle voie dans la production des phénomènes acoustiques, jouent un grand rôle. Les efforts entrepris par les bruitistes italiens en vue de construire de nouveaux instruments avec de nouveaux sons ont été en majeure partie couronnés de succès par les essais avec les tubes amplificateurs comme instrument unique permettant de produire toutes sortes de phénomènes acoustiques. Mais avec cette possibilité on n'a pas épuisé tout ce que l'on pourrait espérer pour une transformation de la musique. Je rappellerai ici l'exellent article de *P. Mondrian: La nouvelle forme dans la musique et les bruitistes italiens* (De Stijl) dans lequel il analyse les bases d'un renouvellement de la création de sons.

Il dit entre autres: "La musique ne peut pas se développer par l'enrichissement des sons ou l'affinement, ni par l'amplification des sons, mais en faisant ressortir la dualité entre l'individuel et l'universel, entre le naturel et le spirituel; c'est-à-dire que l'obtention de l'équilibre de l'homme est le but de toute création." Il dit encore: "Les bruits dans la nature naissent d'une fusion simultanée et continue. L'ancienne musique, en détruisant partiellement cette fusion et cette continuité, a fait dériver des sons de ces bruits et les a ordonnés dans une certaine harmonie. Pour obtenir une forme plus universelle la nouvelle musique devra oser un nouvel ordre des sons et non-sons (bruits spécifiques). L'essentiel est de nous libérer dans la création du "naturel", de "l'animal" dont les traits caractéristiques sont la fusion et la répétition. Veut-on éviter la fusion et ainsi la suprématie de l'individuel, les instruments doivent alors produire des sons de manière à ce que et la longueur d'onde et le nombre d'oscillations restent aussi réguliers que possible. Aussi les instruments doivent-ils être construits de sorte qu'il soit possible d'interrompre d'un seul coup toute oscillation après l'impulsion. On ne peut s'imaginer cette forme sans une autre technique et sans autres instruments".

Ces exigences, dans la mesure où elles peuvent être satisfaites *extérieurement* par des découvertes techniques, seront également réalisées par le recours aux tubes amplificateurs.

Mon effort dans ce même domaine des essais de transformation dans la musique est autre et se trouve étroitement lié aux idées de Mondrian. Je passe dans ce qui suit sur les motivations de la nouvelle création de sons, me contentant d'exposer une possibilité de réalisation à l'aide d'un nouveau moyen d'expression. Je proposais de faire du phonographe en tant qu'instrument de reproduction un instrument de production de manière à ce que le phénomène acoustique se produise lui-même sur le disque sans existence acoustique préalable par la gravure de séries de signes nécessaires.

Etant donné que la description de ce procédé servait là d'exemple à une autre idée, je n'ai énuméré brièvement que les possibilités, mais pas les preuves circonstanciées, qui mènent par ce moyen à la transformation de notre conception musicale.

Spéculativement il est clair que:

1. par l'établissement d'un ABC de signes gravés se trouve créé l'instrument général qui rend superflus tous les instruments existant jusqu'ici.

2. Les signes graphiques permettent l'établissement d'une nouvelle gamme*) grapho-mécanique, c'est-à-dire la création d'une nouvelle harmonie mécanique en examinant les différents signes graphiques et en soumettant leurs rapports à une loi. (Il faut mentionner ici une considération qui paraît encore utopique aujourd'hui: la transposition de représentations graphiques en fonction de strictes normes de rapports dans la musique.)

3. Le compositeur peut lui-même rendre sa composition prête à être reproduite sur le disque, il ne dépend donc pas du savoir absolu de l'interprète. Jusqu'à présent, celui-ci a généralement introduit en cachette ses propres émotions dans la composition écrite en notes. La nouvelle possibilité offerte par le phonographe placera l'éducation musicale actuellement dilettante sur une base plus saine. Au lieu des nombreux "talents de reproduction" qui n'ont rien à voir, ni de façon active ni de façon passive, avec la *véritable* création musicale, les gens seront éduqués de sorte qu'ils seront ou de *véritables* auditeurs de musique ou des compositeurs.

4. L'introduction de ce système lors de représentations musicales aura également un avantage essentiel: l'indépendance à l'égard des grands orchestres; une énorme diffusion des oeuvres originales par un moyen simple.

(L'efficacité du phonographe s'est merveilleusement accrue ces derniers temps grâce à quelques améliorations techniques. Il y a notamment deux découvertes importantes dans ce domaine. L'une fonctionne avec un mécanisme électrique et l'autre avec une nouvelle membrane et reproduit presque parfaitement les oeuvres enregistrées. Je pense que si nous le voulons vraiment, nous serons très bientôt en possession d'appareils parfaits sur le plan technique.)

Les essais pratiques avec le phonographe dans le domaine de la création musicale devraient commencer ainsi à mon avis:

1. Etant donné que les rainures sur le disque réalisé de façon mécanique sont microscopiques, il faut en tout premier lieu trouver un moyen d'obtenir d'un grand disque, qui peut être travaillé facilement à la main des réductions par des moyens techniques mécaniques du format courant des disques actuels. De préférence, on photographiera un disque (de reproduction) d'un phonographe actuel et de cette photographie on fera réaliser par un procédé zincographique, galvanoplastique, un cliché photo ou autotypie. Si ce disque est jouable, ne serait-ce qu'à peu près, la base sera donnée pour poursuivre le travail de cette manière.

2. Etude des signes graphiques des phénomènes acoustiques les plus divers (simultanés et isolés). Utilisation d'appareils de projection. Film. (Il existe déjà à ce sujet des descriptions détaillées dans des études physiques spéciales.)

3. Etudes de sons mécaniques-métalliques, minéraux. Essai pour en tirer une langue spécifique - provisoirement graphique -. Veiller particulièrement aux signes produits par les différentes tonalités.

4. Production - graphique - des plus grands rapports de contraste. (Avant de commencer les essais sur le disque de cire, il est recommandé de suivre avec une aiguille sur les différents disques (de reproduction) de phonographe les lignes des ondes graphiques de la musique dont l'expérimentateur connaît la succession pour se faire une idée de la représentation graphique.)

5. On pourrait alors envisager des *improvisations* sur le disque de cire dont les résultats sonores ne peuvent théoriquement pas encore être prévus mais dont on peut espérer beaucoup d'inspiration, ce moyen nous étant assez inconnu.

*) Notre gamme actuelle a peut-être mille ans et il n'est pas absolument nécessaire d'en respecter l'étroitesse.

Bauhaus-Band. Photo, n.d.

Die Kapelle kommt in Form

Jean Dubuffet

Musikalische Erfahrungen

Als mein Freund, der dänische Maler Asger Jorn, mich Ende des Jahres 1960, um die Weihnachtsfeiertage, zu gemeinsamen Musikimprovisationen eingeladen hatte, war dies für mich der Anlaß, ein Tonband vom Typ Grundig T K 35 zu kaufen, um eine Erinnerung an unsere Zusammenkunft zu bewahren. Die erste Aufnahme mit diesem Gerät machten wir am 27. Dezember: es war der Titel *Nez cassé*, gebrochene Nase. Dem folgten bald viele andere Musikstücke, denn diese musikalischen Experimente faszinierten uns beide so sehr, daß wir uns in den folgenden Monaten sehr oft zu solchen Improvisationen trafen. Asger Jorn hatte einige Erfahrung mit Geige und Trompete; ich konnte meine früher durch lange Praxis erworbenen Klavier-Kenntnisse beisteuern. Aber für die Art von Musik, die uns vorschwebte, brauchte man keine virtuosen Fähigkeiten, denn wir wollten den Instrumenten neue, bisher ungeahnte Töne entlocken. Wir benützten zunächst ein (ziemlich schlechtes) Klavier, eine Geige, ein Cello, eine Trompete, eine Blockflöte, eine Sahara-Flöte, eine Gitarre und ein Tamburin, aber nach und nach kamen alle möglichen anderen Instrumente dazu, die wir zufällig aufstöberten: altertümliche Instrumente wie alte Flöten oder eine Leier, exotische aus Asien, Afrika oder aus der Zigeuner-Kultur, aber auch alltägliche Instrumente wie Oboe, Saxophon, Fagott, Xylophon, Zither, neben Fundstücken aus der Folkloremusik wie Cabrette (eine Art Dudelsack) und Schalmei.

Dabei fanden wir große Unterstützung bei dem Musiker Alain Vian, der in seinem Laden in Paris, in der Rue Grégoire-de-Tours, merkwürdige und seltene Instrumente führt. Er nahm auch ein-, zweimal an unseren kleinen Konzerten teil und kümmerte sich außer-

EXPÉRIENCES MUSICALES

Mon ami le peintre danois Asger Jorn m'ayant, à la fin de l'année 1960, vers Noël, convié à improviser de la musique avec lui, je fis, pour conserver un souvenir de nos réunions, l'acquisition d'un magnétophone du type Grundig T K 35 sur lequel le premier enregistrement de nos jeux fut fait le 27 décembre avec le titre *Nez cassé*, bientôt suivi de nombreux autres car ces expériences musicales nous passionnèrent tous deux si fort que les séances d'improvisation furent fréquentes au cours des mois suivants. Asger Jorn avait quelque expérience du violon et de la trompette; j'en avais pour ma part quelqu'une du piano duquel j'ai fait naguère long exercice. Mais la sorte de musique que nous avions en vue ne requérait nullement des techniques de virtuose car nous entendions utiliser les instruments de manière à en tirer des effets iné-

dits. Outre un piano (assez mauvais) ce furent d'abord un violon, un violoncelle, une trompette, une flûte douce et une flûte saharienne, une guitare et un tambourin, mais vinrent peu à peu s'y adjoindre toutes espèces d'instruments les uns surannés (flûtes anciennes, vielle) ou exotiques (asiatiques, africains, tziganes) les autres plus banaux — hautbois, saxophone, basson, xylophone, cithare, et certains folkloriques comme la cabrette et la bombarde — au hasard de nos trouvailles. Grande aide nous y fut apportée par le musicien Alain Vian qui tient à Paris, rue Grégoire-de-Tours, magasin d'instruments curieux et rares de collection et qui, outre qu'il prit part une fois ou deux à nos petits concerts, s'ingénia par surcroît à nous procurer — voire les fabriquer — des instruments à notre mode.

Ni Asger Jorn ni moi-même ne connaissions à ce moment les productions des musiciens actuels ni notamment des promoteurs de la musique sérielle, dodécaphonique, concrète, électronique, etc. Nous ignorions même ces termes, que je n'ai connus que récemment. Pour ce qui me concerne, mon expérience musicale se limitait à une longue pratique du piano (associée à l'étude, peu approfondie, des musiques classiques) au temps de mon enfance et adolescence, abandonnée vers 20 ans, puis plus tard (à 35 ans) celle de l'accordéon et de la musique « musette » (avec médiocre réussite) et encore, vers 40 ans, le temps d'une année, de nouveau au piano, des partitions de Duke Ellington, assorties d'improvisations à l'harmonium. Après quoi j'avais pris toute la musique européenne en extrême aversion, ne prenant plus plaisir qu'aux musiques orientales (auxquelles je m'étais attaché au cours de mes séjours au Sahara) et extrême-orientales.

Du magnétophone je n'avais bien sûr nulle expérience. C'est par la suite que je pris conscience de l'imperfection de mes enregistrements faits empiriquement sur mon appareil d'amateur au regard de ceux qui sont faits par les professionnels.

Mais, si paradoxal que ce puisse paraître, je ne suis pas convaincu de la supériorité de ces derniers, de même que je préfère souvent des photographies d'amateurs mal outillés à celles des spécialistes. J'ai éprouvé plus tard au contact des techniciens que toutes leurs précautions et installations ont en contrepartie de certains avantages un bien fâcheux effet inhibiteur et aussi que les enregistrements obtenus, pour plus

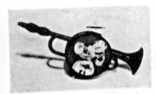

clairs qu'ils soient à l'oreille, plus exempts de bavures et menus accidents, n'en parlent pour cela pas plus à l'esprit. Je crois qu'en tout domaine l'art a tout à gagner à simplifier les techniques auxquelles il doit recourir. Je crois aussi qu'il n'a que faire d'épurations. Je tiens pour les grâces sauvages et sans apprêt contre toutes les parures et les coiffeurs. Mais il y a encore, dans le cas considéré, une raison plus forte. On appelle bon enregistrement celui où les sons sont très clairs et distincts, et donnant l'impression d'émission très proche. Or le monde journalier de notre oreille n'est pas fait que de ces sons-là mais il comporte aussi, et même pour une part beaucoup plus grande, des sons confus et brouillés, très impurs, lointains et plus ou moins mal entendus. Le parti pris de les ignorer conduit à un art spécieux, résolu à ne mettre en œuvre qu'une certaine catégorie de sons qui sont somme toute dans la vie courante assez rares, au lieu que je visais à une musique fondée non sur une sélection mais sur un recours à tous les sons qu'on entend journellement en tous lieux et notamment ceux qu'on entend sans en prendre bien conscience. Mon appareil rudimentaire convenait mieux à cela que les plus perfectionnés. Bien décidé à accueillir et utiliser tous les sons de toutes sortes qui puissent se présenter, ceux que me propose mon magnétophone, même quand ils diffèrent de ceux que j'ai enregistrés, m'intéressent autant que ceux-ci, voire quelquefois davantage. Où les surprises sont à mon gré mauvaises j'efface ou détruis, mais il arrive qu'elles soient remarquablement bonnes.

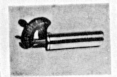

Constituée dès lors en atelier de musique une pièce de ma maison, j'entrepris, dans les intervalles de mes réunions avec Asger Jorn, de faire à moi seul l'orchestre, recourant tour à tour à tous mes instruments (une bonne cinquantaine) et par le moyen, que permet le magnétophone, des *surimpressions*, c'est-à-dire de jouer les parties successivement sur une même bande, qui restitue ensuite le tout ensemble simultané. J'opérais par petits fragments, effaçant et recommençant les séquences mauvaises et organisant à l'aide des ciseaux et du papier collant, des coupures, des soudures et des assemblages. Une telle méthode implique, c'est bien évident, des tâtonnements et une part laissée au hasard : ne pouvant entendre la partie préalablement inscrite au moment que je jouais une nouvelle partie destinée à s'y synchroniser, j'avais de la peine à faire tomber celle-ci juste au point que

je voulais et devais de mencer à mainte re contrôle difficile et part aussi, en contrepartie chance de belles surpri cond magnétophone as assorti d'une boîte de transcrire d'un appareil en écoutant la partie ce fait souvent recomprise ; mais qui dit faite au hasard dit de risques fâcheux, ses. Par la suite un se socié au premier et mixage, me permit de sur l'autre, de jouer préalable, et d'ajouter, effacer et recommencer autant qu'il me plaît sans que mon premier enregistrement s'en trouve par là gâté quand l'effet de l'apport ne me donne pas satisfaction.

La première bande réalisée dans ces conditions est de caractère un peu spécial puisqu'il s'y agit d'un poème, *La fleur de barbe*, déclamé, psalmodié, vague mêlées qui sont toujours la mienne) truments. Les suivantes, dont on procèdent de deux aspirations di et qui d'ailleurs, au moins dans cer crois, simultanément. La première ment chanté (avec plusieurs voix et accompagné par endroits d'instrouvera ci-après la nomenclature, vergentes entre lesquelles je balance tains morceaux, se font jour, je vise une musique d'un accent très

humain, je veux dire où s'ex-
primeraient les humeurs d'un
chacun, les mouvements qui
l'animent, en même temps
qu'aussi les sons, les bains de
sons, les décors de sons, formant l'élément habituel de
notre vie courante, les bruits
les plus communs dans lesquels
nous vivons, qui sont si liés à
nous et qui probablement nous
sont, sans que nous le soupçon-

nions, si chers et si indispensables. Entre cette musique permanente qui nous porte et la propre musique
que nous émettons il y a une osmose; ce ne fait qu'un pour ainsi dire, et ce forme la musique spécifique de l'être humain. Je me plais à nommer cette sorte de musique, dans mon for intérieur, celle qu'on
fait, par opposition à la seconde tout autre, qui m'ex cite aussi beaucoup la
pensée, et que j'appelle en moi-même celle qu'on *écoute*, s'agissant cette
fois, tout au contraire, d'une musique complètement étrangère à nous et à
nos inclinations, non humaine du tout, et suscep tible de nous faire enten-

dre (ou imaginer) des musiques qui seraient émises par les éléments eux-
mêmes, sans que l'homme y ait mis la main. Musi ques supposées extrê-
mement dépaysantes donc comme pourrait être celle qu'on entendrait en
collant notre oreille à quelque bouche ouvrant sur un monde autre que le
nôtre, ou bien s'il nous poussait soudain quelque nou velle ouïe qui nous per-
mettrait d'entendre d'étranges tumultes que nos sens ne nous donnent
pas de percevoir et que font peut-être des éléments apparemment voués à
l'action silencieuse comme l'humus en travail, l'herbe foisonnante, le minéral en mutation.

Il faut observer que dans l'un et l'autre de ces deux ordres de musique et même aussi quand il m'arrive de les fondre en une seule (ce qui
choque la logique mais tant pis) une prédilection se manifeste pour les
sons très composites et comme formés de nombreuses voix évoquant
rumeurs, peuplements, grouillements agités, activités collectives. Je remarque aussi

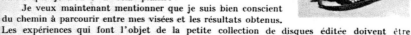

que s'y montre un goût pour des musiques non pas variées,
non pas surtout architecturées en fonction de quelque système, mais uniformes, pour ne pas dire informes, et telles
que les morceaux n'ont pas de commencement ni de fin mais
qu'ils semblent être des prélèvements opérés au hasard sur
des partitions interminablement continues. Il me faut recon-
naître que je trouve à cela plaisir.

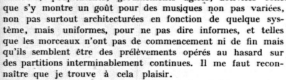

Je veux maintenant mentionner que je suis bien conscient
du chemin à parcourir entre mes visées et les résultats obtenus.
Les expériences qui font l'objet de la petite collection de disques éditée doivent être
considérées comme esquisses d'un programme qui demeure à
exécuter et requerrait, pour être mené à bien, de longues
mises au point dans divers domaines, à commencer par la technique de l'enregistrement, le maniement de chacun des instruments employés, voire aussi la modification de ces instruments
et même la confection d'autres mieux appropriés. Mais encore
faudrait-il d'abord expérimenter tout ce qui peut se faire à
partir déjà de ce qu'on a sous la main. On peut obtenir d'un

seul même instrument, le premier venu, un nombre incroyable d'effets les plus divers, au
point qu'on se demande si c'est bien utile d'en rechercher d'autres. S'agissant de la pratique
des instruments utilisés, de la bonne connaissance méthodique de leur emploi, elle me fait
évidemment grand défaut et je sens bien tout le profit qu'il y aurait à l'acquérir.

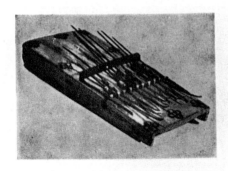

Il se peut cependant qu'à s'y adonner on risque aussi d'y perdre un avantage : celui qu'offre l'emploi à l'improviste d'un instrument dont le maniement correct n'est pas connu, avec les trouvailles imprévues qui en résultent. Tout ceci dit les disques ici réunis ne sont pas présentés dans l'esprit d'œuvres prétendant à s'imposer mais comme premières expérimentations d'un qui s'aventure en un domaine fort mal connu de lui et c'est dans cet esprit que je prie les musiciens de les accueillir.

Avril 1961

Jean DUBUFFET.

NOMENCLATURE DES DISQUES

- Disque N° 1
  Faces I et II   La fleur de barbe   *(janvier 1961)*

- Disque N° 2
  Face   I   1 - Humeur incertaine
               2 - Temps radieux
  Face   II   1 - Trotte matin
               2 - Solennités   *(janvier 1961)*

- Disque N° 3
  Face   I   1 - Pousse l'herbe
               2 - L'eau
  Face   II   1 - Coq à l'œil
               2 - Aguichements   *(février 1961)*

- Disque N° 4
  Face   I   1 - Pleure et applaudit
               2 - Le gai savoir
  Face   II   1 - Le bateau coulé
               2 - Dimanche   *(février 1961)*

- Disque N° 5
  Face   I   1 - Aggravation
               2 - Cris d'herbe
  Face   II   Longue peine   *(mars 1961)*

- Disque N° 6
  Face   I   1 - Délibérants
               2 - Terre foisonnante
  Face   II   1 - Prospère, prolifère
               2 - Diligences futiles   *(avril 1961)*

Éditeur : Galleria del Cavallino, San Marco 1820, Venise.

Photo : Jean WEBER.

dem mit großem Engagement darum, uns geeignete Instrumente zu besorgen, ja sogar herzustellen.

Weder Asger Jorn noch ich selbst kannten zu diesem Zeitpunkt die Arbeiten zeitgenössischer Musiker, insbesondere wußten wir nichts von den Versuchen mit Zwölftonmusik oder mit serieller, konkreter, elektronischer und ähnlicher Musik. Wir kannten nicht einmal diese Begriffe; ich habe sie erst vor kurzem zum ersten Mal gehört. Was mich betrifft, so war meine musikalische Erfahrung damals eher begrenzt: In meiner Kindheit und Jugend hatte ich viele Jahre lang Klavier gespielt (als Teil eines nicht sehr gründlichen Studiums der klassischen Musik), dies allerdings mit etwa 20 aufgegeben; später (mit 35 Jahren) hatte ich mich einige Zeit dem Akkordeon und der "Musette"-Musik gewidmet (mit eher mittelmäßigem Erfolg); und mit etwa 40 hatte ich für ungefähr ein Jahr das Klavier wiederentdeckt, wobei ich mich an Partituren von Duke Ellington versuchte und dazu auch ein bißchen mit dem Harmonium improvisierte. Danach

entwickelte ich eine tiefe Abneigung gegen die ganze europäische Musik und fand nur noch Gefallen an der orientalischen Musik (die ich bei meinen Sahara-Aufenthalten kennen- und liebengelernt hatte) sowie an der Musik aus Fernost.

Mit Tonbandgeräten hatte ich natürlich keinerlei Erfahrung. Erst im Vergleich mit professionellen Arbeiten wurde mir im nachhinein bewußt, wie unvollkommen die Aufnahmen von meinem Amateurgerät waren. Doch auch wenn es paradox klingt, so halte ich die professionellen Tonbandaufnahmen nicht unbedingt für überlegen, genauso wie ich mit bescheidenen Mitteln gemachte Amateurphotos oft lieber habe als Photographien von Spezialisten. Im Kontakt mit Technikern hatte ich dann später das Gefühl, daß alle ihre Vorsichtsmaßnahmen und Installationen zwar gewisse Vorteile bieten, andererseits jedoch einen ärgerlichen Hemmschuh darstellen. Mögen solche Aufnahmen auch klarer für das Ohr sein, fast völlig frei von Fehlern und kleinen Störungen, den Geist können sie des-

halb doch nicht inniger ansprechen. Ich glaube, daß die Kunst in jedem Bereich nur gewinnen kann, wenn sie die notwendigen technischen Hilfsmittel vereinfacht. Ich glaube auch, daß sie Ballast abwerfen muß. Ich halte mich an die natürlichen, ungezähmten Reize, ich bin gegen Schmuck und Ziererei. Aber es gibt in unserem Fall noch einen wichtigeren Grund. Man nennt eine Aufnahme gut, wenn die Töne sehr klar und deutlich sind, wenn man den Eindruck hat, daß sie aus nächster Nähe kommt. Doch in der Alltagswelt unseres Ohres gibt es nicht nur diese Töne, sondern auch - und sogar in einem weit größeren Maße - sehr unreine, undeutliche und verwaschene Töne, die von weit her kommen und mehr oder weniger schlecht zu verstehen sind. Wenn man sich dafür entscheidet, sie zu ignorieren, dann führt das zu einer Schein-Kunst, die nur eine bestimmte Kategorie von Tönen zuläßt - und die sind im täglichen Leben doch eher selten. Mein Ziel dagegen war eine Musik, die sich nicht auf eine Auswahl gründet, sondern die alle Töne, die man täglich an verschiedenen Orten hört, miteinbezieht - und

vor allem die Töne, die man fast unbewußt hört. Mein primitives Gerät war dafür besser geeignet als seine perfekteren Gegenstücke. Töne jeder Art, die entstehen könnten, wollte ich empfangen und benutzen: auch wenn die Töne von meinem Tonbandgerät anders klingen als bei der Aufnahme, so interessieren sie mich genauso, manchmal sogar mehr. Wenn diese Überraschungen nicht nach meinem Geschmack sind, dann lösche oder zerstöre ich sie, aber oft sind sie erstaunlich gut.

Ich hatte inzwischen ein Zimmer in meinem Haus als Musikstudio eingerichtet, wo ich zwischen den Treffen mit Asger Jorn als Ein-Mann-Orchester experimentierte, denn durch die Möglichkeit der Überspielung, die das Tonbandgerät bot, konnte ich meine (mehr als 50) Musikinstrumente einzeln, nacheinander auf dem gleichen Band aufnehmen; das Band gab dann das Ganze zusammen gleichzeitig wieder. Ich arbeitete in kleinen Teilschritten, immer wieder löschte ich schlechte Teile und begann von neuem; mit Hilfe von

Schere und Klebeband nahm das Ganze dann durch Schneiden, Zusammenfügen und Kleben Form an.

Eine solche Methode bedeutet natürlich ständiges Herumprobieren, wobei der Zufall eine wichtige Rolle spielte: weil ich nichts von den vorhergehenden Aufnahmen hören konnte, wenn ich mit einem neuen Instrument den nächsten Teil dazu-synchronisieren wollte, hatte ich große Mühe, immer den richtigen Punkt zu erwischen, und deshalb mußte ich immer wieder von vorne anfangen. Aber wenn man unter so schwer zu kontrollierenden Bedingungen arbeitet, in denen der Zufall eine so große Rolle spielt, dann entstehen als Ausgleich für Ärger und Risiko oft schöne Überraschungen. Später benutzte ich zusätzlich ein zweites Tonbandgerät mit Mischpult und konnte so von einem auf den anderen Apparat überspielen; dadurch war es möglich, beim Musizieren gleichzeitig die vorhergehenden Aufnahmen mitzuhören; auch konnte ich nun neue Töne hinzufügen, löschen oder - wenn ich mit der Wirkung des neuen Teils nicht zufrieden war -

so oft ich wollte wieder von vorne anfangen, ohne daß dadurch meine erste Aufnahme verdorben wurde.

Das erste Band, das unter diesen Bedingungen entstand, ist etwas außergewöhnlich, denn es ist ein Gedicht, *La fleur de barbe*, die Bartblume; es wird aufgesagt, deklamiert, im Sprechgesang vorgetragen (mit mehreren Stimmen, die ich alle selbst gesungen habe) und an manchen Stellen instrumental begleitet. Die nachfolgenden Tonbänder, deren Titel am Ende des Textes aufgelistet sind, entstanden aus zwei gegensätzlichen Bestrebungen, zwischen denen ich schwanke und die übrigens meiner Meinung nach zumindest in einigen Stücken gleichzeitig deutlich werden. Einerseits strebe ich nach einer sehr menschlichen Musik, in der sich die Stimmungen eines jeden ausdrücken sollen, seine Bewegungen und Beweggründe; eine Musik mit den Tönen, in denen wir baden, die als ganz normale Geräuschkulisse unser aller Leben begleiten und schmücken, alltägliche Töne, mit denen wir leben, mit denen wir uns verbunden füh-

len, und die uns wahrscheinlich, ohne daß wir es vermuten, lieb und unentbehrlich geworden sind. Zwischen dieser ständigen Begleitmusik, die uns trägt, und der eigentlichen Musik, die wir hinzufügen, findet eine Osmose statt; alles ist eins, um es einmal so auszudrücken, und das Ganze ist eben die spezifische Musik des menschlichen Wesens. In meinem tiefsten Innern bezeichne ich diese gerne als die Musik, die man *macht*, im Gegensatz zu der anderen Musik, die man *hört* und die mich auch sehr beschäftigt. Letztere ist uns und unseren Neigungen völlig fremd. Sie ist ganz und gar nicht menschlich, und sie läßt uns Musiken hören (oder ahnen), die von den Elementen selbst stammen könnten ohne den Eingriff einer menschlichen Hand. Äußerst befremdliche Musik also, die man vielleicht hören könnte, wenn man das Ohr an einen Mund legen würde, der sich einer anderen, uns unbekannten Welt öffnet, oder wenn uns plötzlich eine neue Art von Gehör wachsen würde, mit dem wir seltsamen Lärm hören könnten, den wir mit unseren jetzigen Sinnen nicht wahrnehmen, und der vielleicht von lautlosen

Elementen wie arbeitendem Humus, schnell wachsendem Gras, mutierenden Mineralien stammt.
Ich habe festgestellt, daß in diesen beiden Musikgattungen und auch in der Verbindung von beiden - was in meinen Werken manchmal vorkommt (das widerspricht zwar der Logik, aber das ist nicht zu ändern) - sehr oft vielfach zusammengesetzte Töne vorkommen; Töne, die an zahllose Stimmen erinnern, an Stimmengewirr, Menschenmassen, Gewimmel und Gemeinschaftsaktivitäten. Außerdem zeigt sich nicht etwa eine Neigung zu abwechslungsreicher, schon gar nicht zu systematisch geplanter und kunstvoll konstruierter Musik, sondern eine Vorliebe für eintönige, um nicht zu sagen unförmige Musik, für Stücke ohne Anfang und Ende, wie wahllos aus sich unendlich fortsetzenden Partituren entnommen. Und ich muß zugeben, daß mir das gefällt.

Ich möchte an dieser Stelle anmerken, daß ich mir der großen Distanz, die noch zwischen meinen Vorstellungen und den vorliegenden Ergebnissen besteht, völlig

bewußt bin. Die bisherigen Erfahrungen, wie sie in dieser kleinen Plattensammlung der Öffentlichkeit vorliegen, sollen nur ein Programm skizzieren, für dessen Verwirklichung noch zahlreiche Verbesserungen in verschiedenen Bereichen nötig sind, angefangen bei der Aufnahmetechnik, der Handhabung der benutzten Instrumente, bei deren Veränderung und sogar bei der Herstellung von anderen, besser geeigneten Instrumenten. Aber vorher sind noch weitere Versuche mit dem jetzt schon zur Verfügung stehenden Material nötig. Man kann schon einem einzigen, x-beliebigen Instrument so unglaublich viele unterschiedlichste Effekte entlocken, daß man sich fragen muß, ob die Suche nach weiteren Instrumenten überhaupt sinnvoll ist. Was nun die praktische Handhabung und methodische Kenntnis der Instrumente angeht, so fehlt es mir daran offensichtlich sehr, und ich ahne sehr wohl, wieviel Nutzen ich aus einem fundierten Wissen ziehen könnte. Andererseits würde man dadurch aber vielleicht einen Vorteil einbüßen: denn das Improvisieren mit einem Instrument, dessen korrekte Handhabung

man nicht kennt, kann unerwartete Entdeckungen ergeben. Nach all diesen Erklärungen sollen die hier zusammengetragenen Platten nicht als Anmaßung verstanden werden, sondern als erste Experimente von jemandem, der sich auf fast völlig unbekanntes Gebiet wagt; und ich bitte die Musiker, die Schallplatten in diesem Sinne anzunehmen.

April 1961

Musical Experiences

When my friend the Danish painter, Asger Jorn, invited me to improvise music with him towards Christmas of 1960, I bought a Grundig T K 35 tape-recorder on

which to keep a record of our sessions. The first recording of our games was made on this on the 27th of December with the title *Nez cassé*, (Broken Nose), and it was soon followed by numerous others as we were both so keenly excited by these musical experiments that we held improvisation sessions frequently over the following months. Asger Jorn had some previous experience with the violin and trumpet; I myself had in the past spent long hours at the piano. But the sort of music we had in mind did not require virtuoso techniques at all since we were intending to use instruments in such a way as to obtain new sounds from them. Besides a piano (not a very good one) our instruments were a violin, a cello, a trumpet, a recorder, a Saharan flute, a guitar and a tambourine at first, but gradually all sorts of other instruments were added to these, some of them antiquated (old-fashioned flutes, hurdy-gurdy) or exotic (Asiatic, African, tsigane), others more banal - oboe, saxophone, bassoon, xylophone, zither, and some folk instruments such as the cabrette (Auvergnat bagpipes)

and the bombarde (Breton oboe) - things we came across by chance. The musician Alain Vian, who sells curious and rare collector's instruments in a shop in the rue Grégoire-de-Tours in Paris, was a great help to us; besides taking part once or twice in our little concerts, he went out of his way to procure - and even to make for us - the sort of instruments we wanted.

Neither Asger Jorn nor myself were at that time familiar with the work of contemporary musicians, or, notably, with the promoters of serial, dodecaphonic, concrete, electronic and other such music. We were not even aware of these terms, which I have only learned recently. As far as I was concerned, my musical experience was limited to prolonged practice of the piano (combined with a superficial study of classical music) in my childhood and adolescence, abandoned at about twenty, then, later (at thirty-five) the accordion and "musette" music (with mediocre results) and, at about forty, the piano again for a year, doing Duke Ellington pieces, together with improvisations on the harmonium. After this I developed an extreme aversion to all Western music and could only appreciate Oriental music (which I had learned to like during my stays in the Sahara) and music from the Far East.

Of course, I had no experience whatever with the tape-recorder. It was only later that I became aware of the imperfections of my recordings, made directly on my amateur's machine, in comparison with those made by professionals. But, paradoxical as it may seem, I am not convinced of the superiority of the latter, in the same way that I often prefer poorly-crafted amateur's photographs to those of the specialists. Later, when I was in contact with technicians, I felt that all their precautions and installations counterbalanced certain advantages with a deplorable inhibitory effect and also that the recordings thus obtained, however much clearer they may be to the ear, however much freer from flaws and minor mishaps, do not speak any louder to the spirit as a result. I believe that in all areas art has everything to gain by simplifying the techniques it is obliged to use. I also believe that all it needs to do is to strip away. I am in favour of untamed, unaffected graces and against all ornaments and window dressers.

But there is a still stronger reason in the present case. A recording in which the sounds are very clear and distinct, giving the impression that their source is very close, is considered to be good. Yet the everyday world of our ears does not consist in only the latter sounds; it is also comprised, and indeed to a far greater extent, of confused and muddled, very impure, distant and more or less misheard sounds. The decision to ignore the latter leads to a specious art, dedicated to only a certain category of sounds which, all things considered, is pretty rare in everyday life. In place of this, I was aiming at a music based not on selection but on all the sounds that are heard daily everywhere and especially those that are heard without being fully registered. My rudimentary apparatus was better suited to this than its most sophisticated rivals. As I was determined to welcome and make use of all sounds of any kind that might occur, those my tape-recorder offered me, even when they were unlike those I had recorded, interested me as much as the latter, sometimes even more. Where these surprises struck me as wrong I cut them out or destroyed them, but they were sometimes remarkably good.

Having set up one of the rooms in my house as a music studio, in the intervals between my sessions with Asger Jorn, I undertook to do the whole orchestra by myself, going one by one through all my instru-

ments (a good fifty or so), using the tape-recorder's capacity to super-impose recordings, that is, playing and recording all the parts one after another onto the same tape, which then reconstitutes them all simultaneously. I worked by small fragments, erasing and redoing the bad sequences and cutting, joining and sticking the tape back together with the aid of scissors and sticky-paper. Such a method obviously implies trial and error and leaving a certain amount up to chance: as I was unable to hear the pre-recorded part when I was playing a new part intended to synchronize with it, it was difficult to get the new part in exactly the right place and I had to do it over and over again. But working with something so difficult to control and letting chance play its part leaves the way open for wonderful surprises to counterbalance the tiresome risks. Later, a second tape-recorder linked to the first and to a mixing-box, enabled me to transcribe from one machine to the other, to play while listening to the part that I had already recorded and to add, erase and redo as much as I liked without ruining my original recording when what I had added was not to my satisfaction.

The first tape I made under these conditions is rather special since it is a poem, *La fleur de barbe*, declaimed, chanted, vaguely sung (with several voices mingled - always my own) and accompanied in places by instruments. The following tapes, whose details are given at the end of the text, originated in two diverging aspirations. I swung from one to the other and in certain pieces at least, I think both are present simultaneously. The first aims at a music with a very human accent, that is, music which could be expressing the mood of anybody; the movements which stir our moods, at the same time as the sounds, or the sound-baths, the sound décor forming the habitual element of our everyday life, the most common noises among which we live, which are so closely linked to us that they are probably necessary and dear to us without our suspecting it. Between this permanent music which carries us along and the real music which we produce an osmosis takes place; it is all one so to speak, and it constitutes the human being's specific music. In my heart of hearts, I like to call this sort of music the music we *make* as opposed to the other very different kind, which I also find highly stimulating, and which I myself call the music to which we *listen*, which is completely strange to us and our inclinations, not human at all, and which might enable us to hear (or to imagine) such music as would be made by the elements themselves, without the help of human hands. This is music as disorientating and other-worldly as might be heard by placing the ear against an opening onto another world, or as we might hear if we suddenly grew a new sense of hearing which allowed us to hear the strange tumults our senses do not permit us to perceive, the sounds that might be made by apparently silent elements like humus decomposing, the grass growing and minerals mutating.

It must be noted that in both of these two orders of music, and even when they become fused into one in my work (which upsets the logic, but never mind), there is a manifest predilection for very composite sounds, sounds like numerous voices evoking murmuring, a human presence, the agitated swarming of people, collective activities. I also notice in my work a taste for music that does not depend on any system for its variety and definitely not for its structure, but is uniform or almost unformed, such that the pieces have no beginning or end, appearing rather as excerpts taken by chance from interminably continuing musical scores. I have to admit that this pleases me.

I want to mention here that I am very aware of the distance between my aims and the results obtained. The experiments featured in the little collection of records published must be considered as the sketches for a programme which has still to be carried out and which would require a great deal of work in various areas, beginning with recording technique, the handling of every instrument used, and indeed the modification of the latter and even the construction of other more appropriate instruments. But it would still be necessary to experiment with everything that can be done using what is already available first. Such an incredible number of extremely diverse effects can be obtained from the first instrument to come to hand alone that one wonders if it is really worth searching for others. Where practical experience and good methodical knowledge of how to play the instruments used is concerned, I am evidently seriously lacking and the benefits of acquiring this knowledge are clear to me. It may be however, that in doing this there is also a risk of losing an advantage: that afforded by the improvised use of an instrument whose proper handling is not known, with the unexpected discoveries that this can bring about. Having said all this, the records collected here are not presented in the spirit of works with any pretentions of their own, but rather as the first experimentations of someone venturing into an area about which he knows practically nothing and it is in this spirit that I ask musicians to accept them.

April 1961

Hans Rudolf Zeller

Medienkomposition nach Cage
(Auszug, vgl. Bibliographie)

"...obwohl die Leute annehmen, sie könnten Schallplatten als Musik verwenden, müssen sie schließlich begreifen, daß sie sie als *Schallplatten* gebrauchen müssen. Und Musik lehrt uns, würde ich sagen, daß der Gebrauch der Dinge, falls er sinnvoll sein soll, eine kreative Handlung ist. Deshalb ist die einzig lebendige Sache, die mit einer Schallplatte geschehen kann, daß man sie auf eine Weise gebraucht, die etwas Neues entstehen läßt. Wenn man zum Beispiel mit Hilfe einer Schallplatte ein anderes Musikstück machen könnte, indem man eine Schallplatte oder andere Geräusche der Umwelt oder andere Musikinstrumente einbezieht, dann würde ich das interessant finden, und tatsächlich habe ich in einem meiner Stücke diese Idee verwirklicht. ... aber die nun entstandene Schallplatte selbst, die eine andere Schallplattenaufnahme enthält, benötigt noch andere Dinge, um lebendig zu werden. Unglücklicherweise benutzen die meisten Leute, die Schallplatten sammeln, sie auf ganz andere Weise: als eine Art tragbares Museum oder als beweglichen Konzertsaal."*

Die Perspektive hat sich seither nicht wesentlich verändert: Komposition verhält sich kritisch gegenüber den verordneten Modellen der Rezeption, wie sie der normierte Mediengebrauch vorschreibt, und umgekehrt ermöglicht die Einsicht in die gesellschaftlich bedingte Struktur der Rezeptionsweisen "kreative Handlungen". Ähnliches gilt für andere, nicht minder fixierte Verhältnisse, wie etwa das von Produktion und Reproduktion. Komposition kann sich im Zusammenhang mit bestimmten Projekten auch darauf beschränken, Voraussetzungen für neue Rezeptionsmöglichkeiten zu schaffen, diese nicht "kausal" zu determinieren. Was das bei Cage dann breit ausgeführte Thema "Unbestimmtheit" meint, ist in einem frühen, lückenlos notierten Stück wie dem Credo die Ungewißheit über die auszuwählende Schallplatte oder das, was aus dem eingeschalteten Radioapparat kommen mag. In den Kompositionen der vierziger und beginnenden fünfziger Jahre für traditionelles Instrumentarium, allem zuvor fürs Klavier (normal oder präpariert), erfaßt sie mit Hilfe von Zufallsoperationen zunächst alle Aspekte der Struktur und bezieht sich am Ende sogar auf die Auswahl des Instrumentariums. Auf dem Weg dahin entstand 1952 die Partitur von *Imaginary Landscape No. 5*, ein Plan "zur Produktion einer Tonbandaufnahme". Sie beginnt mit der Auswahl des "Materials", nämlich von 42 Schallplatten eigener Wahl, wobei sich wiederum zeigt, daß Medienprodukte am besten in Relation

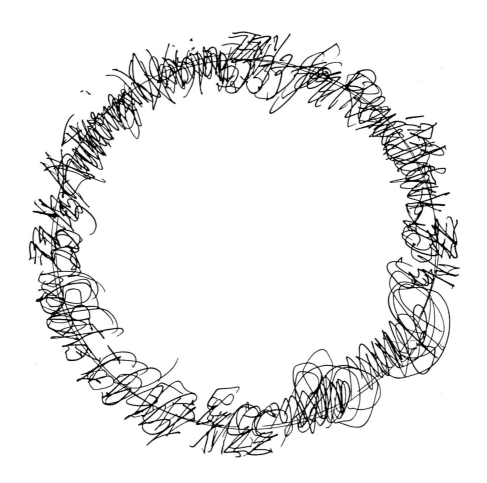

John Cage. *33 1/3.* 1969. Drawing for record label, blue and black ink, 1989

Label for the hundred records used for the installation version of *33 1/3*
(33 1/3   Ambient Music   33 1/3   for René Block   33 1/3   John Cage   33 1/3   1969–1989)

zu einem anderen Medium zu kritisieren sind. (Darin liegt vielleicht eine der Wurzeln des im 20. Jahrhundert entwickelten Verfahrens der Collage, jener Handlung, die fremd gewordene Objekte, gleichsam gefrorene, zur Ruhe gekommene Handlungen in einer Befreiungstat negiert, indem sie sie zerlegt und Teile des Materials neu kombiniert.)

Während die Produktion dieses Stücks noch streng nach Plan zu verlaufen hat, verzichtete Cage in der Folgezeit immer wieder darauf, den Produktionsprozeß, die Verlaufskurve der einzelnen Handlungen mittels ausgeschriebener Partituren festzulegen, besonders dort, wo es um den freien, solistischen oder kollektiven Gebrauch der Medien ging - und vermochte dennoch neue Gebrauchsweisen nahezulegen. In *33 1/3*, 1969 während eines Gesprächs konzipiert, und für 12 Plattenspieler gedacht, soll jeder der 12 Teilnehmer seine eigene Platte auflegen und zur Geltung bringen. Tut's ein jeder - wie zu erwarten - nach Kräften, kommt ein Lärmkonzert dabei heraus. Die rücksichtslose Verfolgung privater Interessen - hier mittels Aufdrehen des Lautstärkereglers - schädigt nicht allein "die anderen", sondern schlägt auf das einzelne egoistische Subjekt zurück, das seine Platte nur hören wird, wenn es wenigstens für Augenblicke bereit ist, den anderen zuzuhören. Schließlich will jeder seine Platte nicht nur sich selber, sondern auch den anderen vorführen.

* zitiert nach der Beilage "Conversations with John Cage, Christian Wolff - Hans G Helms" zur EMI-Schallplatten-Kassette "Music before Revolution" (Ensemble Musica Negativa conducted by Rainer Riehn).

Media Composition According to Cage
(Excerpt, cf. Bibliography)

"...though people think they can use records as music, what they have to finally understand, is, that they have to use them as *records*. And music instructs us, I would say, that the uses of things, if they are meaningful, are creative; therefore the only lively thing that will happen with a record, is, if somehow you would use it to make something which it isn't. If you could for instance make another piece of music with a record, including a record and other sounds of the environment or other musical instruments, that I would find interesting. And in fact one of my pieces has that... but that record itself now which includes a record, needs, in order to become lively, still more things. But unfortunately most people who collect records and use them, use them in quite another way. They use them as a kind of portable museum or a portable concert-hall."*

Up to now, the perspective has not considerably changed: Composition is critical in comparison with the established models of reception, as they are prescribed by the standard use of media, and on the other hand make possible an insight into the socially contingent structure of the kinds of reception-allowed "creative actions". Much the same can be said of relations just as fixed, like that of production and reproduction. Composition, in the context of certain projects, can also limit itself to creating the requirements for new possibilities of reception, while not determining these in a "causal" way. What Cage means with the comprehensive theme "Indeterminacy" is in an early, gapless noted / quoted piece like the Credo, either the uncertainty over the record to be chosen, or that which might come from the switched on radio. In the compositions for traditional instruments, from the forties and early fifties and especially for the piano, (normal or prepared) with the help of random operations, it at first comprehends all aspects of the structure, and in the end, the score even refers to the selection of the instruments. Within this development originated the 1952 score of *Imaginary Landscape No. 5*, a plan "for production of a tape-recording". The score begins with the selection of the "material", namely of 42 records of one's own choice, thereby showing that media products can be critizised best when in relation to another medium. (Perhaps within that lies one of the roots of the 20th century development, collage procedure: that every action which negates alienated objects, frozen actions, which, as it were, have come to rest, does so by means of an act of liberation: by disassembling them and combining parts of the material anew.)

While the production of this piece went strictly according to plan, from then on, Cage did without written scores which determined the production-process - i.e. the graph of each action - especially where the free, solo, or collective use of media was concerned - and was still capable of suggesting new ways of usage. In *33 1/3*, conceived during a conversation in 1969, and was meant for 12 recordplayers, each of the 12 participants should play his own record to bear in the creation of the piece. If everyone does it - as is to be expected - to the best of his ability, the result is a noise-concert. The inconsiderate pursuit of private interests - in this case by turning up the volume control - does not only harm "the others", but backfires on the egoistic individual who will hear his record only if he is willing to listen to the others for a few moments. After all, everyone wants to present his record not only to himself, but to the others as well.

* quoted according to supplement "Conversations with John Cage, Christian Wolff - Hans G Helms" of the EMI-record-cassette "Music before Revolution" (Ensemble Musica Negativa conducted by Rainer Riehn)

La Composition avec media selon Cage
(Extrait, comp. bibliographie)

John Cage. *33 1/3.* 1969. First European installation, daadgalerie, Berlin, 1982

"...bien que les gens pensent pouvoir se servir des disques comme s'il s'agissait de musique vivante, il leur faudra bien comprendre qu'ils doivent les utiliser commes des *disques*. Et la musique nous apprend, dirais-je, que l'usage des choses n'a de sens que s'il est acte créateur. Pour cette raison la seule chose vivante qui puisse se produire avec un disque c'est qu'on l'utilise pour en faire quelque chose qu'il n'est pas. Si l'on pouvait par l'intermédiaire d'un disque créer une autre pièce de musique en faisant intervenir un disque, d'autres bruits de l'environnement ou d'autres instruments de musique, je trouverais cela intéressant; j'ai effectivement réalisé cette idée dans l'une de mes pièces. ...mais le produit, ce disque qui en renferme un autre, nécessite encore autre chose pour devenir vivant. Malheureusement la plupart des collectionneurs utilisent les disques tout autrement: comme une sorte de musée portatif ou de salle de concert ambulante."*

Depuis, la perspective est restée fondamentalement la même: la composition pose un jugement critique sur les modèles de la réception, tels que décrétés par l'utilisation standardisée des mass media, et, inversément, la pénétration des modes de réception et de leur structure socialement déterminée rend possible les "actes créateurs". D'autres relations tout autant fixées, comme celle de la production et de la reproduction, présentent un comportement similaire. Dans le cadre de projets particuliers la composition peut également se limiter à établir les conditions ouvrant la voie à de nouvelles possibilités de réception, sans pour autant les déterminer de façon "causale". L'"indétermination", ce thème largement employé chez Cage, signifie - par exemple dans le Credo, une pièce de jeunesse entièrement notée - l'incertitude concernant les disques à choisir ou ce qui peut résulter de l'intervention d'un poste de radio. Dans les compositions des années quarante et du début des années cinquante pour un effectif instrumental traditionnel - surtout pour le piano préparé ou non - l'indétermination fait appel à des opérations aléatoires; elle englobe d'abord tous les aspects de la structure et finit par impliquer le choix de l'instrumentarium lui-même. Entre ces deux pôles se situe *Imaginary Landscape No. 5*, un plan pour la "production d'un enregistrement sur bande magnétique". Cette partition datant de 1952 commence par la sélection du "matériau", c'est-à-dire de 42 disques au choix, ce qui démontre encore une fois que la critique des produits des mass media s'effectue au mieux en relation avec un autre médium. (C'est peut-être en cela que résident les racines du procédé de collage développé au vingtième siècle: un geste libérateur qui nie les objets aliénés, les actes qui se sont pour ainsi dire figés ou immobilisés, en les décomposant et en recomposant des parties du matériau).

Si la production de cette pièce doit encore se dérouler selon un plan rigoureux, Cage renonça fréquemment par la suite à déterminer au moyen de la partition écrite le processus de production ainsi que le déroulement de actions isolées, particulièrement là où il était question de l'usage libre des mass media par un soliste ou un groupe de participants - et il parvint toutefois à suggérer de nouveaux modes d'utilisation. Dans *33 1/3*, oeuvre conçue en 1969 pendant une conservation et pensée pour 12 tourne-disques, chacun des 12 participants doit jouer son propre disque et le mettre en valeur. Cela se produit-il effectivement, et, comme l'on est en droit de s'y attendre, chacun y met-il de l'emphase, il en résulte un concert cacophonique. La poursuite impitoyable des intérêts individuels, qui se traduit ici par l'amplification du volume, lèse non seulement "les autres", mais se retourne contre le sujet égoïste qui n'entendra réellement son propre disque que lorsqu'il acceptera, au moins pour quelques instants, de prêter l'oreille aux autres. Chacun veut donc se présenter son propre disque en même temps qu'il veut le faire entendre aux autres.

* cité d'après "Conversations with John Cage, Christian Wolff - Hans G Helms", texte accompagnant "Music before Revolution"; disques-cassettes EMI (Ensemble Musica Negativa sous la direction de Rainer Riehn).

Milan Knížák

Broken Music

In den Jahren 1963 und 1964 habe ich Schallplatten zu langsam oder zu schnell abgespielt, dadurch die Eigenart der Musik geändert und so neue Kompositionen geschaffen. 1965 begann ich, Schallplatten zu zerstören: sie zu zerkratzen, Löcher in sie zu bohren, sie zu zerbrechen. Indem ich sie wieder und wieder abspielte (was die Nadel und oft auch den Plattenspieler ruinierte), ergab sich eine völlig neue Musik - unerwartet, nervenaufreibend und aggressiv; Kompositionen, die nur eine Sekunde oder (wenn die Nadel an einem tiefen Kratzer hängenblieb und dieselbe Stelle wieder und wieder spielte) unendlich lange dauerten. Ich entwickelte dieses Verfahren weiter. Ich klebte Klebeband auf die Schallplatten, übermalte sie, verbrannte sie, zerschnitt sie und klebte Teile verschiedener Platten wieder zusammen usw., um eine größtmögliche Klangvielfalt zu erzielen. Eine Klebenaht erzeugte ein rhythmisches Element, das kontrastierende melodische Phrasen voneinander trennte. Später dann arbeitete ich auf dieselbe Weise mit Partituren. Ich löschte

einige Noten, Bezeichnungen und andere Markierungen, ganze Takte (und bestimmte damit - wenn die Pausen regelmäßig waren - zu einem Teil den Rhythmus), fügte Noten und andere Zeichen hinzu, änderte das Tempo usw. Ich veränderte auch die Reihenfolge der Takte, spielte die Komposition rückwärts, stellte die Notensysteme auf den Kopf, kombinierte Teile verschiedener Partituren usw.

Ich benutzte auch Sammlungen populärer Lieder (oder anderer Kompositionen) als Partituren für Orchesterwerke. Jedes Instrument oder jede Gruppe spielt ein anderes Lied. Der daraus resultierende Klang (jede Gruppe behält das originale Tempo, die Intonation und die Länge des jeweiligen Stückes bei) ist eine neue Symphonie.

Und natürlich gab es andere ähnliche Ansätze, nebst ihren Kombinationen und Erweiterungen.

Da Musik, die durch das Abspielen zerstörter Schallplatten zustande kommt, nicht (oder nur unter großen Schwierigkeiten) in eine Notenschrift oder eine andere Sprache übertragen werden kann, können die Schallplatten selber zugleich als Notationen verstanden werden.

Broken Music

In 1963 - 64 I used to play records both too slowly or too fast and thus changed the quality of the music, thereby, creating new compositions. In 1965 I started to destroy records: scratch them, punch holes in them, break them. By playing them over and over again (which destroyed the needle and often the record-player too) an entireley new music was created - unexpected, nerve-racking and aggressive. Compositions lasting one second or almost infinitely long (as when the needle got stuck in a deep groove and played the same phrase over and over again). I developed this system further. I began sticking tapes on top of records, painting over them, burning them, cutting them up and glueing parts of different records back together, etc. to achieve the widest possible variety of sounds. A glued joint created a rhythmic element separating contrasting melodic phrases. Later I began to work in the same way with scores. I erased some of the notes, signatures and other signs, whole bars (and in this way partly determined the rhythm, if the pauses were regular), added notes and signatures, changed the tempo, and so on. I also changed the order of the bars, played the compositions backwards, turned the lines upside down, put parts of different scores together, etc.

I also used collections of popular songs (or other compositions) as scores for orchestral works. Each instrument or section plays one song. The resultant sound (each unit maintains the original tempo, intonation and length of the songs it is playing) is a new symphony.

And naturally, there were other similar approaches, plus their combinations and their offshoots.

Since music that results from playing ruined gramophone records cannot be transcribed to notes or into another language (or if so, only with great difficulty), the records themselves may be considered as notations at the same time.

Broken Music

Durant les années 1963 et 1964 je passais des disques en diminuant ou en accélérant la vitesse, ce qui modifiait les propriétés de la musique et créait ainsi de nouvelles compositions. En 1965 j'ai commencé à détruire les disques en les rayant, en y perçant des trous ou en les cassant. Je les ai laissés tourner sans interruptions (un procédé qui abîme la tête de lecture et souvent aussi le tourne-disque) et il en résultait une musique tout à fait nouvelle, inattendue, énervante et agressive; des compositions qui ne duraient qu'une seconde ou indéfiniment, lorsque par exemple la tête de lecture se prenait dans une rayure profonde et reproduisait sans arrêt la même séquence. J'ai appliqué sur les disques du papier adhésif, je les ai peints, découpés et j'ai collé ensemble des morceaux de disques différents pour obtenir la sonorité la plus variée possible. Une couture exécutée à la colle produisait un élément rythmique qui séparait les phrases mélodiques contrastantes. Par la suite j'ai procédé de la même manière avec des partitions. J'ai effacé quelques notes, différentes indications, des mesures entières, et ainsi, lorsque les silences étaient réguliers, je déterminais partiellement le rythme; j'ai ajouté des notes et autres signes, modifié le tempo etc. J'ai également changé la succession des mesures, joué les compositions à partir de la fin, retourné les systèmes à l'envers et combiné des sections de diverses compositions etc.

J'ai également utilisé des collections de chansons populaires (et autres compositions) comme partitions d'oeuvres orchestrales. Chaque instrument ou chaque groupe joue une chanson différente. Le résultat sonore - chaque groupe conserve le tempo, l'intonation et la longeur d'origine - est une nouvelle symphonie.

Et naturellement il y avait d'autres procédés semblables avec leurs combinaisons et dérivés.

Vue l'extrême difficulté qu'implique la notation de la musique produite par des disques détériorés ou sa transposition dans un autre langage, les disques eux-mêmes peuvent être considérés à la fois comme notations.

Peter Fischli / **David Weiss**. *Popular opposites: true or false*. 1981/82. Unfired clay

Abbreviations

acc	accompaniment
alto-fl	alto flute
alto-h	alto horn
as	alto-saxophone
b	bass
b-cl	bass-clarinet
b-g	bass-guitar
bs	baritone-saxophone
b-sax	bass-saxophone
b-tb	bass-trombone
c	violoncello
cl	clarinet
co	cornet
cond	conductor
dr	drums
el	electronics
el-b	electric-bass
el-g	electric-guitar
el-p	electric-piano
el-v	electric-violin
fl	flute
fl-h	flugelhorn
g	guitar
hpschd	harpsichord
harm	harmonica
ob	oboe
org	organ
p	piano
perc	percussion
sax	saxophone
ss	soprano-saxophone
strings	string section
syn	synthesizer
tb	trombone
tp	trumpet
ts	tenor-saxophone
tu	tuba
v	violin
vib	vibraphone
voc	vocal
xyl	xylophone

ARTISTS' RECORDWORKS

A COMPENDIUM

Das folgende Kompendium verzeichnet Arbeiten von bildenden Künstlern, die mit dem und für das Medium Schallplatte entstanden sind.

Es will mehrere Funktionen gleichzeitig erfüllen: generelle Informationsquelle zum Thema, Handbuch zum wissenschaftlichen Gebrauch, begleitender Ausstellungskatalog und kurzweiliges Bilderbuch.

Es erscheint nur in einer Sprache, in Englisch. Wir halten dies für sinnvoll und zumutbar, da sich die Informationen in den meisten Fällen auf die sachlichen Details beschränken. Die eingefügten Texte wurden in der Regel in der Orginalsprache zitiert.

Das Verzeichnis ist auf Vollständigkeit angelegt, hat aber nur Titel aufgenommen, die konkret zur Katalogisierung vorlagen. Hierbei unterstützten uns Künstler und Leihgeber, die uns auch unabhängig von der Ausstellung ihre Schallplatten und Objekte zur Katalogbearbeitung überließen. Werner Durand, Klaus Ebbeke, Gerti Fietzek, Jon Hendricks und Christian Marclay halfen uns in Einzelfragen.

Einige historische Materialien, zu denen wir keinen Zugang hatten, mußten unberücksichtigt bleiben.

Für die Titelaufnahme haben wir vier Kriterien zu Grunde gelegt:

C over — Schallplattenhüllen, die von einem bildenden Künstler orginal bearbeitet wurden, oder die nach einem eigenen Entwurf entstanden sind

O bject — Schallplatten mit Objektcharakter, Skulpturen unter Verwendung von Schallplatten und solche, denen die Schallplatte ausschließlich als plastisches Material dient

P ublication — Ausstellungskataloge, Bücher, denen als ergänzende Information eine Schallplatte beiliegt

S ound — Schallplatten, bei denen das Klangmaterial selbst von einem bildenden Künstler stammt

Die Künstlernamen im Verzeichnis sind mit den Initialen der jeweils zutreffenden Kriterien gekennzeichnet, häufig trafen mehrere Kriterien zu. In einigen Fällen war die eindeutige Bestimmung problematisch, da mit der Erweiterung des Kunstbegriffs die Kunstsparten sich nicht mehr säuberlich trennen lassen. Auch die Grenzen zwischen bildender Kunst und Musik sind fließend. So war es manchmal unsere persönliche Entscheidung, die zur Aufnahme einer Schallplatte ins Verzeichnis führte.

U.B./M.G.

The following compendium lists works of visual artists created with and for the medium of the record. It wants to fulfill several functions at the same time: a general source of information related to the topic, a reference book for academic use, a catalogue accompanying the exhibition and an entertaining picture book.

It appears in only one language, English. The inserted texts have been cited as a rule in their original language.

The catalogue is designed for completeness, but contains only the titles which were actually present for listing. We were supported by artists and lenders, who left us their records and objects, not only for the exhibition but also for the task of compiling the catalogue. Werner Durand, Klaus Ebbeke, Gerti Fietzek, Jon Hendricks and Christian Marclay helped us with specific problems.

Some historical material, to which we had no access was not included.

The selection of titles is based on four criteria:

C over — Record covers, which are original works by visual artists, or which have been made after the design of a visual artist

O bject — Records with object-character, sculptures which utilize records artistically and sculptures in which records serve the function of a plastic material

P ublication — Exhibition catalogues and books, which contain a record for additional information

S ound — Records, which have sound produced by visual artists

The artists' names in the catalogue are marked with the initials of the appropriate criterion, often, several criteria were applicable. In some cases a definite classification was difficult, because by the extension of the art concept, the art categories are no longer clearly defined.

The boundaries between the fine (visual) arts and music are also flowing. Thus, we sometimes had to make personal decisions to determine which record would be included in the catalogue.

Le présent compendium renferme des oeuvres d'art plastique conçues avec et pour le disque en tant que médium.

Il veut remplir plusieurs fonctions simultanément: source d'information générale sur le sujet, manuel pouvant être utilisé à des fins scientifiques, catalogue complémentaire de l'exposition et livre d'image divertissant.

Il paraît dans une seule langue, l'anglais. Cela nous semble raisonnable, puisque dans la plupart des cas les informations ne concernent que des détails neutres. En règle générale les textes incorporés ont été cités dans la langue originale.

L'index se veut complet, mais il n'inclut que les titres présents lors du classement. A cet effet nous avons bénéficié de l'aide des artistes et des personnes qui, indépendamment de l'exposition, nous ont prêté leurs disques ou objets pour la mise en place du catalogue. Werner Durand, Klaus Ebbeke, Gerti Fietzek, Jon Hendricks et Christian Marclay nous ont conseillé à propos de certains points particuliers. Nous avons dû passer sous silence certains documents historiques auxquels nous n'avions pas accès.

Quatre critères ont déterminé la sélection des titres:

C over — couvertures de disque produites par l'artiste lui-même ou qui ont été fabriquées à partir de ses esquisses

O bjet — disques ayant le caractère d'un objet, sculptures qui utilisent des disques ou dans lesquelles le disque n'a que la fonction de matériau plastique

P ublication — catalogues d'exposition, livres qui renferment un disque en tant qu'information complémentaire

S ound — disques dont le matériau sonore a été produit par le peintre ou le sculpteur

Dans l'index les noms des artistes sont accompagnés de la ou des lettres initiales représentant les qualifications pertinentes. Si dans certains cas plusieurs critères étaient judicieux, dans d'autres la caractérisation univoque posait certains problèmes, car, avec l'extension du concept d'art, les différentes disciplines ne se laissent plus séparer sans restes. Même les frontières entre l'art plastique et la musique sont floues. L'introduction d'un disque au sein du catalogue relève donc parfois de notre seule décision personnelle.

Acconci, Vito
→   Airwaves

Adams, Yura
→   Artsounds Collection

Adler, Jeremy
→   Sound Poetry

Kaiser Wilhelm Museum
Krefeld

Tast- und
Tonbild von
Yaacov Agam

Tableau
Tactile Sonore
par Yaacov Agam

Agam, Yaacov   [S]

Title: Tast- und Tonbild von Yaacov
Agam

Contents: Verwunderung. Beschwörung.
Reproduction of audible examples
of the Touch- and Sound-Picture
from the museum collection.
Realization and recording by the
artist.

ø 17cm, 45 RPM, Kaiser Wilhelm
Museum Krefeld, n.d.

Cover: b/w, photo of a Touch- and Sound-
Picture

Agnetti, Vincenzo
→   Revolutions Per Minute

A I R W A V E S

VITO ACCONCI · LAURIE ANDERSON · JACKI APPLE · CONNIE BECKLEY · JIM BURTON
DIEGO CORTEZ · TERRY FOX · JANA HAIMSOHN · JULIA HEYWARD · LEANDRO KATZ
MEREDITH MONK · RICHARD NONAS · DENNIS OPPENHEIM

Airwaves   [S]

Two Record Anthology Of Artists' Aural
Work & Music

Contents: Vito Acconci: Ten Packed Minutes.
Jana Haimsohn: Hav'a Lava Flow.
Terry Fox: The Labyrinth Scored
For The Purrs Of 11 Different
Cats. Julia Heyward: Mongolian
Face Slap, Big Coup (part one),
Nose Flute, Big Coup (part two).
Dennis Oppenheim: Broken Record
Blues. Meredith Monk: Rally, Pro-
cession. Diego Cortez: Arbiter, You
Pay. Jim Burton: High Country He-
lium. Leandro Katz: Animal Hours.
Connie Beckley: Triad Triangle.
Laurie Anderson: Two Songs For
Tape Bow Violin (Ethics Is The Es-
thetics Of The Few-Ture >Lenin<,
Song For Juanita, 1977), Is Any-
body Home, 1976, It's Not The
Bullet That Kills You - It's The
Hole. Diego Cortez: Cataract
Monologue. Jacki Apple: Black
Holes/blue sky dreams. Richard
Nonas: What Do You Know.

2 LPs, ø 30cm, 33 RPM, 1977,
One Ten Records, New York, No.
OT 001/2, reissue for gelbe Musik,
Berlin, 1982

Cover: b/w, gatefold, text- and photodocu-
mentation

Some generalizations: This record is not an
art object. All the people on this record are
artists. Many of the artists present themselves in a gallery situation: live in performance, electronically through installations.
Often these situations are theatrical. None
of the artists consider themselves actors.
There is no proscenium. It is a floorshow.
Most of the work in the anthology is
musical. Like most of the music in the world
it is predominantly vocal. You can dance to
at least two of the selections. The artists
combine the bravura and risk of the
musician (filter) with the intellect and risk of
the composer (source).
What is heard is often augmented by technology. Technology is a tool, a verb. Sometimes it is avoided because it imposes a
system, another language, on what is
happening. Many of the artists use technology to make things legible. Sometimes
legibility is sacrificed to produce a distinctive
signature.
The concerns here are not the concerns of
painting. Sometimes there are references to
art. Sometimes structure is the subject
matter. Often the subject is the past, or
more precisely personal observations on the
events of the past, or more precisely,
memory. The injection of the self into the
past adds to a feeling of literary-ness.
As in opera, what we hear is influenced by
what we see, how much of the story we
know, and if we understand the language.
As in any performance situation, the energy
generated by the performance is more than,
and perhaps more interesting than, the information presented. You had to be there.
Often what is done is not repeated. This is
a record.

B. George (Covertext)

Albert-Birot, Pierre
→   Sound Poetry

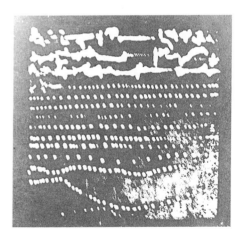

albrecht d.   [C/S]

Title: endless music. (anti-pop-music)

Perf.:   albrecht d. (tabla, cymbal, string-
instruments), Bernd Jaiser (background music), Grit Bäcker (voc),
Axel Knipschild (background music), Thomas Niggl (fl)

ø 30cm, 33 RPM, reflection press,
Stuttgart, 1973/74

Cover: one-color print, part of the issue
two-color print on grey cardboard

YOU PAY Set in the African city, a group of beggars insist: "You pay."
'ESOTERRORISTS' Anya Phillips & Diego Cortez at Chris Makos' opening, Sept. '76
photo: Bobby Grossman
Print: Jimmy DeSana

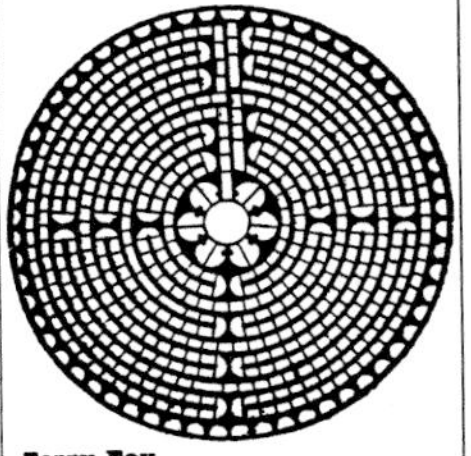

Terry Fox

THE LABYRINTH SCORED FOR THE PURRS OF 11 DIFFERENT CATS The labyrinth at Chartres is a unicursal path winding in 552 steps through 11 concentric rings into the center. In order to hear the sound of this path I have changed the steps into cats purrs. The 552 steps become 5,520 second of purring, each step being equal to 10 seconds of sound. The 11 concentric rings then become 11 different cats, each cat representing one complete ring with all its steps. The stereo balance of the tape corresponds to the directional movement through the labyrinth. The tape begins with 10 seconds of the 1st cat (ring), 10 of the 2nd, 10 of the 3rd, 10 of the 4th then turns left for 130 seconds (steps) of the 5th ring (cat). overlapping into the 6th ring for 140 seconds and so on winding through the labyrinth into the center which is represented by the simultaneous purring of all 11 cats. The entire tape is 95 minutes long, the section represented in this disc is the last few minutes of the tape.

The tape was completed in a live mix engineered by Bob Bileki at the Z.B.S. Foundation in Fort Edward, New York, using 5 prerecorded cats from San Francisco and 6 from Fort Edward in December 1976. Thanks to Tom, Patty, Boogaloo, Miriam, Puffin, Heba, Ferguson, Ernest, Samantha, Spat, Arthur and to the generous help of their "owners" both in San Francisco and New York. This tape was supported in part, by a grant from the New York State Council on the Arts.

Jana Haimsohn

Late September... I unassumingly took a dive into the grey Atlantic. Froze my floundering ass off. This is Coney Island unfortunately. I said, "Take me to the ocean, need a photo in the sea." You see, my image was the Pacific, turquoise-blue, Hawaiian style. I'm clearer near blue-green water and hot for sun-baked local color. But this is 5 or 6 thousand miles later, so I said "Coney Island? Island? O.K."

June... Little New York woman rode out of big city, Hawaii bound. I didn't walk. I rarely walked. It's been bicycle, mass-transit city style, then truck ride, airplane, hitch-hike. I never much figured on my land legs for getting me around. Then I was on Oahu, swimming alot—familiar in that fluid, fluid in that medium—enjoying twisting, floating upside-down, without gravity to down me. And I was asked to go to the big island and Kauai. Kahuna, Hawaiian High-priestess friend said, "Got talk to Pele and tell us what she said." (Pele: Hawaiian Goddess of Fire, of volcanoes). So I headed for volcano, Hawaii, armed with new and strengthened tools, and I found myself talking to the hiking trails, walking alone for hours through nothing but old lava flows. I hiked through Kilauea Iki and Kilauea craters, to Halemaumau crater, and around Mauna Ulu, (Newest U.S. mountain, formed from Pele's 1974 eruption), and Mauna Loa, active steam-venting hot spot of a mountain was drawing my attention. So with sneakers and a minimum of clumsy gear, I started the 18½ mile hike. And as the weight of my scant food supply sank from shoulders to belly, I started half-running my way up that mountain, volcanically propelled.

Hiking alone is fantastic—constant motion, rhythm set in motion, balance and lightness required, moving with the ground over lava. Movement not arbitrary, the terrain dictating the nature of each step, asking for each step to be careful, not to disturb anything on the way. I want to feel the floor, my soles extended two feet beyond the surface line—resigned to be walking through, like wings are on the instep and the soarings down-home base line.

Red hill cabin was my resting spot for the first night. Late afternoon I saw red hill ahead. I said "Oh shit, I hope that's not a mirage." I slept in the cabin, woke for sunrise, and started toward the summit, 11.3 miles further, altitude 13,250 ft. Stayed one night and hiked back to red hill. Couldn't leave. Full-moon and sunsets blazed so fiercely I almost screamed. I heard things I hadn't heard before. Spent hours checking

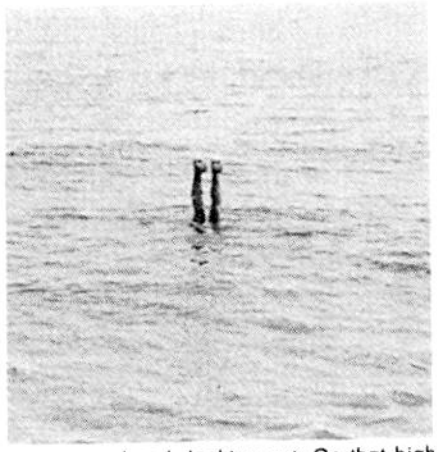

out, eyes closed, looking out. On that high spot, I crouched low, sitting lots, keeping my seat close to volcanic ground me, to Pele—volcanic activity, taking it rectally, anal charge—now I understand. And my bowels moved so fine that week despite total starch desperation diet. And I felt a surge from such space, and clearness, the altitude rising, my attitude rising. And I finally understood why people head for the mountains. I stayed for days. Didn't much want to come down. No more food. Too cold to fast. Had to climb down. Headed for Kauai, north shore, to "secret beach," for time alone, swimming, sun-bathing nude, getting drained by that relentless sun, spending hours crawling in the sand, eyes peeled, picking many tiny tiny perfect amazing minute sand-dollars, the size of a small pimple. *photo: Michael Oblowitz*

Julia Heyward

SOUND DISPLACEMENT: Confusing the sensory hierarchy by separating sound and picture; syncing different sounds with different visuals, dethroning the master sight with incongruous but rhythmic sound and picture co-ordination. Sound displacement by confusing the origin of the sound; I've experimented with speaker placement, with multiple microphone setups, with wireless microphones, with ventrioloquism, with lies and other forms of sensationalism. Ventriloquism; I have combined this technique with audio tape to confuse the sound source. I have recently become more interested in my voice unamplified. I have studied opera—and Mongolian style singing with David Hykes. With the operatic training concentrating on projection and control for a general voice discipline. With the Mongolian style of singing the technique of isolating, amplifying, and projecting the overtone series is a very phenomenal sound displacement experience. The harmonics exist an octave above the fundamental note, and when produced simultaneously with this fundamental note exist spatially separate.

From what I have learned from these two techniques an evolution has begun in the form of a new singing style. I have

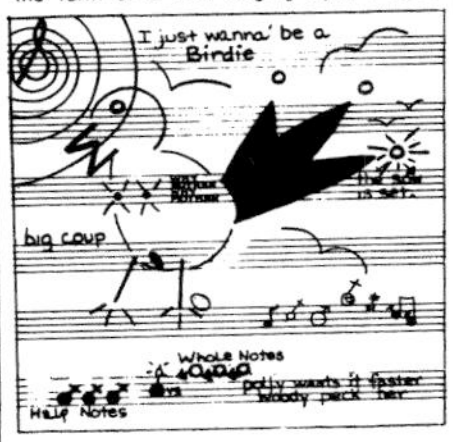

learned to project the sound from my nasal cavity. The sound produced is much like the sound of a flute but not quite as windy. It is a very powerful sound both in volume and beauty. What I later came to discover is that I had been taught the way men sing in Mongolia and that the sound I had accidentally found was similar to the way women sing in Mongolia. So I nurtured my learning process by listening to a bad tape recording of a Mongolian woman with no idea how she was doing what she was doing. After much theory and practice the final singing posture was discovered, which is lips tightly closed or slightly opened using the nostrils as the projecting cavity. This posture works very well for a ventriloquist. I have recently been working with a tape delay so that I can sing with myself live also affording harmony and a fuller sound.

The second singing technique used on this record I call a yodel. The back of my throat is the main production area with modulation achieved by changing the shape and size of my mouth cavity; Also changing the pressure by different breathing exhalation pacings controlled by the diaphragm and the size of the mouth opening. This is a very active sound with many moving parts. Both techniques have an electronic quality to them, but both are produced naturally.

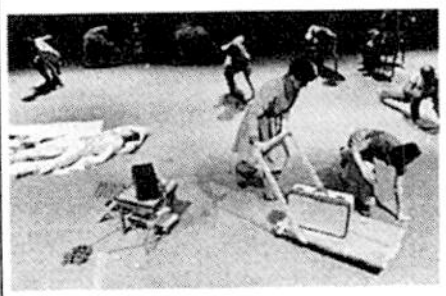

Meredith Monk

QUARRY, an opera composed in 1975-1976, is a mosaic consisting of images, movement, dialogue, film, sound, light and of course music. As in all of my music, it is an exploation of the voice as an instrument i.e. the full range of the voice (pitch, texture, volume, speed, timbre, rhythm, breath, pattern). QUARRY is scored for forty voices, two pump organs, one electric organ (Gibson "Kalamazoo"), soprano recorder and magnetic tape. The score also includes "action sounds": a woman constantly sweeping; a woman shaking uncooked rice on a tray; men and women riding bicycles across the space; bicycle bells ringing in particular pitches; radio static; silverware scraping against glass plates. These sounds are precisely orchestrated within the overall sound structure to occur at particular times. During all of the vocal selections from QUARRY with the exception of the voice and piano solos which were pre-recorded on tape and played through a tiny speaker in the 1940's radio at the center of the space, the singers are moving or dancing. In the Rally, all the singers are simultaneously performing vigorous, calesthenic-like movement; during the Wash, they are performing slow flowing movement patterns in counterpoint to the melodies.

In addition to dealing with these elements abstractly, QUARRY has another layer of content. it is a presentation of World War II or the time of World War II as myth, fantasy, imagination, memory, atmosphere. For my generation World War II exists only as one or more of these things—something in the mind. In QUARRY the consciousness of events is sifted through the mind of a child, more specifically an American child so that all the events are seen either as at a great distance or as completely subjective, internal and irrational. The challenge of working on QUARRY was to find a new and non-linear way of dealing with a historical phenomenon which already conjurs set responses that have been formulated by the extensive information available about it in the mass media and in the memories of those who lived through it. Basically, as in all my theater work, the attempt was to create primarily an ambience pungent with sights, sounds, smells, etc. that evoke and touch upon fundamental psychic experiences. *photo: Johan Elbers*

TOTEM MEMORY AIR
COLUMNS DWELLING
SHRINES ANGLES
NEST PYRAMIDS CLIFFS
LIMIT CUBIC
HISTORICAL PARTITION
CLAN STRUCTURE
ROOMS BAND UNIT
GRAVITY METHOD
REASON PLANE
ARCHAEOLOGICAL CHAIN
MARKING DUALISM

Leandro Katz

Elements of speech sonority, stress, pronunciation, phrasing and intonation arranged as phonetic/musical values by combining distinct voices in parallel recordings and by placing cases of individual speech as collective voice or anthem in states of chaos, coincidence or agreed organization.

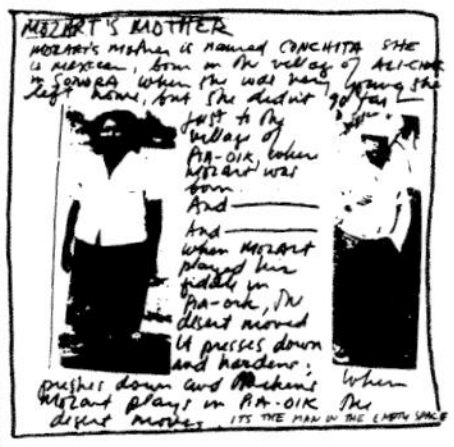

Richard Nonas

What interests me most are the edges, the places where one thing becomes another, where one thing is not quite the other but is still moving; what interests me most are situations whose identity vibrates at the edge of ambiguity.

This tape was originally a book.

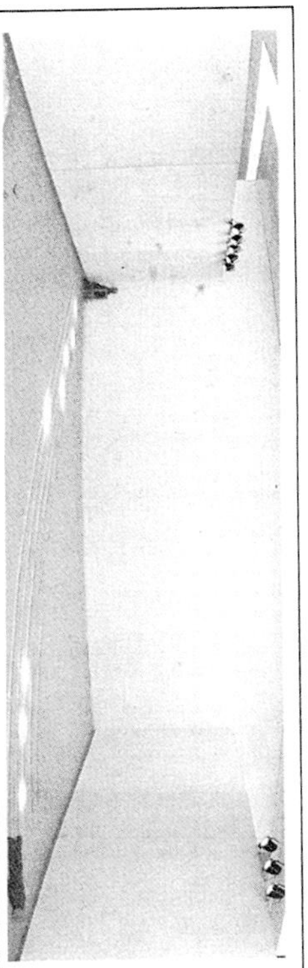

Dennis Oppenheim

BROKEN RECORD BLUES incorporates a single revolution from an early blues record and loops it thereby simulating the effect of a broken record. The notes within this fragment are then plotted with ultra bright lights onto five Drag Marks in blue sand, representing musical bars.

The sound track using the broken record constantly fades in and out of a verbal track describing conditions of stagnation, repetition and the eventual deterioration of a creative process. The five musical bars are sometimes referred to as "scratches on my face that never go away" or "lines of expression that always remain the same" It is also said—"no matter what sound I make it sounds the same, no matter what note I play it's been played before—like finger prints that never change." The scratch marks are referred to as coming from "five fingers that did nothing more than follow the lines that were already there." Finally it asks "I want these lines to go way back, so far back, when the song begins to play—no one has heard it."

Installation at Boymans Museum, Rotterdam, Holland. 1976. Components: two 18" surrogate performers, blue sand, spot lights, stereo sound track.

photo: Wink van Kempen

Airwaves. Cover, right inner side

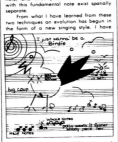

albrecht d. / Joseph Beuys [C/S]

Title: Performance at the ICA London, 1. Nov. 1974

ø 30cm, 33 RPM, n.d., Samadhi Records No. 1003

Cover: one-color print with documentation-photos by Chris Schwarz

The concert took place on occasion of the exhibition *Art Into Society - Society Into Art* in the ICA London.

Special issue: *Ich durchsuche Feldcharakter* 99 copies, numbered and signed by both artists, two-color print with original photo mounted on cover

albrecht d. [S]

Title: Abstract Energy

Contents: endless music goes ZEN. 1970-1985 FIFTEEN YEARS ALBRECHT/d. (Meetings with Bernd Jaiser, "die Stimme" Joseph Beuys, Frans

Weyler, Cosey Fanni Tutti, Genesis P-Orridge, Chris Carter, Katerina Z., Angelika Schmidt, Volker Hamann, Marie Kawazu, Steffen Bremer und Franz Dreyer.)

ø 30cm, 33 RPM, Samadhi Records / reflection Press / Stuttgart, No. 1005

Cover: one-color print, gatefold

8-page supplement with texts and photos of the various actions and performances
Side A is the recording of the solo-performance of Albrecht d. on Feb. 10, 1980, in the Akademie der Künste, Berlin on the occasion of the exhibition *Für Augen und Ohren*

albrecht d.
→ Voices Notes & Noise

Allen, Jo Harvey
→ High Performance

ALMA ART [C/S]
Warszawa, Poland
Series of Polish records with extravagant handmade covers

ALMA ART No. 001 / 1984
Title: Jubileuszowa Orkiestra Helmuta Nadolskiego
Cover: b/w, affixed pencil chips
Design: Andrzej Szewczyk

ALMA ART No. 002 / 1984
Title: Janusz Dziubak tytuł płyty
Cover: b/w, matchbox affixed with blue plastic-strip
Design: Edward Krasinski / Andrzej Szewczyk

ALMA ART No. 003 / 1984
Title: Andrzej Mitan w Swietej Racji
Cover: b/w, red paintblotches
Design: Ryszard Winiarski / Andrzej Szewczyk

ALMA ART No. 004 / 1984
Title: Andrzej Przybielski w sferze dotyku
Cover: covered with black velvet
Design: Jerzy Czuraj / Andrzej Szewczyk

ALMA ART No. 005 / 1984
Title: Miecz Archaniola
Music: Andrzej Bieźan
Cover: b/w, original photo b/w, mounted, title handwritten with blue feltpen
Design: Tadeusz Rolke / Andrzej Szewczyk

ALMA ART No. 006 / 1987

Title: Ptaki. (Birds)
Music and
Singing: Andrzej Mitan and Birds
Cover: b/w, enclosed in mesh-wire
Design: Cezary Staniszewski / Andrzej Szewczyk

ALMA ART No. 007 / 1987

Title: Psalm
Music: Andrzej Mitan
Cover: b/w, enclosed in white cloth
Design: Cezary Staniszewski / Andrzej Szewczyk

ALMA ART No. 008 / 1987
→ Jarosłav Kozłowski

ALMA ART No. 009 / 1987

Title: Lapis. Low Sounds
Music: Krzystof Knittel
Cover: b/w, yellow handwritten name of composer, hairbushels affixed
Design: Włodzimierz Borowski / Andrzej Szewczyk

The Polish artists manufacturing the record sleeves

Altagor
→ Sound Poetry

Altman, Patrick
→ Sound Poetry

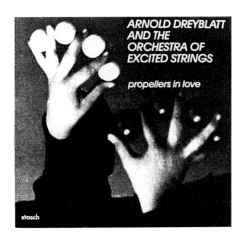

Amerikanische Künstler in Berlin   [P/S]
Supplement: Arnold Dreyblatt And The Orchestra Of Excited Strings

Perf.:   Arnold Dreyblatt, Wolfgang Glum, Jan Schade, Dirk Lebahn, Wolfgang Mettler

Exhibition-catalogue as record-box, white with title sticker, contains loose sheets, 46 pages and a LP-record (ø 30cm, 33 RPM), 1986, Amerika Haus Berlin / Initiative Berlin - USA e.V. The record is a production of the Künstlerhaus-Bethanien, Berlin.

Amirkhanian, Charles
→ Giorno Poetry Systems
→ Revue OU
→ Sound Poetry

Anderson, Beth
→ Giorno Poetry Systems
→ Sound Poetry

Anderson, Laurie   [S]

Title: "It's Not The Bullett That Kills You - It's The Hole." "Break It."

ø 17cm, 45 RPM, 1977, Holly Solomon Gallery, New York

Cover: only in white protective cover

Anderson, Laurie   [C/S]

Title: O Superman. (For Massenet). Walk The Dog

Perf.:   Laurie Anderson (voc, vocoder, v, wooden blocks), Roma Baran (farfisa, casio, vocoder, tenor whistle), Perry Hoberman (fl, sax, walkie-talkies, soprano whistle), D. Sharpe (dr), Brandy (dogs)

ø 17cm, 33 RPM, 1981, One Ten Records, New York

Cover: two-color print, design: Laurie Anderson

Anderson is a composer, but more visibly she is a "performance artist", which gives the first clue to her popularity. Performance art is the fashionable discipline these days, having succeeded painting, theater, dance and video, all of which enjoyed their place in the trend-setting sun over the past two decades. But there is more to her success than that; there are other performance artists, after all. Anderson owes her special recognition to her mixture of music and performance, and specifically to the way she embraced new-wave rock without becoming its slave. In all her guises she is a performer who seizes the attention and holds it. She has a delicious sense of humor, which is not all that common in either punk or the avantgarde. And she is a woman.

Her early pieces were short and clever, owing something to happenings and the post-Cageian avant-garde theater of composers like Ashley. She would play the violin, for instance, but in an unusual situation - like standing in a block of ice - that called fresh attention to this most familiar of actions. She wrote poetry, made conceptual installations in galleries, and recorded short songs and quirky instrumental pieces, all in preparations for her larger projects.

The most ambitious of these projects to date is called *United States I-IV*, an attempt to embrace and understand her native country, the inspiration for which came during her ever more frequent European performances.

All her work, including *United States*, is best described as solo opera - although in her larger-scale recent productions she has had accompanying musicians as well as assistants to help with the sound, lighting, tape recorders and slide and film projectors. Still, it is Anderson alone who is in the spotlight. The effect is like a highly attenuated art-rock concert, a stylized lecture or perhaps a poetry reading writ very large indeed, with every aspect of the poetic concept amplified and counterpointed by aural and visual imagery. The subject is herself on one level, but more generally, in the tradition of all autobiographical artists, her observations on whatever it is that is the subject of a given piece.

Excerpt from John Rockwell: *All American Music*. New York 1983

Laurie Anderson playing her *Viophonograph* (Turntable) mounted on a violin; needle in bow; '45 has 1 note on each band – needle scrapes). (1976)

WALK THE DOG
a song for voice, violin and electronics

I saw a lot of trees today. And they were all made of wood.
Well, they were wooden trees - and they were made entirely of wood.
Well, I came home today, and you were all on fire. Your shirt was on fire.
And your hair was on fire. And flames were licking all around your feet.
And I did not know what to do. And then, a thousand violins began to play.
And I really did not know what to do then.
  So I just decided to go out-
And walk the dog.

I went to the movies, and I saw a dog thirty feet high.
And this dog was made entirely of light. And he filled up the whole screen.
And his eyes were long hallways. He had those long, echoing, hallway eyes.

I turned on the radio and I heard a song by Dolly Parton. And she was singing:
Oh! I feel so bad. I feel so sad. I left my Mom and I left my Dad.
And I just want to go home now.
I just want to go back to my Tennessee mountain home now.
Well, *you* know she's not gonna go back home.
  And I know she's not gonna go back home.
  And she knows she's never gonna go back there.
And I just want to know who's gonna go and walk *her* dog.(Her dog.)

Well, I feel so bad. I feel so sad.
But not as bad as the night I wrote this song.

Close your eyes. OK. Now imagine you're at the most wonderful party. OK.
Delicious food. Uh-huh. Interesting people.
  Uh-mm. Terrific music. Mm-mmh.
NOW OPEN THEM!

5 LPs, ø 30cm, 33 RPM, 1984, Warner Bros. Records Inc., New York, No. 925 192-1

Cover: drawer-box, multi-color print, protective cover of each record with texts, drawings and photos, design: Laurie Anderson

Recorded live at the Brooklyn Academy of Music New York City, February 7-10, 1983.

Further records:
Big Science (Warner Bros. Records, 1982, LP, BSK 3674)
Mister Heartbreak (Warner Bros. Records & WEA International, 1983, LP, 925 077-1)
Home Of The Brave (Warner Bros. Records & WEA International, 1986, LP, 925 400-1)

Several weeks earlier I had played a concert at the Philharmonie in Budapest, and the audience had rioted. That did not disturb me so much as the fact that because of this bedlam they had heard none of the music. So, at my second appearance, I walked out on the concert platform, bowed, and spoke up: "Attendants, will you please close and lock the doors?"
After this was done I reached in under my left armpit in approved American gangster fashion and produced my ugly little automatic. Without a further word I placed it on the front desk of my Steinway and proceeded with my concert. Every note was heard, and, in a sense, I suppose I opened up the way in Hungary for modern music of a non-Bartók-Kodaly variety.

Excerpt from George Antheil: *Bad Boy of Music.* New York 1945

Anderson, Laurie [C/P/S]

Title: let X = X

ø 17cm, 33 RPM, Artforum, February 1982, New York (flexi-disc, transparent, attached), produced by Roma Baran (Biscuit Productions) and Laurie Anderson

Cover: b/w, attached paper-patternchart for cover, design: Laurie Anderson

Anderson, Laurie

→ Airwaves
→ Giorno Poetry Systems
→ Peter Gordon: Love of Life Orchestra
→ Word of Mouth

Antin, Eleanor

→ Revolutions Per Minute

Anderson, Laurie [C/S]

Title: United States

Contents: Parts 1 - 4

Perf.: Laurie Anderson, Peter Gordon, Geraldine Pontius, Joe Kos, Chuck Fisher, Bill Olbrecht, Ann de Marinis, David van Tieghem, Roma Baran, Rufus Harley, Shelley Karson

Technical Realization: Bob Bielecki

Anonymus [C/O/S]

ø 30cm, playable at any speed, 1981

Record with blank grooves is stored between an inverted sandpaper cover, manufactured by ADALOX, NORTON.

Antheil, George

→ Max Ernst
→ Alberto Savinio

Apollinaire, Guillaume [P/S]

Title: Guillaume Apollinaire 1880-1918. A Celebration 1968

Catalogue of the exhibition in the ICA, London, 1968
Folder with 3 pamphlets and different slip-ins and a record (ø 17,5cm, 45 RPM): *Le Pont Mirabeau* read by Guillaume Apollinaire

Appel, Karel [P/S]

Title: Musique Barbare

Contents: Paysage électronique. Poème Barbare. Le cavalier blanc

ø 30cm, 33 RPM, 1963, International Publishing Company Ltd., The World's Window, Baarn, Holland

Cover: book, multi-color print, 24 pages (n.pag), included inside cover + 4 sheets, with text by Jan Vrijman and photos by Ed van der Elsken

The book comes complete with a color-lithography (28 x 38,5 cm) MUSIQUE BARBARE, in a portfolio.

Apple, Jacki [C/S]

Title: The Mexican Tapes

Composer: Joseph Armillas & Zephryn

Perf.: Jacki Apple, Joseph Armillas, Eric Bogosian, Jude Dozier, Henry Korn, Peter Stroud, Zephryn

ø 30cm, 33 RPM, 1980, One Ten Records, New York, No. 003

Cover: multi-color print, cover photo by Sandi Fellman, back cover snapshots by Jacki Apple

THE MEXICAN TAPES is a Super 8 color film and an 8-track stereo mix audio tape soundtrack containing spoken text, music and sound effects.

Jacki Apple (Excerpt from covertext)

Apple, Jacki
→ Airwaves
→ High Performance

Applebroog, Ida
→ Revolutions Per Minute

Arcand, Pierre-André
→ Sound Poetry

Arias-Misson, Alain
→ Sound Poetry

Armajani, Siah
→ Art By Telephone

Arman
→ Art By Telephone

Arp, Hans [C/S]

Title: hans arp liest hans arp

Contents: kaspar ist tot. die wolkenpumpe. dada-sprüche. aus dem "pyramidenrock" (opus 0). im autonomobilen reich. die arabische sanduhr. schnurrmilch. aus "weißt du schwarzt du". straßburgkonfigurationen. gondelfahren. wir bittsteller aber. hinunter hinunter. aus "auf verschleierten schaukeln". engel, sinnende flammen

ø 25cm, 33 RPM, 1964, Verlag Günther Neske, Pfullingen

Cover: three-color print with graphic by Hans Arp

24-page textbook (20,5 x 12,6) as supplement

MUSIC-LANGUAGE
CORRECTED SLOGANS

Side A (Time: 22:45)
Maharashtra, Keep All Your Friends, Imagination I & II, Coleridge vs Martineau, An Exemplification, Postscript to SDS' Infiltration, War Dance I & II, An Harangue, Ergastulum, The Mistakes of Trotsky... Thesmophoriazusae, Louis Napoleon
Side B (Time: 24:06)
Seven Compartments, Petrichenko, Don't Talk to Sociologists..., What Are the Inexpensive Things the Panel Most Enjoys? . . . An International, History, Organization, It's an Illusion, Penny Capitalists, Plekhanov, Natura Facit Saltus

Written, performed* and produced by Art & Language 1973—1976
*Drums and
"A contradiction is the norm
For breaking
Dialectically . . ."
(KAYF): Jesse Chamberlain, It's an Illusion sung by Little Tommy Hobbes

Art & Language [C/S]

Title: Corrected Slogans

Contents: Maharashtra. Keep All Your Friends. Imagination I & II. Coleridge vs Martineau. An Exemplification. Postscript to SDS' Infiltration. War Dance I & II. An Harangue. Ergastulum. The Mistakes of Trotsky... Thesmophoriazusae. Louis Napoleon. Seven Compartments. Patrichenko. Don't Talk to Sociologists... What Are the Inexpensive Things the Panel Most Enjoys?...An International. History. Organization. It's an Illusion. Penny Capitalists. Plekhanov. Natura Facit Saltus

ø 30cm, 33 RPM, 1976, Music-Language / Art & Language New York / Banbury England, No. 1848. 2nd issue 1982, Art & Language and The Red Crayola

Cover: one-color print
2nd issue: b/w, treated photo with song text

Art & Language / [C/S]
The Red Crayola

Title: Born in Flames. The Sword of God

Perf.: M. Thompson

ø 17cm, 45 RPM, 1980, Rough Trade Records, London

Cover: one-color print

Art & Language
→ The Red Crayola

Artaud, Antonin [S]

Title: Pour en finir avec le jugement de dieu. Poème radiophonique enregistré entre les 22 et 29 novembre 1947

Contents: Texte d'ouverture. Tutuguri, le rite du soleil noir. La recherche de la fécalité. La question se pose de... Conclusion.

Perf.: Antonin Artaud, Maria Casarès, Roger Blin, Paule Thévenin

ø 30cm, 33 RPM, 1986, La Manufacture et I.N.A., France

Cover: two-color print

Artaud, Antonin
→ Sound Poetry

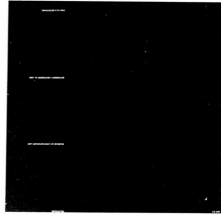

Art By Telephone [P/S]

Title: Art By Telephone. Museum Of Contemporary Art Chicago, November 1 - December 14, 1969

Record as exhibition catalogue ø 30cm, 33 RPM, 1969, Museum of Contemporary Art Chicago

Cover: b/w, gatefold, documentation-photo, texts about the artists and an introduction by Jan van der Marck, design: Sherman Mutchnick

Participating Artists:
Siah Armajani, Arman, Richard Artschwager, John Baldessari, Iain Baxter, Mel Bochner, George Brecht, Jack Burnham, James Lee Byars, Robert H. Cumming, Francois Dallegret, Jan Dibbets, John Giorno, Robert Grosvenor, Hans Haacke, Richard Hamilton, Dick Higgins, Davi Det Hompson, Robert Huot, Alain Jacquet, Ed Kienholz, Joseph Kosuth, Les Levine, Sol LeWitt, Robert Morris, Bruce Nauman, Claes Oldenburg, Dennis Oppenheim, Richard Serra, Robert Smithson, Guenther Uecker, Stan VanDer-Beek, Bernar Venet, Frank Lincoln Viner, Wolf Vostell, William Wegman, William T. Wiley

Shortly after its opening, the Museum of Contemporary Art planned an exhibition to record the trend, incipient then and pervasive today, toward conceptualization of art. This exhibition, scheduled for the spring of 1968 and abandoned because of technical difficulties, consisted of works in different media, conceived by artists in this country and Europe and executed in Chicago on their behalf. The telephone was designated the most fitting means of communication in relaying instructions to those entrusted with fabrication of the artists' projects or enactment of their ideas. To heighten the challenge of a wholly verbal exchange, drawings, blueprints or written descriptions were avoided.

Jan van der Marck (Covertext)

The Artists' Jazz Band [S]

Contents: Looks Like Snow. Is It Addicting? (a love song). Raynershine. Markle-O-Slow

Perf.: Graham Coughtry (tb, pocket tp, fl-h), Harvey Cowan (el-v), Terry Forster (contrabasso), Jim Jones (el-b), Nobuo Kubota (as, bs, ss), Robert Markle (Fender Rhodes el-p, ts), Gerald McAdam (el-g, steel-g), Gordon Rayner (dr, perc), Michael Snow (p, celeste, fl-h, tp, whistling)

2 LPs, ø 30cm, 33 RPM, 1973, Gallery Editions, The Isaacs Gallery, Toronto

Cover: b/w, gatefold, with red printed sticker on plastic sleeve

A boxed set of 9 original prints, 24" x 24", signed and numbered, in a limited edition of 100 sets was produced by the members of the AJB in conjunction with this record.

Artschwager, Richard
→ Art By Telephone

ARTSOUNDS COLLECTION [S]

Title: Artsounds Collection

Contents: Larry Rivers: Nobody Home. Marcel Duchamp: Air de Paris. Connie Beckley: To Faust: A Footnote. Cotten/Prince: Tiny Places. Mineko Grimmer: Tower With Garden. Philemona Williamson: One Day In May. Jeff Gordon: Everyone's An Artist. Tony McAulay: Collaborative Poem. Jonathan Borofsky: Take Your Dreams. Les Levine: Hereditary Language. Burton Van

Deusen: Untitled. Tom Wessel-
mann: Pictures On The Wall Of
Your Heart. Marcy Brafman: I Can't
Get Started/Communfx. Philip
Johnson: Interview. John Burgee:
Interview. Italo Scanga: Untitled
Piece. Thomas Lanigan-Schmidt:
Rite Of Passage. Bob Gruen:
When You're Smiling. Yura Adams:
Dream Of Paradise. Jennifer Bart-
lett: Excerpt from 'History Of The
Universe'

2 LPs, ø 30cm, 33 RPM, 1986,
Created, Produced and Packaged
by Jeff & Juanita Gordon for Zane
Productions, Inc.
Polygram Records Inc., New York,
420273-1

Cover: multi-color print, gatefold, informations about the pieces and portrait photos

Included poster, multi-color print (88,5 x 58,5 cm) with
graphic works by the participating artists. Also available:
Deluxe box containing nineteen 12" x 12" signed and
numbered prints. (Limited issue of 200)

Robert Ashley. *Atalanta*

Ashley, Robert [S]

Title: ATALANTA (ACTS OF GOD)

Contents: Episode I: MAX. Episode II:
WILLARD. Episode III: BUD

Perf.:   Robert Ashley, Thomas Buckner,
Jacqueline Humbert, Carla Tato
(voc), 'Blue'Gene Tyranny
(keybords & electronics), Rebecca
Amstrong, David Van Tieghem
(voices: pre-recorded chorales)

3 LPs in a box, 1985, Lovely
Music, New York, No. VR 3301-3

Cover: multi-color print, design: by Design,
cover image: Lawrence Lemak
Brickman

Included brochure (libretto), 24 p. (n.pag.).
Recorded live at the Teatro Olimpico, Rome, March 1985

<u>ATALANTA (ACTS OF GOD)</u>, whose theme
is "architecture", is the first part of a trilogy
of narrative works ("operas"), of which
<u>PERFECT LIVES</u>, whose theme is
"agriculture", is the second part, and <u>NOW
ELEANOR'S IDEA</u>, whose theme is "genea-
logy", is part three.

Excerpt from brochure

This is an opera, parts of which are sung in
Italian with Tenor Tom Buckner and Carla
Tato. This is an opera that has a peripheral
relationship to other operas you have heard,
though has none of the forced theatricality
or minimalism of other modern operas. The
accent's on words of course, all sung and
spoken in that relaxed Robert Ashley style.
Ashley's later pieces have been compared
to watching a baseball game, a series of
patterns and sporadic events that disturb the
patterns. The music is all by "Blue Gene"
Tyranny at his best, one minute loungey
Farfisa and rhythm box, the next orchestral
synthesizers doing melodious washes.

From: New Music Distribution Service, Annual 1988

Discography:
Untitled Mixes. Wolfman. From: The Bob
James Trio "Explosions". (ESP-Disk, New
York, 1965, LP, No. 1009)

In memoriam CRAZY HORSE (Symphony).
From: Music from the Once Festival.
(Advance Recordings, Tucson, Arizona,
1966, LP, No. FGR -5)

She was a visitor. From: Extended Voices
(Odyssey, New York, LP, No. 32160156)

Purposeful Lady Slow Afternoon. From:
Sonic Arts Union - Electric Sound.
(Mainstream, New York, LP, No. MS 5010)

*In Sara, Mencken, Christ and Beethoven
there were men and women.* (Cramps, Nova
Musicha, Milano, 1974, LP, No. 3)

Private Parts. (Lovely Music, New York,
1977, LP, VR 1001)

Automatic Writing. (Lovely Music, New York,
1979, LP, VR 1002)

Sonata. From: "Blue" Gene Tyranny: Just
for the Record. (Lovely Music, New York,
1979, VR 1062)

Perfect Lives. (Private Parts). The Bar.
(Lovely Music, New York, 1980, LP, VR
4904)

*"The Lessons" from Perfect Lives (Private
Parts).* (Lovely Music, New York, 1981, LP,
VR 4908)

Ashley, Robert
→   Giorno Poetry Systems
→   Jasper Johns
→   Perfo 2
→   Rosenfest
→   Sound Poetry
→   Source Magazine

Asins, Elena
→   Sound Poetry

Aspen Magazine [P]

Published by Roaring Fork Press Inc., New
York. Phyllis Johnson, Editor and Publisher.
Each issue is of a different format and was

designed by a different artist. Various contributions exist, a.o. brochures, slips of paper and records.

No. 1 (1965)
record-supplement (flexidisc, ø 17cm, 33 RPM):
The Mellow Sounds of Traditional Jazz *St. James Infirmary Blues*. The Exploratory Sounds of Modern Jazz *Israel*. (Bill Evans Trio '65.)

No.2 (1966)
designed by Frank Kirk
record-supplement (flexidisc, ø 20cm, 33 RPM) :
Alexander Scriabin *Tenth Sonata*

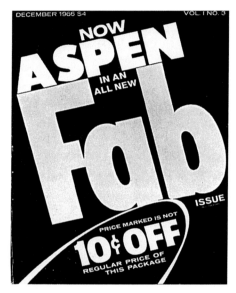

No. 3 (1966) *FAB*
designed by Andy Warhol and David Dalton
record-supplement (flexidisc, ø 17cm, 33 RPM):
The Velvet Underground *Loop* (John Cale), Peter Walker *White Wind*

"Here it is - the Fab issue of Aspen, designed by Andy Warhol and David Dalton. An exploration of this productoriented Pop McLuhan world which has paradoxically produced a mass avant-garde movement among all ages, testing and discaring all the boundaries. As Bob Dylan put it, it doesn't have anything to do with chronological age at all, but who's alive and who's in suspended animation, who's still growing and who's given up and gone to sleep..."he not busy being born is busy dying."

No. 4 (1967)
The Medium
designed by Quentin Fiore
record-supplement (flexidisc, ø 17cm, 33 RPM):
Gordon Mumma *Horn*, Mario Davidovsky *In Memoriam Edgard Varèse*

No. 5 + 6 (1967)
'for Stephane Mallarmé'
guest editor-designer Brian O'Doherty; guest art directors David Dalton, Lynn Letterman
5 LPs as supplement (flexidiscs, each ø 20cm, 33 or 16 2/3 RPM):
Samuel Beckett *Text for Nothing No.8*, read by Jack MacGowran.
William Burroughs *Nova Express*, (excerpts), read by the author.
Alain Robbe-Grillet *Now the shadow of the southwest column* from *Jealousy*, read by the author.
John Cage *Fontana Mix-Feed*, realized by Max Neuhaus.
Morton Feldman *The King of Denmark*, Morton Feldman/Max Neuhaus, percussion.
Merce Cunningham, Interview. *Space, Time and Dance*, read by the author.
Marcel Duchamp *The Creative Act*, read by the author. Some texts from *A L'Infinitif*, read by the author.
Richard Huelsenbeck, four poems from *Phantastische Gebete*, read by the author.
Naum Gabo/Noton Pevsner *The Realistic Manifesto*, read by Gabo.

No. 7 (1969)
designed by John Kosh
two records as supplement (flexidiscs, ø 20cm, 33 RPM):
Yoko Ono *Songs for John*. John Lennon *Radio Play*. Christiopher Logue reads *New Numbers*. John Taverner *Three Songs for Surrealists*. (Magritte, Ernst, Dali)

No. 8 (1970)
Art / Information / Science
Dan Graham, guest editor; George Maciunas, guest designer
record-supplement (flexidisc, ø 20cm):
La Monte Young *Drift Study 31.1.69.* (May be played at any constant speed from 16 2/3 to 78 RPM).
Jackson MacLow *Young Turtle Asymmetries*

No. 9 (1970)
Dreamweapon
designed by Hetty MacLise
record-supplement (flexidisc, ø 20cm, 33 RPM):
Spontaneous Sound. (Played spontaneously by Christopher Tree on a collection of 150 instruments from many parts of the world).
The Joyous Lake

Atelier Kramer   [C/S]

Title: Atelier Kramer. Effekt ist Wirkung ohne Ursache

Contents: Zusammenschnitt aus einem Referat für das Internationale Künstlergremium

ø 17cm, 33 RPM, 1986

Cover: b/w

Printed as invitation for the exhibition: Das Atelier Kramer der Gesamthochschule Kassel zu Gast bei der Marielies Hess-Stiftung im Hause des Hessischen Rundfunks, Frankfurt.

Atkinson, Conrad
→   Revolutions Per Minute

Attersee / Christine Jones   [C/S]

Title: Weihnacht zu zweit

Contents: Das Christkind kommt. Du schau mich an. Klingeling am Butterbrot. Kein Wein, Kein Bier. Es wird scho glei du mpa. Side B Himmlische Ruh (blank)

Perf.:   Christian Ludwig Attersee, Christine Jones (voc), Tommy Böröcz (perc), Erwin Kienast (syn), Mischa Kraus (b), Hans Salomon (sax), Robert Schönherr, Peter Schrammel (keyboards), Peter Paul Skrepek (g, accordion, choir)

ø 30cm, 33 RPM, 1983, Yedermann Productions, Wien, No.
150142

Cover: multi-color print, design: Attersee

Attersee / Gerhard Rühm   [C/S]

Title: Attersee und Rühm. Klaviertreiben

Contents: Schwarzer Peter. Halbe Gans. Ro-
te Punkte. Tastenkinder. Weiss-
zwang. Klaviertreiben. Blaue
Punkte. Zebra

Perf.: pianos played by Attersee and
Rühm

ø 30cm, 33 RPM, n.d., limited
edition of 400, Galerie Heike
Curtze, Düsseldorf / Wien, No. 001

Cover: one-color print from a painting by
Attersee

Documentation of a concert on the occasion of the opening of the Attersee-exhibition: *Die Tischzärte*. Galerie Heike
Curtze, Düsseldorf, 4.12.1980

Attersee   [C/S]

Title: Atterseemusik. Lieder von Wetter
und Liebe

Contents: Ich will dich. Brautgewieher
(Fleisch und Blut). Hand in Hand
(Heut ist Hochzeitstag). Mein Fin-
nisch. Schreibe von Liebe. Mutti-
mädel. Frucht und Form (Lilly und
Gaby). Hackepeter. Flotter Morgen.
Weisst du wieviel

Perf.: Christian Ludwig Attersee (voc, p)

Technical Realization: Erwin Reith-
meier (Edek Bartz)

ø 30cm, 33 RPM, 1985, Extraplatte
Wien, No. EX 43

Cover: multi-color print, design: Attersee

Included folding-page, two-colored print with song-texts and
portrait-photos of Attersee

Attersee   [C/S]

Title: Atterseezigeuner

Contents: Schöpfungsstück oder Weg der
Liebe und Do you really want to
kiss me. Ich will dich. Old man
please. Fleisch und Blut (Brautgewieher). I don't want to sing Bob
Dylan songs. Kommt ein Glaserl
geflogen. Summertime. Rampi
Rampi. Rock'n Roll I want to shine
your shoes

Perf.: Attersee und das Ferry Trio Live in
München, Sept. 1987

ø 30cm, 33 RPM, 1987, Extra
Platte, Wien No. EX 72

Cover: multi-color print, design: Attersee

Attersee

→   selten gehörte Musik

AUDIO ARTS / ORCHARD GALLERY

Audio Arts   [S]

Title: Audio Arts / Orchard Gallery

ø 30 cm, 33 RPM, 1984, Audio
Arts London, No. AA 002

Cover: multi-color print with 2 segments of
city-maps (Londonderry / London-
Brixton)

This publication is produced as part of an
Audio Arts Exhibition at the Orchard Gallery,
Londonderry, in May and June, 1984.
All the material heard on the record was derived from original recordings made out on
the streets in Londonderry and Brixton
during January and February, 1984. The
tapes then produced by Audio Arts in May,
1984.
Textsheet as supplement

Audio Arts   [S]

Title: Accent For A Start

Contents: Accent for a Start. Canny, In Re-
lation to What? Uniform. Warm.
Song for Edwina. It's About Time.
Canny Place. Everything You
Could Possibly Want. Fri-
day/Saturday Night. Bucklets of
Sand. Mint

ø 30cm, 33 RPM, 1987, Audio
Arts, London, MMW 004 AA 006

Cover: two-color print

NE

AUDIO ARTS

ACCENT FOR A START

This LP by Audio Arts arises out of a series of voice recordings made on the streets in Newcastle-upon-Tyne. In combination with a number of environmental sounds from the same location, most notably the interior of the Tyne Bridge's South Tower, these recordings have undergone various musical and rhythmic treatments.

Passers by were stopped at random in Newcastle's city centre and asked questions about their attitudes towards living in the North East and their perceptions of cultural, economic and social differences which might exist between the North and the South. Subsequently, key words, sentences and phrases were removed and orchestrated, in order to focus on and express specific issues and concerns within the material. As well as what is said, it is how things are said - that is, accent, humour and intonation - which has given rise to particular tracks on the LP.

Press release

AUDIO ARTS

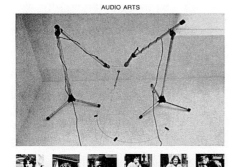

INTERIM ART

Audio Arts [S]

Title: The Difference. Head Low

ø 17cm, 45 RPM, 1987, Interim Art, London, AA 004

Cover: two-color print

This single was published as part of the exhibition *In So Many Words* at Interim Art.

Azeredo, Ronaldo
→ Sound Poetry

Baacke, Rolf-Peter [P]

Title: LUXUS. TON NOT. NOT TON

Contents: Boogi Woogi für'n Stück Pappe. Marsch für kotzende Tauben unterm S-Bahnbogen. Die Postmoderne, unvollendetes Singspiel. Heftige Blechmusik für Avantgarde ohne Puste und ohne Saxophon. Triangel für fliehende Horizonte bei mittäglichem Stadtlärm inmitten herumassozierender Stille

Perf.: Retina-Band and the Orchestra Oriental and Okzidental

ø 17cm, 45/33 RPM, 1982, gleichsam, (Sonderheft) zweitschrift 10, Underwood Sehraub Records Berlin

Cardboard-records in sealed protective cover

Babel, Tara
→ Perfo 2

Bärtschi, Werner
→ Dominik and Manuel Süess

Bakhchanyan
→ Voices Notes & Noise

Baldessari, John
→ Art By Telephone

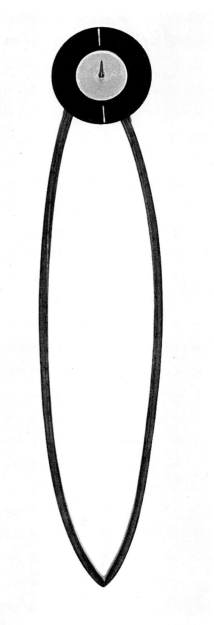

Fritz Balthaus. *Der Schallplatten*

Balestrini, Nanni
→ Sound Poetry

Ball, Hugo
→ dada For Now
→ Sound Poetry

Balla, Giacomo
→ dada For Now
→ musica futurista
→ Sound Poetry

Ballabeni, Franco
→ Sound Poetry

Balthaus, Fritz [O]

Title: Der Schallplatten. 1986

Single, label painted orange on both sides, on reverse side sticker with handwritten title and signature. In the center-hole of the record, a bicycle-valve is installed, attached to it, the flat inner tube.

Balthaus, Fritz
→ Views beside...

Baren, Peter [C/S]

Title: Hearth

red flexidisc, ø 17cm, 33RPM, 1987, Century Edition, Stichting OKO Amsterdam

---

Cover: b/w

Here gathers Nameless Energy. Audio and light performance.

Covertext

Barg, Barbara
→ Sound Poetry

Baroni, Vittore
→ Sound Poetry
→ Voices Notes & Noise

Bartlett, Jennifer
→ Artsounds Collection

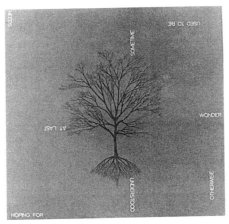

Barry, Robert [C/S]

Title: Otherwise

ø 30cm, 33 RPM, 1981, Van Abbemuseum, Eindhoven

Cover: two-color print

Baschet, Bernard et François [S]

Title: Structures Sonores

Composer: Jacques Lasry

Contents: Rhapsodie de Budapest. Quatuor pour trois. Moelle de lion. Paludisme. Jeux d'ombre

Perf.: Bernard + Francois Baschet (with their homemade instruments), Jaques Chollet + Daniel Ouzounoff

---

(perc, "tubes graves"), Roger Simon (cl), Lucie Rapp (voc)

ø 30cm, 33 RPM, 1976, BAM, Paris, BAM 5878

Cover: multi-color print, gatefold

Baschet, Bernard et François [S]

Title: 4 ESPACES SONORES

Contents: Resurgence. Errance. Polykinese. Iranon

Perf.: Bernard Baschet, Michel Deneuve, Alain Dumont

2 LPs, ø 30cm, 33 RPM, 1982, Pizzicato, PIZ 62013

Cover: multi-color print, gatefold

Baschet, Bernard et François
→ The Sounds of Sound Sculpture

Bates, Bob
→   Sound

Baumann, Katharina
→   Das ist Schönheit

Baxter, Iain
→   Art By Telephone

Bean, Anne
→   Perfo 2

van Bebber, Claus   [S]

Title: Stück für Stück

Perf.:   Claus van Bebber, Ronny Schmidt, Toto Thelosen

    ø 30cm, 33 RPM

Cover: b/w, design: Günni & Udo

Recorded live at "Guckkasten", Bad Soden, W-Germany, May 1977

van Bebber, Claus
→   Das Heinrich-Mucken Saalorchester

van Bebber, Claus   [O]

Title: Fund-Büro No. 0017. n.d.

Approximately 25 records, burned in different degrees, melted and baked together. (Found object from the collection *Fund-Büro*)
Size: ø appr. 19 cm, height appr. 7 cm

van Bebber, Claus   [O]

Title: Fund-Büro No. 0018. n.d.

Scorched record-rack with appr. 15 records burned in different degrees and remainders of the cover. (Found object from the collection *Fund-Büro*)
Size: 18 x 32 x 18 cm
Material: wood, wire, vinyl, paper

van Bebber, Claus   [O]

Title: "Single-Club". 1986

1 recordplayer with 4 speeds and built-in loudspeaker
5 prepared records (ø 17,5 cm), 1 rubber-stopper to connect tone arm with record
Size: appr. 17 x 39 x 32,5 cm

Claus van Bebber. *Fund-Büro No. 0018*

Becker, Konrad
→ Monoton

Beckett, Samuel
→ Aspen Magazine

Beckley, Connie
→ Airwaves
→ Artsounds Collection

Bedaux, Jacoba
→ Perfo 2
→ Relly Tarlo

Bekaert, Jacques
→ Revue OU

Belgian Institute for World Affairs
→ Perfo 2

Bell, Grace
→ Sound

van Bemmel, Marcelle
→ Perfo 2

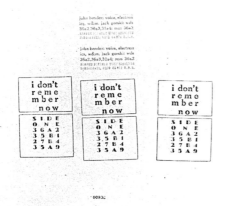

Bender, John   [C/S]

Title: I don't remember now. I don't want to talk about it

Perf.:   John Bender (voc, el, wds & mus), Jack Gorski (wds & mus)

ø 30cm, 33 RPM, n.d., numbered, Record Sluts, Cincinnati / Ohio

Cover: cardboard, stamped with title-information and other different-colored motives

Bender, John   [C/S]

Title: Plaster Falling

Contents: Station. Plaster. Women. People. Something. Records. Knuckles. Cities. Street

Perf.:   John Bender (voc, el, wds & mus)

ø 30cm, 33 RPM, n.d.(1982), Record Sluts, Cincinnati / Ohio, No. RS 003

Cover: cardboard covered with latex, title sprayed on, further information stamped

Print: "Sealed In Latex For Your Protection." "To Open: Pull String Along Taped Edge."

Bender, John
→ C.A.G.E.

Bense, Max
→ Sound Poetry

Berberian, Cathy
→ Eugenio Carmi

Bergamini, Giacomo
→ Sound Poetry

Bernstein, Alex
→ Sound

Bertini, Giani
→ Bernard Heidsieck

SONAMBIENT

LPS 10570

Bertoia, Harry   [S]

Title: Sonambient

Contents: Bellissima, Bellissima, Bellissima. Nova

ø 30cm, 33 RPM, n.d. (1979), No. LPS 10570

Cover: b/w, picture of 'the Bertoia sounding sculptures' and textinformation, cover photo by Guy Tomme

Harry Bertoia, whose creations, in addition to refined tactile values, have equal appeal for the ear and the eye. This artist - whose first claim to fame was the "Bertoia" chair, in 1952, and who has since provided major decorative elements for public buildings all over the nation - has been showing, in a group of recent works on display at the Staempfli Gallery in New York, a number of extraordinary *Sounding sculptures*. These are somewhat difficult to describe, and illustration does them but partial justice. They consist, basically, of seried ranks of tall slender metal rods, placed either upright or at special slants in rectangular formations. These metallic fasces are not rigid, but "give" when stoked - at the same time releasing lingering musical chords of a weirdly haunting quality, like some otherwordly harps. Monotony is ruled out, since there never can be an exact repetition, and it is obvious also that the familiarity of possession would not bring about a surfeit but rather heighten and deepen the spell.

D'Otrange Mastai (Excerpt from covertext)

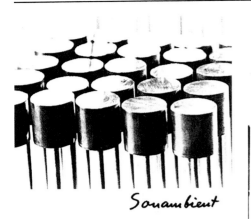

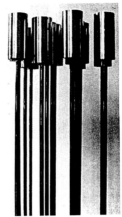

Bertoia, Harry [S]

Title: Sonambient

Contents: Space Voyage. Echoes Of Other Times

ø 30cm, 33 RPM, n.d., No. F/W 1023

Cover: b/w

Bertoia, Harry [S]

Title: Sonambient

Contents: Unfolding. Sounds Beyond

ø 30cm, 33 RPM, n.d., No. F/W 1025

Cover: b/w

Bertoia, Harry [S]

Title: Sonambient

Contents: All And More. Passage

ø 30cm, 33 RPM, n.d., No. F/W 1027

Cover: b/w

Bertoia, Harry [S]

Title: Sonambient

Contents: Swift Sounds. Phosphorescence

ø 30cm, 33 RPM, n.d., No. F/W 1024

Cover: b/w

Bertoia, Harry [S]

Title: Sonambient

Contents: Gong Gong. Elemental

ø 30cm, 33 RPM, n.d., No. F/W 1026

Cover: b/w

Bertoia, Harry [S]

Title: Sonambient

Contents: Energizing. Mellow Top

ø 30cm, 33 RPM, n.d., No. F/W 1028

Cover: b/w

Bertoia, Harry
→ The Sounds of Sound Sculpture

Bertrand, Jean-Pierre
→ La France à la Biennale

Bertoia, Harry [S]

Title: Sonambient

Contents: Continuum. Near And Far

ø 30cm, 33 RPM, n.d., No. F/W 1029

Cover: b/w

Bertoia, Harry [S]

Title: Sonambient

Contents: Ocean Mysteries. Softly Played

ø 30cm, 33 RPM, n.d., No. F/W 1031

Cover: b/w

GABRIELE MAZZOTTA EDITORE

Beuys, Joseph [C/S]

Title: Ja Ja Ja Nee Nee Nee

ø 30cm, 33 RPM, n.d. (1970), limited edition of 500, numbered and stamped, Gabriele Mazzotta Editore Milano

Cover: gatefold, two-color print with attached photos, 12 pages (n.pag)

The recording derives from a Fluxus Concert of same name in the Staatliche Kunstakademie Düsseldorf, 1968, and is based on a compositional idea by Henning Christiansen.

Beuys, Joseph [O]

Title: Sonnenscheibe. 1973

Limited edition of 77, numbered and signed, Verlag Schellmann & Klüser, Munich

Record master-mould (copper, nickeled on incised side, other side plain), with two brown-stamped pieces of felt, in a cardboard box (38 x 38 x 4 cm)
Master-moulds for the record *Schottische Symphonie. Requiem of Art*

Bertoia, Harry [S]

Title: Sonambient

Contents: Swinging Bars. Vulcans Play

ø 30cm, 33 RPM, n.d., No. F/W 1030

Cover: b/w

Bertoia, Harry [S]

Title: Sonambient

Contents: Here And Now. Unknown

ø 30cm, 33 RPM, n.d., No. F/W 1032

Cover: b/w

Beuys' thinking about music always finds a way into his work whenever acoustical processes are to be considered within the complex of a sculptural perception: Thus in many of his objects there is a bridge between the potential visual and auditory interpretations [Noiseless Blackboard Eraser, Silence (Das Schweigen), Bone Gramophone (Grammophon aus Knochen), Tape in Stacked Felt (Tonband in Filzstapel)]: one hears through careful observation, one sees through attentive listening. Latent sound is the observer's sculpture. -- Conveyors of music and sound lie dormant between stacked layers of sound-absorbing felt as in a sarcophagus.

The Noiseless Blackboard Eraser arouses in the observer the unpleasant and undesireable noise (although unheard) associated with cleansing a blackboard, rather than the more pleasant, noiseless wiping: the perfect negative acoustic sculpture. In other objects as well the communication between "transmitter" and "receiver" is achieved through nonrealisation, through sound latent in the object, but which has meaning through its prospective potency (Evervess, Telefon: S --E). In this "art of silent sound" the relativity of the invariability of a work of art is well substantiated.

With Beuys the parameters of sound are not accidental. Thus in his Actions the music is often a vehicle for the perception of time parallel to that of the spatial dimension.

The music of Henning Christiansen is incorporated into Beuys' work to create a Time-Space. This might seem superfluous, to the extent that, as Robert Ashley observed in an interview with John Cage, our consciousness of time has become so acute that we don't have to be informed about it constantly through the medium of sound.

The experience of the time, then, in the Actions of Beuys, is reinforced by the music played during them (Bloch also sees music as a space for listening to measurements).

In a theater performance during Experimenta, Beuys used as instrumental accompaniment two cymbals. In a statement about Iphigenie he said: "Sculptural and musical, all organs play through the larnyx." -- Further, the phonograph records used in Beuys' work are not only conveyors of sound, but more often carriers of objects when he intends to create a sculpture with the assistance of "anti-music": Phonograph with skeletal parts or metal pieces affixed to them. In another work, called "Ocean Symphony", a small lighthouse is mounted upon a recording of Carmen.

Excerpt from: Reiner Speck: *Beuys und Musik*. In: *Joseph Beuys*. (cat.) Kasseler Kunstverein, Kassel 1975 (translated by Ann Noël and Emmett Williams)

Joseph Beuys. *Musikbox*. 1962/63

Joseph Beuys. *Sonnenscheibe*

HENNING CHRISTIANSEN: OP. 50 REQUIEM OF ART   AUS „CELTIC"

JOSEPH BEUYS/HENNING CHRISTIANSEN: SCHOTTISCHE SYMPHONIE   AUS „CELTIC"

2 LPs, ø 30cm, 33 RPM, 1982, Edition Block, Berlin No. EB 113/114

Cover: b/w, gatefold, photo of Maciunas and documentary photos (Ute Klophaus) of the concert

Live-recording of the Fluxus-Soirée of the René Block Gallery in the Auditorium of the Staatliche Kunstakademie Düsseldorf

Special issue in a wooden box with *Felt Wedge* (5,5 x 8,5 x 25 cm) by Joseph Beuys, *Primeval Piano* (appr. 11 x 32 x 52 cm) by Nam June Paik, limited edition of 47, certificate signed and numbered, 1984

See illustration below

Beuys, Joseph / Henning Christiansen   [S]

Title: Schottische Symphonie. Requiem Of Art

         2 LPs, ø 30 cm, 33 RPM, 1973, limited edition of 500, numbered, Bernd Klüser / Jörg Schellmann München

Cover: gatefold, multi-color print of a photo by Manfred Tischer, design: Michael Stahl

Schottische Symphonie (Aus *Celtic*), recording: College of Art, Edinburgh, 21.8.1970
Requiem of Art (Aus *Celtic*) (Fluxorum Organum II).
2nd issue 1986, 800 copies, 90 + XXX copies for portfolio "für Joseph Beuys", supplement (8 pages, n.pag.) with colored scores by Henning Christiansen, gatefold cover, b/w

Beuys, Joseph / Nam June Paik   [S]

Title: In memoriam George Maciunas. Klavierduett. 7.7.1978

Beuys, Joseph   [C/S]

Title: Sonne statt Reagan

Contents: Sonne statt Reagan. Kräfte sammeln

Perf.:   Joseph Beuys, Klaus Heuser, Wolf Mahn, Susanne Stenchly, Gunne Wagner, Steve Borg, Alain Thomé, Helmut Rüssmann, John, K.H. Pütz

         ø 30cm, 45 RPM, 1982, EMI Electrola (Musikant), Köln, No. 1C K 052-46 614 Z

Cover: two-color print, design: Joseph Beuys, Adam Backhausen, Manfred Boecker

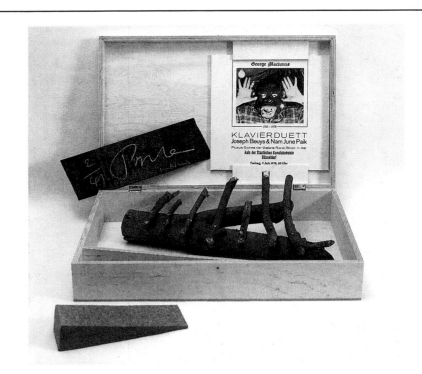

BEUYS/CHRISTIANSEN
SCHOTTISCHE SYMPHONIE
REQUIEM OF ART

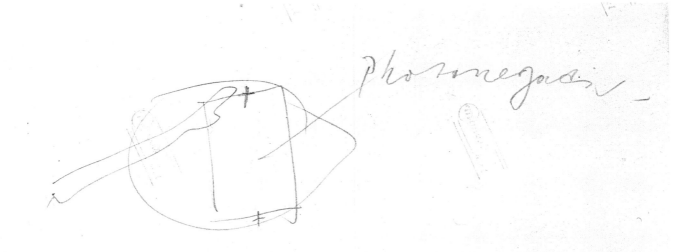

Joseph Beuys. *Stummes Grammophon*. 1958

Beuys, Joseph
→   albrecht d.
→   Henning Christiansen
→   Terry Fox
→   Revolutions Per Minute

BEI EINEM WESENSGE
MÄSSEN BESCHREIBEN
DES GESCHEHENS ZUR
BEFREIUNG DER VON
DER FÄHIGKEIT GETRA
GENEN ARBEIT IST ES
DOCH LOGISCH, DASS
DAS TRAGENDE ZUERST
BEFREIT WERDEN MUSS.

Bianchi, Maurizio
→   Sound Poetry

Bielz, Gudrun
→   Fünfzehn Tonspuren

Bijl, Guillaume
→   Perfo 2

Bissett, Bill
→   Sound Poetry

Joseph Beuys (Untitled. Grammophon mit Blutwurst und Lautsprecher) 1969/81

THE BLACKIE
CHRISTMAS ORATORIO

THE BIRTH OF
A BUILDING

The Blackie Christmas Oratorio [S]

Title: The Blackie Christmas Oratorio

Contents: The Birth Of A Building. Symphony In Sea

Perf.: The Blackie Christmas Oratorio was created by Dave Gollancz, assisted by Simon Holland and Rikke Riggelson; with contributions from Bill Harpe, Wendy Harpe, Charlie Stuart, Duncan Curtis, Sally Morris and Stevie Smith.
Symphonie in sea was created by Gerda Koetja and Fred de Borst, with Martin Brems and others

ø 30cm, 33 RPM, 1980, Great George Community Liverpool

Cover: three-color print, design: Judy Bates

Contains folding-sheet with project-description and brochure (24 x 24,5 cm), 8 p.(n. pag.), with texts. Documentation of the Great Georges Project (reconstruction and first cultural activities in a former church in Liverpool)

Blaine, Julien
→ Radiotaxi
→ Sound Poetry

Blake, Peter [C]

Title: Sgt. Pepper's Lonely Hearts Club Band

Music: The Beatles

ø 30cm, 33 RPM, 1967, Odeon / EMI, SHZE 401

Cover: gatefold, multi-color print, staged by Peter Blake and Jann Haworth, photographed by Michael Cooper

Lock groove at end of side two. Maybe the first (voluntary) lock groove?

Christian Marclay. In: Extended Play. (cat.) New York 1988

"Blue" Gene Tyranny
→ Perfo 2
→ Robert Ashley
→ Rosenfest

Bleus, Guy
→ Sound Poetry

Blum, Eberhard
→ Sound Poetry

Blumenschein, Tabea
→ Die Tödliche Doris

Bob & Bob [C/S]

Title: We Know You're Alone (L.A.). We've Been Seeing Things (N.Y.C.)

Music: P. Velick, F. Shishim

Produced by Jeff Gordon

ø 30cm, 33 RPM, 1983, Polygram Records, New York, 422-813 395-1 Y-1

Cover: multi-color print, original cover art: Bob & Bob

Bob & Bob
→ High Performance

Bochner, Mel
→ Art By Telephone

Bodde, Jan
→ Perfo 2

Bodde, Sievert
→ Perfo 2

Bodin, Lars-Gunnar
→ Sound Poetry

Bodin, Svante
→ Sound Poetry

Boegel and Holtappels
→ Perfo 2

Böhmler, Claus [C/S]

Title: Materialien zur Postmoderne in Bild und Ton

Contents: Rahlstedt. Nacht. Innen. Tonbandkomposition in 3 Sätzen.(1982) Chers amis du meubler perdu, chers auditeurs! Design beim Wort genommen.(1984)

Technical Realization: Holger Hiller

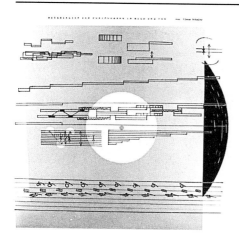

ø 30cm, 45 RPM, 1986, Edition Block, Berlin, No. EB 120

Cover: two-color print of a drawing by Claus Böhmler

White record, score included

By acoustic revision, the sequence of the recitation is made brittle, pointed, and - again through arrangement of simple elements - the message is decomposed and multilayered.

Böhmler, who designs media-furniture, is a polyglot: he speaks and writes music for all. His living room lecture "Chers amis du meubler perdu, chers auditeurs! Moble party, verehrte wörldstars!" is analytical, many-voiced, and playful in language; it is a compositional essay, more witty than many a clever appeal. "Alles nur gewohnung, Fritz!"

Michael Glasmeier

Böhmler, Claus   [O]

Title: Aus einer LP ausgekoppelte Single. 1987

Single, ø 17cm, cut out off a LP, ø 30cm.

Claus Böhmler works with the media. Since they seem to function so well, he takes them apart, examines them, and then, perhaps, assembles them anew. This process doesn't create chic elements for the living rooms of the communication-theorists, the sociologists, or the simulation-apocalyptic, but rather the same sort of rudimentary raw material as found in notebooks, drawings, miniature cameras, radios, photostats, and cassettes. It's these poor media that open eyes and ears. Not bound to a cultural-bureaucratic administrative machinery, they stand their ground by presenting an opulence of idea-productions that fragmentate, ferment, combine, and experiment, because "according to Böhmler, every substance is good for thinking" (K. Gallwitz).

Especially language materializes, for to Böhmler it is not only commentary, but also a starting point, composition, confusion, and instruction at the same time. Imagine a rhinoceros as a gramophone. With the apt title *Materialien zur Postmoderne in Bild und Ton*, Böhmler's record for this device presents a complex, compact matter. Side A composes three movements with magnetic tape. The concatenation of tapped, blown, plucked, and played sound produces a changing atmosphere and, as with any series of fragments, could go on sounding forever.

The enclosed score of this Muzak for progressive idyllists, housewives, and cardrivers - all of whom are not annoyed by sporting airplanes - was written during the recording of the white colored record; its coverdesign mixpickles Stockhausen, Rams, typewriter-esthetic, and fashion.

The other side of the record includes a speech by Böhmler about the new German design ("die kombi-nation steht Kopf!").

Böhmler, Claus

→   Das ist Schönheit

→   Kunstproben

Claus Böhmler showing his *Record archive on videotape*. 1987. Photo (René Block) and drawing (Claus Böhmler)

Bogosian, Eric [S]

Title: Selections From Voices Of America. Selections From Men Inside

ø 30cm, 33 RPM, 1983, Neutral New York, No. Neutral 10

Cover: b/w, design: Jo Bonney, portrait photos: Paula Court

Voices of America premiered at Corps de Garde, Groningen Holland, under the direction of Van Lagestein, in April 1982. It made its New York premiere at Joseph Papp's Public Theater in July 1982. Men inside premiered at Franklin Furnace, New York in February 1981. Recorded live at the ICA London, on October 1982 as part of the ICA / NY performance season under the direction of Michael Morris.

Boltanski, Christian [C/S]

Title: RECONSTITUTION DE CHANSONS QUI ONT ÉTÉ CHANTÉES A CHRISTIAN BOLTANSKI ENTRE 1944 ET 1946

Contents: Fais dodo Colas mon petit frère. Il était un petit navire. Sainte-Elisabeth

ø 17,5 cm, 45 RPM, 1971/72

Cover: Original (collage incorporating remainders of yellowed photos by Christian Boltanski)

Boltanski, Christian
→ La France à la Biennale

Bonis, John
→ obscure

Bonk, Ecke
→ Fünfzehn Tonspuren

Borillo, Mario
→ Voices Notes & Noise

Borofsky, Jonathan
→ Artsounds Collection

Bory, Jean-François
→ Radiotaxi
→ Sound Poetry

Brafman, Marcy
→ Artsounds Collection

Brau, Jean-Louis
→ Poesie Physique
→ Sound Poetry

Branca, Glenn
→ Dan Graham
→ Giorno Poetry Systems
→ Just Another Asshole
→ Roberto Longo

Brandauer, Christina
→ Fünfzehn Tonspuren

Braga, Edgard
→ Sound Poetry

Brauer, Arik [C/S]

Contents: Oho Halali. Die Jause. Sie hab'n a Haus baut. Wie a Hund. Warum ist er so dumm. Sein Köpferl im Sand. Reise nach Afrika. Der Surmissui. Der Spiritus. Rostiger die Feuerwehr kommt. Serenade. Dschiribim-Dschiribam

ø 30cm, 33 RPM, n.d., Polydor in Co-production with ORF, Wien, No. 2371224

Cover: multi-color print, gatefold

Brauer, Erich [P/S]

Title: Brauer

catalogue (19,8 x 21 cm, 12 p. (n.pag.)) with the single "Brauer singt seine Malerei. Lieder zu Bildern bei Peithner-Lichtenfels 1965". ø 17cm, 45 RPM, Galerie Peithner-Lichtenfels, Wien 1965

Contents: Mond-Tag. Die Olivenbraut. Glaub nicht an das Winkelmaß. Das Rostauto. Ein Mann mit seinem Huhn

Brecht, George
→ Art By Telephone
→ Record of Interviews...

Brehmer, K.P.
→ Das ist Schönheit
→ Philip Corner

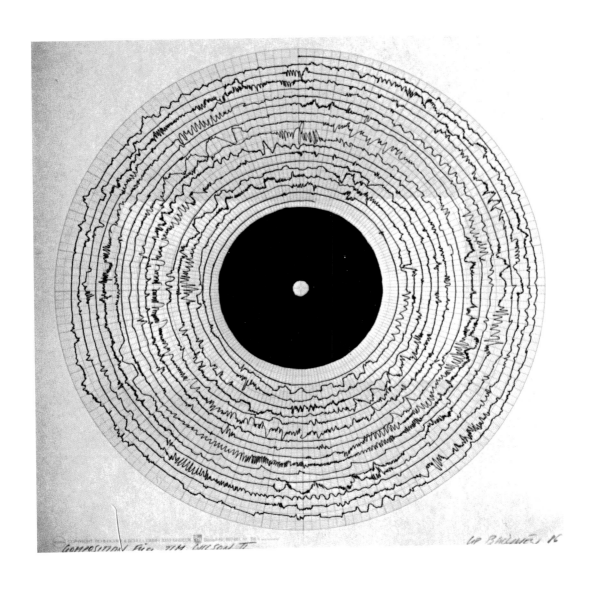

KP Brehmer. *Komposition für Tim Wilson II*. 1986. Drawing 33 x 33 cm, Indian ink and tempera on graph paper

The 33 year old Englishman, Tim Wilson, has the ability to read records. When, for example, the complete recorded symphonies of Beethoven were shown to him, he could identify in detail the unlabeled records. (dpa   Oct. 1985)

Bremer, Claus
→   Sound Poetry

Breuss, Lisi + Rose
→   Fünfzehn Tonspuren

MACHINE GUN

ma·chine' gun automatic
gun for fast, continuous
firing. THE PETER BRÖTZMANN OCTET

Brötzmann, Peter   [C/S]

Title: Machine Gun

Music: The Peter Brötzmann Octet

Contents: Machine Gun. Responsible. Music For Han Bennik I

ø 30cm, 33 RPM Mono, 1968, Peter Brötzmann, BRÖ 2

Cover: two-color print, frontcover with silk-screen by Peter Brötzmann, back-cover with photos by Paul Gerhard Deker

Recorded May 1968, "Lila Eule", Bremen

THE PETER BRÖTZMANN SEXTET / QUARTET

Brötzmann, Peter   [C/S]

Title: Nipples

Music: The Peter Brötzmann Sextet / Quartet

ø 30cm, 33 RPM, 1969, Prod. by Manfred Eicher + Jazz by Post. Calig Verlag München, No. CAL 30604

Cover: b/w, with mounted leporello: photographs of the musicians and statements of artist friends (Tomas Schmit, Nam June Paik, Evan Parker)

Brown, Earle
→   Franz Kline

Brunner, Reinhold
→   Voices Notes & Noise

Dichtung und Musik
PANISCHES LIEDERBUCH

Günter Brus
zum 50. Geburtstag
überreicht
vom
1. Deutschen Trivialeum

Brus, Günter   [C/S]

Title: Panisches Liederbuch

Contents: Dichtungen von Günter Brus aus den Jahren 1973-1988

Perf.:   Arnulf Meifert (voice), Arnulf and Franziska Meifert (perc, fl and other instruments), Peter Fürmetz and Manfred Hölzel (electronic sounds and instruments)

ø 30cm, 33 RPM, limited edition of 500 copies, Die Taubnessel 1, Das Hohe Gebrechen 1988, Balance Music, West-Germany, BAL 3003

Cover: b/w, cover illustrations according to drawings by Günter Brus from *Nullte Muse*

To Günter Brus for his 50th birthday presented by the 1st German Trivialeum

Brus, Günter
→   selten gehörte Musik
→   Sound Poetry

Bruscky, Paulo
→   Sound Poetry

Brush, Leif
→   Sound Poetry

Bruynèl, Ton
→   Sound <=> Sight

Buchloh, Benjamin
→   Subkultur Berlin

Buckley, Timothy
→   Perfo 2

Büttner, Werner
→   Die Rache der Erinnerung

Burden, Chris
→   Revolutions Per Minute
→   Word Of Mouth

Buren, Daniel
→   La France à la Biennale
→   Word Of Mouth

Burgee, John
→   Artsounds Collection

Burnham, Jack
→   Art By Telephone

Burnham, Linda
→   High Performance

Burroughs, William

→ Aspen Magazine
→ Giorno Poetry Systems
→ Revolutions Per Minute
→ Revue OU
→ Sound Poetry

Burton, Jim

→ Airwaves

Byars, James Lee

→ Art By Telephone

THE 25-YEAR RETROSPECTIVE CONCERT OF THE MUSIC OF
JOHN CAGE

Recorded in performance at Town Hall, New York, May 15, 1958

Cage, John   [S]

Title: The 25-Year Retrospective Concert
           of the Music of John Cage

Contents: Six Short Inventions For Seven In-
           struments (1934). Construction In
           Metal (1937). Imaginary Landscape
           No. 1 (1939). The Wonderful
           Widow Of Eighteen Springs (1942).
           She Is Asleep (1943). Sonatas And
           Interludes (1946-48). Music For
           Carillon (1954). Williams Mix
           (1952). Concert For Piano And
           Orchestra (1957-58)

Perf.:   Manhattan Percussion Ensemble,
           Arline Carmen (contralto), John
           Cage (p), Maro Ajemian (p), David
           Tudor (electric carillon/p), Merce
           Cunningham (cond)

           Recorded in performance at Town
           Hall, New York, May 15, 1958, by
           Robert E. Blake

           3 LPs, ø 30cm, 33 RPM, 1959,
           George Avakian, New York

Cover: box with three records, design:
           Jerry Liebermann

12 double-sided score- and text-sheets. A 16-page supplement with texts and photos by Bob Rauschenberg, Bob
Cato, Remy Charlip and George Moffett. The concert was
produced by Impresario Inc., Emile de Antonio, Jasper
Johns, Bob Rauschenberg.

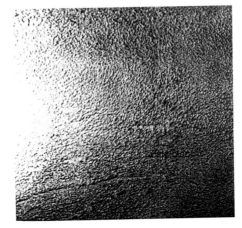

Cage, John   [S]

Title: live John Cage

Contents: Sonata XIII. Music for Marcel Du-
           champ. Song Books I-II / Empty
           Words III

Perf.:   John Cage (voice), Peter Roggen-
           kamp (p), Schola Cantorum Stutt-
           gart, Clytus Gottwald (cond)

           ø 30 cm, 33 RPM, 1976, Wergo
           Mainz No. WER 60074

Cover: two-color print of a profile-drawing
           of Marcel Duchamp; backside,
           scores by John Cage

Concert recordings Stuttgart 22.6.1975. Text supplement
with scores, a photo-portrait of John Cage and text by Dieter Schnebel (German/English)

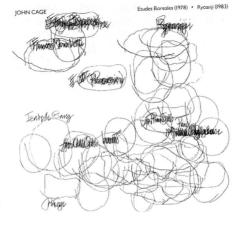

Selected discography since 1982

A nearly complete discography until 1982 is found in: *A
John Cage Reader in celebration of his 70th birthday.* New
York 1982

Freeman Etudes I-VIII. Paul Zukofsky (v).
(Musical Observations, New York, 1983, LP,
CP^2/12)

Sonatas & Interludes For Prepared Piano.
Gerard Fremy (p). (Etcetera Records B.V.,
Amsterdam, 1983, 2 LPs, ETC 2001)

Sixteen Dances. New Music Concerts,
Toronto; Paul Zukofsky (cond). (Musical Observations, New York, 1984, LP, CP^2/15)

Freeman Etudes I-XVI. János Négyesy (v).
(Lovely Music, New York, 1985, 2 LPs, VR
2051-2)

Etudes Boreales (1978). Ryoanji (1983).
Frances-Marie Uitti (cello), Michael Pugliese
(p, perc), Isabelle Ganz (mezzo-soprano).
(Mode Records, New York, 1985, 2 LPs,
Mode 1/2)

Works for piano & prepared piano.(1943-
1952). Contents: A Room. She Is Asleep. In
A Landscape. Seven Haiku. Totem Ances-
tor. Two Pastorales. And The Earth Shall
Bear Again. Waiting. For M.C. And D.T.
Joshua Pierce (p), Jay Clayton (voice), The
Paul Price Percussion Ensemble. (Wergo
Schallplatten, Mainz, 1986, LP, WER 60151)

Atlas Eclipticalis with Winter Music. The
New Performance Group, John Cage (cond).
(Mode Records, New York, 1986, 4 LPs in
a box, Mode 3/6)

Empty Words Part IV. John Cage reads.
(Edition Michael F. Bauer, Frankfurt a.M.,
1987, 2 LPs, MFB 003-004)

Etudes Australes for Piano (complete).Grete
Sultan (p). (Wergo Schallplatten, Mainz,
1987, 4 LPs in a box, WER 60152/55)

Thirty Pieces for Five Orchestras. Music for
Piano. Szombathelyi Szimfonikus Zenekar,
Péter Eötvös (musical direction), Zoltán
Jeney (p), László Vidovszky (p), László Sáry
(p), Barnabás Dukay (p). (Hungaroton,
Budapest, 1987, LP, SLPD 12893)

The First Meeting of the Satie Society. John
Cage (voice), Klaus Schöning (voice), Grete
Wehmeyer (p), Bonner Ensemble für Neue
Musik. (Edition Michael Frauenlob Bauer,
Frankfurt a.M., 1988, 2 LPs, MFB 014-015)

Cage, John

→ Aspen Magazine
→ Marcel Duchamp
→ Giorno Poetry Systems
→ Sound Poetry
→ Word Of Mouth

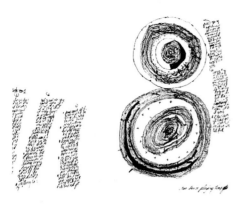

C.A.G.E. [C/S]

Title: C.A.G.E. (Cincinnati Artists' Group Effort), C.C.G. (Cincinnatti Composers' Guild)

Contents: Gerhard Samuel: Circles. (The Percussion Group). Martin Sweidel: Split Shot Study No. 1. (Martin Sweidel prep. guitar). Henry Gwiazda: Say Watt? (Henry Gwiazda el. guitar). Jay Bolot: Serpent Sun. Jan Harrison: Animal Tongue. Thom Middlebrook: Five Guidelines for an Emotional Breakdown. Kip Eagen: The Tinkers Trouble. Hudson/Buzz Tone Outlet: Love Answered Phone. John Bender: Decomposition. Art Holes (P. Trupin, J. Wood with P. Alaxander and N. Mountel): Experimental Animals. Victoria Mansoor: Two Hours Playing Time

ø 30cm, 33 RPM, 1981, C.C.G./-C.A.G.E. Records, Cincinnati, Ohio

Cover: b/w, with drawn record

de Campos, Augusto
→ Sound Poetry

de Campos, Haroldo
→ Sound Poetry

Cangiullo, Francesco
→ Sound Poetry

Cantsin, Monty
→ Sound Poetry

Caroompas, Carole
→ High Performance

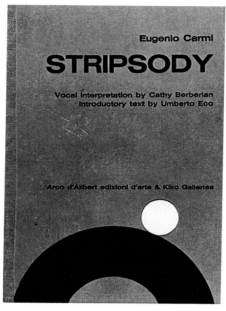

Carmi, Eugenio [P/S]

Title: Stripsody

Perf.: Vocal interpretation Cathy Berberian

Book (29 x 20 cm), 18 p.(n.pag.), backcover with pocket containing record (ø 17cm, 33 RPM)
Arco d'Alibert edizioni d'arte, Roma and Kiko Galleries, Houston, Texas 1966

Introductory text by Umberto Eco. *Stripsody* has been composed in March 1966. First performance in Bremen - May 1966 - during "the contemporary music show" (MUSICA NOVA) hold in Bremen's Radio

Carstensen, Claus [P/S]

Title: RØDBLIND

Contents: Kræftens Bekæmpelse (The beat ist bad). Boykot (Looking for a sound)

Catalogue, Claus Carstensen: RØDBLIND (20 x 20 cm), 60 p., record ø 17 cm, 45 RPM, attached to backcover, Galleri Prag, Hellerup 1988

Castano, Loriana
→ Walter Marchetti

Castelli, Luciano / Kiddy Citny [C/S]

Title: Mackie Messer. B-Luft

Music: Weill-Brecht, Paul Lincke
ø 17 cm, 45 RPM, 1986, FAUX PAS, Berlin, 86.1

Cover: multi-color print, cover-photo: Birgit Hoffmeister

Castelli, Luciano
→ Geile Tiere

Cena, Sergio
→ Sound Poetry

Chant, Michael
→ Sound Poetry

Charlier, Jacques
→   Perfo 2

Chenard, Laure
→   Perfo 2

Chlebnikov, Velemir
→   Sound Poetry

Chopin, Henri
→   Radiotaxi
→   Revue OU
→   Sound Poetry

Christiansen, Henning   [C/S]

Title: Betrayal, opus 144 (1981)

Contents: Intrada. Thoughts. Remembrance. 'Drying out'. I don't believe you. Betrayal. Love-Story. Be in Love. Deceit. Sad Message-Bad Message. Beginning and Ending

Perf.:   Laura Helasvuo Simonsen (v), Hans Andersen (tu), Lise Errboe (vib)

ø 17cm, 33 RPM, 1982, limited edition of 500, signed and numbered, Borgen Records, No. 5202-8

Cover: colored reproduction of a picture by Ursula Reuter Christiansen

Record in a box (18,7 x 18,7 cm) with supplements: 5 pieces of cardboard printed yellow on both sides to accompany 10 musical pieces, 3 different colored serviettes, 1 guarantee-card

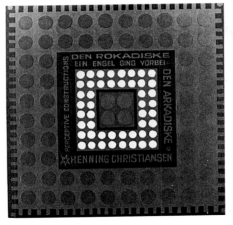

Christiansen, Henning   [C/S]

Title: Konstruktioner (1964-1967)

Contents: Perceptive Constructions. Den Rokadiske. Und ein Engel ging vorbei. Den Arkadiske

Perf.:   Kjeld Mardahl (fl), Elisabeth Sigurdsson (cl), Søren Bagger (b-cl), Klaus Gottlieb (co), Stig Sønderriis (tb), Rolf Sandmark (tb), Einar Nielsen (perc), Sindre Lindal (perc), Ulla Andresen Schmidt (perc), Hans Stengaard (v), Lars Geisler (cello), Thomas Jensen (cond), Carl Nielsen Kvartetten, Jens Schou (cl), Peder Elbaek (v), Rosalind Bevan (p)

ø 30cm, 33 RPM, 1982, Paula Records, Give / Denmark, No. Paula 19

Cover: three-color print, design: Paul Gernes

Christiansen, Henning   [C/S]

Title: Fluxid (Musik Essayistik)

Contents: Hulemåned (Höhlenmonat). Sulemåned (Fressmonat)

Perf.:   Thomas Jensen (fl), Ib Herman (cello), Michael Petersen (sax)

ø 30cm, 33 RPM, 1983, Borgen Records, Valby, Denmark, No. 5475-6

Cover: two-color print, design: Henning Christiansen

MUSIK ESSAYISTIK

Christiansen, Henning   [C/S]

Title: Fluxyl (Musik Essayistik)

Contents: Kong Frost (König Frost). Maskenmåned (Maskenmonat)

Perf.:   Bjørn Carl Nielsen (ob), Svend Age Mott (tp), Hans Andersen (tu)

ø 30cm, 33 RPM, 1984, Borgen Records, Valby, Denmark, No. ISBN 87-418-7146-4

Cover: two-color print, design: Henning Christiansen

Christiansen, Henning   [C/S]

Title: Kirkeby and Edvard Munch (op. 136, 1981)

Contents: Through Kirk'by's gate. A walk down "Karl Johan Street". Kirk'by's queen-song. Venereal woman. Kirk'by's space. Hunting the critic. Kirk'by and the end of the world. The dance of life. Kirk'by's railing. "I do not paint what I have seen, but what I saw". "I am the prisoner

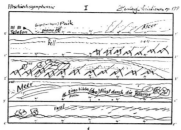
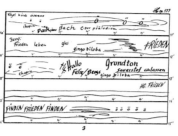
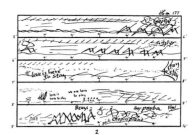
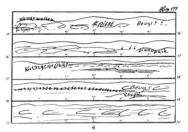

of painting". "A terrible painting, a bad painting by Edvard Munch"

Perf.: Hans Andersen (tu), Henning Christiansen (voice)

ø 30cm, 33 RPM, 1982, Weltmelodie, Borgen Forlag, No. WM LP 4718

Cover: multi-color print of a painting by Per Kirkeby

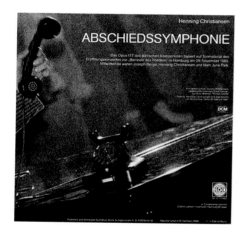

Christiansen, Henning   [S]

Title: Abschiedssymphonie

Perf.: Henning Christiansen (p), Nam June Paik (p,voice), Joseph Beuys (Telefon)

ø 30cm, 33 RPM, 1988, Edition Block, Berlin + Lebeer Hossmann, Hamburg / Brüssel, No. EB 118

Cover: one-color print

The opus 177 of the Danish composer is based on sound-material of the opening-concert to the "Peace Biennale " in Hamburg, November 29, 1985

Paik og Henning Christiansen ved tangenterne i Hamburg

Die Kunst ist ein Träger der Ideen.

Früher hat Beuys immer „es ist doch klar" usw. gesagt. Langsam übernahm das „logisch" die Bedeutung, weil die Sätze weniger klar wurden, aber mehr logisch.

Es ist kein einfacher Satz, den er uns übers Telephon bei der Friedensbiennale in Hamburg hinterlassen hat. Es geht um einen neuen Anfang, neuen Boden, neue Gedanken, neue Vorstellungen, die wir uns erkämpfen müssen, um unsere Fähigkeiten zur Geltung zu bringen. Der Mensch muß sich ständig darüber im klaren sein, was ihn geschieht, so daß „die Befreiung der von der Fähigkeit getragenen Arbeit" immer „freikommt", z. B. daß Systeme ihn nicht hemmen, täglich hemmen. Es werden immer neue Systeme auftauchen, aber jeder Mensch muß ständig dafür sorgen, daß das Tragende betreit wird.

Das Tragende? Was ist das Tragende. Es ist ein Rätsel, wenn man bedenkt, wie verschieden die Menschen sind, wie verschiedene Bedürfnisse wir haben. Grundsätzlich brauchen wir Essen und Wärme. Sie hängen schön zusammen, Essen und Wärme, aber darum geht es wohl nicht in unseren wohlgenährten Zeiten – WestZeit – aber Wärme doch. Beuys hat auch über den „Wärmecharakter des Denkens" geredet. Die Wärme wird in Denken umgesetzt, und das eben in Fähigkeiten unter Menschen, die Energie muß zurück, der Generator muß ewig laufen, und dazu haben wir heute die Möglichkeiten, weil wir doch sehr viel über Zusammenhänge wissen, z. B. die Zusammenhänge zwischen Ökonomie und Kriegen, zwischen Ökonomie und Unrecht und über den Zwang der repräsentativen Demokratie, die Kräfte freiläßt, die wir eher unterbinden sollten durch Fähigkeiten, die als Menschensumme genau das Tragende sind, wenn man das ewige Generatorprinzip durchdenkt.

Es war eine FRIEDENSBIENNALE, die in Hamburg eröffnet wurde. Den Frieden nicht Krieg als tragendes Element zu sehen ist wohl klar. Unter seinem Flügel lag eine Oxygenflasche, und durch das Telephon hat Joseph Beuys Felisch gebeten, den Sauerstoff loszulassen, als Energiebild oder auch das Tragende. Lange haben wir ökologische Fragen in und um beschäftigt. Soweit ich Beuys kenne, geht es in dieser Frage nicht (nur) um das Überleben der Menschheit, das ist doch selbstverständlich klar, aber als logisch gilt es, die Fähigkeiten zu entwickeln, uns sinnlich zu bereichern, klüger zu werden, und dazu brauchen wir die Ökologiebalance als das Tragende.

Als Frage von Rene Block gefragt wurde, ob er bei dem Eröffnungskonzert mit Paik und Christiansen mitmachen wollte, stimmte er sofort zu. Am 29.11.1985 war es plötzlich saukalt und bestimmt nicht klug für einen Herzkranken nach draußen zu gehen, aber er hatte sofort eine Lösung: „Ich mache übers Telephon mit". Block sollte nur die Pedale von Beuys' Flügel abschrauben und oben auf dem Flügeldeckel stellen, vielleicht als unter dem auch das Tragende. Lange haben eine Tafel mit einem Stück Kreide dazustellen und unter den Fuß der Oxygenflasche hinlegen und sie verwenden, wenn er übers Telephon darum bat. Er wollte dann als Zeichen für den Konzertanfang anrufen.

Das Eröffnungskonzert der Friedensbiennale fiel unter dem Motto „Der Frieden muß aktiv werden" Der Raum wurde voll von Lautsbildern. Paik spielt von Pferdegröße-Reitergeige, und Christiansen spielt einen Klaviervogel. Auf seinem Flügel steht ein weißes Kanarienweibchen, das ständig hin und her hüpft und pip sagt. Ein Friedensvogel der wie der Mensch im Käfig geboren ist und leibt und lebt und singt und hüpft. Christiansen schlägt zwischen den Akkorden mit seinen Armflügeln und singt unterwegs ein paar Worte „Love is here to stay" – We are here to play." Paik geht zum Fernseher und zeigt nun das Tokvideen, ein Konzert mit ihm und Beuys, das es ein Thema aufnimmt und sich in Japan verständlich macht. Auf Tonband läuft im Saal das Meer und SYMPHONY NATURA und die Wölfe singen mit Beuys' ö-ö zusammen saang-saang (koreanisch – zusammen). Es erinnert an Beuys' Slogan für die DEUTSCHE STUDENTENPARTEI. Es ist die größte Partei der Welt, die meisten Mitglieder sind Tiere."

Paik greift seinen Flügel voller Liebe an und spielt Chopin. Christiansen akkompaniert den fliegend auf seinem Flügel, dabei fällt Paiks Makrophon aus und Chopin flattert in der großen Halle herum. Nach dem Applaus ist nur noch ein Klingeln und das Kanarienweibchenpipsen im Meer zu hören – Ruhe.

Während des Konzertes hat Beuys sich telephonisch gemeldet. Der Sauerstoff ist ausgelassen, und er hat den schönen Satz BEI EINEM WESENSGEMÄSSEN usw. durchgesagt und Felisch hat ihn auf der Tafel mit Kreide niedergezeichnet, mit dem Dreieck und der Vierzahl – und nach Wiederholung des Satzes durch Beuys und seiner Frage „Gut so" und nach Felischs „Ja", hat Beuys uns allen „Auf Wiedersehen" – gesagt.

Keiner konnte wissen, daß es zugleich ein Abschiedskonzert wurde. Viele waren darüber enttäuscht, daß er nicht persönlich kommen konnte – er fehlte und fehlt immer noch, auch weiler so stark mit dem Begriff des aktiven Friedens verbunden ist.

Fähigkeit zur Liebe. Fähigkeit neue Ideen für den Frieden zu entwickeln das ist Kunst. Es ist „Wärmecharakter im Denken".

Henning Christiansen, Berlin, 29.11.1987

Per Kirkeby. Cover for Henning Christiansen *Kirkeby and Edvard Munch*

Henning Christiansen. *Jouez ma pipe*. 1986

Christmann, G.S. [S]

Title: Audio-Plastic No.4. Sydney 1974-77 (Jew's Harp & Traffic)

Technical Realization: EMI (Australia) Ltd.

ø 30cm, 33 RPM, 1977, limited edition of 200, signed and numbered

Cover: white, contains only number and signature

Ciani, Piermario
→ Sound Poetry

Cibulka, Heinz
→ selten gehörte Musik

Citny, Kiddy
→ Luciano Castelli

Claire, Paula
→ Sound Poetry

Clark, Thomas A.
→ Sound Poetry

Claus, Carlfriedrich
→ Sound Poetry

Clemente, Francesco [C]

Title: Primitive Cool

Music: Mick Jagger

ø 30cm, 33 RPM, 1987, CBS, Holland, No. 4601231

Cover: b/w, package concept and illustrations by Francesco Clemente

Cobbing, Bob
→ Revue OU
→ Sound Poetry

Cocteau, Jean [S]

Title: Jean Cocteau Reads His Poetry and Prose

Contents: Les voleurs d'enfants plain chant. L'ange heurtebise. Hommage à Manolete. Un ami dort. Le discours du Sphinx. De l'innocence criminelle. De la responsabilité, selection. Le paquet rouge

ø 30cm, 33 RPM, 1962, Caedmon Records, New York, No. TC 1083

Colette

Schallplatten an der Wand

Eine Schallplatte hat eine wunderbare Form. Mit ihrem 30 cm Durchmesser ist es ein gutes Gefühl, sie in die Hände zu nehmen und anzuschauen.

Die feinen Rillen sind voll von Mysterium und dazu das Loch in der Mitte, das man genau beobachten muss, wenn man die Schallplatte auf sein Grammophon legt. Wenn der Grammophonarm über das schwarze Rondell läuft und tanzt und die Geräusche, die Musik, den Gesang unsere Kulturbilder tönen lässt, dann ist es ein Wunder, das aus dem Lautsprecher kommt.

Ich möchte aber auch gerne hören, was meine Pfeife erzählen könnte, als grüner Pick-up, über die Zeit in der ich sie geraucht habe.

Ich habe auch eine Schallplatte festgenagelt, weil diese runde Form (Disco) mich als Objekt fasziniert - als festgefrorenes Schweigen.

Nageln Sie die Schallplatte an die Wand als teuerbares Kulturgut - damit wir weiterlaufen können in unserer Suche nach der neuen Weltordnung - Festgenageltes Kulturgut.

Henning Christiansen

Christiansen, Henning
→ Joseph Beuys
→ Rosenfest

Colette [C/S]

Title: Justine And The Victorian Punks

Music: Peter Gordon

Contents: Beautiful Dreamer. Still You

Perf.: Love of Life Orchestra, Justine (voc)

ø 30cm, 33 RPM, 1979, 1000 copies of the issue signed, Colette is Dead Co. Ltd.

Cover: one-color print with photos of a store window-action of Colette on 24. September 1979 in Graz, Austria

Il Concento Prosodico
→ Sound Poetry

Contò, Agostino
→ Sound Poetry

Copley, William
→ S.M.S.

Corner, Philip [C/O/S]

Title: Playing With The Elements

Contents: Breath: Rubbing Rock. Boiling Water. Terra Cotta (Heated Stone)

ø 30cm, 33 RPM, 1985, limited edition of 100 signed and numbered copies, Editions Lebeer Hossmann Brüssel / Hamburg

Box (31,2 x 31,5 x 3,3 cm) made of grey cardboard, hinged, with black silk-screen print of a diagram by Philip Corner.
The box contains: one diagram *Boiling Water*, one cloth bag with printed directions for use of the contained Terra Cotta Stone, crumpled tissue paper with same diagram as box and one record

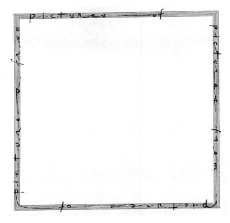

Corner, Philip [C/S]

Title: Pictures of Pictures from Pictures of Pictures

Perf.: Philip Corner (p)

ø 30cm, 33 RPM, 1988, Edition Block, Berlin, EB 106

Cover: b/w, gatefold, according to a drawing by Philip Corner

Special issue of 20 copies contains besides the record 11 pages (21,5 x 35,5 cm) of score (photostats), hand-colored, numbered and signed by Philip Corner and 10 etchings (53 x 67 cm), b/w, signed and numbered, by KP Brehmer.

Modest Moussorgsky wrote *Pictures at an Exhibition* in 1874, inspired by his impressions of an exhibition of visual works by his deceased friend Victor Hartman. Brehmer's 10 etchings transpose Moussorgsky's music back into visual terms. The *Promenades*, the recurring motif that unites the individual pictures, are left out. The titles of the etchings are identical with those of the 10 pictures set to music.
The transposition of the music was effected at the Institute for Communication Studies at the Technical University, Berlin. The respective motifs for each piece were translated into a sonagram. Brehmer transferred these sonagrams onto etching plates and copied in the titles. Philip Corner reactivated the 10 graphics once again in his musical compositions.

Corner, Philip
→ Radiotaxi

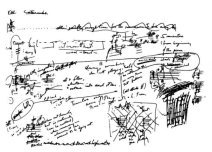

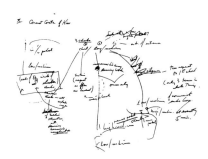

Philip Corner. Scores for *Pictures of Pictures from Pictures of Pictures*

Bilder einer Ausstellung
10 Radierungen von
KP Brehmer (1975)

Modest Mussorgsky schrieb die Musik „Bilder einer Ausstellung" im Jahre 1874, bewegt von den Eindrücken, die eine Ausstellung seines Freundes Victor Hartman hinterließ. Die 10 Radierungen Brehmers übersetzen Mussorgskys Musik ins Visuelle zurück. Die Promenaden, Mussorgskys immer wiederkehrendes, die einzelnen Bilder verbindendes Motiv, bleiben unbeachtet. Die Titel der Radierungen sind identisch mit den Titeln der 10 vertonten Bilder.
Die Rückübersetzung der Musik erfolgte im Institut für Kommunikationswissenschaften der Technischen Universität Berlin. Das jeweilige Hauptmotiv wurde in ein Sonagramm übersetzt. Brehmer übertrug die Sonagramme auf die Radierplatte und kopierte Titel ein. Die 10 Grafiken regten Philip Corner wiederum zu seiner Komposition an.

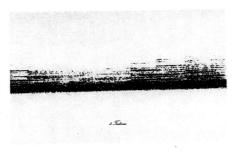

Pictures at an Exhibition
10 Etchings by
KP Brehmer (1975)

Modest Moussorgsky wrote "Pictures at an Exhibition" in 1874, inspired by his impressions of an exhibition of visual works by his deceased friend Victor Hartman. Brehmer's 10 etchings transpose Moussorgsky's music back into visual terms. The Promenades, the recurring motif that unites the individual pictures, are left out. The titles of the etchings are identical with those of the 10 pictures set to music.
The transposition of the music was effected at the Institute for Communication Studies at the Technical University, Berlin. The respective motifs for each piece were translated into a sonagram. Brehmer transferred these sonagrams onto etching plates and copied in the titles. Philip Corner reactivated the 10 graphics once again in his musical compositions.

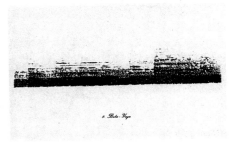

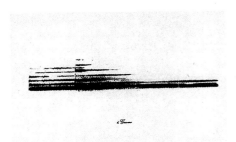

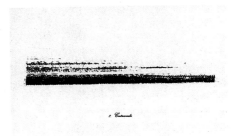

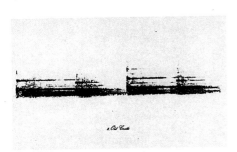

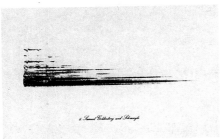

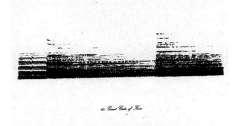

Costa, Corrado
→ Sound Poetry

Cortez, Diego
→ Airwaves

Cotten / Prince
→ Artsounds Collection

Coughtry, Graham
→ The Artists' Jazz Band

Cowan, Harvey
→ The Artists' Jazz Band

Cumming, Robert H.
→ Art By Telephone

Cunningham, Merce
→ Aspen Magazine
→ John Cage

Cuomo, Raffaele
→ Sound Poetry

Curran, Alvin [P/S]

Title: The Magic Carpet

Music: Alvin Curran / Paul Klerr

record ø 25cm, 33 RPM, as supplement in *Source*, music of the avant garde, Sacramento, California, No.9, 1971

The original *Magic Carpet* consisted of two basement rooms of the Gallery Arco D'Alibert (Rome, Italy) which were threaded with about 300 meters of colored strings in cotton, wool, gut, nylon and steel, creating a web of geometric patterns which changed with the viewer's perspective. Eighty metallic sliding intersections enabled the viewer/participant to modify the structure at will. Suspended from an independent set of strings were twelve groups of chimes with from five to seven elements each. They were made of bars and tubes of hard and soft aluminium, brass, and steel, 8 to 35 centimeters in length. A wooden frame and sound box was fitted into the passage-way between the rooms and supported thirty-five steel strings maintained in tension by piano-tuning pegs. The whole formed a kind of walk-through harp. There were no chimes in the first room, and only one waxed wool string was made to sound (if rubbed). In

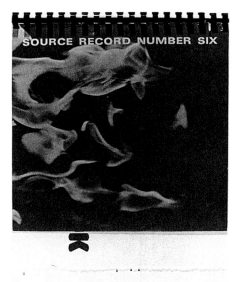

corners of the second room, strings converged into small metallic "sound boxes", which also housed contact microphones. The sound of these "wall guitars", as well as those of the "harp", were picked up by eight microphones in all, amplified and heard on speakers in two other rooms in the gallery. No conscious attempt was made to tune these instruments or to indicate what to do with them. The public was quick to move from the novelty of making sounds to the pleasure of making its own "public music".

Excerpt from Source

Discography:

Canti e vedute del giardino magnetico (Ananda No. 1, Roma, 1975, LP)
Fiori chiari, fiori oscuri (Ananda No. 4, Roma, 1975, LP)
The Works (Fore 80 No. 2, Raretone Music Library, Milano, 1980, LP)
Canti illuminati (Fore 80 No. 7, Rartone Music Library, Milano, 1982, LP)
For Cornelius. Era ora (New Albion Records, San Francisco, 1986, Na 011, LP)

Curtis, Jackie
→ Giorno Poetry Systems

Customer Service
→ Sound Poetry

Czchoch, Saskia
→ Das ist Schönheit

dada For Now [S]

Title: dada For Now. A Collection of Futurist and Dada Sound Works

Contents: Antonio Russolo: Corale and Serenata, 1921. Hugo Ball: Karawane, 1916; Wolken, 1916; Katzen und Pfauen, 1916; Totenklage, 1916; Gadji beri bimba, 1916; Seepferdchen und Flugfische, 1916. Arthur Honegger: Pacific 231, 1923. Tristan Tzara / Marcel Janco / Richard Huelsenbeck: L'amiral cherche une maison à louer, 1916. Kurt Schwitters: Simultangedicht kaa gee dee, 1919; WW, 1922; boo, 1926; naa, 1926; bii büll ree, 1936; Obervogelsang, 1946; Niesscherzo e Hustenscherzo, 1937; Cigarren, 1921; The real disuda of the nightmare, 1946. Raoul Hausmann: Soundrel, 1919. Giacomo Balla: Discussione sul futurismo di due critici sudanesi, 1914; Macchina Tipografica, 1914; Paesaggio + Temporale, 1914. Luigi Russolo: Veglio di una citta, 1914

Perf.: Ball, Tzara-Janco-Huelsenbeck, and Schwitters: Trio Exvoco (Hanna Aurbacher, Theophil Maier, and Ewald Liska). Balla: Luigi Pennone, Arrigo Lora-Totino, and Sergio Cena. Honegger: L'Orchestre de la Suisse Romande, Ernest Ansermet (cond)

ø 30cm, 33 RPM, 1985, ARK Liverpool, Dove 4

Cover: b/w, design: Colin Fallows according to a photo by Reg Cox

Included folder with photos and manifestos

Dallegret, François
→ Art By Telephone

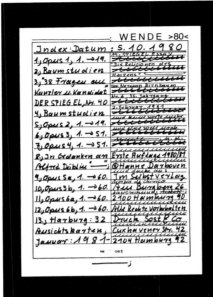

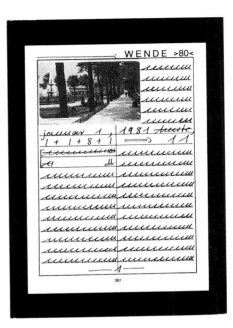

Darboven, Hanne [C/S]

Title: Wende >80<. 1980/81

Contents: Index Opus 1 - 6 b. Opus 1. Opus 2. Opus 3. Opus 4. Opus 5a. Opus 5b. Opus 6a. Opus 6b.

11 LPs, ø 30cm, 33 RPM, limited edition of 250, signed, Selbstverlag Hamburg, Am Burgberg, 1980/81

Cover: box made of grey cardboard, sticker, b/w, with printed handwritten informations

A second box (43,5 x 31,4 x 8,7 cm) with same decor contains 415 score sheets (each 42 x 29,7 cm), b/w

VIERJAHRESZEITEN
1981/82

hAnNEdArsOVEn
"DER MOND IST AUFGEGANGEN"

Darboven, Hanne [C/S]

Title: Vierjahreszeiten. Opus 7 "Der Mond ist aufgegangen"

ø 30cm, 33 RPM, 1981/82, Selbstverlag Hanne Darboven

Cover: two-color print

Hanne Darboven. Four pages of *Wende >80<*

Darreg, Ivor
→ Sound

Das ist Schönheit [C/S]

Title: Das ist Schönheit. Hamburg Mai 80

Sound: Peter Reitberger, Rima Lucia Mardoyan, Walter Thielsch, Thomas Fehlmann, Rainer Oehms, Holger Hiller, Angela Marcus, Karin, Insook, Oliver Hirschbiegel, Saskia Czchoch, Jürgen Heimes, Jelle Fargo, Katharina Baumann, Claus Böhmler, Andre Rademacher

2 LPs, ø 30 cm, 33 RPM, 1980/81/82, parts of the issue signed and numbered, published by the artists

---

Cover: gatefold, white, each cover with an original Gouache, different colored and feltpen-drawings by various artists
Coordination: Walter Thielsch, Thomas Fehlmann

The production originated during a workshop by Conrad Schnitzler in May 1980 at the Kunsthochschule Hamburg. With special thanks to Carl Vogel, K.P. Brehmer und Claus Böhmler. Photostat supplement with title informations

Davis, Douglas
→ Revolutions Per Minute

Davis, Hugh
→ Revue OU

DeMarinis, Paul
→ Sound

Dencker, Klaus Peter
→ Sound Poetry

Depero, Fortunato
→ Sound Poetry

Desforges, Christophe
→ Voices Notes & Noise

Desiato, Guiseppe
→ Radiotaxi

van Deusen, Burton
→ Artsounds Collection

Dias, Antonio [C/S]

Title: The Space Between

Contents: The Theory of Counting. The Theory of Density

ø 30cm, 33 RPM, 1971, limited edition of 180, signed and numbered, Antonio Dias

Cover: padded mailing envelope (33 x 36,5 cm), mounted postcard, b/w

---

with red lettering according to a photo by Ruy Bastos

The Space Between, an album published by Dias, is the recording of the intermittent, and then continuous, scansion of two sounds: an alarm clock and breathing. First the record has three seconds of sound followed by three seconds of silence, observing a pre-established pattern in order to stress the acoustic effect of the full and the empty, or sound and silence. In the second part attention is focused on the continuum of breathing with its natural drawing and expelling of breath, again positive and negative.

Germano Celant: *The Record As Artwork.* (cat.) Fort Worth, Texas 1978, p. 70 and 74

Dibbets, Jan [C/S]

Title: Afsluitdyk 1969, the sound of driving 5 km on a straight road with a constant speed of 100 km an hour
Das Geräusch einer Fahrt von 5 km auf einer geraden Strecke mit einer konstanten Geschwindigkeit von 100 Stundenkilometern

ø 15 cm, 33 RPM, 1969, Museum Haus Lange, Krefeld

Cover: front cover b/w, back cover multicolor print of a map showing the dyke

Dibbets, Jan
→   Art By Telephone

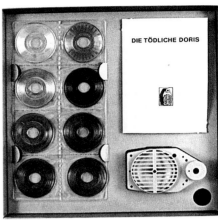

nicht beobachtet. Haare im Mund. M. Röck: Rhythmus im Blut. Kavaliere. fliegt schnell laut summend. Robert. Über-Mutti. In der Pause

ø 30cm, 33 RPM, n.d. (1982), ZICKZACK Hamburg, No. ZZ 123

Cover: multi-color print with special high gloss printed photo motif, and texts

---

Die Tödliche Doris   [C/S]

Title: Die 7 tödlichen Unfälle im Haushalt

Contents: 7 tödliche Unfälle im Haushalt. Tanz im^2. Avon-Gard. Stop der Information. Der Krieg der Basen. Der Astronaut und der Kosmos

ø 30cm, 45 RPM, n.d. (1980), ZICKZACK Hamburg, No. ZZ 35

Cover: b/w with drawing and text

Die Tödliche Doris   [C/S]

Title: "Die tödliche Doris"

Contents: stümmel mir die Sprache. Posaunen der Liebe. Der Tod ist ein Skandal. Panzerabwehrfaust. Wie still es im Wald ist. Sie werden

---

Die Tödliche Doris   [O/S]

Title: Chöre & Soli

Limited edition of 1000, gelbe Musik Berlin, Pure Freude Düsseldorf, 1983

Green box (31,3 x 31,3 x 5,6 cm) with black titles, contains 8 mini-records (ø 6cm) of different colors in plastic bag, play-back device (flesh-color) with battery and a booklet (16,9 x 12 cm) with 32 photos from the Photo-Documentary-Archive and texts (prose and songs) by Wolfgang Müller, Nikolaus Vermoehlen, Käthe Kruse and Tabea Blumenschein.

The title "you see we come as friends" appeared as one of 16 titles on 8 mini-records, together with a battery operated phonograph in a box called *Chöre & Soli*. It was released by Gelbe Musik, Berlin and Pure Freude, Düsseldorf 1983.

Mini-records and their respective phonographs are usually components of talking dolls and laughing sacks.

After Die Tödliche Doris had released a 12 inch and a LP, she began to get bored. One LP follows the other and then the comparison starts. The critic speaks of the "development" of the group in this or in that direction, guarantying the new release a positive development ("the music has be-come more elaborate and more thoroughly composed"), or a negative one ("sadly the strength of the first LP is lacking"). Through the format of "Chöre & Soli" this couldn't happen. Towards the independence from records and phonographs, as in our LP's "Unser Debut" and "Sechs" and equally through a third immaterial LP (order the poster "Throw away your crutches!" from Die Tödliche Doris, Lützowstr. 23, D-1000 Berlin 30), an important contribution was achieved. Don't worry!
Die Tödliche Doris

Die Tödliche Doris   [P/S]

Title: Naturkatastrophen (Natural Disasters)

Catalogue (22,5 x 21 cm) of homonymous exhibition in *gelbe Musik* Berlin, 36 p., record (ø 17cm, 45 RPM) attached, limited edition of 1000, gelbe Musik Berlin, 1984

Texts by "Die Tödliche Doris", Dietrich Kuhlbrodt, Christian Borngräber, Ursula Block (German/English). Materials of *Natural Disasters*: video - objects - photos - texts from the period 1982 - 1984

Die Tödliche Doris [C/S]

Title: Unser Debut. Wie geht es dir jetzt

Contents: Südwestwind - The Sound of Bells.
           Ungerechtigkeit (hinter Glas oder
           Folie). Noch 14 Vorstellungen.
           Nachdenken, Gedächtnis und
           Gesang. Auf dem Lande, b) Tat-
           sachen. Unser Debut / dtsch.-engl.
           Ungerechtigkeit Teil II (20 Pfennig
           Finderlohn). Lieblingslied / Verun-
           glückt (5). Weltkonferenz Hochal-
           pen

           ø 30cm, 33 RPM, 1985, AtaTak
           Düsseldorf, No. WR 33 LP

Cover: multi-color print with photo and text
           information

Die Tödliche Doris [C/S]

Title: Die Tödliche Doris 6. Jetzt ist alles
           gut

Contents: Windstille. Grünland in der Grenz-
           schlade. Eine Frau zur selben Zeit

an einem anderen Ort. Wir be-
grüßen den neuen Tag. Beim
Rechtsanwalt, a) Zopf. Not true.
Ortsgespräch 1986. Im Tief. Finale
der Plattenseite B

ø 30cm, 33 RPM, 1986, AtaTak
Düsseldorf, No. WR 35 LP

Cover: multi-color print with photos and
           titles

Recommendation of the artists: to play this record parallel
to *Unser Debut*. As a result in Japan these two records
were issued as a double album, WAVE, No. SP 36-6020-
21.

Die Tödliche Doris [S]

Title: Liveplaybacks. Wien - Hamburg -
           München - Helsinki - Berlin -
           Budapest - New York - s'Hertogen-
           bosch - Bonn - Frankfurt -
           Bruxelles - Villingen-Schwenningen
           - Paris - Bordeaux - Amsterdam

           ø 30cm, 33 RPM, 1986, Reinhard
           Wilhelmi Berlin, No. 8

Cover: b/w, title- and textinformation

Printed protective cover

"With this record Die Tödliche Doris
presents you a 40-minutes lasting musicpro-
gram of her biggest Live-successes in
continious gradual Playback-operation. This
incursion will lead us to the internationally
renowned arthalls, tents or private abodes."

Dimitrijević, Braco [O]

Title: Njeqove dovke glas. His pencil's
           voice

           ø 17cm, 16, 33, 45, 78 RPM,
           1973, record of white cardboard,
           on one side groove pressed in by

a pencil, Galerija studentskog
centra i muzički salonteatra ITD
Zagreb

Cover: b/w, photos by Fedor Vučemilović
           and Sven Stilinović

Dine, Jim
→   Record Of Interviews ...

Döhl, Reinhard
→   Sound Poetry

Dokoupil, Jiri Georg [C]

Title: Wirtschaftswunder: Salmobray

Music: Wirtschaftswunder (Angelo Galizia,
           Jürgen Beuth, Tom Dokoupil, Mark
           Pfurtscheller)

           ø 30cm, 33 RPM, n.d., Zick Zack
           Platten, Hamburg, ZZ 20

Cover: two-color print

Dorner, Felix

→   Fünfzehn Tonspuren

Downsbrough, Peter   [C/S]

Title: From

Contents: a place to be / and brought back to. to be and repeat / and then again here. assign a place to / arrive and depart from. to be here and / there are in place. about to arrive at / and brought to or. a place to place / here to be there. there to be here

Perf.:   Gordon Meyer (p, voice), Patrick Blackburn, Mimi Wheeler, Jennifer Albright, Dorothy Topham, Martine Rapin, Susan Lemak, Leila Gastil, John Merrill (voice)

ø 30cm, 33 RPM, 1982, The Stedelijk Van Abbemuseum, Eindhoven

Cover: two-colorprint, design and photos: Peter Downsbrough

Supplement with photo and listing of the pieces and interpreters

Doyon, Jacques

→   Sound Poetry

Draper, Ronald

→   Sound Poetry

Dreyblatt, Arnold

→   Amerikanische Künstler in Berlin
→   Ellen Fullmann

Driscoll, John

→   David Tudor

Droprarchief

→   Perfo 2

Droese, Felix

→   p. 131

Drucker, Heidi

→   Sound Poetry

Dubuffet, Jean   [C/S]

Title: Expériences Musicales

Contents: La fleur de barbe. Humeur incertaine. Temps radieux. Trotte matin. Solennités. Pousse l'herbe. L'eau. Coq à l'oeil. Aguichements. Pleure et applaudit. Le gai savoir. Le bateau coulé. Dimanche. Aggravation. Cris d'herbe. Longue peine. Délibérants. Terre foisonnante. Prospère, prolifère. Diligences futiles

6 LPs, ø 25cm, 33 RPM, 1961, limited edition of 50, signed and numbered, Galleria del Cavallino, Venezia

Cover: box (29,5 x 28,5 x 5,5 cm) with black linen, signature and year in white relief print

The fronts of the 6 covers contain 6 reproduced drawings (b/w) by the artist. 4-page pamphlet with photos of Jean Dubuffet and his instruments, and a text by the artist.

→   p. 59 - 71

Dubuffet, Jean   [S]

Title: La fleur de barbe

ø 20,5cm, 33 RPM, 1961, de Luca, Rom

Cover: b/w, title and portraitphoto

Dubuffet, Jean [C/S]

Title: Musical Experiences

Contents: Aguichements. L'eau. Délibérants. Pleure et applaudit. Humeur incertaine. Bateau coulé. Diligences futiles. Gai savoir

ø 30cm, 33 RPM, 1973, Finnadar Records, USA, No. SR 9002

Cover: b/w, design: Jean Dubuffet

Duchamp, Marcel [O]

Title: Rotoreliefs (Optical Discs)

Set of six discs (ø 20cm), with a drawing on each side printed in color by offset lithography, to be seen as they rotate at the speed of 33 RPM.

First disc
front: Rotorelief No. 1 *Corolles*
back: Rotorelief No. 4 *Lampe*

Second disc
front: Rotorelief No. 2 *Oeuf à la coque*
back: Rotorelief No. 3 *Lanterne chinoise*

Third disc
front: Rotorelief No. 5 *Poisson japonais*
back: Rotorelief No. 6 *Escargot*

Fourth disc
front: Rotorelief No. 7 *Verre de Bohême*
back: Rotorelief No. 8 *Cerceaux*

Fifth disc
front: Rotorelief No. 9 *Montgolfière*
back: Rotorelief No. 10 *Cage*

Sixth disc
front: Rotorelief No. 11 *Éclipse totale*
back: Rotorelief No. 12 *Spirale blanche*

Several editions were issued: 1935 Paris, 1953 New York, 1959 Paris, 1963 New York, 1965 Milan

We are reproducing and showing the version of 1965, Milan:
"A signed and numbered edition of the remaining 150 sets of discs of the original 1953 edition was issued under the supervision of Duchamp. In each set one disc is signed on the outer edge, in ink M.D. Each wall-hanging unit, designed by Duchamp on the basis of the 1963 edition, bears on the back of the front panel a brassplate on which Duchamp etched his signature, date (1965), and number of the example (1/150 to 150/150); at the bottom of the plate, in printed letters, set as two lines, has also been etched: "Rotorelief 1935 -1953 / Edition Galerie Schwarz, Milan".

According to Arturo Schwarz: *The Complete Works of Marcel Duchamp.* London 1969

The wall-hanging unit consists of a wooden box (37,5 x 37,5 x 8,5 cm), which is covered with black velvet; the motor is behind, in the center of the box, and drives a revolving magnetized turntable (ø 24,8 cm) which enables one to use, according to the discs to be shown, either one of the two circular magnetized black frames of different widths supplied with this unit.

Dubuffet, Jean [C]

Title: The Pillory

Music: Jasun Martz

ø 30cm, 33 RPM, 1981, Neoteric Music, Los Angeles, No. NEO 61853

Cover: three-color print

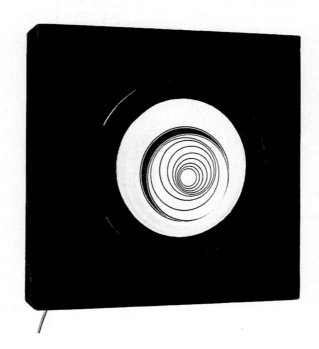

Marcel Duchamp. Rotorelief No.3. *Lanterne Chinoise* on the wall-hanging unit

Duchamp, Marcel [P/S]

Title: Some Texts from A 'Infinitif (1912-1920). The Creative Act (1957). (A paper presented to the Convention of the American Federation of Arts at Houston, Texas, April 1957). Read by the author

ø 20cm, 33 RPM, as supplement of Aspen Magazine No. 5 + 6, New York 1967

Duchamp, Marcel [P/S]

Title: Marcel Duchamp and John Cage. Reunion along with Teeny Duchamp, David Tudor, Gordon Mumma, David Behrman, Lowell Cross

Book (15,5 x 21,5 cm), 180 p. (n.pag.) with 1 blue flexidisc (ø 13cm, 33RPM), limited edition of 500 numbered copies, published by Takeyoshi Miyazawa, 1968
Photo- and text-documentation of a game of chess on March 5, 1968 in the Ryerson Theatre in Toronto, chessboard by Lowell Cross, photos by Shigeko Kubota. The record contains acoustic signals produced by the individual moves during the game. Technical realization: David Behrman

Duchamp, Marcel [C/S]

Title: Ives / Duchamp / Cage

Contents: Charles Ives: Three Quarter-Tone Pieces. Marcel Duchamp: Le Mariée mise à nu par ses Célibataires, même. Erratum musical. John Cage: A Book of Music for Two Prepared Pianos

Perf.: Mats Persson/ Kristine Scholz (p)

ø 30cm, 33 RPM, 1982, Caprice, No. CAP 1226

Cover: two-color print of a drawing of Marcel Duchamp "avoir l'apprente dans le soleil", design: Ulf Anderson

Included folder with informations and photos of the composers and interpreters. Texts by Per-Anders Hellqvist and Bengt Emil Johnson

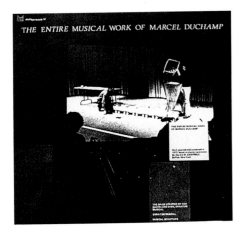

Duchamp, Marcel [S]

Title: The Entire Musical Work of Marcel Duchamp

Contents: La Mariée mise à nu par ses Célibataires, même. Erratum musical. 1.3 Voices: Erratum musical. Musical Sculpture

Perf.: S.E.M. Ensemble: Petr Kotik (alto-fl, voc), James Kasprowicz (tb), William Lyon Lee (celeste, voc), John Bondler (glockenspiel, voc)

ø 30cm, 33 RPM, 1976, Multipla Records, Milano, No. 1

Cover: gatefold, two-color print with photo- and textinformations

Duchamp, Marcel / John Cage [S]

Title: Marcel Duchamp: The Bride Stripped Bare by her Bachelors, Even. Erratum Musical. John Cage: 27'10.554" For a Percussionist.

Perf.: Donald Knaack (perc)

ø 30cm, 33 RPM, 1977, Finnadar Records, New York, No. SR 9017

Cover: b/w, with portraitphoto of Marcel Duchamp, designed by Lynn Breslin

Musical sculpture.
lasting and
Sounds leaving from
different places and
forming
sounding
a sculpture which lasts.

Duchamp, Marcel

→ Artsounds Collection
→ John Cage
→ S.M.S.

p. 128 / 129. **Marcel Duchamp.** *Rotoreliefs*

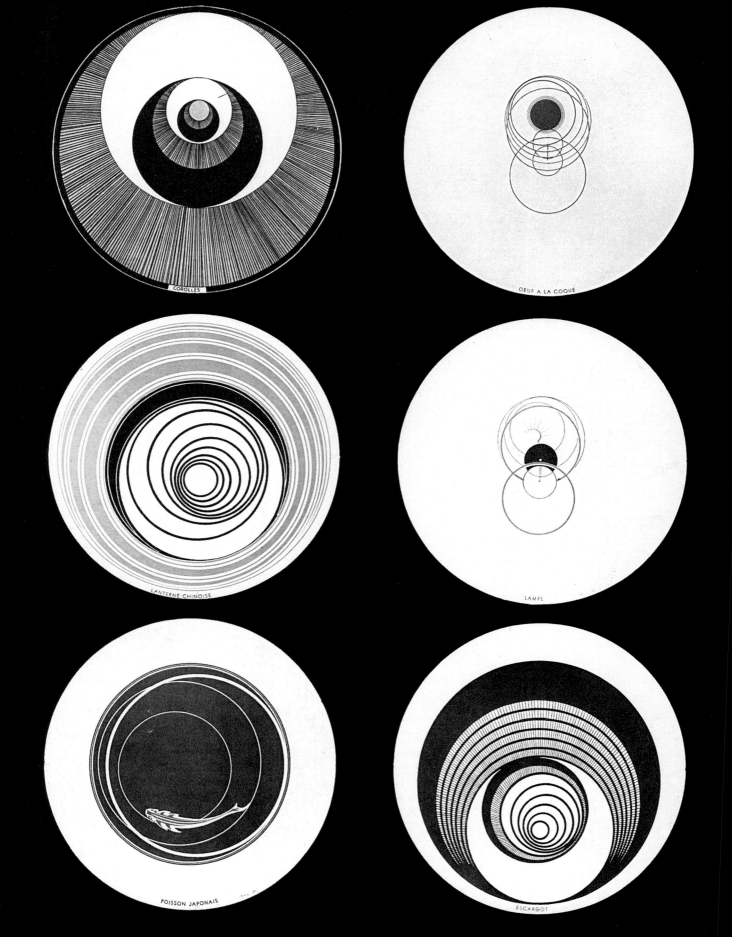

COROLLES

OEUF A LA COQUE

LANTERNE CHINOISE

LAMPE

POISSON JAPONAIS

ESCARGOT

VERRE DE BOHEME

CERCEAUX

MONTGOLFIERE

CAGE

ECLIPSE TOTALE

SPIRALE BLANCHE

Dufrêne, François

→ Poesie Physique
→ Revue OU
→ Sound Poetry

DUTCH "DIFFICULT" MUSIC [S]

Title: Dutch "Difficult" Music. a selective view

Contents: Motobs: Low, Low Spirit. Harrie de Wit: Thin Cities. Peter Zegveld: Dynamica Tumultus (fragment). Noodband: Sono Koubaly. Niew Hip Stilen: Mud. Remko Scha & The Machines: HGM 2. Jacques Palinckx: De Kamermachine / Do The Doomdoom-Doom / Het Huilen Van Urgje / Blin / Meer Groeten. Loos: Edge. Moniek Toebosch & Michel Waisvisz: Killpik

ø 30cm, 33 RPM, n.d., Eksakt Records, Tilburg, Holland, Eksakt 021

Cover: multi-color, design: Huib Simons

Included double-sheet with photos and text information

Dugal, Réjean

→ Sound Poetry

Duncan, John

→ Sound

Dunlap, Richard

→ Sound

Eckert, Karl-Heinz [O]

Title: Panorama vom Inselsberg. 1983

Cardboard-telescope (ø 9,6cm, length 60cm) mounted on adjusted tripod, picture-disc (woodgraving, ø 30,5cm) on recordplayer (tone-arm as red and white toll-gate) without pick-up, 16 RPM. Cardboard-sign (12,5 x 39 cm) *Panorama vom Inselsberg*

Egg, Loys

→ Peter Weibel

Einhorn, Nikolaus

→ Sound Poetry

Felix Droese. *Leuchtturm.* 1981. 28 x 26 x 17 cm

van Elk, Ger [C]

Music:	Willem Breuker/ Leo Cuypers
Title:	Live in Shaffy
Contents:	Aandeel 1+2. Rabbit. Für Leo und Wim. Ham & Egg Stango. Once there was. Churchy. Bouquet Mélancolique
	ø 30cm, 33 RPM, 1974, BVHAAST, Amsterdam, No. 005
Cover:	multi-color print, triangular shape (lateral length 61/51,5/51,5 cm), typography: Evelien de Vries Robbé

Live recording of a concert on September 28, 1974 in the Shaffy Theater, Amsterdam

Engels, Pieter [S]

Title:	Fabulous Oldest Hits. (One Fan Can't Be Wrong) (Pieter Engels, Simon Es tape-recording 1963)
Contents:	"Big Fat Girl". "Cadillac". Oral Signature. ditto
	Double-single, ø 17cm, 45 RPM, n.d. (1972), publication of 'atlas voor een nieuwe metropole', Rotterdam in co-operation with 'engels third institute', Amsterdam, Holland
Cover:	b/w, gatefold

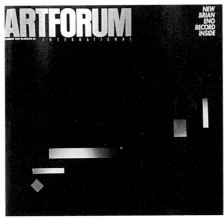

Eno, Brian [P/S]

Title:	Glint. (East of Woodbridge)
	Artforum Summer 1986, New York, transparent flexidisc enclosed, ø 17cm, 33 RPM

Eno, Brian
→ obscure

Entgrenzte Grenzen [P/S]

Sound:	Josef Klammer / Seppo Gruendler "Razionalnik"
	Single, ø 17cm, 45 RPM, as supplement to the catalogue: Entgrenzte Grenzen (88 p.), 1987, Graz, Austria. Concept: Richard Kriesche

Erb, Elke
→ Sound Poetry

Ernst, Max [C/S]

Title:	La Femme 100 Têtes
Music:	George Antheil
Perf.:	David Albee (p)
	ø 30cm, 33 RPM, 1984, CRI SD 502
Cover:	two-color print of an etching by Max Ernst from the folder La Femme 100 Têtes

...This unusual set of visionary etudes, inspired by La Femme 100 Têtes, a book of collaged etchings assembled by the surrealist painter Max Ernst from their original sources in volumes of 19th Century picture storybook, and each given subtitles with hauntingly suggestive overtones, typifies Antheil's music during what the composer himself referred to as earlier "mechanistic" period (1922-25)...

Charles Amirkhanian (Excerpt from covertext)

Ertl, Fedo
→ Werner Schmeiser

Ess, Barbara
→ Just Another Asshole

ÉTANT DONNÉS [C/S]
(Eric and Marc Hurtado)

Title:	LE SENS POSITIF
Contents:	La nuit si calme et si transparente. Entre 4 étoiles. La montée au ciel. Mon coeur 2 âmes. Déjà le blé

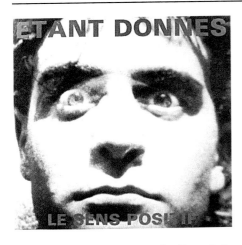

pleure son désespoir. Une étoile c'est le ciel

ø 30cm, 33 RPM, n.d., D.M.A., Bordeaux, D.M.A. 006

Cover: multi-color print with photos

ÉTANT DONNÉS [C/S]

Contents: PLUTOT L'EXIL DU CINQ DORÉ. MONDE ET CHAIR. LES FOURS A CHAUX

ø 17cm, 45 RPM, 1983, VITA NOVA, Grenoble, France

Cover: two-color print

Evans, Dennis
→ Sound

Export, Valie / Monsti Wiener [C/S]

Title: wahre Freundschaft

Music: a.o. Raimund, Bayer/Rühm, Schubert, Léhar

Contents: anfang. hab sonne im herzen. futi. wenn gott will. sahara. froh zu sein. salomon. wahre freundschaft. honolulu. hobellied. bananen. die bluse. guten abend. my bonnie. am brunnen. alkohol. frère jacques. müllers lust. weana madln. immer nur lächeln. soldat am wolgastrand. schlucken

Perf.: Valie Export, Monsti Wiener, Michael Schwabe

ø 30cm, 33 RPM, 1978, signed and numbered by both artists, heimproduktion, berlin-kreuzberg

Cover: b/w

Single for "die zweitschrift" No. 8, special issue, "m.u.(z.i.e.k)²", 1981, with the pieces *Caprifischer. Bananen*

Extended Play [P/S]

Title: Extended Play

catalogue (for a record exhibition curated by Christian Marclay & Ursula Block) in the format of a box (18 x 18 x 1,5 cm) including 51 single sheets (with texts, statements of the artists) and 1 flexidisc, ø 17cm, 33 RPM, with excerpts from exhibited records. Emily Harvey Gallery, New York 1988

Farfa
→ Sound Poetry

Fargo, Jelle
→ Das ist Schönheit

Farioli, Daniel
→ Perfo 2

Fay, Jane
→ Sound Poetry

Faye, Jean-Pierre
→ Sound Poetry

Fehlmann, Thomas
→ Albert Oehlen
→ Das ist Schönheit

Feininger, Lyonel [C/S]

Title: Dichter und Maler als Komponisten. Poets and Painters as Composers

Klavierwerke von Boris Pasternak, E.T.A. Hoffmann, Lyonel Feininger

Contents: Lyonel Feininger: Fuge I für Klavier (1921), Fuge III (Gigue) für Klavier (1921)

Perf.: Annie Gicquel (p)

ø 30cm, 33 RPM, 1981, Fono Schallplatten Münster, No. FSM 53210 EB

Cover: multi-color print of a painting by Lyonel Feininger, design: Heinrich Lehmann

Fekner, John
→ Sound Poetry

Feldman, Morton
→ Aspen Magazine
→ Franz Kline

Ferlinghetti, Lawrence
→ Sound Poetry

Fier, Bruce
→ Sound

Fischer, Hervé
→ Sound Poetry

Fischli / Weiss   [O/P]

Title: Schallplatte

record of Beracryl, ø 30cm, 1988, limited edition of 120, numbered and signed, special issue of PARKETT No. 17
RECORD. 1988

The two collaboration-artists present a record as part of the special edition of Parkett No. 17. But Peter Fischli and David Weiss did not produce it in a Sound-Studio. The record described here is an object with the title "Record". However, you can actually play this Fischli/Weiss-record. If you're not afraid to ruin your recordplayer or stylus, you will hear a kind of average disco-music. Average, in this case, also means a reduction of the possible fidelity: HiFi-fetishism devours itself.

The record represents one of the favourite and most widespread articles for domestic use. It belongs to a household like the potted plant, the furniture, the pots and pans, the car, the newspapers, and the jam. But we probably have never encountered a self-made, self-molded species record. Only Fischli/Weiss bring us this sympathic, bulk article near to the custom-tailored dress, the home-assembled bookshelf, or the self-built house. They refer to that fine line between the ridiculous and the special, which is unique to such objects. This record is an imitation.

Here we remember the antique legend of the bird who tried to pick a painted cherry, because painting had imitated nature so perfectly.

Fischli/Weiss confront us with an object that shows the cherry as a record and the bill of the bird as the stylus.

In one of the small sculptures of the series "Plötzlich diese Übersicht", Fischli/Weiss already dealt with this problem by plastically forming the signet of "His Master's Voice". Not only does the question arise whether the dog follows the real or unreal, the right or the wrong voice of his master, but also whether the trademark reproduced by Fischli/Weiss is still valid as a trademark.

The material which the Fischli/Weiss record is made of is Beracryl and is similar to the material that the artists use for their so-called "rubber"-sculptures. Thus "rubber" can sometimes imitate rubber; but, in our case, acryl imitates vinyl...

Bice Curiger

Fishbein, Sue
→ Sound Poetry

Fisk, Steve
→ Sound Poetry

Fischli / Weiss

Fletcher, Leland

→ Voices Notes & Noise

Flying Klassenfeind [C]

Contents: Sun City. Venus in Furs. Ulan Bator. Out Demons Out

Perf.: a.o. Markus Oehlen (g, dr, syn), Diedrich Diederichsen (keyboards, voc, dr, voc), Jörg Gülden (g)

ø 30cm, 45 RPM, 1982, Line Music, Hamburg, No. LMMS 3026AG

Cover: b/w, design: Flying Klassenfeind

Förg, Günther [C]

Title: Zwei Quintette

Music: Rüdiger Carl

Perf.: Rüdiger Carl (ts, cl), Phil Wachsman (v, el), Stephan Wittwer (g,

el), Irene Schweizer (p), Jay Oliver (b)

2 LPs, ø 30cm, 33 RPM, 1987, Free Music Production, Berlin, No. FMP 1210/20

Cover: two-color print, gatefold, design: Günther Förg

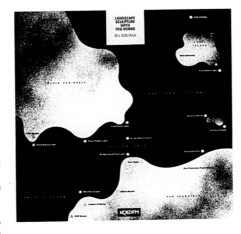

Fontana, Bill [S]

Title: Landscape Sculpture With Fog Horns

Contents: Landscape Sculpture With Fog Horns, Installation Version, 1981. Landscape Sculpture With Fog Horns, Live Radio Version, 1982

ø 30cm, 33 RPM, 1982, KQED-FM, San Francisco

Cover: multi-color print, design: Bill Anton, Dennis Favello

The sculpture site of this version... was created for the New Music America '81 Festival. At the sculpture site, listeners walked along the 600 foot pier, on a trajectory towards Angel Island (3 miles away). At the end of the pier, all of San Francisco bay is visible. For 300 feet of this walk, listeners would pass under a sequence of eight loudspeakers. Each of these played a live broadcast of ambient sound from each of eight different and distant microphone locations around San Francisco Bay...

Bill Fontana (Excerpt from covertext)

Fontana, Bill [S]

Title: Sounds Of The Bay Area

Contents: A Ride on a San Francisco Cable Car. California Sea Lions in Monte-

rey Harbour. A Mockingbird in a Tree. Resonating Exhaust Ducts at the PG&E Power Plant at Elkhorn Slough. Passing Flocks of Redwing Blackbirds at Dawn. Dawn in the Cliffs above the Entrance to Bodega Bay. Fog Horns and Surf under the Golden Gate Bridge. Amtrak Trains going through Level Crossings in Berkeley

ø 30cm, 33 RPM, 1983, KQED-FM, San Francisco

Cover: hand-painted pieced photograph by Bruce Handelsman

Fontana, Bill [S]

Title: Field Recordings Of Natural Sounds

Contents: The Mating Dance of Sage Grouse near Mammoth Lake California. Multi-Channel Recording of a Woodpecker and Other Birds on a Lake in the Adirondack Mountains. Spring Peepers in the Adirondack

Mountains. Birds along a River's Edge in a Chaparral South of Monterey. Birds in a Rainforest in Southeastern Australia. Waves Breaking on Rocks along the Northeast Australian Coast

ø 30cm, 33 RPM, 1983, Sierra Club, San Francisco, CA

Cover: three-color print, design: Bill Anton, photo: Luis Espinosa Casanova, 1929

As a composer, I have been concerned with exploring the occurrence of musical form in the ambient sounds of the natural and man-made environment. I have also been concerned with finding suitable artistic mediums in which to express these naturally occurring musical forms...

The recordings on this album were all made in natural environments, and explore a variety of natural sound textures. All of the recordings are in real time, they are not edited. This sense of real time is necessary for preserving and communicating the natural symmetry of these sound textures, which like the environments they come from, possess a certain timelessness.

Bill Fontana (Excerpt from covertext)

Fontana, Bill
→　　　Sound

Fontana, Giovanni
→　　　Sound Poetry
→　　　Voices Notes & Noise

Forster, John
→　　　Sound Poetry

Forster, Terry
→　　　The Artists' Jazz Band

Four Horsemen
→　　　Giorno Poetry Systems
→　　　Sound Poetry

Fournier, Micheline
→　　　Sound Poetry

Fox, Terry　　　　　　　　　　[P/S]

Title: Isolation Unit. Düsseldorf Kunstakademie, 11-24-70, 7:00 P.M.

FISH FOX KOS

DeSAISSET MUSEUM & ART GALLERY, UNIVERSITY OF SANTA CLARA.
FEB. 2 - 28, 1971 reception & event feb.2,7:30·10

Perf.: Terry Fox (pipes), Joseph Beuys (seeds)

Record (ø 17cm, 45 RPM, 1970) as supplement to the catalogue 'FISH FOX KOS', 7 loose sheets (23,3 x 23,3 cm) with photos of the performance and text, DeSaisset Museum & Art Gallery, University of Santa Clara, CA

The record contained in this catalogue was pressed from a tape made during an event in the Kunstakademie in Düsseldorf, Germany, November 24, 1970. The record presents the final twelve minutes of the event, which lasted approximately one hour.

The performance was a collaboration between Terry Fox and Joseph Beuys involving many elements of sound. The first sound heard on the record is Terry Fox striking an eight-inch pipe with a one-inch iron pipe. The mouth of the pipe is directed toward a window frame containing four panes of glass. The pipe is struck and acoustically dead spots are searched for in the glass by listening to the echo. When those spots are found, the glass is shattered.

There is a candle burning behind the window frame. When all of the panes are broken, the wooden cross is knocked out of the frame and an attempt is made to bend the candle flame with the sound wave enamating from the pipe.

Then the small pipe is struck on the floor in search for the dead spots in the glass of a burning light bulb. At this time, Beuys begins eating a Cherimoya fruit, spitting the seeds one at a time into a small silver bowl at his feet. These two sounds continue simultaneously until the fruit is consumed.

Fox, Terry　　　　　　　　　　[C/P/S]

Title: Linkage (Acoustic Wire Sound)

Contents: Drumming. Pulling. Bowing. Beating. Scraping. Ether. The News. The Vicar And The Cowboy. The Bear. Sign Off

Catalogue (31,2 x 31,5 cm), 36 p.(n.pag.), with enclosed LP ø 30cm, 33 RPM, Kunstmuseum Luzern, 1982.

In the field of "acoustics" and "space" Terry Fox has also made a significant contribution, quite distinct from that of other endeavors in the visual art, especially those of the Fluxus movement. Terry Fox works with acoustics as resonance, as sound produced by the space within which the resonance occurs. The space becomes a sounding box in which he appears merely as a catalyst for

the sounds. Thus he makes the spatial features of resonance and sound visible, on the one hand, while, on the other, transforming space itself with acoustic devices. His material, physical intervention serves only to assist in the creation of these space instruments or spaces as instrument. His person, his body recedes more into the background than in earlier performances. The spaces, the characteristics, the story of the spaces are given voice and replace the actor telling his story. Thus Terry Fox still remains well within the bounds of the visual arts while opening them up to a vast field - acoustics as a spatial dimension. His work can, of course, also be seen in the light of musical development, though only if it is understood as a rejection of music in the frame of a work with acoustics. In this context, his work is revolutionary as well, since it does not reverse John Cage's slogan, "any sound is music", but turns it upside down. Not "all music is sound"; instead, the entire range of sound as such is not merely music. The installation Linkage and the accompanying disc pressed here in Lucerne present an optimally record of Terry Fox's acoustic work in the exhibiton at the Kunstmuseum Lucerne.

Martin Kunz (Excerpt from catalogue)

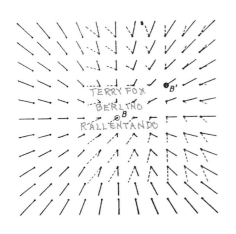

Fox, Terry [S]

Title: BERLINO / RALLENTANDO

Perf.: Terry Fox, Paul Panhuysen, Jan van Riet, Mario van Horrik

ø 30cm, 33 RPM, 1988, Het Apollohuis, Eindhoven, Apollo Records AR 088807

Cover: b/w, diagram from a book found by Terry Fox in a Berlin fleamarket 1980

LP with Folder (enclosed)

Fox, Terry

→ Airwaves
→ Sound
→ Revolutions Per Minute

La France à la Biennale [S]

Contents: Pierre Bertrand: Un camion freine - Voiture de police - La musique passe. Sarkis: "Sérénades opus 2" pour 12 kornemuses. A "ma mémoire est ma patrie". Christian Boltanski: Reconstitution de chansons qui ont été chantées a Christian Boltanski entre 1944 et 1946. Bertrand Lavier: Madrugada / Reine de musette. Daniel Buren: L'Indicible

ø 25cm, 33 RPM, 1985, Association Française d'Action Artistique Paris

Cover: gatefold, three-color print, design: MINIMUM

Included pamphlet, 16 pages (n.pag.), with illustrations and texts (Spanish, French, English) by Michel Nuridsany about the artists
The record was produced on occasion of the Biennale in São Paulo (October, 4 - December, 15, 1985)

Franken, Ruth

→ Bernard Heidsieck

Fréchette, Jean-Yves

→ Sound Poetry

STENCILLED LETTERS ON WHITE JACKET 1960's

STENCILLED LETTERS ON BLACK JACKET 1760's

Friedman, Ken [O]

Title: Zen For Record

A phonograph record with no sound on it (1966). A prototype of *Zen for Record* was made with a blank record acquired at E.S.P.Disk Records while Ken Friedman worked there in September / October 1966. Variant versions were made with blank, empty record jackets and with painted records and jackets. The piece is an oblique homage to Nam June Paik's *Zen for Film*.

Fritsch, Katharina [S]

Title: Regen

ø 30cm, 33 RPM, 1987, Verlag der Buchhandlung Walther König, Köln

Cover: two-color print

Regen

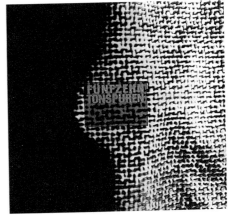

Fünfzehn Tonspuren [C/S]

Contents: Hans Weigand: Blue. Gudrun Bielz: Kid-Ding. Lisi + Rose Breuss: Ezechiel. Karl Kowanz: Beherztes Geschwätz. Tommy Schneider: Tausend X Täglich. Rupert Putz: Ai-No Korida. Inge Graf + ZYX: Automaten-Programm Tempo 127. Ebba Sinzinger + Anna Petschinka: Alle Niederreissen. Christina Brandauer + Ralph Ralph: Lektion 7. Helmut Rainer: Twang. Gary Texas: Black Helicopterlanding. Eva Schlegel: F→T (TV-Break). Romana Scheffknecht + Ecke Bonk: Proben für ein Finale. Günther Schrom: Schnucki Alpha Adaption?. Felix Dorner und Gäste: In den Rossbreiten

ø 30cm, 33 RPM, 1984, Hochschule für angewandte Kunst, Wien (Oberhuber / Kowanz)

Cover: three-color print

15 sound-tracks for fifteen non-materialized S-8 films + videos

Fuller, R. Buckminster

→ Revolutions Per Minute

Fullman, Ellen [S]

Title: The Long String Instrument

Contents: Woven processional. Langzaam. Swingen. Memory of a Big Room (For Matthew). Dripping music

Perf.: Ellen Fullman, Arnold Dreyblatt as guestperformer

ø 30cm, 33 RPM, 1985, Het Apollohuis, Eindhoven, AR 11 85 01

Cover: b/w, design: Ton Homburg / Hans Arnold

My interest in sound began by using contact microphones to amplify objects. I made collages of these sounds with tape machines and used them in performances. I gradually developed an interest in tonality, yet had no desire to play a traditional instrument. My previous background in sculpture and in performance art coelesced in the making of my own instruments...

Ellen Fullman (Excerpt from covertext)

Futurism
→ musica futurista

Gabo, Naum / [P/S]
Noton Pevsner

Title: The Realistic Manifesto (1920) Read by Gabo

ø 20cm, 16 RPM, as supplement in Aspen Magazine No. 5 + 6, New York, 1967
Posted in Moscow, Aug. 5, 1920; Recorded by Aspen, November 1967

Gagnon, Jean-Claude
→ Sound Poetry

Galas, Diamanda
→ Giorno Poetry Systems

Galas, Philip-Dimitri
→ High Performance

Garnier, Ilse
→ Sound Poetry
→ Voices Notes & Noise

Garnier, Pierre
→ Sound Poetry

Geile Tiere [S]

Title: Geile Tiere. Chinatown

Perf.: Salomé, Luciano Castelli, Luise, Yoshio Yabara (voc)

ø 17cm, 45 RPM, 1980, Salomé, Berlin

Cover: b/w with a photo by Scirocco

Geile Tiere [O/S]

Title: Geile Tiere Berlin

Contents: Berlin Nite. Neon Herz. U-Bahn. Whiskybar. Johnny

Perf.: Salomé (voc), Luis Walter (voc), Luciano Castelli (b, g), Udo Jünemann (perc), Eschi Rehm (g, syn, p, org, choir)

ø 25cm, 33 RPM, 1980, Geile Tiere Records Berlin, No. C 81

Cover: red printed plastic carrying-bag (33 x 28 cm), design: Geile Tiere, with a photo by Scirocco

Geile Tiere [C/S]

Contents: Rosa/Hellblau. Ich bin ein Huhn. Place des alpes. Liebst du mich? Supergeil. Plastic. Ausbildung. Interview. Kein Gefühl. Just in case. Love you (live)

ø 30cm, 33 RPM, 1981, GeeBeeDee, GBD 0022

Cover: two-color print, design based on an idea of Salomé and Castelli

Geissbühler, Rolf
→ Sound Poetry

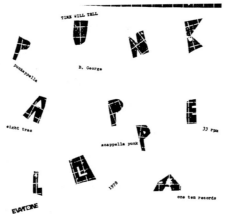

Genzken, Isa [O/S]

Title: Tri-Star

ø 17cm, 45 RPM, 1979, Düsselton Düsseldorf, No. TS 2779

75 copies of the issue numbered, painted grey on one side, signed and dated (Oct. 81) by Gerhard Richter, black cover

George, Bob [S]

Title: acapella punk. punkappella

transparent flexidisc, ø 17cm, 33 RPM, instead of label a circle of paperclips, One ten records, New York, 1978

Cover: b/w

Direction: Mono, Solo, Play Yery Loud

George, Bob
→ Voices Notes & Noise

George, Ron
→ Sound

Gernes, Paul
→ Henning Christiansen

Gerrets, Borris
→ Perfo 2

Gette, Paul Armand
→ Bernard Heidsieck

Giacomucci, Ubaldo
→ Sound Poetry
→ Voices Notes & Noise

Gibbs, Michael
→ Sound Poetry

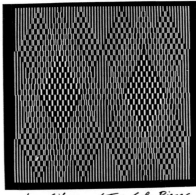

Jon Gibson / Two Solo Pieces

Gibson, Jon [C/S]

Title: Two Solo Pieces

Contents: Cycles (1973). Untitled (1974)

Perf.: Jon Gibson (org, alto-fl)

ø 30cm, 33 RPM, 1977, Chatham Square Records

Cover: frontside with a graphic score by Jon Gibson, backside with photo and text information, design: Katherine Landman

Gils, Gust
→ Sound Poetry

Ginsberg, Allen
→ Giorno Poetry Systems
→ Sound Poetry

Giorno, John
→ Art By Telephone
→ Giorno Poetry Systems
→ Sound Poetry

Giorno Poetry Systems Records
The Dial - A - Poem Poets, New York

Open the lines to the poets! We used the telephone for poetry. They used it to spy on you. Poetry plumbers unite! We invite you to do it yourself. Start your own Dial-A-Poem in your own hometown. Get hooked up to the telephones. Call your local telephone company business office; order a system and put on it these LP selections; put on your own local poets and we'll supply you with more poets.

Excerpt from covertext

Selected discography:

Title: Disconnected

2 LPs, ø 30cm, 33 RPM (GPS-003), 1974
Contributions by: Charles Amirkhanian, John Ashbery, Imamu Amiri Baraka, Bill Berkson, Paul Blackburn, Joe Brainard, Michael Brownstein, William S. Burroughs, John Cage, Jim Carroll, Tom Clark, Clark Coolidge, Gregory Corso, Robert Creeley, Diane Di Prima, Ed Dorn, Larry Fagin, Allen Ginsberg, John Giorno, Frank Lima, Michael McClure, Gerard Malanga, Frank O'Hara, Charles Olson, Peter Orlovsky, Maureen Owen, Ron Padgett, John Perreault, Charles Plymell, Ed Sanders, Jack Spicer, Lorenzo

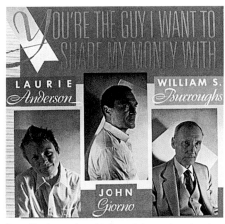

Thomas, Chogyam Trungpa Rinpoche, Diane Wakoski, Anne Waldman, Philip Whalen, John Wieners

Title: Biting off the Tongue of a Corpse

LP, ø 30cm, 33 RPM (GPS-005), 1975
Contributions by: Helen Adam, John Ashbery, Ted Berrigan, William S. Burroughs, John Cage, Edwin Denby, Diane Di Prima, Robert Duncan, John Giorno, Kenneth Koch, Denise Levertov, Frank O'Hara, Charles Olson, Ed Sanders, Charles Stein, Gary Snyder, John Wieners

Title: A D'ARC PRESS SELECTION

2 LPs, ø 30cm, 33 RPM (GPS 006-007), 1975
William S. Burroughs / John Giorno

Title: Totally Corrupt

2 LPs, ø 30cm, 33 RPM (GPS 008-009), 1976
Contributions by: Charles Amirkhanian, Imamu Amiri Baraka, Ted Berrigan, Michael Brownstein, Charles Bukowski, William S. Burroughs, John Cage, Jackie Curtis, Ed Dorn, Allen Ginsberg, John Giorno, Bernard Heidsieck, Susan Howe, Erica Huggins, Ken Kesey, Bill Knott, Joanne Kyger, Michael McClure, Jackson MacLow, Taylor Mead, Frank O'Hara, Charles Olson, Maureen Owen, Rochelle Owens, Sylvia Plath, Jerome Rothenberg, Ed Sanders, Jack Spicer, Tony Towle, Anne Waldman, Tom Weatherly, William Carlos Williams

Title: A Kulchur Selection

2 LPs, ø 30cm, 33 RPM (GPS 010-011), 1977
John Giorno / Anne Waldmann

Title: Big Ego

2 LPs, ø 30cm, 33 RPM (GPS 012-013), 1978

Contributions by: Helen Adam, Laurie Anderson, Robert Ashley, Jim Brodey, Otis Brown, William S. Burroughs, Jackie Curtis, Mona Da Vinci, Kenward Elmslie, The Fugs, John Giorno, Philip Glass, Anthony J. Gnazzo, Ted Greenwald, Steve Hamilton, Bernard Heidsieck, Joe Johnson, Michael Lally, Denise Levertov, Robert Lowell, Meredith Monk, Eileen Myles, Frank O'Hara, Claes Oldenburg, Joel Oppenheimer, Ron Padgett, Ishmael Reed, Ed Sanders, Harris Schiff, Patti Smith, Lorenzo Thomas, Steve & Gloria Tropp, Anne Waldman, Larry Wendt, Robert Wilson & Christopher Knowles

Title: The Nova Convention

2 LPs, ø 30cm, 33 RPM (GPS 014-015), 1979
Contributions by: Laurie Anderson, William S. Burroughs, John Cage, Allen Ginsberg, John Giorno, Philip Glass, Brion Gysin, Julia Heyward, Timothy Leary, Les Levine, Peter Orlovsky, Ed Sanders, Patti Smith, Terry Southern, Anne Waldman, Robert Anton Wilson, Frank Zappa

Title: Sugar, Alcohol & Meat

2 LPs, ø 30cm, 33 RPM (GPS 018-019), 1980
Contributions by: Kathy Acker, Miguel Algarin, Beth Anderson, John Ashbery, Barbara Barg, Regina Beck, Charles Bernstein, Ted Berrigan, William S. Burroughs, William S. Burroughs Jr., John Cage, Tom Carey, Charlotte Carter, Didi Susan Dubelyew, Cliff Fyman, Allen Ginsberg, John Giorno, Daniela Gioseffi, Bernard Heidsieck, Peter Gordon, Bob Holman, Rochelle Kraut, Mitchell Kreigman, Steve McCaffery, Robin Messing, Charlie Morrow, Eileen Myles, The Nuyorican Poets, Miguel Piñero, Ron Padgett, Rene Ricard, Patti Smith, Gary Snyder, Ned Sublette, Paul Violi, Andrei Vosnesensky, Anne Waldman

Title: You're The Guy I Want To Share My Money With

2 LPs, ø 30cm, 33 RPM (GPS 020-021), 1981
Contributions by: Laurie Anderson, William S. Burroughs, John Giorno

Title: Who You Staring At?

LP, ø 30cm, 33 RPM (GPS 025), 1982
Glenn Branca / John Giorno

Title: Life Is A Killer

LP, ø 30 cm, 33 RPM (GPS 027), 1982
Contributions by: Amiri Baraka, Brion Gysin, William S. Burroughs, Rose Lesniak, Jim Carroll, Ned Sublette, Jayne Cortez, Four Horsemen, John Giorno

Title: You're a Hook. The 15 Year Anniversary Of Dial-A-Poem

LP, ø 30cm, 33 RPM (GPS 030), 1983
Contributions by: Laurie Anderson, William S. Burroughs, Jim Carroll, Allen Ginsberg, John Giorno, Philip Glass, Lenny Kaye, Patti Smith, Frank Zappa

Title: Lenny Kaye Connection: I've Got A Right

LP, ø 30cm, 33 RPM (GPS 032), 1984

Title: Better An Old Demon Than A New God

LP, ø 30cm, 33 RPM (GPS 033), 1984
Contributions by: David Johansen, John Giorno, William S. Burroughs, Psychic TV, Lydia Lunch, Meredith Monk, Jim Carroll, Anne Waldman, Richard Hell, Arto Lindsay

Title: A Diamond Hidden In The Mouth Of A Corpse

LP, ø 30cm, 33 RPM (GPS 035), 1985
Contributions by: Hüsker Dü, David Johan-

sen, John Giorno Band, William S. Burroughs, Sonic Youth, Cabaret Voltaire, Diamanda Galas, Coil, Michael Gira, David van Tieghem, Jessica Hagedorn & The Gangster Choir

Title: Smack My Crack

LP, ø 30cm, 33 RPM (GPS 038), 1987
Contributions by: Butthole Surfers, Einstürzende Neubauten, Diamanda Galas, William S. Burroughs, Swans, John Giorno Band, Chad & Sudan, Tom Waits, Chris Stein, Nick Cave

Girouard, Tina
→　　Lawrence Weiner / Richard Landry

Giroud, Michel
→　　Sound Poetry

Glass Jr., Jesse
→　　Sound Poetry

Glass, Philip / Robert Wilson　　　　　[S]

Title: Einstein on the Beach
(An opera in four acts)

Contents: Knee Play 1. Act I: Train. Trial. Knee Play 2. Act II: Dance 1. Night Train. Knee Play 3. Act III: Trial/Prison. Dance 2. Knee Play 4. Act IV: Building/Train. Bed. Spaceship. Knee Play 5

Philip Glass (Music / Lyrics)
Robert Wilson (Design / Direction)

Perf.: Philip Glass Ensemble: Jon Gibson (ss, fl), Philip Glass (org), Iris Hiskey (voc), Richard Landry (fl, ss,b-cl), Kurt Munkacsi (sound mix), Richard Peck (as, fl), Michael Riesman (org, syn bass, additional keyboard)

Small Chorus, Large Chorus
Actors: Lucinda Childs, Samuel M. Johnson, Paul Mann, Sheryl Sutton
Christopher Knowles (voice)
Paul Zukofsky (v)

Box with 4 LPs, 33 RPM, The Tomato Music Company, New York, 1979, second edition CBS Masterworks No. M4 38875

Cover: multi-color print, design: Milton Glaser

Included booklet (24 p.) with texts and photos.
This recording contains all the music, lyrics and speeches from the original production of *Einstein on the Beach* as performed in Europe in the Summer and Fall of 1976 and at the Metropolitan Opera House in New York City in November 1976.

Glass, Philip
→　　Giorno Poetry Systems

Goedhart, Johan
→　　Paul Panhuysen

Goldstein, Jack　　　　　[O/S]

Series of 10 sound effect records, ø 17 cm, 45 RPM, in different colors, Jack Goldstein, New Yorck. Cover: b/w

A German Shepherd, 1976, No. 45-7610
A Swim Against the Tide, 1976, No. 45-7611
A Faster Run, 1976, No. 45-7612
The Tornado, 1976, No. 457613
Two Wrestling Cats, 1976, No. 45-7614
Three Felled Trees, 1976, No. 45-7615
The Lost Ocean Liner, 1976, No. 45-7616
The Burning Forest, 1976, No. 45-7617
The Dying Wind, 1976, No. 45-7618
The Six Minute Drown, 1977, No. 45-7619

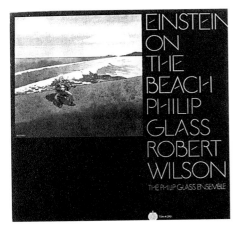

THE BURNING FOREST

© Jack Goldstein, 1976

Sound effect records create a picture of a fragmented part of nature. This fragmented part of nature, as record, is a picture in place of its fragmentation.
Without distance one hears too many indiscernible things. Sound is the space that frames an image as image from its object. Sound is the time of image that locates the spectator outside. Sound is the silence of image that limits the image as finite. Sound is the distance of image that defines dark from light. Sound is the memory of image that dislocates the origin from it's object. Sound is the location of image that fixes the image in time.

Jack Goldstein in *Extended Play* (cat.) New York 1988

Goldstein, Jack　　　　　[S]

The Quivering Earth. 1977, ø 30cm + rim, 33 RPM
The Murder. 1977, ø 30cm, 33 RPM
The Unknown Dimension. 1978, ø 30cm

Goldstein, Jack　　　　　[S]

Title: Planets

6 records, ø 25cm, 33 RPM, n.d. (1986), in a brown painted box. The records have black labels without defining text anywhere, they are packed in green protective covers. Neutral Records, New York, No. 7

Collected from special effects sound libraries, the music - like Jack Goldstein's paintings - communicates in images. The records are "spaces" for the imagination. Recollections of half-forgotten sci-fi soundtracks, they hover between the known and the unknown. The sound/images are shadowy remembrances gleaned from our all available culture of surveillance. In their

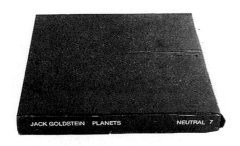

recorded form they bear only a shadow of their former cultural life (of soundtrack movie music).

From: New Music Distribution Service, Annual 1986

Gomringer, Eugen
→ Sound Poetry

Gordh, Bill
→ High Performance

Gordon, Jeff
→ Artsounds Collection

Gordon, Jim
→ Sound

Gordon, Peter   [C/S]

Title: Love of Life Orchestra

Music: Gordon, Peter

Contents: Beginning of the heartbreak. Don't don't. Extended niceties. Reprise

Perf.:   Love of Life Orchestra: Peter Gordon (keyboard), David Van Tieghem (dr, perc, synare) with David Wooford; Ernie Brooks (b), Randy Gun, Larry Saltzman, David Byrne, Arto Lindsay (g), Rik Albani (tp)

           ø 30 cm, 45 RPM, 1980

Cover: two-color print, concept: Laurie Anderson/Peter Gordon, design: Catherine Churko according to a photo and video by John Sanborn

Gordon, Peter   [C/S]

Title: Love of Life Orchestra. Casino

Music: Peter Gordon, David Van Tieghem

Contents: Siberia. Casino. Jocks on Ice$_o$. Roses on Bond Street. Condo. Jocks on Ice$_{oo}$

Perf.:   Love of Life Orchestra: Peter Gordon (sax, syn, org, p, voc), David Van Tieghem (dr, acoustical perc, marimba, syn, voc, shortwave radio) and guest musicians

           ø 30cm, 45 RPM, 1982, Expanded Music, Bologna, Italia

Cover: two-color print, design: Peter Gordon, Anna Persiani and Oderso, including a cover photo by Paolo Pellion di Persano of Joan Jonas in performance of Robert Ashley's Atalanta in Genazzano, Italy

Gordon, Peter
→ Giorno Poetry Systems
→ Lawrence Weiner

Goufas, Alexis
→ Sound Poetry

Goulart, Claudio
→ Perfo 2

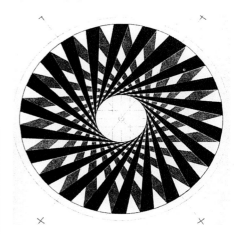

Graf, Franz   [O/S]

Title: Picture-Disc

Music: Franz Graf / Johanna Arneth

           ø 30cm, 33 RPM, limited edition of 540, stamped, numbered and signed, Kunstverein für die Rheinlande und Westfalen, Düsseldorf, Jahresgabe 1988

Cover: b/w

Graf, Inge
→ Fünfzehn Tonspuren

DAN GRAHAM

PAVILIONS

12. März – 17. April 1983

KUNSTHALLE BERN

Graham, Dan [P/S]

Title: Pavilions

Music: Glenn Branca

Catalogue (27 x 21 cm) with record, ø 17cm, 45 RPM, *Acoustic Phenomena*, Kunsthalle Bern, 1983

Direction: "Play loud"

Graham, Dan
→ Aspen Magazine

Graham, Roberta
→ Perfo 2

Greenham, Lily
→ Sound Poetry

Greenham, Peter
→ Sound Poetry

Grimmer, Mineko
→ Artsounds Collection

Groh, Klaus
→ Sound Poetry

Grosvenor, Robert
→ Art By Telephone

Gruen, Bob
→ Artsounds Collection

Grupo Texto Poetico
→ Sound Poetry

The Guerrilla Art Action Group
→ Radiotaxi

Guhl, Andy
→ Norbert Möslang

Gusella, Ernest [S]

Title: JAPANESE TWINS AND WHITE MAN

Contents: Star In The Art Whirl. Down On The Forsyth Street. Stinkin' Badges. Andy Warhol. Words. Dirty Ernie Hates Clams. The Bride Stripped Bare. Voice From The Underground. Punch-Up Of 1912. Arrows

Perf.: Ernest Gusella (words and music),

ø 30cm, 33 RPM, 1977, Tomiyo Sasaki for Ear Wax Records, New York

Cover: b/w with portrait photos of the artist by Gabe Tellez

Gutmann, Benny KH [O]

Title: Schallplatte. Schalldämpfer. 1986

Partitur für Schallplatte und Schalldämpfer
Score for disc (soundproducer) and sound absorber

1. Condition: Water is continually dripping, at a certain time interval, from a height of about two meters into a drinking glass.

2. The disc (sheet zinc ø 30cm) is placed on the glass. The water is dripping onto the sheet zinc, the glass amplifies the dripping acoustically.
Playing time: Until the disc is completely covered with water.

3. Use of the sound absorbers: Up to 20 newspaper clippings (ø 30cm) are piled one by one on top of the sheet zinc until the impact of the waterdrops cannot be heard anymore.

Benny KH Gutmann

Gysin, Brion
→ Giorno Poetry Systems
→ Revue OU
→ Sound Poetry

Haacke, Hans
→ Art By Telephone

Haimsohn, Jana
→ Airwaves

Hamilton, Richard [C]

Title: The Beatles

Music: The Beatles

2 LPs, ø 30cm, 33 RPM, 1968, Apple Records, London, 1C 192-04173/4

Cover: gatefold, white with imprinted title and serial number

Included poster with texts, photos and four color-starphotos

Hamilton, Richard
→ Art By Telephone

Hammarberg-Åkesson, Jarl and Sonja
→ Sound Poetry

Hanimann, Alex
→ Norbert Möslang

Hanson, Sten
→ Sound Poetry
→ Revue OU

Harding, Bill
→ High Performance

Harrison, Helen and Newton
→ Revolutions Per Minute

Harrison, Margaret
→ Revolutions Per Minute

Hausmann, Raoul
→ dada For Now
→ Revue OU
→ Sound Poetry

Hayman, R.I.P   [O]

Title: ∞ Disc Design, 1983
design for random endless play record

This is a design for an endless random play record. It allows the ballistics of stylus action to create music by the disc medium itself. The sound material would be flute, voice, and drum cut onto the disc in segments. Realization of a pressable master would require the combination of a finer computer design interfaced to direct a disc master lathe with variable motion cutting head.
Once pressed the disc could be played by any turntable. Each turntable would track differently by its minute difference in skating action.

The design is based upon my work at Sterling Sound mastering studios with Robert Ludwig and CBS Records studios with Daniel Lentz. Graphic by Jujana Easterly

R.I.P. Haymann in *Extended Play* (cat.) New York 1988

Hamilton, Richard /   [C/S]
Dieter Roth

Title: Canciones de Cadaques

Contents: Barks from Cadaques. Hundelieder

Perf.: Chispas Luis (voc), Richard Hamilton, Dieter Roth (voc, g)

2 singles, ø 17cm, 45 RPM, 1976, limited edition of 500, 60 copies numbered and signed, Hansjörg Mayer Stuttgart / London / Reykjavik and Galeria Cadaques

Cover: gatefold, multi-color print, photos by Rita Donagh

Heidsieck, Bernard   [P/S]

Title: Partition V

Contents: Poème-partition. Poème-partition B2 B3. Le quatrième plan. La pénétration. La convention collective. La cage. La mer est grosse. Quel age avez-vous? Bilan ou macher ses mots. La semaine. Ruth Franken a téléphoné

book (19 x 19 cm, 149 p.), 6 included flexidiscs (ø 17 cm, 33 RPM), limited edition of 1125, 1-250 signed and numbered, Le Soleil Noir, Paris (= Le Soleil Noir, No. 132), 1973

Cover: 1 included flexidisc, design: Ruth Franken

Heidsieck, Bernard [P/S]

Title: D 2 + D 3 Z. Poèmes Partitions. 1958 1961

Contents: Poème-Partition D 2 (11 poèmes sur des peintures de Jean Degottex). Poème Partition D 3 Z (3 mouvements sur 7 Métasignes de Jean Degottex)

book (26,5 x 21 cm), 96 p.(n.pag.), 2 singles as supplement (ø 17cm, 33 RPM), limited edition of 550, printed for Henry Chopin and his Collection OU, 1973

Heidsieck, Bernard [P/S]

with G. Bertini and P.A. Gette

Title: Poème partition B 2 B 3. Exorcisme

book (21 x 18 cm), 16 p.(n.pag.), included flexidisc (ø 17cm, 45 RPM), limited edition of 60, signed and numbered by the artist, Edition du Castel Rose, Collection "L'Ornière", Paris, 1964

Heidsieck, Bernard [S]

Title: Trois Biopsies + Un Passe-Partout

Contents: Qui je suis: 1 minute. Portrait-Pétales. Couper n'est pas jouer. La Poinçonneuse. 1967-70

ø 30cm, 33 RPM, Multi-Techniques, Paris

Cover: b/w

Heidsieck, Bernard / Françoise Janicot [S]

Title: Encoconnage

Contents: passe-partout no 9 / version no 1 (1971-72). passe-partout no 9 / version no 3 (1971-72)

ø 30cm, 33 RPM, 1974, limited edition of 500, numbered and signed by Françoise Janicot and Bernard Heidsieck, Guy Schraenen Antwerpen, D / 1974 / 2059/3

Cover: b/w, gatefold with attached documentation 12 p.(n.pag.): reproductions of photos made during the performance of Françoise Janicot, scores and textsheet

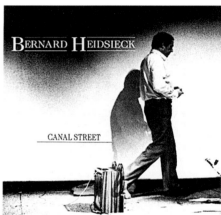

Heidsieck, Bernard [S]

Title: Canal Street. 1974-1976

Contents: Canal Street 1, 2, 3, 4, 5, 6, 7, 8, 9, 10, 11, 12, 13, 14, 15, 16, 17, 18, 19, 20, 21, 22, 23, 24, 25, 26, 27, 28, 29, 30, 31, 32, 33, 34, 35

box with 3 LPs, 33 RPM, 1986, limited edition of 550, signed and numbered

Cover: b/w

2 included sheets with texts and photos

Premier temps
New York. Mai 1973. Canal Street...et son double flot inversé, ininterrompu, vacarme dingue, de camions et de camions, de camions et de camions, de camions et de camions, toutes tailles, marques, catégories and Co.
Canal Street, trottoir de droite en direction du Bowery: une promenade, à pas crispés/ nonchalants, une promenade, oui, un instant tout simple de tiède laisser-aller, énergétique cependant, aigu/tendu, dans ce

bain flou/net de vapeur d'essence et de foule.

L'évocation de ce lieu impose ici et maintenant, celle de George Maciunas, disparu il y a moins d'un mois, bouillonnant <boss> de FLUXUS. C'est en effet d'une boutique spécialisée dans la vente d'objets en plastique, située sur le trottoir d'en face, à la même hauteur, que proviennent, notamment, les célèbres boîtes Fluxus, réalisées par les différents éléments du groupe et dont il assurait la diffusion.

Bernard Heidsieck (Excerpt from included text)

Heidsieck, Bernard [S]

Title:	Poème Partition B2 B3 "Exorcisme"
	ø 17cm, 45 RPM, 1962

Heidsieck, Bernard

→ Giorno Poetry Systems
→ Radiotaxi
→ Revue OU
→ Sound Poetry

Heimes, Jürgen

→ Das ist Schönheit

Heino [C]

Title:	Alpenglühen. Blau, Blau, Blau blüht der Enzian
	ø 30cm, 45 RPM, 1985, Virgin Records, No. 602 052

Special edition of 500 copies, white, with a feltpen-drawing by Heino, signed, numbered and with a stamp: "völlig harmlos"

Das Heinrich-Mucken Saalorchester [P/S]

Title:	Frühling-Weg. Sommer-Orchesterprozesse. Herbst-Weg. Winter-Landwehr
Perf.:	Claus van Bebber, Karl van Betteraey, Michael Breihann, Clemens Drissen, Kerstin Kühn, Helmut Lemke, Heiner Linne, Leo Neikes, Dieter Schlensog, Karl Schlüter, Joachim Schwarz, Henning Schweichel, Klaus Seelig, Hans-Wilhelm Specht, Michael Vorfeld

Hans Ulrich Kreß / Rainer Weichert: *Jahreszeiten*. Künstler arbeiten in der Landschaft. Landart und Performance.
Book with enclosed single ø 17cm, 45 RPM, Edition Aragon, Moers, 1986

Recorded "live" during the Symposion *Jahreszeiten* 1985 Binnenheide / Winnekendonk

Heißenbüttel, Helmut

→ Sound Poetry

Helms, Hans G.

→ Sound Poetry

Heyward, Julia

→ Airwaves
→ Giorno Poetry Systems

Hidalgo, Juan [S]

Title:	TAMARAN.(Gocce di sperma per dodici pianoforti) 1974
Perf.:	Juan Hidalgo, assistance: Walter Marchetti
	ø 30cm, 33 RPM, 1974, Cramps Records, Milano, nova musicha n. 2
Cover:	gatefold, one-color print with photos by Antonio de Gregorio and Ummarino srl., covertext: Gianni-Emilio Simonetti

Inner sleeve with a photo and excerpt of musical score

Hidalgo, Juan [C/S]

Title:	Rrose Sélavy. 6 pezzi ammuffiti per 6 fontane sonore. Un eccetera ZAJ senza fine
Contents:	Rrose Sélavy (Solo). Belle Haleine. Rrose Sélavy (Trio). Eau de Voilette. Rrose Sélavy (Quintetto) L.H.O.O.Q.

ø 30cm, 33 RPM, 1977, Cramps Records, Milano, nova musicha n. 13

Cover: gatefold, one-color print, photos by Roberto Masotti, Adolfo Keim and Man Ray (Rrose Sélavy) on the cover and inner sleeve

Hidalgo, Juan
→ Walter Marchetti

Higgins, Dick
→ Art By Telephone
→ Sound Poetry

High Performance [P/S]
Title: Artists Doing Songs

With: Jo Harvey Allen, Terry Allen, Jacki Apple, Bob & Bob, Linda Burnham, Carole Caroompas, Philip-Dimitri Galas, Bill Gordh, Bill Harding, Citizen Kafka, Kipper Kids, Jill Kroesen, Paul McCarthy, Michael Peppe, Bill Talen, Johanna Went, Martha Wilson

2 LPs, ø 30cm, 33 RPM, High Performance, The Original Performance Art Magazine, Volume 6, No. 3, 1983

Cover: two-color print, gatefold

High Performance was established in 1977 by Linda Burnham as a quarterly primarily devoted to documentation and coverage of Performance Art (performance works by visual artists)

Hiller, Holger [S]
Title: Holger Hiller with Chris Lunch and Walter Thielsch

Contents: Ich kann nicht mehr warten. Ein ganz normaler Kuss. Dingdonggefühl. Herzmuskel. R IN S/W

ø 17 cm, 45 RPM, 1980, ATATAK, Düsseldorf, No. WR 004

274 AO-SONG
weniger Spielraum für die volle Entfaltung der Initiative lassen als die Angriffsoperationen.

Hiller, Holger / Walter Thielsch [C/S]
Title: Konzentration der Kräfte

Contents: Sieht leicht aus. Kleinere zu besiegen. Ernst und peinlich. Dann ist es das Wichtigste

ø 17cm, 45 RPM, RP 17117

Cover: two-color print

Hiller, Holger [S]
Title: Ein Bündel Fäulnis in der Grube

Contents: Liebe Beamtinnen und Beamte. Blass schlafen Rabe... Budapest - Bukarest. Jonny (du Lump). Hosen, die nicht aneinander passen. Akt mit Feile (für A.O.). Mütter der Fröhlichkeit. Chemische und physikalische Entdeckungen. Ein Bündel Fäulnis in der Grube. Das Feuer. Ein Hoch auf das Bügeln

Perf.: Holger Hiller, Moritz Oswald (perc), Jürgen Keller (b), Catherine Lienert (emulator)

ø 30 cm, 33 RPM, 1983, AtaTak Düsseldorf, No. WR 20

Cover: two-color print

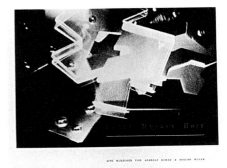

Hiller, Holger / Andreas Dorau [S]
Title: Guten Morgen Hose (Kurzoper)

Perf.: Andreas Dorau, Catherine Lienert, Moritz Reichelt, Hagar Groeteke,

Erika Kochs, Holger Hiller, Sol Rubio, Jochen Liedisch, Claudia Kaloff

ø 30cm, 45 RPM, 1984, AtaTak Düsseldorf, No. WR 28

Cover: two-color print, design: Feuer

Hiller, Holger
→ Claus Böhmler
→ Albert Oehlen
→ Das ist Schönheit

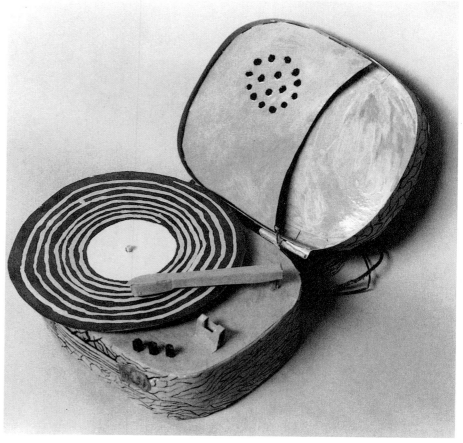

This is a RECORD COVER. This writing is the DESIGN upon the record cover. The DESIGN is to help SELL the record. We hope to draw your attention to it and encourage you to pick it up. When you have done that maybe you'll be persuaded to listen to the music - in this case XTC's Go 2 album. Then we want you to BUY it. The idea being that the more of you that buy this record the more money Virgin Records, the manager Ian Reid and XTC themselves will make. To the aforementioned this is known as PLEASURE. A good cover DESIGN is one that attracts more buyers and gives more pleasure. This writing is trying to pull you in much like an eye-catching picture. It is designed to get you to READ it. This is called luring the VICTIM, and you are the VICTIM. But if you have a free mind you should STOP READING NOW! because all we are attempting to do is to get you to read on. Yet this is a DOUBLE BIND because if you indeed stop you'll be doing what we tell you, and if you read on you'll be doing what we've wanted all along. And the more you read on the more you're falling for this simple device of telling you exactly how a good commercial design works. They're TRICKS and this is the worst TRICK of all since it's describing the TRICK whilst trying to TRICK you, and if you've read this far then you're TRICKED but you wouldn't have known this unless you'd read this far. At least we're telling you directly instead of seducing you with a beautiful or haunting visual that say never tell you. We're letting you know that you ought to buy this record because in essence it's a PRODUCT and PRODUCTS are to be consumed and you are a consumer and this is a good PRODUCT. We could have written the band's name in special lettering so that it stood out and you'd see it before you'd read any of this writing and possibly have bought it anyway. What we are really suggesting is that you are FOOLISH to buy or not buy an album merely as a consequence of the design on its cover. This is a con because if you agree then you'll probably like this writing - which is the cover design - and hence the album inside. But we've just warned you against that. The con is a con. A good cover design could be considered as one that gets you to buy the record, but that never actually happens to YOU because YOU know it's just a design for the cover. And this is the RECORD COVER.

Hipgnosis [C]

Title: Go 2

Music: XTC

ø 30cm, 33 RPM, 1978, Virgin Records, London V2108

Cover: b/w

4 pages supplement, multi-color print

Hirschbiegel, Oliver
→ Das ist Schönheit

Hobart, Jim
→ Sound

Hodell, Åke
→ Revue OU
→ Sound Poetry

Hofter, Sibylle [O]

Title: Plattenspieler. 1986

Portable cardboard recordplayer (32 x 24 x 12 cm), with cardboard record ø 27cm, painted in oil

Hollis, Doug
→ Sound

Hompson, Davi Det
→ Art By Telephone

Honegger, Arthur
→ dada For Now

Horobin, Pete
→ Voices Notes & Noise

Hubert, Pierre-Alain
→ Voices Notes & Noise

Hubaut, Joel
→ Sound Poetry

Huelsenbeck, Richard [P/S]

Title: Four Poems from Phantastische Gebete (1916)
Read by the author

ø 20cm, 33 RPM, as supplement in Aspen Magazine No. 5 + 6, New York, 1967

Huelsenbeck, Richard
→ dada For Now
→ Sound Poetry

This is a RECORD COVER. This writing is the DESIGN upon the record cover. The DESIGN is to help SELL the record. We hope to draw your attention to it and encourage you to pick it up. When you have done that maybe you'll be persuaded to listen to the music - in this case XTC's Go 2 album. Then we want you to BUY it. The idea being that the more of you that buy this record the more money Virgin Records, the manager Ian Reid and XTC themselves will make. To the aforementioned this is known as PLEASURE. A good cover DESIGN is one that attracts more buyers and gives more pleasure. This writing is trying to pull you in much like an eye-catching picture. It is designed to get you to READ IT. This is called luring the VICTIM, and you are the VICTIM. But if you have a free mind you should STOP READING NOW! because all we are attempting to do is to get you to read on. Yet this is a DOUBLE BIND because if you indeed stop you'll be doing what we tell you, and if you read on you'll be doing what we've wanted all along. And the more you read on the more you're falling for this simple device of telling you exactly how a good commercial design works. They're TRICKS and this is the worst TRICK of all since it's describing the TRICK whilst trying to TRICK you, and if you've read this far then you're TRICKED but you wouldn't have known this unless you'd read this far. At least we're telling you directly instead of seducing you with a beautiful or haunting visual that may never tell you. We're letting you know that you ought to buy this record because in essence it's a PRODUCT and PRODUCTS are to be consumed and you are a consumer and this is a good PRODUCT. We could have written the band's name in special lettering so that it stood out and you'd see it before you'd read any of this writing and possibly have bought it anyway. What we are really suggesting is that you are FOOLISH to buy or not buy an album merely as a consequence of the design on its cover. This is a con because if you agree then you'll probably like this writing - which is the cover design - and hence the album inside. But we've just warned you against that. The con is a con. A good cover design could be considered as one that gets you to buy the record, but that never actually happens to YOU because YOU know it's just a design for the cover. And this is the RECORD COVER.

Hipgnosis

von Huene, Stephan
→   The Sounds of Sound Sculpture

Hummel / Homeyer
→   Voices Notes & Noise

Hunt, Bryan
→   Word of Mouth

Huot, Robert
→   Art By Telephone

Hurst, Paul
→   Voices Notes & Noise

Hurtado, Eric and Marc
→   ÉTANT DONNÉS

Iannone, Dorothy   [C/P/S]

Title: I Am Tender I Am Just

Contents: Und Du, Herr Hoffmann. Follow Me

Perf.:   Dorothy Iannone (voc), Jochen Ruopp (p)

Single, ø 17cm, 45 RPM, as supplement to the catalogue *Follow Me*, 25 x 19,8 cm, in form of a leporello, Berliner Künstler-programm des DAAD, 1978

Immendorff, Jörg
→   Die Rache der Erinnerung

Insook
→   Das ist Schönheit

Isou, Isidore
→   Sound Poetry

Iwata, Hiroko
→   Sound Poetry

Jacobs, David
→   The Sounds of Sound Sculpture

Jacquet, Alain
→   Art By Telephone

James, Robin
→   Sound Poetry

Janco, Marcel
→   dada For Now
→   Sound Poetry

Jandl, Ernst
→   Sound Poetry

Janicot, Françoise
→   Bernard Heidsieck

Janssen, Servie
→   Perfo 2

Jelloun, Tahar Ben
→   Sound Poetry

Jenkins, Tom
→   Sound

Johnson, Bengt Emil
→   Revue OU
→   Sound Poetry

Johansson, Sven Åke   [C/S]

Title: Idylle und Katastrophen

Music: Sven Åke Johansson, Alexander von Schlippenbach a.o.

Perf.:   Sven ÅKe Johansson (voc, accordion, perc), Alexander von Schlippenbach (p, drahtklavier, celeste), Maarten Altena (double b, c), Derek Bailey (g, voc), Günter Christman (tb), Wolfgang Fuchs (b-cl, sopranino), Paul Lovens (perc, zither, säge), Candace Natvig (v, voc)

ø 30cm, 33 RPM, 1980, Po Torch Records, Aachen PTR/IWD6

Cover: multi-color print, according to a drawing by Marina Kern

Johansson, Sven Åke   [C/S]

Title: Kalfaktor A. Falke und andere Lieder

Music: Sven Åke Johansson, Alexander von Schlippenbach

Contents: Der Borkenkäfer. Weghobel. China-man (when you were in Europe). Der herrenlose Koffer. Alhambra-fliegen. Deutsches Pilsner. Kal-faktor A. Falke. Waldbelustigungen. Die als Bremse verkleidete Stech-fliege. Karamell-Socken. The Blue Tent. Spiegelung im Glas. Total Time. Kalifornische Rosinen. Das Nashorn und das Zebra. I'm Gonna Sit Right Down. Wo es weht. Pfiff

Perf.: Sven Åke Johansson (voc), Alexander von Schlippenbach (p)

ø 30cm, 33 RPM, 1982, Free Music Production, Berlin, FMP 0970

Cover: three-color print, design: Sven Åke Johansson

Johansson, Sven Åke [C/S]

Title: Blind aber hungrig - Norddeutsche Gesänge

Music: Sven Åke Johansson, Alexander von Schlippenbach

Contents: der einäugige Karpfen. meilenweit von dattelpalmen. Kleinbrahm. in den flachbaukonstruktionen. falsett-träger Bräll. moonshine über kal-tenkirchen. vorposten. herrlich ... blind aber hungrig

Perf.: Sven Åke Johansson (voc), Alexander von Schlippenbach (p)

ø 25cm, 33 RPM, 1986, Free Music Production, Berlin, FMP S15

Cover: two-color print, design: Sven Åke Johansson

Johansson, Sven Åke

→ Peter Brötzmann

Johns, Jasper [C]

Title: MUSIC FROM MILLS

These records were published: In Celebra-tion of the Centennial of the Chartering of Mills College 1885-1985. A selection of works featuring composers and performers from the Mills College Music Department and Center for Contemporary Music

Compositions by: Elinor Armer, Robert Ash-ley, David Behrman, Luciano Berio, Anthony Braxton, Dave Brubeck, Howard Brubeck, Janice Giteck, Anthony Gnazzo, Lou Harri-son, Katrina Krimsky, Darius Milhaud, Pandit Pran Nath, Pauline Oliveros, Maggi Payne, Larry Polansky, Steve Reich, Terry Riley, David Rosenboom, Ramon Sender, Morton Subotnick, "Blue" Gene Tyranny

3 LPs, ø 30cm, 33 RPM, 1986, Mills Col-lege, Oakland

Cover: b/w with a print of *The Critic Sees* by Jasper Johns, from the collec-tion of the Mills College Art Gallery

Johns, Jasper

→ John Cage
→ Record of Interviews

Johnson, Philip

→ Artsounds Collection

Jones, Christine

→ Attersee

Jonas, Joan

→ Word Of Mouth

Jones, Jim

→ The Artists' Jazz Band

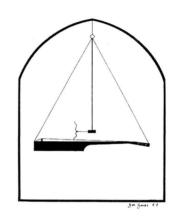

Jones, Joe [C/S]

Title: Joe Jones in Performance. Tone Deaf Musik Co.

Perf.: Joe Jones and music machines

ø 30cm, 33 RPM, 1977, limited edition of 500, numbered and signed, Harlekin Art records, Wies-baden

Cover: one-color silk-screen print based on a drawing of the artist

Jones, Joe

→ Yoko Ono

Jongsma, Hans

→ Perfo 2

Jori, Marcello

→ Radiotaxi

Julius [C/S]

Title: Walzer für ein Dreieck

Edition Giannozzo - Berlin

JULIUS: WALZER FÜR EIN DREIECK

Contents: Walzer für ein Dreieck. Afrikan. Klavierkonzert No. 2. Konzert für eine große Wiese. Elefantenmusik

ø 17cm, 45 RPM, 1982, Edition Gianozzo Berlin

Cover: b/w, design: Julius

Limited edition of 100, single with 6 sheets of texts and information in a white box (19,5 x 19,5 cm)

JULIUS

'Lullaby for the fishes'

Julius [S]

Title: Lullaby for the fishes

Contents: Musiklinie - Konzert für einen Strand. Lullaby for the fishes. Lied für einen Morgen. Altes Klavierkonzert (für die Weser). Zwergenmusik. Minutenblues

ø 30cm, 33 RPM, 1985, Künstlerhaus Bethanien, Berlin, No. 66.23713

Cover: b/w, design: Ton Homburg, Hans Arnold

JULIUS is the archetypal "sound artist". He paints with sound, he colors with pitch, and his work demands the attention and open-mindedness who embrace modern art. He collects found sounds, and mixes them with prerecorded single tone notes which are then, electronically modified and filtered through tiny loudspeakers, becoming transformed into music. Depending on the surface texture where the loudspeaker has been placed - wall, floor or outdoors - these objects resonate and "breathe" sound. His music is a mixture of all these sounds; a carefully calculated and conceived creation. He sculpts sound to define space, creating a musical environment where subtle changes occur.

Brooke Wentz (Excerpt from covertext)

Julius
→   Views beside...

Jung, Dieter [C]

Title: Friedrich Nietzsche Klaviermusik

Music: Friedrich Nietzsche

Perf.: Jorge Zulueta (p)

ø 30cm, 33 RPM, 1980, Edition Theater am Turm Frankfurt, No. PHL 8001

Cover: multi-color print

Includes information sheet

FRIEDRICH NIETZSCHE KLAVIERMUSIK
JORGE ZULUETA

EDITION

Jung, Dieter [C]

Title: Friedrich Nietzsche Lieder

Music: Friedrich Nietzsche

Perf.: Angela Dellert, Judy Roberts (voc), Peter Hahn (voice), Jorge Zulueta (p)

ø 30cm, 33 RPM, 1981, Edition Theater am Turm Frankfurt, No. PHL 8003

Cover: multi-color print, design: Dieter Jung

Included song texts

Jupitter-Larsen, Gerald
→   Sound Poetry

Just Another Asshole [P/S]

with contributions by about 80 artists
No. 5 of the magazine Just Another Asshole as a record, ø 30cm, 33 RPM, n.d.(1981)
Editors: Barbara Ess and Glenn Branca

Cover: b/w

Kafka, Citizen
→   High Performance

Kagel, Mauricio [S]

Title: Staatstheater. (Scenic Composition)

Contents: repertoire (Scenic Concert Piece). einspielungen (Music for Loudspeakers). ensemble (Music for sixteen voices). debüt (for sixty voices). saison (Sing-Spiel in 65 Tableaux). spielplan (Instrumental Music in Action). Kontra→danse (Ballet for

Mauricio Kagel

Der Umweg zur Höheren SubFidelität

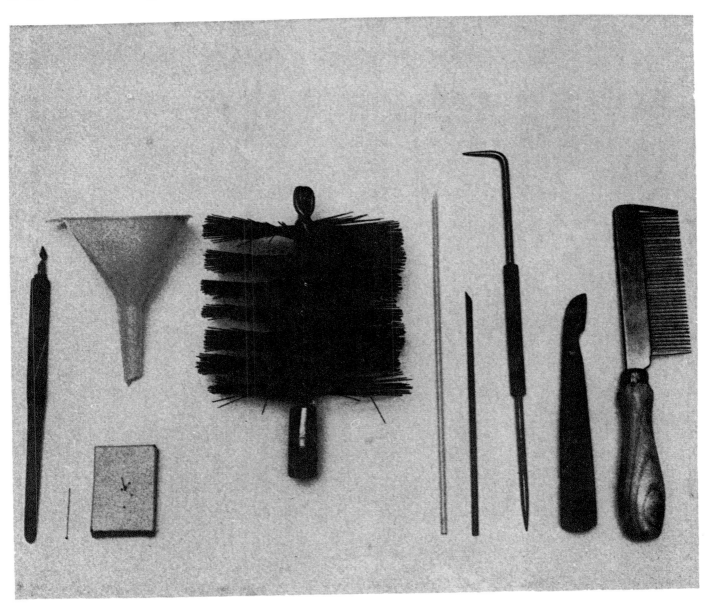

Noch immer legt die überwiegende Mehrzahl der Musikfreunde in aller Welt bei Stereo-Wiedergabe im Heim eine Kunststoffscheibe auf den Plattenteller, deren Tonschrift mit der Spitze eines Tonabnehmers abgetastet wird. Alle Anzeichen sprechen dafür, daß dies auch noch während längerer Zeit so bleibt. Hier eine Neuentwicklung, die in ihrer Preisklasse echte Maßstäbe setzt. Präzision steckt in jedem dieser Tonabnehmer. Auch im kleinsten und preiswertesten.

Zur subjektiven Prüfung des Jaulens und Wimmerns eines Plattenspielers eignet sich am besten Klaviermusik, vorzugsweise langsame Passagen mit lang ausgehaltenen Tönen. Eine gewisse Art des Jaulens wird besonders gut hörbar bei Solostellen von Holzblasinstrumenten, zum Beispiel der Klarinette.

Die besten Tonabnehmerpatronen (es sind auch immer die teuersten) arbeiten für gewöhnlich selbst bei der niedrigsten für sie angegebenen Auflagekraft noch einwandfrei, sofern sie in Tonarmen höchster Qualität verwendet werden. Bei der Festlegung der Auflagekraft für einen Tonabnehmer ist es im allgemeinen am günstigsten, mit dem höchsten zulässigen Wert zu beginnen und schrittweise die Auflagekraft so lange herabzusetzen, bis diejenige Einstellung gefunden ist, bei der die Patrone in dem verwendeten Tonarm am besten arbeitet. Bevor man diese Einstellung endgültig beläßt, führt man zweckmäßigerweise noch eine Überprüfung mit der am schwierigsten abzuspielenden Platte des eigenen Repertoires durch; es ist diejenige mit den lautesten und orchestermäßig am stärksten besetzten Passagen etwa z.B. das „Dies Irae" im Requiem von Berlioz.

Ausgangspunkt für die während der letzten Jahre erfolgte außerordentliche Verbesserung der Tonarme ist der Stereo-Tonabnehmer gewesen. Er bewirkte, daß jeder existierende Tonarm unzureichend wurde und damit überholt war.

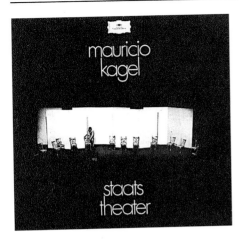

Non-Dancers). freifahrt (Sliding Chamber Music). parkett (Concertante Tutti Scenes)

2 records, ø 30cm, 33 RPM, in a box, multi-color print, included brochure 32 p. (n.pag.) with texts, photos, and scores, Deutsche Grammophon, No. 2707060

Recorded on the occasion of the world premiere at the Hamburg State Opera, April 1971. Musical direction and stage production: Mauricio Kagel.
Besides the classical Kagel uses a newly invented and conceived instrumentarium, this forms the kernel of the "opera", which draws together the various spheres.

Two examples of "directions" for performers:
Self-strangulation: The actor carries a steel spiral about two meters long in his right hand, which he swings over his head like a lasso; and an enormous hissing noise results. As the arm is lowered, the spiral coils round the performer's throat. While this is happening, he goes hastily to the back of the stage. A hand from behind the wings grabs him, and pulls him offstage by the spiral.
Acoustic: The player, his back bowed low, carries a polystyrol sheet, from which six spirals are suspended, which trail across the floor. Suddenly, the player interrupts his transit across the stage, so that a point of complete stillness occurs. In a second action, the same plate is lowered from the stage roof, and steered laterally in such a way that, once again, the spirals drag across the floor. Through this combination of two actions with the same aural result, the acoustic takes on a clearly dialectical tension, stemming from the alienated effort.

English text from included brochure

Kamenskij, Vasilij
→ Sound Poetry

Kapielski, Thomas   [O/S]

Title: Rosa Rauscht

Box (31,7 x 31,7 x 2 cm) covered with white linen and title-sticker. Contains: Circular saw-blade (300/80/0,2) in protective cover, one LP record "37 Stücke", a second LP record "Rosa Rauschen", a spiral note-book (30 x 30 cm). 80 p.(n.pag.) of photostat texts and drawings, original drawings, original photos, 1 "flying object" (balloon). Motto (Michel Serres): "The degree between hiss/-noise and signal/information is jagged, coincidental, stochastic."
1982, limited edition of 12, numbered and signed, published by the artist

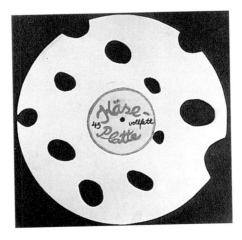

Kapielski, Thomas   [O]

Title: Käseplatte. 45 vollfett. 1986

Compressed cardboard, ø 43 x 0,4 cm, yellow varnish, with cheese holes, label with handpainted title, backside signed and inscribed "2nd cheeseplate"

Kapielski, Thomas   [C/S]

Music: Thomas Kapielski, Frieder Butzmann

Title: War Pur War

Contents: Freebeer. Damit des Ergetzens auf Erden kein Ende seyn möge. Die Luftmatratze. Der Garagenschlager. Pavel from Prague. Incendio - (Versione per danza)-. Do the VoPo. Zweitstimme. Wunderbar. Wurmberg. Rolle der Frau. Quak pur qua. Con fermezza. HAACKE & GROSS. Kurzstück. Ein beglockendes Rauschen

Perf.:   Thomas Kapielski, Frieder Butzman, and guests

           ø 30cm, 33 RPM, 1987, Zensor Musikproduktion, Berlin, No. 480099

Cover: multi-color print, cover photo by Thomas Kapielski

Motto: "Good people are bad musicians"

Kapielski, Thomas
→ Views beside ...

Kaprow, Allan   [C/S]

Title: How to Make a Happening

           ø 30cm, 33 RPM, n.d. (1966), Mass. Art. Inc. No. M-132

Cover: b/w, photo: Sol Goldberg from Allan Kaprow's Happening "Household", Cornell University, 1964. Special issue with silk-screen on plastic cover by Alison Knowles

In 1957 Allan Kaprow decided to try out the possibility that the "action" of Action Painting was a ritual act of creation, not just an incidental frenzy of movement that produced wild canvases. That decision effectively ended his growing career as a painter. Since then he has given to the world a word: the Happening. From Murray the K's radio program to the Revlon commercials, to peace marches and sit-ins, to the campaigns of politicians - that word seems to have satisfied a need to evoke the zest, freakishness and game of the life around us. Kaprow himself finds the Cape Kennedy rocket launchings among the most powerful quasi-Happenings. And one embittered cynic recently compared the war in Viet Nam to a "Happening gone out of control".

Excerpt from covertext

Karam, Dyali
→   Sound Poetry

Karin
→   Das ist Schönheit

Kastner, Bernd
→   Strafe für Rebellion

Katz, Leandro
→   Airwaves

Kern, Bliem
→   Sound Poetry

Kern, Marina
→   Sven Åke Johansson

Key-Åberg, Sandro
→   Sound Poetry

Kienholz, Ed
→   Art By Telephone

Kippenberger, Martin   [C/S]

Music: Martin Kippenberger, Christine Hahn, Eric Mitchell

Title: Luxus

Contents: New York - Auschwitz. Pretty Good. Love Song. Falsch verbunden

ø 17cm, 45 RPM, n.d. (1979), S.O. 36 Records Berlin No. SO 36

Cover: b/w, 3 printed sheets with photos and title information, stapled together with the protective cover

Kippenberger, Martin /   [C/S]
Albert Oehlen

Title: Weiß und Doof

Contents: Rio Clamoso Part I. Rio Clamoso Part II

Perf.:   Martin Kippenberger, Albert Oehlen

ø 17cm, 45 RPM, n.d., Z Records No. 66.11757-01

Cover: b/w

Kippenberger, Martin /   [C/S]
Albert Oehlen

Title: The Knowhow Knockers

Contents: Knocking for Jazz. Scheiß Schuhe

Perf.:   Martin Kippenberger, Albert Oehlen

ø 17cm, 45 RPM, n.d., Z Records No. 66.11756-01

Cover: two-color print

Kippenberger, Martin /   [C/S]
Albert Oehlen

Title: Live in Rio. The Alma Band

Contents: The Way. The Way Out

Perf.:   Martin Kippenberger, Albert Oehlen

ø 17cm, 45 RPM, n.d., Z Records, No. 66.11758-01

Cover: b/w with colored characters, according to photos by Ursula Böckler

Kippenberger, Martin
→   Die Rache der Erinnerung
→   Christian Traut

HOW TO MAKE A HAPPENING

Allan Kaprow

Kipper Kids
→ High Performance

Kirkeby, Per
→ Henning Christiansen

Klauke, Jürgen
→ Perfo 2

YVES KLEIN

Klein, Yves [C/S]

Title: Conférence à la Sorbonne. 3 Juin 1959

2 LPs, ø 30cm, 33 RPM, n.d. (1959), limited edition of 500, numbered, CNAC Paris

Cover: gatefold, Yves Klein - blue (IKB-International Klein Blue) and a b/w portrait photo by P. Descargues

---

Pierre Restany commenting on the performance (March 9, 1960) of Yves Klein's musical master piece "Symphonie Monoton-Silence":

...Then Yves came, dressed in a black tuxedo. At his signal, the orchestra started with the symphony, and the models with the body-prints, either flat on the floor or pressed against the wall. Yves Klein conducted the whole action-spectacle which lasted fourty minutes, the duration of the symphony.[1]
Fourty minutes which, for Klein, turned into fourty centuries of concentration and nervous tension. After a certain surprise-effect, the audience reacted positively. The spectacle was of an incontestable, poetic beauty. The presence of the naked flesh, intensified by the blue color, the lighting, the technical ballet of bodies which was emphasized by the persistent music and finally transcended through the silence: all that, perfectly guided by the deus ex machina, impressed and moved the trained audience which was sensitive to the high precision of the event and its magical character.

1 After the first rendition of 1949 and two versions from the years 1957 and 1960 respectively Yves Klein in 1961 wrote, under the final title, "Symphonie Monoton-Silence 1949-1961", the last version, changing the structure of the orchestra (20 singers in two seperate choruses, 10 violins, 3 contrabasses, 3 flutes, 3 oboes, 3 horns) and giving the following instructions: duration 5 or 7 minutes and 45 minutes of absolute quiet. Nobody in the orchestra makes a move. The very lively and intense interpretation continues on. No attack should be heard, not even the strike of the bow.

Klein, Yves [S]

Title: Prince of Space. Musik der Leere von Yves Klein. Tanz der Leere

Contents: Als die Holländer kamen, waren die Indianer schon da. Weißes Rauschen. Concert Vacuum. Gefrorener Knall

Perf.: Outer Space Philharmonic Orchestra, solist: Cosmos Berthold Finkelstein (Helikon), Charles Wilp (cond)

ø 30cm, 33 RPM, n.d. (1959), Sight & Sound Production No. T 74975

Cover: b/w list of titles

Klerr, Paul
→ Alvin Curran

Kline, Franz [C]

Title: Feldman / Brown

Music: Morton Feldman, Earle Brown

Contents: Durations (Feldman). Music for Violin, Cello, and Piano (Brown). Music for Cello and Piano (Brown). Hodograph I (Brown).

ø 30cm, 33 RPM, n.d., Mainstream Records, New York MS/5007

Cover: b/w, gatefold, according to a painting by Franz Kline

Klintberg, Bengt af
→ Sound Poetry

Knight, Cheri
→ Sound Poetry

Sight & Sound Production

‹Prince of Space›

Musik der Leere

von

Yves Klein.

Charles Wilp

dirigiert das

„Outer Space

Philharmonic Orchestra"

Solist:

Cosmos Berthold Finkelstein

(Helikon)

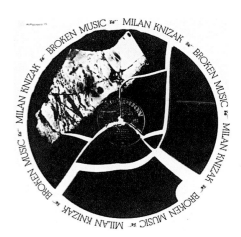

Knížák, Milan [C/S]

Title: Broken Music

Contents: Composition N. 1 - 5

ø 30cm, 33 RPM, 1979, Multhipla Records Milano No. 5

Cover: gatefold, multi-color print with picture of record objects, revised scores and a portrait photo, biography, and statement

Knížák, Milan [O/S]

Title: Destroyed Music

Record with glued on record fragments, (ø 30cm), 1963-79, original, signature on backside

Knížák, Milan [O/S]

Title: Untitled

A cut-out cross shape from a record (16 x 17 cm), 1985, signature on backside

Knížák, Milan [O/S]

Title: Untitled

Record (ø 30cm) with glued on record-square (17 x 17 cm) and circle segments (21cm long), 1985-88, signature on backside

Knížák, Milan [O/S]

Title: Untitled

Record with 7 penetrating safety-pins, (ø 30cm), 1985-88, original, signature on backside

Knížák, Milan [O/S]

Title: Untitled

Charred record (ø 30cm) with glued on record-fragments and a mounted Electron ECHO MINI PIANO, 1988, original, signature on backside

Knížák, Milan [O/S]

Title: Untitled

Record (ø 30cm) with mounted bridge over which 5 strings are screwed up attached by a wooden construction on the backside and 5 L-hooks on the frontside, 1985-88, original, signature on backside

Milan Knížák. *Destroyed Music*. 1963-1979

Milan Knížák. *Untitled*. 1963-1987

Milan Knížák. *Untitled*. 1963-1985

Milan Knížák. *Untitled*. 1963-1985

Knoebel, Imi [C]

Title: "Pst"

Music: S.Y.P.H.

ø 30cm, 33 RPM, n.d. (1980), Pure Freude Düsseldorf No. 06 CK 3

Cover: multi-color print, design: Imi Knoebel

Knoebel, Imi [S]

Title: 'Bismarckstrasse 50'. Raum 4 - 28.8.1983

Green flexidisc, ø 17cm, 45 RPM, as supplement to the invitation card for the opening of the exhibition: *Imi Knoebel in the Rijksmuseum Kröller-Müller in Otterlo (13.4.1985)*

Knowles, Alison

→ Allan Kaprow
→ Sound Poetry

Knowles, Christopher

→ Giorno Poetry Systems
→ Philip Glass

Knox, Sonia

→ Perfo 2

Køpcke, Arthur [O/S]

Title: Music while you work. Piece No. 1

Piece No. 1 from *Continue*, where all pieces by Køpcke from the years 1958-64 were published in the form of an "idea-file" in a limited edition of 150, signed and numbered. Examples 1-30 in a case (26 x 36 x 21 cm) with objects, including this record: ø 25cm, with stamped Label and spots of glue. Edition Block, Berlin 1972
Piece No. 1: "... the record/music starts and the exponent has to work (i.e. clean the stage). when the gramophone-needle hits the scotchtape, the music stumples and the actor has to begin the record again every time. the piece is over a) when the work is finished b) if the record ends ..."

Komar and Melamid

→ Perfo 2
→ Revolutions Per Minute

de Kooning, Willem [C]

Title: Music To Paintings

Music: Edvard Lieber

Contents: Twenty-Four de Kooning Preludes. Prelude to Jackson Pollock's 'Autumn Rhythm' etc.

ø 30cm, 33 RPM, 1983, No. EL -1

Cover: multi-color print, according to a painting by Willem de Kooning

Koopman, Eduard

→ Perfo 2

Kostelanetz, Richard

→ Sound Poetry

Kosugi, Takehisa [S]

Title: Violin Solo by Takehisa Kosugi

Contents: Soundscape I. Soundscape II

ø 30cm, 33 RPM, 1981, Bellows Records, New York 003

Cover: two-color print, design: Tomiyasu Shiraiwa

Kosugi utilizes a number of instruments, including violin, voice and electronic devices, which he has developed himself. His musical performances are improvisations based partly on his compositions and

Arthur Køpcke. *Music while you work.* 1966

prompted by a specific setting of the performance. He combines visual as well as musical activities, believing that music should create events in time/space, thus stimulating equally the audio and visual senses.

"A performance should give the feeling of the invisible side of a situation, it should suggest the mysterious ... seeing sounds as well as hearing sounds." (Takehisa Kosugi)

Excerpt from covertext

Kosugi, Takehisa [C/S]

Title: EN BAN. Takehisa Kosugi, Takashi Kazamaki Live At The Strange Fruit, Tokyo

Perf.: Takehisa Kosugi (v, voc, pipe), Takashi Kazamaki (perc, dr, harm, gong)

ø 30cm, 33 RPM, 1983, Fool - 002, Tokyo

Cover: two-color print, according to a drawing by Mariko Arai

Kosugi, Takehisa [S]

Title: Catch Wave. Sounds Speeding On Lights, Light Speeding On Sounds. Music Between Riddles & Solutions

ø 30cm, 33 RPM, 1975, CBS/Sony, Tokyo, SOCM - 88

Cover: two-color print, design: Aritsune Terada & Shizuo Ishizuka

Kosuth, Joseph
→ Art By Telephone

Kowalski, Piotr
→ Revolutions Per Minute

Kowanz, Karl
→ Fünfzehn Tonspuren
→ Pas Paravant

Kowanz-Kocer, Renate
→ Pas Paravant

Kozłowski, Jarosław [C/S]

Title: THE GOLDEN VIOLIN

Contents: Solo. Octet

Perf.: Jarosław Kozłowski (v)

ø 30cm, 33 RPM, 1987, edition of 800 + 200, Klub Muzyki Nowej REMONT, Warszawa, Płyta Nr. 008 ALMA ART

Cover: grey cardboard. Frontside with relief print of artist's name and title, sprayed in gold. Backside with informations

Included sheet (30 x 30,5 cm) with photos of live-performance of the artist. His violin performance in April and June 1985 was part of his *The Show/The Exhibition* in the daadgalerie, Berlin 1985. Compare catalogue to the exhibition

Kramer, Harry
→ Atelier Kramer

Krempelsauer, Joseph
→ Perfo 2

Kriesche, Richard
→ Entgrenzte Grenzen

Kriwet, Ferdinand [C/P/S]

Title: CAMPAIGN. WAHLKAMPF IN DEN USA

Contents: Campaign '72 (Democratic National Convention 1972). Campaign '72 (National Republican Convention 1972). Campaign (Hörtext IX, radio-text IX, 1972/73)

3 LPs, ø 30cm, 33 RPM, and a book (31 x 31 cm), 114 p. with texts and photos by Ferdinand Kriwet in a box (31,6 x 31,6 x 2,3 cm), one-color print, Droste Verlag GmbH, Düsseldorf, 1974. Signed and numbered special issue of 100 copies for the members of the Kunstverein für die Rheinlande und Westfalen

Kroesen, Jill
→ High Performance

Kručënych, Aleksej
→ Sound Poetry

JAROSŁAW KOZŁOWSKI

THE GOLDEN VIOLIN

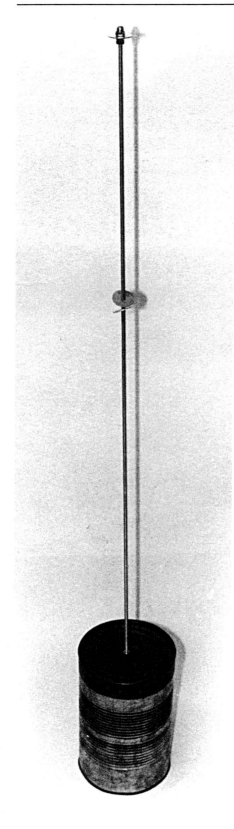

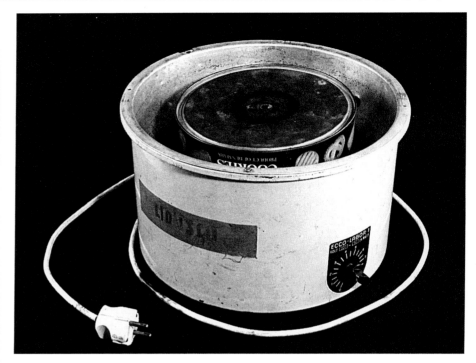

Krüger, Nils [O/S]

Title: LID ISCO (Rhythmuszentrifugator). Grob. 1982

A disassembled test-tube centrifuge (ø 30,5cm, height 18,5cm) is used as a sounding lid-player. Lids or cans made of different materials should be placed onto the rotating axis. The circular hurl creates rhythmic and unrhythmic accidental structures of free sound.

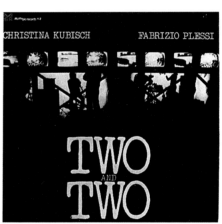

Kubisch, Christina / [C/S]
Fabrizio Plessi

Title: Two and Two

Contents: Earth. Fire. Air. Water

Perf.: Christina Kubisch (alto-fl., voc., Swanee whistle, el-metronome), Fabrizio Plessi (c, el-vibrator, contact microphone on ventilator, acc, waterjet on steel-dr)

ø 30cm, 33 RPM, Multhipla Records Milano, No. 2

Cover: two color-print, gatefold, design: Fabrizio Plessi, photos by Roberto Bruzzo

Krüger, Nils [O/S]

Title: Fallplattenspieler. Fein. 1984

Flatbed washers (ø 33cm) descend slowly down a threaded rod (length 100cm, falling-time 2 min.). The acoustic sound-spheres which are produced become audible through the use of a tin can (ø 15,5cm, height 25cm) serving as a sound resonator.

DIVerso n.10
KUBIS
SCH-PI
LESSI
tempo liquido

Kubisch, Christina / Fabrizio Plessi [S]

Title: tempo liquido

ø 30cm, 33 RPM, 1979, Cramps Records Milano, No. 5206210 (=DIVerso n. 10)

Cover: two-color print, photos of the performance and text

Protective cover with pictures of the score and photos

christina kubisch

night flights

Kubisch, Christina [S]

Title: Night Flights

Contents: The Cat's Dream. Night Flights. Circles

ø 30cm, 33 RPM, n.d., Auf Dem Nil/A.D.N. DMM 004 R

Cover: one-color print

After numerous performances as a flutist specialized in contemporary music in 1975 she renounces at the career as an instru-mental performer, concentrating her work on her own compositions, multi-media performances and video productions. Since 1980 Christina Kubisch works mostly in the field of soundinstallations and environmental concerts. Her installations are often presented in non-conventional places like parks, abondoned factories, shipyards, basements, monasteries and so on.

Excerpt from included information sheet

Kubisch, Christina
→ Sound

Kubota, Nabuo
→ The Artists' Jazz Band

Kubota, Shigeko
→ Marcel Duchamp

das Kümmerling Trio [S]

Title: Kümmerling Trio Nr.1, Danneckerstr. 32, 23. Mai 1979. Kümmerling Trio Nr.2, Hassmannstr. 198-204, 29. Mai 1979, Vivace

With: Hansjörg Mayer, Dieter Roth, Emmett Williams

ø 30cm, 33 RPM, limited edition of 300, Edition Hansjörg Mayer Stuttgart/London No. 122

Cover: gatefold, multi-color print, photos, drawings, texts

Riddling With Kuemmerling:

1. Once upon a time a great magician from King Arthur's Court crawled into Kuemmerling. Can you find the famous magician?
2. A mischievous child once stuck a ruler into Kuemmerling. Do you see his majesty?
3. Kuemmerling was visiting the Musée du Louvre one day, and quite by accident swallowed a Chinese vase. Can you identify the dynasty?
4. Kuemmerling's father was a shipbuilder, which accounts for the fact that Kuemmerling's bone structure resembles part of a ship. Do you know which part?
5. Kuemmerling has a great quantity of beer in him. Look carefully, and find out how much.
6. Kuemmerling ate a long, slippery fish for dinner last night. Do you see it inside him?
7. Kuemmerling's great-grandfather came from the land where the shamrocks grow. Can you find evidence of Irish ancestry in his name?
8. Kuemmerling was a great glutton, and once, during a visit to Switzerland, he gulped down a whole river. Can you name this river?

Emmett Williams

Küntzel, Tilman
→ Kunstproben

Kunkel, Christopher David
→ Sound Poetry

Kunstproben [P/S]

Title: Kunstproben. Studenten der Hochschule für Bildende Künste Hamburg im Forum Junger Künstler. Koordination Prof. Claus Böhmler

Exhibition catalogue (29,8 X 21 cm), 110 p. 2 of the participating artists have made an acoustic contribution on flexidisc: Dong-Sik Rim *Tonkreis* (1987), ø 17cm, 33 RPM; Tilman Küntzel *The Platte / Deja-Vu Ciyermasa* (1987), ø 17cm, 45 RPM

Kunzelmann, Dieter
→   Subkultur Berlin

Kushner, Robert
→   Word Of Mouth

Laaban, Ilmar
→   Sound Poetry

La Barbara, Joan
→   Sound
→   Views beside ...

Lacaz, Guto   [O]

Title: Edison Laser. 1987

Compact Disc, showing a painting of Edison, mounted on a single record, both mounted on a record, ø 25cm, height 8cm.
"*Mr. Thomas A. Edison listening to his brandnew phonograph with electric motor and wax cylinder.* Shown in the Universal Exhibition of 1889. Emilio Belini [Emile Berliner] invented the record which allows the reproduction of industrial recording, 78 RPM - 33 RPM - 45 RPM - Compact Disc."

Guto Lacaz

Ladik, Katalin
→   Sound Poetry

LAIBACH

REKAPITULACIJA 1980–84

PREŠLA BO SODBA VEKA
IN NAŠIH DNI STREMLJENJE,
IN NAROD VSTAL BO SLAVEN
V MOGOČNO POMLAJENJE!

WALTER ULBRICHT SCHALLFOLIEN

Laibach   [C/S]

Title: Rekapitulacija 1980-84

Contents: Reskription. Resektion. Restauration. Resolution

Walter Ulbricht Schallfolien, Hamburg, 1985, Wulp 003/4

Box, b/w, with 2 LPs, 33 RPM, 4 graphics (29 x 29 cm), brochure (29 x 29 cm), two-color print, 12 p. (n.pag.), with texts, reproduced woodcuts and drawings by the artists

Art and Totalitarianism do not exclude one another.
Totalitarian regimes repeal the illusion of the revolutionary, individual freedom of art.
Laibachart is the principle of conscious renunciation of personal taste, judgement, conviction...
Free depersonalization,
voluntary assumption
of the role of ideology,
unmasking and recapitulation
of the regimes - postmodernism...

Laibach

Laibach   [C/S]

Title: Krst pod Triglavom-Baptism

Contents: Scipion Nasice (Klangniederschrift einer Taufe)

Box, multi-color print, with 2 Lps, 33 RPM, in additional cover, multi-color print, brochure, 16 p. (n.pag.) with texts and pictures of the theater work of the artists, and 2 folded posters (62 x 93 cm).
Sub Rosa Sub, Bruxelles 33006-7/9, Walter Ulbricht Schallfolien, Hamburg, Wulp 005-6, 1986/87

Laibach   [C/S]

Title: Sympathy For The Devil II

Contents: Germania. Sympathy for the devil. (Who killed the Kennedys). 300,000 V.K. Sympathy for the devil. (Soul to waste)

ø 30cm, 45 RPM, Mute Records London, 1988, MUTE INT 126.898

Cover: two-color print, design: Slim Smith

Laibach   [C/S]

Title: Let It Be

Contents: Get back. Two of us. Dig a pony. I me mine. Across the universe. Dig it. I've got a feeling. The long and winding road. One after 909. For you blue. Maggi Mae

ø 30cm, 33 RPM, Mute Records London, 1988, MUTE INT 146.845

Cover: multi-color print, design: Collectivism Studio / Slim Smith according to paintings by Irwin

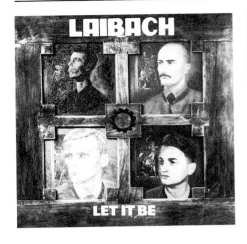

Laibach [C/S]

Title: Across the Universe

Contents: Across the universe. Maggi Mae. Get back

ø 30cm, 45 RPM, Mute Records London, 1988, MUTE INT 126.899

Cover: three-color print, design: New Collectivism Studio / Slim Smith

Laibach [C/S]

Title: Sympathy For The Devil

Contents: Sympathy for the devil (Time for a change). Sympathy for the devil (Dem Teufel zugeneigt). Dreihunderttausend verschiedene Krawalle - Symathy for the devil (Anastasia)

ø 30cm, 33 RPM, Mute Records London, MUTE INT 126.893

Cover: two-color print, design: Slim Smith

Lamers, Herman
→ Perfo 2

Lanigan-Schmidt, Thomas
→ Artsounds Collection

Larsen, Jupiter
→ Voices Notes & Noise

Lavier, Bertrand
→ La France à la Biennale

Lebel, Jean-Jacques
→ Sound Poetry

Lehmann, Ann Holyoke [C]

Title: AXOLOTL. THE WILD BEASTS

Music: Morton Subotnick

Perf.: Morton Subotnick (el), Joel Krosnick (cello, el), Virko Baley (p, el)

ø 30cm, 33 RPM, 1981, Nonesuch Records, Los Angeles / New York, N-78012

Cover: multi-color print of a portrait of Morton Subotnick

Lema, Vincente Zito
→ Sound Poetry

Lemaître, Maurice
→ Sound Poetry

Lennon, John
→ Aspen Magazine
→ Yoko Ono

Lerman, Richard [S]

Title: TRAVELON GAMELON. Music for Bicycles

Contents: Promenade version (Boston, Mass. July 2, 1979). Concert version (Pittsburgh, Pa., June 6, 1981). Promenade version (Amsterdam, the Netherlands, April 27, 1982). Concert version (Amsterdam, April 27, 1982)

ø 30cm, 33 RPM, 1982, Folkways Records, New York FX 6241

Cover: two-color print with a photo-portrait of the artist by Michiel Hendryckx design: Ronald Clyne

6-page folder (28 x 21,7 cm) (n.pag.) with a text by Richard Lerman

TRAVELON GAMELON. Why music for bicycles? The title came first. A gamelan orchestra is a large group of percussive instruments, usually metallic, from SE Asia. In fact, the sound of such a group is not unlike the timbre of amplified bicycles. The rhyme of the title, and its implication of a 'travelling' gamelan, seemed too good an idea to pass up. I was further intrigued with using the bicycle as a sound source, as an instrument and as an image. Memories from childhood of attaching cards to wheels to strike the spokes provided another impetus to pursue the pieces.
I had briefly amplified a bicycle in 1963 for an early tape music piece by jamming a microphone against the frame and recording

the sound for future use. This would have been impossible in live performance --- too much feedback. Using phono cartridges which I took apart, the first performance of an earlier version happened on Feb. 4, 1977. Four of the six cartridges broke. Over the next 6 months I developed a way to safely house the cartridges in plastic and also increase their response.

It occurred to me that another version could be performed outdoors with riders and I conceived the Promenade version. This necessitated designing and building 25 small battery powered amplifiers, getting horn-type loudspeakers to attach to the bicycles, making pickups, and organizing the event. With each rider individually amplified, the Promenade version was first given in May, 1978 at U. Mass. - Boston.

Richard Lerman (Excerpt from covertext)

Les Salopettes
→   Sound Poetry

Letarte, Geneviève
→   Sound Poetry

Lévesque, Marie
→   Sound Poetry

Levine, Les
→   Art By Telephone
→   Artsounds Collection
→   Giorno Poetry Systems
→   Revolutions Per Minute

Lewitt, Sol
→   Art By Telephone

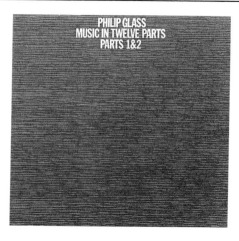

Lewitt, Sol   [C]

Title:	Music in Twelve Parts. Parts 1 & 2
Music:	Philip Glass
	ø 30cm, 33 RPM, 1974, Virgin Records London No. CA 2010
Cover:	two-color print according to a drawing by Sol Lewitt

Lichtenstein, Roy
→   Record of Interviews ...

Lille, Christer Hennix
→   Sound Poetry

Lockwood, Anna   [S]

Title:	Glass World of Anna Lockwood. An exploration into the complexity of sounds drawn exclusively from glass

ø 30cm, 33 RPM, 1970, Tangent Records, London TGS 104

Cover:	multi-color print, design: Robert Morgan, photos, drawings (by the artist) and text information

Many types, shapes, and sizes of glass are used, singly or combined, and are manipulated in a variety of ways so as to extract from them their latent sounds. The glass used has not been specially prepared or shaped as with musical instruments; pieces of glass have been used which are not normally seen - fragments picked up from factory floors, such as small glass discs which are rubbed together, and sea-green glass rocks which are knocked against each other.

Excerpt from covertext

Lockwood, Anna
→   Source
→   Sound Poetry

Logue, Christopher
→   Aspen Magazine

Longo, Roberto   [C]

Title:	The Ascension
Music:	Glenn Branca
	ø 30cm, 33 RPM, 1981, Ninety Nine Music, New York
Cover:	b/w

Lora-Totino, Arrigo
→   Sound Poetry
→   Source

Luca, Gherasim
→   Sound Poetry

Lucier, Alvin
→   Source

Luigetti, Serse
→   Sound Poetry

Luis Chispas
→   Richard Hamilton/Dieter Roth

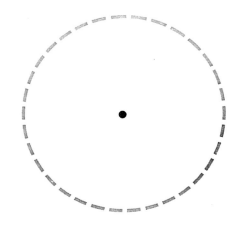

Lunds Konsthall   [P/S]

Title: Lunds Konsthall 1965. Le Merveilleux Moderne. Det Underbara Moderna. Det Underbara Idag

Exhibition catalogue (20 x 20 cm), 88 p. (n.pag.). Frontpage with mounted flexidisc (ø 17cm), the centerhole is drilled through the entire catalogue.

Lyytikäinen, Olli
→   J.O. Mallander

Mac Adams, Lewis   [P/S]

Title: Beirut

Music: Dark Bob

Perf.:   Lewis Mac Adams (voc), Wippo (g, b, dr), Aseley Otten (g), Wippo, Dark Bob, Twinka Thiebaud (voc)

ø 17cm, 45 RPM, High Performance, Los Angeles, CA. 1982

This record is not for sale, it's for white magic.

Maciunas, George
→   Aspen Magazine
→   Yoko Ono

Maciunas Ensemble   [C/S]

Title: Music for Everyman

Contents: Easy Take. Jota Rock. A wide, white World

Perf.:   Paul Panhuysen (p, voc, motor on Fender guitar), Jan van Riet (Fender guitar, b-g, sound mix), Leon van Noorden (cello), Mario van Horrik (slit drum, motor on Eko guitar), Horst Rickels (b-sax, p, motor on Sho-Bud steel guitar), Michiel van Eeden (sound mix)

ø 30cm, 33 RPM, 1986, Apollo-records, Eindhoven No. AR 028605

Cover: one-color print, *A score for Hélène* by Paul Panhuysen

MacLow, Jackson
→   Aspen Magazine
→   Giorno Poetry Systems
→   Radiotaxi
→   Sound Poetry

Maggi, Ruggero
→   Voices Notes & Noise

Magli, Valeria
→   Sound Poetry

Majakovskij, Vladimir
→   Sound Poetry

Malevič, Kasimir
→   Sound Poetry

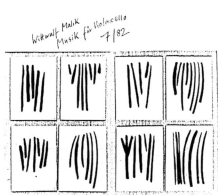

Malik, Wittwulf   [C/S]

Title: Musik für Violoncello 7/1982

Contents: 5 Sätze für Violoncello Solo aus Italien, Herbst 1981. Improvisation am 9.7.1982

ø 25cm, 33 RPM, 1982, record exists in 2 numbered and signed copies, published by the artist

Cover: mounted photostat of score, handwritten title, mounted typed table of contents

Malik, Wittwulf [C/S]

Title: Zwei Performance-Musiken mit Violoncello Mai und November 1982, in Hamburg

Contents: Musik vom Dach. Cello-LKW-Performance

Perf.: Wittwulf Malik (cello), Ingo Hauss (drumbox, el)

ø 30cm, 33 RPM, 1983, only 1 signed copy of this record, published by the artist

Cover: mounted photostat of portrait-photo, handwritten table of contents, typed title-sticker

2 Din A4 leaflets with further information as supplement

Mallander, J. O. [C/S]

Title: Extended Play

Contents: Two Pieces by J.O. Mallander. Forward! "1962". "1968"

ø 17cm, 45 RPM, 1968, Eteenpäin! NG-97, Finland

Cover: b/w

2nd issue by Love Records, 1977. The pieces of *Extended Play* are now labeled: *Kekkonen*, 1962. *Kekkonen*, 1968. Front cover (b/w): Olli Lyytikäinen

Mallander, J.O. [S]

Title: Decompositions

Contents: Bound. Variation On A Theme By Haydn. A Fifth. Blues-A-Version. Degnahc Ev'Uoy

ø 17cm, 33 RPM, 1970, Love Records LREP 108, Helsinki, Finland

Cover: b/w

Mandiargues, Andre Pieyre de
→ Sound Poetry

Marchetti, Walter [S]

Title: La CACCIA (da "Arpocrate Seduto sul Loto" 1965)

Perf.: Walter Marchetti, Assistence: Juan Hidalgo

ø 30cm, 33 RPM, 1974, Cramps Records, Milano, nova musicha n.4

Cover: one-color print, gatefold with photos and text by Walter Marchetti

Inner sleeve with an excerpt of the score

Marchetti, Walter [S]

Title: In terram utopicam

Contents: J'aimerai jouer avec un piano qui aurait un grosse queue. Adversus. Osmanthus fragrans

Perf.: Walter Marchetti, Juan Hidlago (p), homemade electric music

ø 30cm, 33 RPM, 1977, Cramps Records, Milano, nova musicha n.15

Cover: two-color print, gatefold, photos on cover and inner sleeve by Giorgio Colombo, Fernando Arreche Goitosolo

Marchetti, Walter [C/S]

Title: Per la sete dell'orecchio

Contents: Da nulla e verso nulla. Per la sete dell'orecchio

Perf.: Walter Marchetti, Giorgio Battistelli (Marimba, Maracas, Raspa, Nastro magnetico)

ø 30cm, 33 RPM, 1984, Vandalia
Records No. 10584

Cover: multi-color print, design: Loriana
Castano

Marchetti, Walter

→ Juan Hidalgo

Christian Marclay plays to this fetish-association we have with records. He tropes on the record as an object *and* as a bearer of sound, engaging the device both in performance and in static physical manipulation. Furthermore, he allows the metamorphoses rendered on one aspect of the record to effect the other aspect. That is, when Marclay takes several records and montages them, inserting shards of one into slots cut into the other or mismatching pie slices or constructing checkerboard patterns or whatever method he employs to subvert (or even pervert) the wholeness and continuity of normal records, he does so in order to invent a new hybrid record which gives both visual and sonic evidence of its, her, parentage. A leopard-spotted disk is oddly lovely to look at - and startling to listen to. The visual patterns that result from the intercutting of different-colored vinyl are matched by the sound resulting from their play: a rhythmic seguing from one music to another, totally different music. The segues are rapid hiccups, not slow fade-out-fade-ins; contrast, not continuity, is Marclay's standard - although the segues occur so fast that the sounds blend into a pattern that (exactly like the visual appearance of the violated record) makes sense only as a whole but teases the ears with intimations of the originals.

Excerpt from Peter Frank: *Christian Marclay*. In: *FRI.ART made in Switzerland*. (cat.) New York 1985

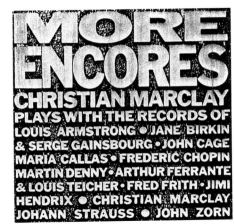

Marclay, Christian   [C/S]

Title: More Encores

Contents: Christian Marclay plays with the records of Louis Armstrong, Jane Birkin & Serge Gainsbourg, John Cage, Maria Callas, Frederic Chopin, Martin Denny, Arthur Ferrante & Louis Teicher, Fred Frith, Jimi Hendrix, Christian Marclay, Johann Strauss, John Zorn

ø 30cm, 33 RPM, 1988, No Man's Land, Würzburg, W-Germany, nml 8816

Cover: b/w, design: Garland & Marclay

Direction: Play back at high volume

Marclay, Christian   [O/S]

Title: Record Without A Cover

Manipulated records on multiple turntables

ø 30cm, 33 RPM, 1985, Recycled Records New York

One side of the record playable; on the other side, titles and textinformation have been pressed in. Direction: Do not store in a protective package.

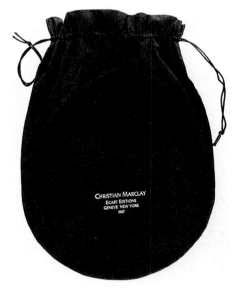

Marclay, Christian   [O]

12" black vinyl grooveless record with golden label in black suede poche with gold lettering

Edition of 50, signed and numbered, Ecart Editions, Genève / New York, 1987

Christian Marclay. (Untitled). 1983

Christian Marclay. 1982

Christian Marclay. Installation at gelbe Musik, Berlin 1988

Christian Marclay. (Untitled). 1983

Marcus, Angela
→ Das ist Schönheit

Marden, Eric
→ Word Of Mouth

Mardoyan, Rima Lucia
→ Das ist Schönheit

Marge, Bellee Etienne
→ Sound Poetry

Marinetti, Filippo Tommaso
→ musica futurista
→ Sound Poetry

Marioni, Tom
→ Sound
→ Word Of Mouth

Markle, Robert
→ The Artists' Jazz Band

Martel, Richard
→ Sound Poetry

Martin, Henry [C/S]

Title: Concerto per un quadro di Adami

ø 30cm, 33 RPM, n.d., Edizioni Studio Marconi, Milano, HA 001

Cover: b/w, gatefold, included folded poster (62 x 85 cm), multi-color print *Universität Leipzig*

Masquelier, Baina
→ Voices Notes & Noise

Matusow, Harvey
→ Sound Poetry

Mayröcker, Friederike
→ Sound Poetry

Mazza, Italo
→ Sound Poetry

McAdam, Gerald
→ The Artists' Jazz Band

McAulay, Tony
→ Artsounds Collection

McCarthy, Paul
→ High Performance

McCough, Peter
→ Perfo 2

McDermott, David
→ Perfo 2

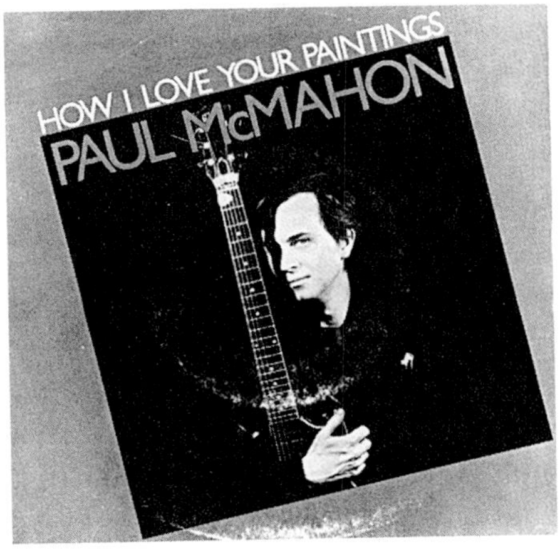

McMahon, Paul [C/S]

Title: How I Love Your Paintings

Contents: How I Love Your Paintings. Movie Star

Perf.: Paul McMahon (voc), Brooke Halpin (p, marimba), David Hofstra (b), Peter Moser (perc), Peter Gordon (sax)

ø 17cm, 45 RPM, 1981, Live Bait Music, Eos Records, New York

Cover: two-color print, cover photos by Robert Mapplethorpe, design: Anthony McCall

Mead, Taylor
→ Sound Poetry

Medalla, David
→ Perfo 2

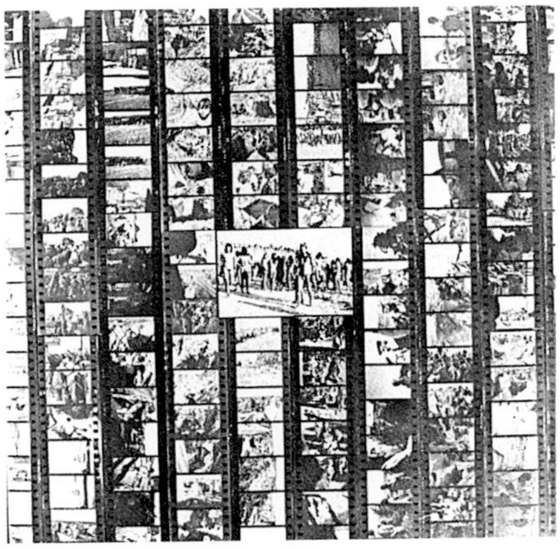

Meireles, Cildo [C/S]

Title: PESQUISA: SAL SEM CARNE. Salt Without Meat

ø 30cm, 33 RPM, 1974/75, Galeria Luiz Buarque de Hollanda & Paulo Bittencourt, CM - 003

Cover: b/w

Meireles, Cildo [C/S]

Title: PESQUISA DE AUDIO. I MEBS. II CARAXIA

ø 17cm, 33 RPM, 1970/71, edition of 500, Cildo Meireles, Brasil, 1971

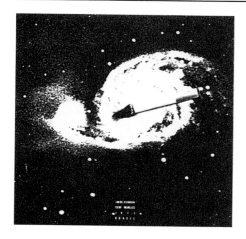

Cover: b/w, the picture of a burning cigarette and a real burned hole

The idea of this record - made up with a frequency oscillator - was to construct sonorous sculptures, that is to say, to project a spatial image through auditory perception. So, the band MEBS would be the sonorous graph of the Moebius'ribbon, while CARAXIA refers to render sonorous a spiral.

Cildo Meireles

Melamed, Brad [O]

Title: Records To Listen To The Radio By

Cover: b/w

Record, ø 30cm, on both sides with stencil-spray-paintings

Mellnäs, Arne
→ Sound Poetry

Melo e Castro, E.M. de
→ Sound Poetry

Merzbow [C/S]

Title: Antimonument

Contents: Tatara. Bardo Song. 1560° C Saiseikam No Owari. Pleasure Dome. Grid Module

picture-disc of paintings by Hasami Abtectonics, ø 30cm, 33 RPM, 1986, C & P ZSF Product Tokyo

Cover: transparent plastic-cover with title sticker and transparent protective cover. Art direction AD Suprex

Métail, Michèle
→ Sound Poetry

Meyer, Moe
→ Perfo 2

Meyer, Peter R.
→ Sound Poetry

Miccini, Eugenio
→ Radiotaxi

Mills, Neil
→ Sound Poetry

Minarelli, Enzo
→ Sound Poetry

Minus Delta T [C/S]

Title: Das Projekt. Le Projet. The Project. Minus Delta T. The Bangok Project

Contents: Child of God. Muslim Pulse. Bugo Schligo. Dallas. Ata Etno Turk. Tripoli. Turkish March. Don't Cry My Little Girl. Bus. Dervich Furioso. Cedar Babies. Damascus. This Is My Life. Excuse Me. Motorhead. Traditional Thai Music And Dance. Schiraz. Malang Dervishes. Ventilator Dance. Euphorie. Waterpump. Savadikap. Concert Of The Labor-Day/Workers. China

1 LP, ø 30cm, 33 RPM, 1 Single, ø 17cm, 45 RPM, 1984, Ata Tak Düsseldorf, LC 8372 (WR 21-LP) (WR 22.7)

Cover: 4-way unfolding, multi-color print with documentary material, table of contents, project description, trilingual

After numerous conferences, performances, radiointerviews, and live interventions, here the first record of the Bangok project (starting in Southwales/England) composed of documentary sounds, overdubbed documentations, and musical works of the group Minus Delta T from 1982 to 1983 (the 50 minutes musics are extracts from the 250 hours soundarchive of the trip)

Minus Delta T [C/S]

Title: Opera Death

3 LPs, 33 RPM, n.d.(1987), Ata Tak, Düsseldorf, No. 82Ø 36-38

Cover: multi-color print

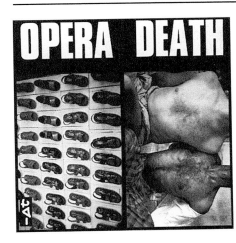

Miti, Luca

→ Sound Poetry

Mixed Band Philanthropist [C]

Title: The Impossible Humane

Contents: I) The beginnings of a once great loneliness II) Some were animated by their purest motives III) Confusion in the mind of the otherwise healthy boy IV) The industry of children and machines V) Horus man (enclaved by wisdom) VI) The impossible humane

With: P 16.D4 a.o.

ø 30cm, 33 RPM, n.d. (1986), Selektion, Mainz, No. SLP 007

Cover: original painting, concept: Swimming Behavior Of The Human Infant

Möslang, Norbert / Andy Guhl [C/S]

Title: Voice Crack

Perf.: Norbert Möslang, Andy Guhl: geknackte Alltagselektronik

ø 30cm, 33 RPM, 1984, Uhlang-Produktion St. Gallen, No. 03

Cover: b/w, coverdrawings by Josef Felix Müller, 2nd inside cover red/white with documentary photos and titles

Recorded live on March 23, 1984, during the exhibition of Josef Felix Müller at the gallery Corinne Hummel in Basel, Switzerland

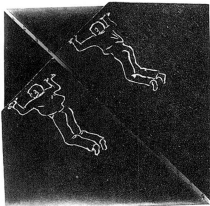

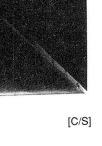

Möslang, Norbert/ Andy Guhl [C/S]

Title: Kick That Habit

Perf.: Norbert Möslang, Andy Guhl: geknackte Alltagselektronik

ø 30cm, 33 RPM, 1986, Uhlang-Production St. Gallen No. 05

Cover: original woodcut (66 x 44 cm) by Alex Hanimann, b/w, folded to coversize, yellow protective cover with titles and text

Recorded live on May 31, 1986 at the Southern Dancework Studio Birmingham, Alabama

Mol, Kees

→ Perfo 2

Molero, Herminio

→ Sound Poetry

Mon, Franz

→ Sound Poetry

Monk, Meredith [C/S]

Title: Our Lady of Late

Perf.: Meredith Monk (voice and glass), Collin Walcott (percussion for glass)

ø 30cm, 33 RPM, 1973, MINONA Records

Cover: two-color print, design: Meredith Monk, incorporating an own drawing and a portait photo by Peter Moore

Selected discography:
Candy, Bullets And Moon (Monk/Preston, ø 17cm, 33 RPM, New York 1967)
key (Increase Records, New York, 1970, LP),
key, reissue (Lovely Music (New York, 1977, LML 1051, LP)
Songs From The Hill/Tablet (Wergo spectrum, Mainz , 1979, SM 1022, LP)
Dolmen Music (ECM Records, München, 1981, ECM 1197, LP)
Turtle Dreams (ECM Records, München, 1983, ECM 1240, LP)
Our Lady of Late (Wergo spectrum, Mainz, 1986, SM 1058, LP)
Do You Be (ECM Records, München 1987, ECM New Series 1336, LP)

Monk, Meredith
→ Airwaves
→ Giorno Poetry Systems

Monoton   [S]

Title: Monoton

Music: Konrad Becker

Contents: Ein Wort. Dubwise. Wirklichkeit. Leben im Dschungel

Perf.: Konrad Becker (el, voc, sax, v, steeldrum), Eugenia Rochas (b, g), Albert Grieman (el)

ø 30cm, 33 RPM, 1980, Monoton Produkt Wien, No. 02

Cover: one-color print on blue cardboard

Red protective cover with informations, record (blue). Included folding sheet *Ich weiß nichts* (Monoton Produkt 04)

Morandi, Sergio-Emilio
→ Sound Poetry

Morgan, Edwin
→ Sound Poetry

Morgenstern, Christian
→ Sound Poetry

Morris, Robert
→ Art By Telephone

Morrow, Charlie
→ Giorno Poetry Systems

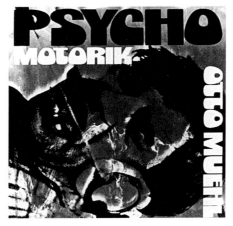

Muehl, Otto   [S]

Title: Psycho Motorik. Für Jugendliche unter 21 Jahren verboten

Contents: Jetzt wird's geil. Akt natur. Der fliegende Bösendorfer. Futschaas. Hygiene. Aestheten-Schweinerei. Ein schrecklicher Gedanke. Mein Testament. Jodler. Hygiene. Meine Mutter. Klavierkonzert K

ø 30 cm, 33 RPM, n.d.

Cover: two-color print with portrait by Otto Muehl

S1
einschrecklicher gedanke
meine mutter
Klavier Konzert
mein testament
jodler
hygiene
ästhetenschweinerei
an der schönen blauen donau

S2
jetzt wird's geil
der fliegende bösendorfer
kaiser ebersdorf

Muehl, Otto   [S]

Title: Ein schrecklicher Gedanke

Contents: meine mutter. klavierkonzert. mein testament. jodler. hygiene. ästhetenschweinerei. an der schönen blauen donau. jetzt wird's geil. der fliegende bösendorfer. kaiser ebersdorf

ø 30cm, 33 RPM, n.d.(1972)

Cover: one-color print, gatefold, with a text by Franz Knödel, Vienna 1972

Muehl, Otto   [S]

Title: AAM 1. Aktions Analytische Musik

Contents: Musikalische Selbstdarstellungen 1974/75. Eberhard - Blues. Freie Sexualität. Vorstadtblues. Jealousy

ø 30cm, 33 RPM, AA Verlag, Wien

Cover: multi-color print, gatefold

Included brochure, 20 p., Kurt Schmäles talking with Otto Muehl

THE AA COMMUNE

the AA kommune is in its fifth year and is the most significant social model presently existing. the AA kommune consists of 100 people at the moment, 7 of them are children. in the AA kommune, principles are realized which humanity has dreamed of for thousands of years in vain: FREE SEXUALITY, COMMON PROPERTY, COMMON PRODUCTION in various enterprises. the AA kommune is an ideal example of how children can grow up without nuclear family damages. the important thing is not the upbringing and education of the children, but the satisfaction of their needs. (the commune children are not forced to do anything, for the cc there is no compulsive division of time forced on them by adults, neither by breast feeding, eating, nor sleeping). the AA kommune was begun in vienna. two years after its founding, friedrichshof was purchased and rebuilt into a country commune. up until 1973 we still had two-person relationships and private property in the commune. in 1972 we began to develop the actions analysis. we realized that the nuclear family man is a damaged human, incapable of living together with other humans in a social context.

through the actions analysis we were able to resolve the aggressions and fears to such an extent that a new consciousness evolved in the group, the famous AA consciousness, recently discussed in the club of rome, which made the individual capable of free sexuality and common property. since 1974 the actions analysis has developed into the actions analytical selbstdarstellung, the spontaneous self-expressive action in front of the group.

English text from included brochure

Müller, Josef Felix
→   Norbert Möslang

musica futurista   [S]

Contents: Francesco Balilla Pratella: La Guerra (1930). Giorno di Festa (1930). Silvio Mix: Due preludi da *Gli stati d'animo* (1922). Profilo sintetico Musicale di Marinetti (1923). Franco Casavola: Preludio a *Prigionieri* (1925). Danza della scimmie (1926). Filippo Tommaso Marinetti: Cinque sintesi radiofoniche (1933). Daniele Napoletano: Estratti Musicali (1933). Luigi Russolo: Risveglio di una città (1913). Esempi sonori di... Antonio Russolo: Corale. Serenata. Virgilio Mortari: Fox-Trot del Teatro della Sorpresa (1921). Luigi Grandi: Aeroduello (1935). Cavalli +

Acciaio (1935). Filippo Tommaso Marinetti, Aldo Giuntini: Sintesi Musicali Futuristiche (1931). Aldo Giuntini: The Indian Rubber Man (Fox-Trot) (1931). Alfredo Casella: Pupazzetti (1915). Filippo Tommaso Marinetti: La Battaglia di Adrianopoli (1924). Definizione di Futurismo (1924)

Perf.: Daniele Lombardo (p), Filippo Tommaso Marinetti (voc), Aldo Giuntini (p), *intonarumori* by Russolo, which have been reconstructed by M. Abate and P. Verardo in 1977

2 LPs, ø 30cm, 33 RPM, 1980, Daniele Lombardi for Cramps

Piotr Nathan: *Ansicht einer Revolution.* 1982

Records Muthipla, No. 5204002, reissue 1986, Fonit Cetra FDM 0007

Cover: gatefold, multi-color print with pictures: Russolo e Piatti con gli intonarumori; Balla: Progetto per copertina di disco. Text by Luigi Rognoni. Inner sleeve with detailed explanations by Daniele Lombardi

Naif Orchestra

→ Sound Poetry

Nannucci, Maurizio [C/S]

Title: World symphony / outdoor atmosphere

ø 17cm, 33 RPM, 1971, limited edition of 200, numbered and signed

Cover: b/w, design: Maurizio Nannucci

Six original outside registrations in collaboration with the radio stations of six different parts of the world: RAI Radio Televisiona Italiana, Radio Canada, Nhk (Tokyo), Radio Diffusion Côte d'Avoir, Australian Broadcasting commission, Radio Venezuela

Nannucci, Maurizio

→ Sound Poetry
→ Views beside ...

Nathan, Piotr (Sobieralski) [O/S]

Title: Absicht einer Revolution. 1982

→ p. 185

The object exists of: a recordplayer (34,5 x 23 x 5 cm), a loudspeaker (18 x 8 cm), a preserving jar containing the inner technical parts of the recordplayer. The tone-arm is a mounted wing of a sea-eagle, a record ø 30cm with speeches by Lenin is played, a red flag serves as background. Of this object exists a recording on a transparent flexidisc with an installation photo in spiral binding.

The stylus jumps back and forth between the two cables which I have glued onto the record. This movement - at the same time the movement of the wings - deforms the content of the record. One hears parts of the speeches and words.
A record with speeches by Lenin.

Piotr Nathan

Piotr Nathan. *Snowflakes.* 1987
→

Nathan, Piotr (Sobieralski) [O]

Title: Negativform Snowflakes. 1987

Unlimited series of records (ø 30cm) with cutout *snowflakes* on top of found (orange painted) sculptures (animals in different sizes)

The tension between incompatible states and languages - between music and its notation, for example - is Nathan's real place of exile, a chosen ground where difference becomes so everyday that ontological differentiation becomes a blur. There is nothing rarified about this process. On the contrary, Nathan does everything he can to emphasize the dailiness of the activity. Sitting at a jig-saw that resembles a sewing-machine, he has carved records into shapes that occur to him as he goes along, shapes that (not surprisingly) are abstract but pregnant with figurative associations. Then these shapes are mounted on walls in grid formations of fifty or more, and the result - always with the title *Snowflakes* - exists as a homage to the decorative, perhaps the only mode of classic Modernism capable of encapsulating, even resolving, the rupture between disparate realms which so obsesses him. The black snowflakes present a repetition, a structure, an infinite suggestiveness, above all the refusal to coalesce into thought, which are properties of music. And they turn notation into the *real thing* - bearing in mind, of course, that in this case the real thing has no tangible form.

They are the culmination of his record sculpture. That, at least, is one way of viewing them. The other would be to see them as a running critique of the more pragmatic side of Nathan's work - his series of sliced gramophone records mounted on silk, named after the underground stations on the line that runs through East Berlin without stopping there, with the grooves radiating from the central cut like lines of force or like indications of importance in strip cartoon, or like shock waves from the sound of the trains passing through. Politics is implicit at every point in Nathan's work, not least in the simplicity by which the snowflakes succeed in avoiding fixity, or associations of waste, or waste salvaged, or waste salvaged which has become the material for transcendence. Whatever role music plays in Nathan's life, it is logical to assume that it has nothing to do with escapism. And for *music* read *art* in general: a constant gesture of escape within permanent, and perhaps irreconcilable, boundaries. It is in the repetition of the gesture that some salvation may reside. Or, more realistically, a better grasp of the terms that define us.

Excerpt from an unpublished essay by Stuart Morgan

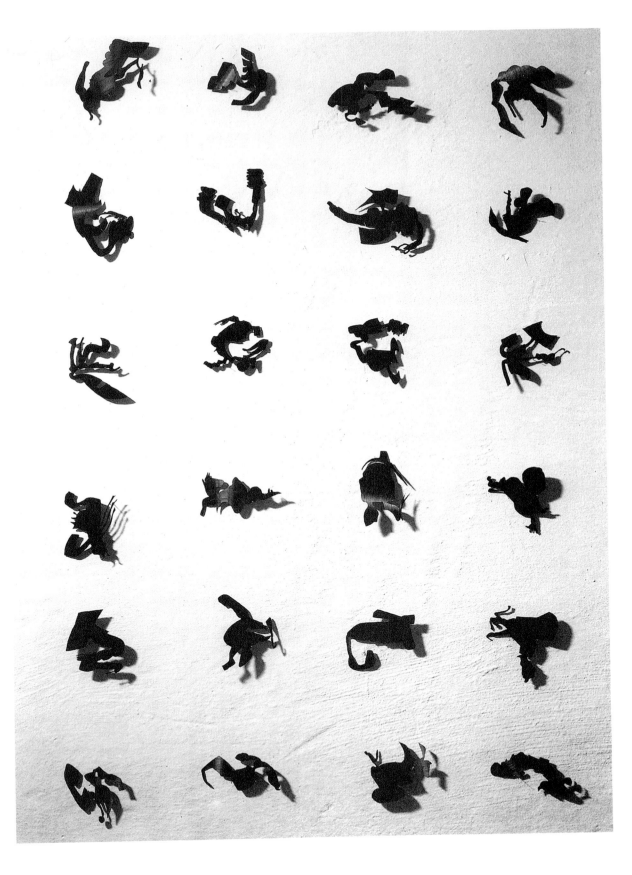

Nauman, Bruce
→   Art By Telephone

Nebel, Otto
→   Sound Poetry

Neuhaus, Max
→   Aspen Magazine

Neveu, Angeline
→   Sound Poetry

Niesporek, Lutz
→   Sound Poetry

Niikuni, Seiichi
→   Sound Poetry

Nitsch, Hermann   [S]

Title: Akustisches Abreaktionsspiel

A recording of WDR (Westdeutscher Rundfunk, Köln)

ø 30cm, 33 RPM, 1972, the issue is partially signed, Galerie Klewan Wien, No. 30-382

Cover: mailing-box with photo of a performance by Hermann Nitsch

Nitsch, Hermann   [S]

Title: Requiem für meine Frau Beate. 56. Aktion - Bologna 1977

Box with 3 LPs, 33 RPM, 1977, Edizione Morra, Napoli

Cover: black box with silver inscription

Includes score of the performance (66 x 59 cm) and a booklet 40 p. (n.pag.) with directions and photos
This performance was realized on June 1, 1977 in Bologna in the Chiesa Santa Lucia, Via Castiglione.

First page of the directions:

über der mitte des kirchenraumes ca. einen halben meter über dem boden, hängt an 2 von den beiden seitenwänden herabhängenden seilen ein geschlachtetes abgehäutetes schaf (schaf 1, kopf nach unten) die hinterbeine des schafes sind an den seilen so befestigt, dass sie weit auseinandergezogen werden, der geöffnete brustkorb von schaf 1 ist durch ein holzstück aufgeklafft, unter dem schaf ist weisser stoff ausgelegt.

2 m entfernt von dem aufgeklafften schaf (richtung stirnwand der kirche) liegt auf einer auf einem tisch liegenden tragbahre nr.1. er ist bekleidet, seine augen sind mit weissem verbandstoff umwunden, er ist mit einem weissen tuch verhüllt.

an der stirnwand der kirche ist ein geschlachtetes abgehäutetes schaf (kopf nach unten) wie gekreuzigt genagelt. schaf 2 ist mit einem weissen Tuch verhüllt rechts neben dem altar ist orchester 1, das lärm orchester gruppiert. es besteht aus 20 mann es enthält folgende instrument gruppen:

trillerpfeiferl

flöten

ratschen

leichtes schlagzeug (becken, klingel, glocken, es wird ein rauschendes zischendes geräusch verlangt)

schweres schlagzeug (trommeln, pauken)

bläser (1. bläsergruppe)

links neben dem eingang und rückwärts auf dem chor kirche, ist ein vollzähliges blasor-

chester gruppiert (2. orchester, 2. bläsergruppe). das blasorchester enthält auch das dafür übliche schlagzeug, becken und pauke. trotzdem reagiert es nur auf das einsatzsignal für bläser und tutti, und setzt immer insgesamt ein.
(nur bei orchester 1 werden die instrument gruppen jeweils gesondert eingesetzt).

Nitsch, Hermann   [S]

Title: 60. aktion berlin 1978

Perf.:   Frank Dolch (org.), Punk Rock Group P.V.C.

ø 30cm, 33 RPM, 1979, limited edition of 500, Dieter Roth's Verlag, Stuttgart, JST 236

Cover: b/w, documentary photos and cutouts of a score

Music of the 60. performance, Berlin 1978, organized by Galerie Petersen

Nitsch, Hermann   [S]

Title: ISLAND eine sinfonie in 10 sätzen

Contents: 1. satz: kreuz + dionysos. 2. satz: adagio. zwillingsgestirn. 3. satz:

nordlicht. 4. satz: 1.teil -opferung des lammes-. 2.teil -die freuden des lammes / das essen der pflanzen / vorahnung der auferstehung-. 5. satz: scherzo. 6. satz: lava. 7. satz: fuge. 8. satz: vatnajökull. 9. satz: die zerreißung des lammes. 10. satz: auferstehung des lammes

Perf.: Hermann Nitsch (p, org) and an orchestra of Icelandic musicians conducted by Hermann Nitsch

Technical Realization: Björn Roth, Bali Mosfellssveit

6 LPs, 33 RPM, 1980, limited edition of 200, Dieter Roth's Verlag, Luzern

Cover: box, b/w

The orchestra-musicians also sing and play car-horn, tin- and miniature instruments in addition to the conventional instruments.

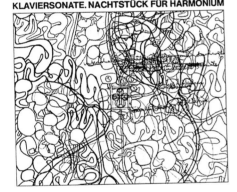

HERMANN NITSCH
KLAVIERSONATE. NACHTSTÜCK FÜR HARMONIUM

Nitsch, Hermann [C/S]

Title: Klaviersonate. Nachtstück für Harmonium

Perf.: Hermann Nitsch (p, harmonium)

ø 30cm, 33 RPM, Yedermann No. 29838

Cover: b/w, gatefold, according to a drawing by Hermann Nitsch, design: Wittigo

Recordings of performances at Galerie Heike Curtze, Düsseldorf, on 7.5.1984 and Vienna on 27.6.1984

Nitsch, Hermann [S]

Title: ORGELKONZERT. das zürcher konzert

HERMANN NITSCH

ORGELKONZERT
das zürcher konzert

~ 16/150

Contents: Die Geburt. Die Tiefe des Alls. Der dritte Hahnenschrei. Dornenkrönung. Kreuzweg und Auferstehung

Perf.: Hermann Nitsch (org)

2 LPs, 33 RPM, 1988, limited edition of 150, numbered and signed, Schedle & Arpagaus, Zürich, S & A 1988, 01/2

Cover: gatefold, b/w, design: HG Kestel

Included sheet with photos and texts by HG Kestel

Nitsch, Hermann

→ selten gehörte Musik
→ Sound Poetry

Le Noble, Jean [C/S]

Title: soundlines '79

Contents: Part 1 - 17 KHZ. Part 2 - 17^5 KHZ. Part 3 - 18 KHZ. Part 4 - 18^5 KHZ. Part 1 - 19 KHZ. Part 2 - 19^5 KHZ. Part 3 - 20 KHZ

ø 30cm, 33 RPM, 1979, limited edition of 250, numbered and signed, Edition Artist, Haarlem, Holland

White hinged box with printed white drawing, textsheet (Dutch and English)

This record is a direct consequence of my immaterial drawings and reliefs, in which I try to give expression to that, what is not, or hardly to be seen, and try to draw the attention of the spectator to the existence of apparently not measurable fields of tension, which are present in the world, surrounding us. the noise, brought on this record, lies in a frequency-area, which we can't perceive in

sensory perception, namely from seventeen till twenty khz; the sustaining tone, which is raising with one half khz, and is continuing with intervals during five to six minutes, I experience as a line of sound-lines; I draw as it were, seven sound-lines.

Jean Le Noble

NON + SMEGMA

SMEGMA + NON

NON + SMEGMA [S]

Title: Non + Smegma

Contents: Smegma: Can't Look Straight. Flashcards
Non: 1-3 Sound Tracks - Multi Speed Multi Axis, 4 Mode of Infection 33 RPM - Multi Axis. 5 Knife Ladder 33 RPM - Multi Axis

Perf.: Boyd Rice (voc, noise manipulation unit, iona rotaguitar-tapes, altered drum machine), Robert Turman (noise manipulation unit-tapes)

ø 17cm, 33 RPM + multi speed (16-33-45-78), 1980, Mute Records, London, No. 007

Cover: b/w

Nonas, Richard
→ Airwaves

Novák, Ladislav
→ Sound Poetry
→ Revue OU

obscure [C/S]

series of 10 records ø 30cm, 33 RPM, produced by Brian Eno, Island Records, London, 1975-78

Cover: multi-color print, design: John Bonis

The series of Obscure Records was founded in 1975 as a Special-Price-Label by Brian Eno, who was supported in the selection by Bryars and Nyman. This record-company should propagate a new generation of experimental music from Great Britain, a music that would reflect the influence of the systemic compositions of the American Minimal-School of La Monte Young, Steve Reich, Phil Glass, and Terry Riley, but which at the same time would experience a transformation and expansion through a recourse upon a European concept of music to the point of that peculiar British "taste", especially in the music of Bryars, Nyman, and the Penguin Café Orchestra in which associative, "obscure" fantasy, sentimentality, and the sense of wit, humor and parody are the guide for the arrangement of musical and non-musical fragments and whole genres. The variety of references to the non-musical, the association with other art species, the shameless approach to music-history, and the amiable, nevertheless subversive infiltration of well-kept boundaries between the music-branches make these composers accomplices to the expansion of the music- and art-concept.

Excerpt from: *London Minimal.* In: *Der Hang zum Gesamtkunstwerk.* (Additional brochure). Berlin 1984

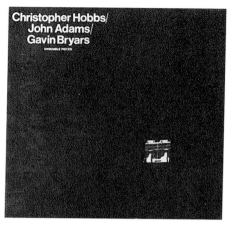

No.2 Christopher Hobbs / John Adams / Gavin Bryars: *Ensemble Pieces*

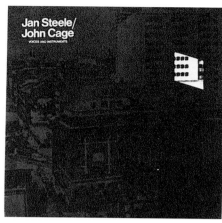

No.5 Jan Steele / John Cage *Voices and Instruments*

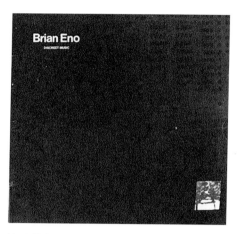

No.3 Brian Eno *Discreet Music*

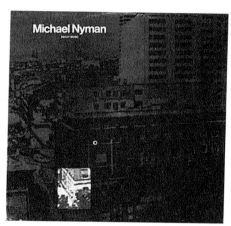

No.6 Michael Nyman *Decay Music*

No.1 Gavin Bryars *The Sinking of the Titanic*

No.4 David Toop / Max Eastley *New and Rediscovered Musical Instruments*

No.7 Music From The Penguin Cafe

No.8 John White / Gavin Bryars
Machine Music

No.9 *Irma*. An Opera by Tom Philipps.
Music by Gavin Bryars. Libretto by Fred
Orton

No.10 Harold Budd
The Pavillion Of Dreams

Oehlen, Albert [C]

Title:	Let's Go Swimming
Music:	Arthur Russell
Contents:	Coastal Dub. Gulf Stream Dub. Puppy Surf Dub
	ø 30cm, 45 RPM, 1986, Rough Trade Records, Upside Records, RTT 184
Cover:	two-color print, design: Albert Oehlen

Palais Schaumburg
'Macht mich glücklich wie nie'

Zick Zack 23

Oehlen, Albert [C]

Title:	Rote Lichter. Macht mich glücklich wie nie
Music:	Palais Schaumburg (Hiller/Fehlmann)
	ø 17cm, 45 RPM, n.d., ZickZack Platten, Nc. 2723
Cover:	two-color print, design: Albert Oehlen

Oehlen, Albert

→ Martin Kippenberger
→ Die Rache der Erinnerung

Oehlen, Markus [C/S]

Title:	Mittagspause
Contents:	Testbild. 3 x Nordpol. Intelnet. X - 9200. Militürk. InnenStadtFront. Deutschland. Derendorf. Überblick. In der Tat. Ernstfall.
Perf.:	Franz Bielmeier (g), Peter Hein (voc), Markus Oehlen (perc), Thomas Schwebel (g)
	ø 30cm, 33 RPM, 1983, Pure Freude Düsseldorf, No. PF 18 CK 9
Cover:	two-color print according to a woodcut by Markus Oehlen (1982)

Oehlen, Markus [C/S]

Title:	beer is enough. gut und boese

ø 30cm, 45 RPM, Ed. Zickzack. What's so funny about. Hamburg. LC 8963 (SF 07)

Cover: two-color print

Thanks to H. Hiller, Ziggy XY, U. Gabriel

Oehlen, Markus
→ Flying Klassenfeind
→ Die Rache der Erinnerung

Oehms, Rainer
→ Das ist Schönheit

O'Hara, Frank
→ Giorno Poetry Systems

O.J. [C/S]

Title: ...ojee!!

Music: all Songs by A.M. Wijnen and M. Postma

Contents: The warning of the walrus. De zandbank. De blaue veer. Waarom giraffen lange nekken hebben. De spiegel van eenzaamheid. Telefunken. L'ours blanc. De koolmees. De jongen en het meisje en de drie angsten. Filles commes moi. You betrayed me. Du lügst - der Lügner. De krokodil en de W.C. Mambo obscure. Nitsjewo. Het meisje en de reus.

ø 30cm, 33 RPM, 1983 Stemra No. KS 09571

Cover: two-color print

Includes folding sheet with texts and drawings

Olbrich, Jürgen O.
→ Voices Notes & Noise

Oldenburg, Claes
→ Art By Telephone
→ Giorno Poetry Systems
→ Record of Interviews...

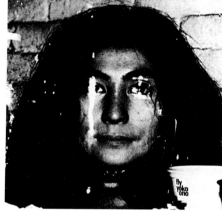

Ono, Yoko [C/S]

Title: fly

Contents: Midsummer New York. Mind Train. Mind Holes. Don't Worry Kyoko. Mrs. Lennon. Hirake. Toilet Piece / Unknown. O'Wind (Body is the scar of your mind). Airmale. Don't count the waves. You. Fly. Telephone piece

Perf.: Yoko Ono (voc, claves), John Lennon (g, p, org), Klaus Voorman (b, g, bells, cymbal), Chris Osborne (dobro), Jim Keltner (dr, perc, tabla), Eric Clapton (g), Ringo Starr (dr), Jim Gordon (dr, tabla), Bobby Keyes (claves), Joe Jones (tone deaf music co. with John Lennon)

2 LPs, ø 30cm, 33 RPM, n.d.(1971), Apple Records, No. SVBB - 3380

Cover: gatefold, outside multi-color print, portrait of Yoko Ono, design: John Lennon. Inside b/w, photo-collage a.o. Joe Jones with tone deaf music co., design: George Maciunas

Protective covers printed with texts and drawings by Yoko Ono. Included poster (58 x 58 cm), b/w
Included order card *A Hole To See The Sky Through* for *Grapefruit* by Yoko Ono

i was always fascinated by the idea of making special instruments for special emotions - instruments that lead us to emotions arrived by their own motions rather than by our control. with those instruments, i wanted to explore emotions and vibrations which have not been explored as yet in music.

i thought of building a house on the hill which makes different sounds on a windy day by the wind that goes through different windows, doors and holes. (re: grapefruit paperback edition)

then i've met joe jones who's been making such instruments for 10 years almost unnoticed. joe built me 8 new instruments specially for this album which can play by themselves with minimum manipulation (turning switches only)

Yoko Ono

Ono, Yoko
→ Aspen Magazine

Opalka, Roman [C/S]

Title: 1965/1 - ∞

Contents: Detail 1 987 108 - 2 010 495. Detail 2 136 352 - 2 154 452

ø 30cm, 33 RPM, 1977, limited edition of 400, Edition René Block, Berlin in collaboration with the Berlin Artist program of the DAAD, RO 1001

Cover: gatefold, 2 multi-color prints of photographic self-portraits, 1 picture-segment (M 1:1) and a trilingual text by the artist

In my attitude, which constitutes a program for my lifetime, progression registers the process of work, documents and defines time.

Only one date appears, 1965, the date when the first *detail* came into being, followed by the sign of infinity, as well as the first and last number of the given *detail*.

I am counting progressively from one to infinity, on *details* of the same format (*voyage notes* excluded), by hand, with a brush, with white paint on a grey background, with the assumption that the background of each successive *detail* will have 1 % more white than the *detail* before it. In connection with this, I anticipate the arrival of the moment when *details* will be identified in white on white.
Every *detail* is accompanied by a phonetic registration on a tape recorder and a photographic documentation of my face.

Roman Opalka

Opalka, Roman [P/S]

Title: Opalka 1965/1 - ∞

Contents: Detail 2 981 421 - 3 008 116

book (32,5 x 32,5 cm), 164 p. (n.pag.) with LP (ø 30cm, 33 RPM), limited edition of 600 numbered copies, published by Roman Opalka and Ottenhausen Verlag, München 1980

On the record Roman Opalka is counting from 2 981 421 up to 3 008 116. The book shows some of the photographic documentation accompaning his work.

Oppenheim, Dennis
→ Airwaves
→ Art By Telephone
→ Perfo 2

Orlan
→ Perfo 2

Orlovsky, Peter
→ Sound Poetry

Oshita, Gerald
→ Sound

Otte, Hans [S]

Title: On Earth, Klangraum 1978

Perf.: Elisabeth Weber, Wilfried Grimpe (voice), Hans Otte (direction)

ø 30cm, 33 RPM, 1979, limited edition of 200, numbered and signed, Kölnischer Kunstverein (Edition 2)

Recording of the performance on June 13, 1979 in the Cologne Kunstverein

Paalvast, Peter
→ Sound Poetry

Pacquee, Ria
→ Perfo 2

Padgett, Ron
→ Giorno Poetry Systems

Paik, Nam June [C/S]

Title: My Jubilee ist unverhemmet

ø 30cm, 33 RPM, 1977, limited edition of 100, numbered and signed, Editions Lebeer Hossman, Hamburg and Brüssel

Cover: b/w, design and text: Nam June Paik

For one side of the record Nam June Paik used a piece by Schoenberg *Verklärte Nacht* and played it 4 times slower (from 78 RPM to 16 RPM), on the other side a graphic sign is printed in grey color.

In 2 weeks I will be 45. It is time for *Archeology of Avantgarde*. I lived in Korea in the 40's, where only available informations were from Japanese books printed before World War II. Therefore it was a great luck that I heard the name of Arnold Schoenberg in 1947 or so. He immediately interested me, because he was written as a devil or the most extreme avantgarde. How-

ever there were no record or scores of Schoenberg available in Korea in 1947, except a pirate edition of his op 33 a piano piece. It took 2 or 3 years of desparate struggle to find the only available record, which was released in the pre-war Japan, *Verklärte Nacht*. I will not forget forever the excitement of holding this fragile 78 RPM record in my hand like a jewel from the Egyptian tomb. And I cannot forget the disappointment of this record, which was purely Wagnerian Quatsch.
Korean war came soon after.
25 years after this experience I found the same record of Schoenberg in a flea market in New York. I played this record 4 times slower (on 16 RPM) in a Merce Cunningham dance event. Merce smiled and said: "You improved Schoenberg".
Hamburg 2/7/1977 Nam June Paik

P.S.
I question myself now, why was I interested in Schoenberg? Only because he was described as the most extreme avantgarde. I question again myself why was I interested in "most extreme"? It is because of my Mongolian DNA. - Mongolian - Ural - Altair horse back hunting people moved around the world in prehistoric age from Siberia to Peru to Korea to Nepal to Lappland. They were not center-oriented like Chinese agrarian society. They saw *far* and when they *see* a new horizon *far* away, they had to go and *see far* more -
Tele-vision means in Greek to *see* far.
see far = fernsehen = Tele-vision

Covertext

Paik, Nam June
→ Peter Brötzmann
→ Joseph Beuys
→ Dieter Roth

Paik, Nam June / Takis [S]

Title: Duett Paik / Takis. Takis Klang-raum

Perf.: Nam June Paik (hpschd, p, voc), Takis (three metal sculptures, three string objects)

Technical Realization: Klarenz Barlow, Walter Zimmermann

ø 30cm, 33 RPM, 1979, limited edition of 200, signed by both artists, Kölnischer Kunstverein (Edition 1)

Cover: gatefold, with b/w prints of documentary photos

Direction: Paik-side 16 RPM resp. 78 RPM playable

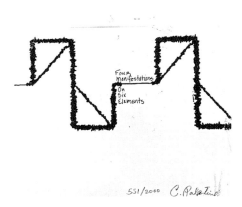

Palestine, Charlemagne [C/S]

Title: Four Manifestations On Six Elements

Contents: Two Perfect Fifths A Major Third Apart Reinforced Twice. One +

Two + Three. Perfect Fifths In The Rhythm 3 Against 2. For Piano Sliding Fifths For Piano. Three Perfect Fifths A Major Second Apart Reinforced Twice

2 LPs, ø 30cm, 33 RPM, 1974, edition of 2000, numbered and signed, Sonnabend Gallery New York

Cover: gatefold, b/w, with glued on streamer with a reproduced drawing of Charlemagne Palestine

Palestine, Charlemagne [C/S]

Title: Strumming Music

ø 30cm, 33 RPM, n.d.(1977), Shandar, Paris, No. 83517

Cover: two-color print, front drawing, back writing Charlemagne Palestine, back photo Carol Parker

STRUMMING MUSIC is a work developed over the past five years utilizing a note alternation technique with the sustain pedal of the piano constantly depressed. This technique allows the undampened strings to resonate and compound with each other creating complex mixtures of pure strummed sonority and their overtones. No electronics or special tunings are utilized; only the finest instruments available today, the Rolls Royce of pianos, *Bösendorfer* of Vienna, all of Mr. Palestine's piano works have been composed especially for this marvellous instrument.

Charlemagne Palestine (Covertext)

Panhuysen, Paul / [S]
Johan Goedhart

Title: Long String Installations. (1982-1985)

Contents: The Twins. Standing Waves. Circus. Two Symmetric Automats. Jan Huygen I. Jan Huygen II. The Paal. Day-Glo. Steelband. Spider. Splitlevel. Carillon. Gymnasium. Requiem. The Paal. Two Symmetric Automats

Perf.: Paul Panhuysen / Johan Goedhart (strings, voc), Jon Rose (cello, el-v, strings), Shelley Hirsch (voc)

Technical Realization: Ellen Fullman, Michiel van Eeden

3 LPs, ø 30cm, 33 RPM, 1986, Apollorecords Eindhoven, No. AR 088502 - 4

Cover: box with color picture of an installation and list of titles

Photo- and text documentation (29 x 29 cm), 40 p.(n.pag)

Panhuysen, Paul
→ Maciunas Ensemble
→ Terry Fox

Papp, Tibor
→ Sound Poetry

Parsons, Will
→ Sound

Pas Paravant [S]

Title: Brot und Spiel

Music: Renate Kocer (cymbals, computer), Karl Kowanz (as, ss, computer), Wolfgang Poor (bs, cymbals, computer)

ø 30cm, 33 RPM, 1986, Austro Mechana, No. 120929

Cover: two-color print, design: Peter Kogler

Pas Paravant [S]

Title: Musik aus -Zwei Zimmer- / Pas Paravant und Gäste

Music: Renate Kowanz-Kocer (perc), Karl Kowanz (as, ss), Wolfgang Poor (bs)

ø 30cm, 33 RPM, 1988 Austro Mechana, No. 150076-1

Cover: gatefold, outside b/w, inside multi-color print, design: Karl Kowanz, W. Stengl

Pas Paravant is founded 1980 as open formation of visual artists and musicians with the purpose of working together.
-Zwei Zimmer- is conceived as a performance series by Pas Paravant and alternating guests.

-Zwei Zimmer- is not substantial architecture but a reality that enables parallel courses and creates space.

Excerpt from press release

Pastior, Oskar
→ Sound Poetry

Penck, A. R. [C/S]

Title: Gostritzer 92

Contents: Einzug des Kellers. Ta Ba Ti Ti Ba. A + B = O. Frih Jazz. Soul Soul. Gostritzerstr. 92. Die Damen an die ...

Perf.: ML (as), HG (tp,dr), RW (dr,g,voc), FG (tp), HJ (g,p,b), HH (imaginär perc)

ø 30cm, 33 RPM, n.d., Weltmelodie, No. WM LP 0100

Cover: multi-color print, design: A.R. Penck

Penck, A.R. [C/S]

Title: 4 mm. Die Geschichte der 4

Contents: Westkeller. Endstation

Perf.: Frank Wollny (g), Heinz Wollny (g), Detlev Kessler (p, syn), A.R. Penck (dr, p, syn)

ø 30cm, 33 RPM, 1983, M. Werner, Weltmelodie, WM LP 4719

Cover: gatefold, multi-color print, design: A.R. Penck

Penck, A.R. [C/S]

Title: 3+1

Contents: Nachtfahrt. Vision

Perf.: Frank Wollny (g), Heinz Wollny (b), A.R. Penck (dr), H. Georg Kohnert (syn)

ø 30cm, 33 RPM, 1983, Wau-Wau Records WW-LP 46831

Cover: gatefold, b/w, design: A.R. Penck

Ralf Winkler (A.R. Penck), since his emigration to the West, has been increasingly involved with music. He participates in the production of many Free-Jazz-Records.
"The music was always there. Usually, I play drums and, together with a group, I have made records in the Free Jazz style. It is a very important medium for me to express myself in. By its means, I can release my aggressions. Music is also a better medium than painting for communicating with the audience. It is a very direct and emotional form of expression;

something which I especially need after a period of isolation." (Interview Blum, 1980)

"I play piano. I give concerts. I also make records .... At any rate, I'm mostly interested in discovering systems or signs which allow me to communicate with the future." (Interview Davvetas, 1984)

"I want to create a coherence among optics, meaning and sound, but not in the tradition of the *Gesamtkunstwerk* but by a coherence which relies more on a principle." (Interview Groot, 1979)

Schlieker: "When you play the piano in one of our exhibitions, are you inspired by the paintings around you?"

A.R. Penck: "Not really, painting and making music are two different forms of thought. But music can influence people's approach to painting. Suddenly a picture takes on a different appearance. I could create a connection, but music and painting remain in their own separate fields." (Interview Schlieker, 1983).

Excerpt from: *A.R. Penck.* (cat.) Nationalgalerie Berlin, Kunsthaus Zürich, 1988

Perf.:   Peter Kowald (b), Luigi Trovesi (sax,cl), A.R. Penck (p)

ø 30cm, 33 RPM, Kunsthalle Bern No. 30-771

Cover: gatefold, b/w, drawings by A.R. Penck and a photo by Michael v. Graffenred

Penck, A.R.   [C/S]

Title: London underground with Billi. Experiment 2

Perf.:   Billi Bang (dr, v), Frank Wollny (g), Heinz Wollny (b), A.R. Penck (p, dr)

ø 30cm, 33 RPM, n.d.

Cover: b/w, according to a drawing by A.R. Penck

Penck, A.R.   [C/S]

Title: Nachtcafé Deutschland. A + B = C? oder was ??

Perf.:   A.R. Penck (b, minisyn)

2 LPs, ø 30cm, 33 RPM, 1980, Weltmelodie No. WM LP 4717/1+2

Cover: gatefold, multi-color print, design: A.R. Penck

Penck, A. R.   [C/S]

Title: Konzert Bern 14.8.81

Music: Kowald Trio I

Penck, A.R.   [C/S]

Title: 3+2 = $\begin{smallmatrix} x\ x \\ x \\ x\ x \end{smallmatrix}$

Contents: We met Frank and Butch in town. Our sound unity

Perf.:   Frank Wright (sax), Butch Morris (co), Frank Wollny (g), Heinz Wollny (b), A.R. Penck (dr)

ø 30cm, 33 RPM, 1984

Cover: three-color print, according to a drawing by A.R. Penck

Penck, A.R.   [C/S]

Title: Bristol Concert. Dialog I. Abschied

Perf.:   Frank Wollny (g, b, voc), Heinz Wollny (b), A.R. Penck (dr, g), Andreas X (dr)

ø 30cm, 33 RPM, n.d.

Cover: one-color print, according to a drawing by A.R. Penck

A.R. Penck

Penck, A.R. [C/S]

Title: WTLSKREEEL

Contents: CRHDU DNU DRUHC. RHDUC NUD CHDRU. sccniee oiiftnc

Perf.: Frank Wollny (g, perc), Detlev Kessler (dr, perc), A.R. Penck (perc, syn)

ø 30cm, 33 RPM, 1984, Weltmelodie, WM LP 4719

Cover: b/w, according to a drawing by A.R. Penck

Penck, A.R. [C/S]

Title: Hinter der Wüste sterben die Gespenster, Jazz Rock. Afrika Paranoia, Archaik-Fri-Jazz

Perf.: W. (g), Y. (dr), F. (sax)

2 LPs, ø 30cm, 33 RPM, 1980, Weltmelodie, WM LP 4715/1+2

Cover: gatefold, multi-color print, design: A.R. Penck

Penck, A.R. [C/S]

Title: 5

Contents: xtrmpieee. N.Y. situation I. Isle in the ocean. N.Y. situation II

Perf.: Billy Bang Walker (v), Frank Lowe (sax), Frank Wollny (g), Heinz Wollny (b), A.R. Penck (dr)

ø 30cm, 33 RPM, 1984

Cover: three-color print, according to a drawing by A.R. Penck

Penck, A.R.
→   Rache der Erinnerung

Peppe, Michael
→   High Performance

Perfo 2 [P/S]

including the Symphonie Perfomantique (Catalogus Performancefestival van 12 t/m 19 mei 1984)

Participating artists:

Robert Ashley, Anne Bean, Belgian Institute for World Affairs, Marcelle van Bemmel, Guillaume Bijl, Jan Bodde, Boegel en Holtappels, Timothy Buckley, Jacques Charlier, Laure Chenard, Droparchief, Daniel Farioli, Borris Gerrets, Claudio Goulart, Roberta Graham, Servie Janssen, Hans Jongsma, Jürgen Klauke, Sonia Knox, Komar en Melamid, Eduard Koopman en Sievert Bodde, Joseph Krempelsauer, Herman Lamers en Vivien Rowe, David McDermott en Peter McCough, David Medalla, Moe Meyer, Kees Mol, Dennis Oppenheim, Orlan, Ria Pacquee, Tom Puckley, Claude Sandoz, Joseph Semah, Michal Shabtay, Stuart Sherman, SiropA, Andre Stitt en Tara Babel, Relly Tarlo en Jacoba Bedaux, Henk Tas, Blue Gene Tyranny, Marieken Verheyen, Wackenhut, Robin Winters, De Zaak, Sylvia Ziranek

ø 30cm, 33 RPM, 1984, Lantaren Venster Records Rotterdam No. LAT 8442

Cover: gatefold, multi-color print, design: Tom van den Haspel

Supplement 24 p. with text- and photo-documentation of the performance-festival in Rotterdam. Organization: Lantaren/Venster in collaboration with Wink van Kempen

Petasz, Pawel
→   Voices Notes & Noise

Peters, Steve
→   Sound Poetry

Pétronio, Arthur
→   Sound Poetry

Petschinka, Anna
→   Fünfzehn Tonspuren

Pevsner, Noton
→   Naum Gabo

Pezzati, Marko / [O/S]
Leslie Stevens

Title: 33

ø 22,5cm, 33 RPM, 1981

Cover: transparent plastic bag (33 x 26,5 cm) with plastic naps

Transparent flexidisc, included transparent plastic-foil (31,5 x 24,8 cm) with engraved title-information and direction: "These sounds are intended to be played at maximum volume levels, other levels are not remotely suitable".

Perf.: Tom Phillips, Jill Phillips, John Tilbury, Laurie Baker, Morray Walsh

ø 30cm, 33 RPM, mono, 1975, limited edition of 500, Edition Hansjörg Mayer, Stuttgart

Cover: two-color print, design: Tom Phillips

Phillips, Tom
→ obscure

Pieper Marxhausen, Reinhold
→ The Sounds of Sound Sculpture

Pignatari, Decio
→ Sound Poetry

Pintò, José M. Pezuela
→ Sound Poetry

Plessi, Fabrizio
→ Christina Kubisch

Pokorny, Jaroslav
→ Sound Poetry

Pomeroy, Jim
→ Sound

Poole, Harry C.
→ Voices Notes & Noise

Poor, Wolfgang
→ Pas Paravant

Pl6.D4
→ Sound Poetry
→ Mixed Band Philanthropist

Puckley, Tom
→ Perfo 2

Putz, Rupert
→ Fünfzehn Tonspuren

Raaijmakers, Dick
→ Sound <=> Sight

Phillips, Tom   [C/S]

Title: Words and Music. LXXIV

Contents: Excerpt from the opera IRMA op. XII. Literature for four pianos, op.XI,No.3. Lesbia Waltz, op. XV. Ornamentik, op. IX. Extracts from A HUMUMENT

Poesie Physique   [P/S]

Title: Poesie Physique

Book with spiral binding, 18 x 18 cm, one-color print, contains 2 small original pictures and 3 singles, ø 17cm, 45 RPM. François Dufrêne: Crirythme. 1965. Jean-Loius Brau: Instrumentation verbale. 1963/64. Gil J. Wolman: Megapneumies. 1963

Die Rache der Erinnerung   [C/S]

Title: Die Rache der Erinnerung

Contents: Intro. Goin' Up The Country. Billy Beat It. Bang Bang. Nobody

Knows You. Rock On. One & One Is One. Yuppi Du. Little Red Book. Sexual Healing. Sympathy For The Devil. Drei Lilien

Perf.: Schinni Schinthelm (keyboard, voc, b, g), Albert Oehlen (voc, harm, perc), Markus Oehlen (perc, voc, keyboard), Gerd Schäfer (g, b), Markus Reschtnewki (viola, keyboard, voc), Jörg Immendorff (voc), Werner Büttner (voc, perc, fl), Martin Kippenberger (voc), Berthold Locke (g, b), Günter Tuzina (sax), A.R. Penck (voc, g)

ø 30cm, 33 RPM, 1984, ZickZack Hamburg No. ZZ 205

Cover: two-color print, design: A.R. Penck

Included poster (43,5 x 60,5 cm) of a photo-collage, which shows the artistis in a sauna

Rademacher, Andre
→ Das ist Schönheit

$$\Sigma = a = b = a + b$$

eliane radigue

Radigue, Eliane [S]

Title: "Pour Farhi". $\Sigma = a = b = a + b$

2 records, ø 17cm, 1969

Cover: b/w, gatefold, 18,5 x 18,5 cm

250 double copies of this record were made. 20 were packaged in a box designed by Farhi, to whom this work is dedicated. 200 copies were signed and numbered. Side A and B of these two identical records can be played simultaneously in infinite combinations and at any speed 78, 45, 33, or 16 RPM.

RADIOTAXI©
vibrazioni del sonoro
1

SARENCO & FRANCO VERDI
"SANREMANDO"

EDIZIONI LOTTA POETICA & STUDIO MORRA, VERONA - NAPOLI

RADIOTAXI©
vibrazioni del sonoro
8

PHILIP CORNER
"2 WORKS FOR GAMELAN ENSEMBLE"

EDIZIONI LOTTA POETICA & STUDIO MORRA, VERONA - NAPOLI

RADIOTAXI [P/S]

Title: RADIOTAXI vibrazioni del sonoro

Edizioni Lotta Poetica & Studio Morra, Verona, Napoli, cover-design: Sarenco & Franco Verdi

Radiotaxi 1. Sarenco & Franco Verdi: Sanremando. (LP 0717), 1979, supplement "Lotta Poetica" No. 2/3 (1982)

Radiotaxi 2. Paul De Vree: Toute Predication. (LP 0718), 1979, supplement "Lotta Poetica" No. 4 (1982)

Radiotaxi 3. Henri Chopin: Audiopoems. (LP 0719), recorded 1973 - 1979, supplement "Lotta Poetica" No. 5/6 (1982)

Radiotaxi 4. Sarenco & Franco Verdi: Viva il Futurismo! (LP 0720), supplement "Lotta Poetica" No. 7/8 (1982)

Radiotaxi 5. Sarenco: Armaniana. (LP 0721), supplement "Lotta Poetica" No. 9 (1982)

Radiotaxi 6. Franco Verdi: Cut Up. (LP 0722), supplement "Lotta Poetica" No. 10 (1982)

RADIOTAXI©
vibrazioni del sonoro
11

JACKSON MAC LOW
"CONCERT AT THE KITCHEN 1980"

EDIZIONI LOTTA POETICA & STUDIO MORRA, VERONA - NAPOLI

Radiotaxi 7. Bernard Heidsieck: P Puissance B. (LP 0723), recorded 1962 - 1975, supplement "Lotta Poetica" No. 11/12 (1983)

Radiotaxi 8. Philip Corner: 2 Works for Gamelan Ensemble. (LP 0724), supplement "Lotta Poetica" No. 13 (1983)

Radiotaxi 9. Eugenio Miccini: Concerti di Poesia. (LP 0725), recorded 1966 - 1982, supplement "Lotta Poetica" No. 14 (1983)

Radiotaxi 10. The Guerrilla Art Action Group: Action-Interview at WBAI Radio Station-N.Y. (LP 0726), recorded 1970, supplement "Lotta Poetica" No. 15/16 (1983)

Radiotaxi 11. Jackson MacLow: Concert at the Kitchen 1980. (LP 0727), supplement "Lotta Poetica" No. 17 (1984)

Radiotaxi 12. Marcello Jori: Moldau (B. Smetana) on Moldau. (LP 0728), supplement "Lotta Poetica" No. 18 (1984)

Radiotaxi 13/14/15. Hermann Nitsch: 56ª Azione Chiesa S. Lucia Bologna. (3 LPs 0729), recorded 1977, supplement "Lotta Poetica" No. 19/20 (1984)

Radiotaxi 16/17/18. Attersee, Brus, Nitsch, Rainer, Roth, Rühm, Steiger, Wiener: Das Berliner Konzert. (3 LP 0730), recorded 1974, supplement "Lotta Poetica" No. 21 (1984)

Radiotaxi 19. Giuseppe Desiato: Ave Maria. (LP 0731), n.d.

Radiotaxi 20. Sarenco: Io Grido e Canto. (LP 0732), n.d.

Radiotaxi 21. never published

Radiotaxi 22. Julien Blaine: Passé/Futur. (LP 0734), n.d.

Radiotaxi 23. Jean-François Bory: Game Over. (LP 0735), n.d.

Robert Rauschenberg

Radovanovic, Vladan
→   Sound Poetry

Rainer - Roth   [C/S]

Title: Ratio - Konditio

Contents: Ratio-Gespräch Wien, am 17.3.79 im Radiostudio RAKORO. (Entwederoder): "HART INS GERICHT - ZART INS GESICHT"

ø 17cm, 45 RPM, 1979, limited edition of 500, Edition Lebeer-Hossmann, Brüssel/Hamburg; Edition Hansjörg Mayer; Dieter Roth's Verlag, Stuttgart

Cover: two-color print, design: Dieter Roth

Rainer, Arnulf
→   selten gehörte Musik
→   Roth & Rainer

Rainer, Helmut
→   Fünfzehn Tonspuren

Ralph, Ralph
→   Fünfzehn Tonspuren

Rasmussen, Steen Moller
→   Sound Poetry

Rauschenberg, Robert   [C]

Title: Speaking Tongues

Music: Talking Heads

---

transparent record, ø 30cm, 33 RPM, 1983, Sire Records Company / Warner Bros. Music Ltd. No. 92-3771-1

Cover: transparent plastic package with 3 overlapping movable foils in LP-size, printed in yellow, red, blue with collages by Robert Rauschenberg

Rauschenberg, Robert
→   John Cage
→   Record of Interviews

Rawcliffe, Susan
→   Sound

Rayner, Gordon
→   The Artists' Jazz Band

Recchion, Tom
→   Sound
→   Voices Notes & Noise

Record of Interviews   [S]

Title: Record of Interviews with Artists Participating in the Popular Image Exhibition. The Washington Gallery of Modern Art, April 18 - June 2, 1963

Contents: Interviews with Jim Dine, George Brecht, Jasper Johns, Roy Lichtenstein, John Wesley, Robert Watts, Tom Wesselmann, Andy Warhol, Claes Oldenburg, Jim Rosenquist, Robert Rauschenberg

---

ø 30cm, 33 RPM, 1963, Billy Klüver No. PB-474/475

Cover: white cover with mounted record-label

The Red Crayola with Art & Language   [C/S]

Title: Kangaroo?

Contents: Kangaroo? A Portrait of V.I. Lenin In the Style of Jackson Pollock: Part I, II. Marches Number 23, 24 and 25. Born to Win (Transactional Analysis With Gestalt Experiments). Keep All Your Friends. The Milkmaid. The Principles of Party Organization. Prisoner's Model. The Mistakes of Trotsky. 1917. The Tractor Driver. Plekhanov. An Old Man's Dream. If She Loves You

Perf.:   Lora Logic, Epic Soundtracks, Allan Ravenstine, Ben Annesly, Gina Birch, Mayo Thompson ø 30cm, 33 RPM, 1981, Rough Trade Records Ltd. London, No. Rough 19

Cover: multi-color print of a painting referring to Baselitz' style

The Red Crayola with Art & Language [S]

Title: Zukunftsflieger

Contents: Zukunftsflieger. Rattenmensch / Gewichtswächter

ø 17cm, 45 RPM, 1981, Konkurrenz Schallplatten / Rough Trade, No. 6005184 (Kon12)

Cover: multi-color print

The Red Crayola with Art & Language [S]

Title: Black Snakes

Music: Michael Baldwin, Mel Ramsden, Mayo Thompson

Contents: Black Snakes (Version). Ratman, the weightwatcher. The sloths. The Jam. Hedges. A portrait of V.I. Lenin in the style of Jackson Pollock, part 1. Future Pilots. A portrait of you. Words of love. Cafe twenty-one. Gynaecology in ancient Greece

Perf.: Ben Annesly (b), Allan Ravenstine (syn, sax), Chris Taylor (dr), Mayo Thompson (g, voc), Sue Johnson (managment, organisation)

ø 30cm, 33 RPM, 1983, ALRC London, Rec Rec Zürich, Pure Freude Düsseldorf, No. ALRC-1849

Cover: two-color print

Song-texts printed on protective cover

The Red Crayola

→ Art & Language

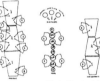

Reich, Steve [C/S]

Title: Drumming

for eight small tuned drums, three marimbas, three glokkenspiels, male and female voices, whistling, and piccolo

Perf.: Steve Reich and musicians: Art Murphy, Steve Chambers, Russ Hartenberger, James Preiss, Jon Gibson, Joan la Barbara, Judy Sherman, Jay Clayton, Ben Harms, Gary Burke, Frank Maefsky, James Ogden

2 LPs, ø 30cm, 33 RPM, 1971, John Gibson and Multiples, New York and Los Angeles

Cover: b/w, gatefold with printed photos, drawings ad handwritten texts by Steve Reich

A limited edition of 500 signed and numbered copies was issued 1972 together with a printed score in form of a leporello, 30 p. (n.pag.), 35,4 x 28 cm

Reitberger, Peter

→ Das ist Schönheit

Reitzenstein, Reinhard [C/S]

Title: According

Music: Gayle Young

Contents: According to the Moon. In Motion. Theorein

ø 30cm, 33 RPM, 1980, JWD Music, Canada, WRC1-1265

Cover: multi-color print, design: Reinhard Reitzenstein, Gayle Young

All these compositions were commissioned by Reinhard Reitzenstein to form an integral part of the three visual environments. Photographic documentation of the installations in a 24 p. booklet enclosed

Reservation-Henk-Jockec

→ Sound Poetry

The Residents [S]

Title: Eskimo

Contents: The Walrus Hunt. Birth. Arctic Hysteria. The Angry Angakok. A Spirit Steals A Child. The Festival of Death

ø 30cm, 33 RPM, 1979, Ralph Records, San Francisco, ESK 7906

Cover: two-color print

North of Greenland, well with the Arctic Circle, and on the floating ice continent surrounding the North Pole, lived a nomadic

The Residents [C/S]

Title: The White Single

Contents: Safety is a cootie wootie. This is a man's man's man's world

ø 17cm, 45 RPM, 1984, Ralph Records San Francisco

Cover: Transparent plastic cover with red print

White record

Reuter Christiansen, Ursula
→ Henning Christiansen

Revolutions Per Minute [C/S]

Title: Revolutions Per Minute (The Art Record)

Contents: Jud Fine: Polynesian / Polyhedron. Eleanor Antin: Antinova Remembers. Terry Fox: Internal Sound. Margaret Harrison: First Lines. Les Levine: Would Not Say No To Some Help. Hannah Wilke: Stand Up. Douglas Davis: How To Make Love To A Sound. Komar and Melamid: Russian Language Lesson. Helen and Newton Harrison: A Memoriam To John Isaacs. Vincenzo Agnetti: Pieces of Sound. Chris Burden: The Atomic Alphabet. Piotr Kowalski & William Burroughs: You Only Call The Old Doctor Once. Ida Applebroog: Really, Is That A Fact? Edwin Schlossberg: Vibrations / Metaphors. SITE: Comments on SITE. R. Buckminster Fuller: Critical Path. Thomas Shannon: Smashing Beauty. Conrad Atkinson: The Louis XIV Deterrent. David Smyth:

Typewriter in D. Todd Siler: Think Twice. Joseph Beuys: Excerpt From Cooper Union Dialogue

2 LPs, ø 30cm, 33 RPM, 1981/82, Ronald Feldman Fine Arts New York

Cover: gatefold, outside: grey cardboard, inside: b/w, with titles and text-information, design: Juanita Gordon

4 page folding sheet, b/w, with photoportraits of the artists and an introduction by Robert C. Morgan. Special edition of 500 copies: LP and portofolio of twenty-one original photo lithographs created as album cover proposals by the artists. All prints are signed and numbered.

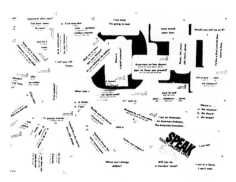

REVUE OU [P/S]

REVUE OU
Cinquième Saison
Editor: Henri Chopin, Paris

Elaborately styled magazine with folding-sheets, posters, booklets, graphics and records of international artists and poets in a folder (27 x 26 cm), each conceived by a different artist. Records in the following issues:

20/21 (1964). Record (ø 25cm, 33 RPM) with contributions by Brion Gysin, Bernard Heidsieck, Henri Chopin

23/24 (1965). Record (ø 25cm, 33 RPM) with contributions by Rotella, François Dufrêne, Bernard Heidsieck, Brion Gysin, Henri Chopin

26/27 (1966). Record (ø 17cm, 33 RPM) with contributions by Raoul Hausmann, Bernard Heidsieck, Henri Chopin

28/29 (1967). Record (ø 25cm, 33 RPM) with contributions by François Dufrêne, Paul de Vree, Henri Chopin

30/31 (1967). Record (ø 25cm, 33 RPM) with contributions by Henri Chopin

tribe of Mongolian descendants known as the Eskimo.

Their culture was passed down through generations in the form of adventurous tales and ceremonial music.

This album attempts to recreate not only the Eskimo ceremonial music, but also a living context for its existence, in the form of Eskimo stories. Although on the record the stories are told purely with sound, a written account is provided to aid your appreciation of this unique culture. For maximum enjoyment, this record should be listened to with headphones while reading the enclosed verbal accounts of what you hear. The disc should be played in its entirety and in the proper sequence of sides. A relaxed state of mind is essential. Warm clothing or a blanket should be within easy reach.

Epilogue: All the stories on this record are expressed in the past tense. This is because the Eskimo, particularly the Polar Eskimo on which this album is based, was "rescued" from the "miserable" lifestyle by welfare in the late sixties. The Polar Eskimo has been relocated entirely into government housing, and now spends most of the day watching reruns on TV.

Excerpt from covertext

"The Eskimos are the Residents" (Fast Forward)
"Not all Eskimos are Residents" (Werner Durand)

REVOLUTIONS PER MINUTE (THE ART RECORD)

Introduction by Robert C. Morgan

Means are, then, media when they are not just preparatory or preliminary . . . A phonographic disc is a vehicle of an effect and nothing more.

— John Dewey, *Art As Experience* (1934)

The image of a spiral is a marking in relation to time. It represents both the containment (storage) and the processing (retrieval) of coded information. It has literal as well as allegorical connotations in high technology. In the present circumstance, phonograph records contain sets of spirals pressed into a hard plastic vinyl. These spirals store electro-magnetic signals in a linear sequence which, when properly activated, will produce sound.

Throughout history — in fact, a *record* of time — the image of spirals has recurred in various forms and in different symbolic contexts; it is one of our most potent and primitive signs, indelibly pressed on the human consciousness. The significance of the spiral can be found in numerous representations of natural and cultural life. It usually appears in the gestural imagery of children somewhere between two and three years, a period when many children begin to draw by rotating the arm or wrist in a steady rhythmical motion. These "scribbles" and other spiral markings are observable in both abstract and concrete permutations throughout the natural/physical sciences and in the social sciences as they apply directly to everyday objects and events.

For the philosopher John Dewey, phonographic discs were regarded as a technological media capable of reproducing sound *effects.* Contingent upon the listener's discretion, of course, any record which manufactured these effects could incite various impulses and sensations which, on a superficial level, had all the attributes of a genuine experience. According to Dewey, such a response to a sound removed from its originating source could only produce a surrogate experience for the listener. His essential concern was that mimesis should not be confused with art. Indeed, the reality felt in experiencing a work of art first-hand was a reality that went beyond that of effects. To touch or hear or see or feel this reality, one had to experience the phenomenon directly as part of being in the world. A real experience was one which unfolded in time. Yet the vitality was such that it could be felt much beyond the time of the actual encounter; ideally, it would become part of the beholder, fully absorbed into consciousness.

In spite of the mind-boggling, computerized sound-splitting devices routinely used in recording studios of the 1980's, the concern for a meaningful aesthetic posture, of a human sort, is no less of an issue today. The problem as to how one experiences reality — regardless of the terms applied to it — through a qualitative sensory/mind process never ceases to be a viable concern. Today it appears as a shared universal concern. Communications technology has made information about the "good life" increasingly more apparent to everyone. (Corporations still make profits, even in a severely recessionary economy.) Yet the reality of art as a truly heightened experiential encounter with life in the present environment seems far removed from the notion of reality currently acknowledged by the status quo, including educated people whose careers have advanced concomitant to the advances of the most recent technology.

One indication of this separation between art and everyday life is the recent retreat to purely decorative and imagistic motifs. Formerly embedded within a functional context in late Nineteenth Century artisanry, these updated motifs have been revived as relics of a post-modern redundancy. Instead of attempting to synthesize profound individual feelings with a shared sense of everyday reality, artists are encouraged to fill the vapidity of technopolis with mindless adjunctive euphoria. Ideologically, this resignation toward aesthetic detachment disguises art as something both "safe" and visually

commodifiable. Yet if it is to remain viable in our culture, art cannot be removed from the reality of today's world. There is a certain privilege involved in recognizing this reality; from the fact of global consciousness, there can be no turning back.

Given the current priority toward absence of intentionality in serious art-making — wherein the content of emotional expressivity is exuberantly detached and self-effacing — the belief in an essential human experience becomes ever more crucial and necessary. With the manipulation of various media — electronically, economically, and politically — often beyond immediate comprehension, the challenge to our perceptual modes of cognition and our sensibilities has become imminent.

The fact that records are capable of transmitting a variety of sound effects with ultra-precision in reproductive quality has made it increasingly difficult to differentiate a "real time" event from that of a recording. This issue, in particular, is addressed on the album with Piotr Kowalski's "Time Machine II" in which spoken phonemes are reversed in time a fraction of a second and then laminated beside the forward progression of time: a concept most appropriate to the fantasmagorical configurations spoken by William Burroughs. In essence, the sound industry has been able to achieve mimesis with uncanny accuracy. The delivery of reproductive effects is utterly convincing.

For the majority of artists represented here, the record's primary function is that of a tool. In most cases, the content is less involved with mimesis or effects, and more directed toward communication. Although different in spirit and content, Edwin Schlossberg and Douglas Davis — two of the record's contributors — are interested in communicating ideas and feelings on an intimate one-to-one scale. Records have opened up another possibility for their narrative works: a direct channel for the spoken word. Davis is interested in inhabiting the listener's space, of forming a dyad with the listener, and thereby appropriating the feeling of being in the present-tense. Schlossberg sees the recording medium as a convenient technology for contemplating poetic language aloud and for projecting "metaphors" into time.

As a group of performances, this record/exhibition carries a certain iconoclastic underpinning; this is metaphorically stated within the album's title: *REVOLUTIONS PER MINUTE (The Art Record).* Not only is the exhibition an accessible one, existing outside as well as inside the gallery location, it is also an exhibition which can be played on a turntable almost any time of day or night. It can be heard simultaneously by people in various parts of the world. In theory, there are no spatial or geographical boundaries — other than political ones.

Rather than decry the missing "aura" of art, *REVOLUTIONS PER MINUTE (The Art Record)* celebrates the potential of art as a means transformed into media. To echo Dewey's idea, the record has the potential to move outside the preparatory or preliminary stages and toward a sense of inspired communication with the listener; this is not a condition, however, which can be imposed. Inspired communication can only be suggested through the way the medium is used. Whether we are listening to Buckminster Fuller discuss his economic and evolutionary rites of passage or Margaret Harrison's brilliant recitation of opening lines by various women authors situated over a history of two-hundred years, we are getting information on a first-hand basis. It is not an attempt at documentation so much as a prepared situation in the studio or home transformed into a reality of its own; each message

is unique to itself and is received on a different level of comprehension by each listener.

Inevitably, the question will arise as to the real distinction (if any) between an "art record" and any other type of record. (It is curious that the term "recording artist" has by now become common fare in the industry.) Records by artists — other than musicians, composers, and comedians — are by no means a recent phenomenon in the history of the avant-garde. There are Dada records, Bauhaus records, and post-war Nouveaux Realistes records — to name a few; — so what makes *REVOLUTIONS PER MINUTE (The Art Record)* all that "revolutionary"? Is there, perhaps, some new criteria at stake involving issues of formal/technical restraint in relation to the art world and the commercial recording industry? (The final issue is indirectly related to Duchamp's restraint in his choice of Readymades.)

In listening to this particular record, one might consider the following three interpretations:

1) **Literal Interpretation** — The phonographic disc revolves in time and space as we hear it (Moholy-Nagy: time + space = motion). The purely mechanical operation is not any different from the operation of other records. The only distinction is a theoretical one — that the album's title compels us to consider the "literal" means of the record more openly. In doing so, a plethora of investigations moves into the realm of creative/communicative possibility.

2) **Instrumentalist Interpretation** — The infrastructure peculiar to "art records" may defy the notion of any category given to traditional aesthetic modes. Instead of isolating "the arts" according to a mediumistic definition, the experience of art evolves through the interaction of various disciplines in which psychological, social, economic, and political interactions are clearly apparent. As Joseph Beuys has remarked on several occasions: either art exists as inclusive of the whole social structure or it holds no relevance. Of course, not everybody wants to participate in art. Even so, a person's decision to abstain from art should be an open choice, not one of social exemption or coercion. Records are informational media with the potential of exhibiting art ideas across broad socio-economic strata and in many types of situations.

3) **Contextual Interpretation** — Each artist on this album has used the medium as a context in which to apply a specific locus of ideas. In other words, the album is not made up of "recording artists", but of artists who have discovered a possibility for appropriating a standardized technology to meet their terms of work.

> A gramophone record, the musical idea, the written notes, and the sound-waves, all stand to one another in the same internal relation of depicting that holds between language and the world.
>
> — Ludwig Wittgenstein,
>
> *Tractatus Logico-Philosophicus* (1922)

Both as a political/social/artistic tool and in terms of specific content, *REVOLUTIONS PER MINUTE (The Art Record)* functions on many levels. Some artists regard the medium as a carrier of metaphors, while others prefer to deliver more explicit ideas and information. There are essentially five types of recordings (categories of intentionality) on this album:

1) **Sound Work Compositions** — These tracks emphasize properties of abstract ("concrete") sound. Terry Fox and David Smyth perform works without any spoken text, while Jud Fine and Piotr Kowalski rely specifically upon verbalized information. Vincenzo Agnetti uses both instrumentation and text in a composite

form, playing one against the other sequentially.

2) **Allegorical Narratives** — Less related to abstraction, these narrative works have a more accessible "literary" content; this category of recordings includes works by Margaret Harrison, Chris Burden, Conrad Atkinson, Eleanor Antin, Douglas Davis, and William Burroughs (with Piotr Kowalski).

3) **Situations and Encounters** — The emphasis is given to an event, either real or fabricated. In the work of Komar/Melamid, the event is staged in "real time" as a theatrical skit. In Ida Applebroog's "Really, Is That A Fact?", the party dialogues are manipulated electronically to stimulate a situation which, in fact, never existed. With Beuys, Edwin Schlossberg, and the architectural group SITE, the concern is not with fiction, but with actual documentation of an experience.

4) **Songs** — Three songs have been contributed by Les Levine, Thomas Shannon, and Hannah Wilke. In the country-western style lyrics of Les Levine, a current topical issue is addressed in a humorous, straight-forward manner. Thomas Shannon's song reflects a counter-cultural position in current song-writing by using sci-fi lyrics and special sound effects. In Hannah Wilke's "Stand Up", the commentary is intended as an operative social metaphor; the implications are clearly sexual with a curiously obverse relationship to Duchampian iconography.

5) **Heuristic Texts** — These tracts include artists' theories in action or theories embedded within some type of narrative structure. Included are contributions by Buckminster Fuller, Newton and Helen Harrison, and Todd Siler. Joseph Beuys and Edwin Schlossberg overlap between this category and "Situations and Encounters" in that the heuristic content of their verbalizations is essential to the feeling of presence in their art. With Beuys, the ideas are structured in relation to a "Public Dialogue" which is the context from which he is speaking. With Schlossberg, his unrehearsed spoken meditation is an intensely private affair.

The purpose of this Introduction is not one of critical-historical commentary; rather it is to assist in the location of a theoretical framework which appropriately presents a method for addressing the works in this album. In recent years, with alternative networks allowing for air play of artists' records plus the converging of mainstream electronic rock music with that of "new wave" concept albums, the energetic force of such ventures in the commercial marketplace has broadened the appeal of these works considerably. The likelihood of expanding the art networks into the commercial mainstream is dependent upon three important factors: promotion, education, and the willingness of major record companies to take the risk.

In spite of an uncertain economy, the decade of the 80's has brought a more open-ended structure of dissemination for recordings by artists both in Europe and in the United States. By seeking out avenues of financial backing, access to recording equipment, and expertise in advanced production techniques, experimental composers and performance artists have re-introduced a more significant use of recording media. Such outlets will continue to prove valuable among artists whose works are otherwise restricted to irregular engagements in lofts, galleries, colleges, and museum settings. *REVOLUTIONS PER MINUTE (The Art Record)* is one example of how such exhibitions can be packaged. Undoubtedly, it will set a precedent for other related works to follow.

Rochester Institute of Technology

February — March 1982

33 (1968). Record (ø 17cm, 33 RPM) with contributions by Gil J Wolman, Bernard Heidsieck, François Dufrêne, Henri Chopin

34/35 (1969). Record (ø 25cm, 33 RPM) with contributions by François Dufrêne, Bob Cobbing, Henri Chopin

36/37 (1970). Record (ø 25cm, 33 RPM) with contributions by Ladislav Novák, Hugh Davis, Sten Hanson, Henri Chopin, Bernard Heidsieck

38/39 (1971). Record (ø 25cm, 33 RPM) with contributions by Bengt Emil Johnson, Henri Chopin, Stan Hanson, Jacques Bekaert

40/41 (1972). Record (ø 25cm, 33 RPM) with contributions by William Burroughs, J.A. da Silva, Brion Gysin, Bernard Heidsieck, Henri Chopin

42/43/44 (1973). Record (ø 25cm, 33 RPM) with contributions by Arthur Rimbaud, Charles Amirkhanian, Ladislav Novák, Henri Chopin, Åke Hodell

Rheinsberg, Raffael [P/S]

Title: Wörtliche Fotografie

Book (14.7 x 21 cm), 148 p. (n. pag.) with mounted colorphoto and single record ø 17cm, 45 RPM. Limited edition of 200, Edition Giannozzo Berlin, 1981

Raffael Rheinsberg: ... I see something, I point the taperecorder in the direction of what I have seen, the taperecorder reproduces the sound of the camera, I make a note of what I have seen.

Rhizotomes

→ Sound Poetry

Rice, Boyd / NON [C/S]

Title: NON

Contents: Mode of Infection. Knife Ladder

Perf.: Boyd Rice, Robert Turman

ø 17cm, 16, 33, 45, 78 RPM, n.d., No. MR oo

Cover: two-color print, design: Boyd Rice, according to a photo from Kamera ZIE

Record with 2 holes. Printed directions on the inside cover: "multi axis, multi speed. soundtracks designed for play at 16, 33, 45 and 78. engineered to permit remixing at home. maximum volume suggested. this record is absolutely unbreakable."

Rice, Boyd / NON [S]

Title: pagan muzak

ø 17cm, n.d.(1981), Gray Beat, SLP/3000

Cover: b/w, single in LP sleeve

Two center holes and 17 lock grooves. Playable at any speed. Maximum volume suggested.

I have been releasing records of my music for a decade now. I started simply due to the fact that I did not particularly care for any of the music available to me at the time and so I felt compeled to create my own. The only instrument I had mastered at the time was imagination. Now, I'm solely dependent on it, having no knowledge whatsoever of instruments or anything else related to the creation or performance of music. To this day I cannot read a single note of music or play any traditional instrument. As soon as I had decided I wanted to release records, I also knew I wanted to exploit whatever possibilities might exist for playing with the format. Instantaneously, my head began to fill with ideas; in five or six minutes I had generated more ideas than I will propably be able to apply. My output so far represents a very small fraction of some of those possibilities, a few that seem to me the most interesting or fruitful. Although I haven't made use of alternative formats in my last several recordings, I haven't abandoned them - they continue to fascinate me, because instead of saying something to the listener, they show something to the listener. There is obviously a big difference about the two and I have always been aware of that difference and always endeaver to reflect that awareness in what I do. I try to make music into something to experience rather than just something to listen to. And the use of alternative format has been only one aspect of that intent.

Boyd Rice. In: *Extended Play.* (cat.) New York 1988

Richard, Alain-Martin

→ Sound Poetry

Richter, Gerhard [C]

Title: Daydream Nation

Music: Sonic Youth

Contents: Teen Age Riot. Silver Rocket. The Sprawl. Cross The Breeze. Eric's Trip. Total Trash. Hey Joni. Providence. Candle. Rainking. Kissability. Trilogy: a) The Wonder b) Hyperstation z) Eliminator Jr

2 LPs, 33 RPM, 1988, Torso, No. 33088

Cover: multi-color print, gatefold, design: Slim Smith, cover paintings by Gerhard Richter, front *Kerze* 1983, back *Kerze* 1982

Richter, Gerhard
→ Isa Genzken

Rickels, Horst
→ Maciunas Ensemble

Riedl, Josef Anton
→ Sound Poetry

Rietveld Audio Visueel [C/S]

Contents: The Dead Capital. Luctor et Emergo. A Touch of Fleshness. Verzet. 5/6. Wie-Tja-Poe, Collage, Traplopen, Hinderpaal. Moritori Te Salvant. Statue V. Tandboor, I Can't Stand It, Leiluun, Funk. In de Bedstee. My Strategy Towards Your Throat. Aloha From A

ø 30cm, 33 RPM, 1986, Rietveldprojekt 44, Werkstukken in het kader van lessen in geluid van Dick Lucas, Holland

Cover: original painting

Rim, Dong-Sik
→ Kunstproben

Rinnstein, Tommy
→ Sound Poetry

Rivers, Larry
→ Artsounds Collection

Robbe-Grillet, Alain
→ Aspen Magazine

Robertson, Clive
→ Sound Poetry

Robson, Ernest
→ Sound Poetry

Roche, Maurice
→ Sound Poetry

Roqué, Mariaelena
→ Carles Santos

Rosamilia, Enzo
→ Sound Poetry

Rosenberg, Marilyn R.
→ Voices Notes & Noise

Rosenfest [P/S]

Title: Rosenfest. Berlin, 1984

Contents: Fragment XXX. Akt 1 (Giancarlo Schiaffini). Akt 2 (Robert Ashley / "Blue" Gene Tyranny). Akt 3 (Henning Christiansen)

Perf.: Carlo Tatò, Giancarlo Schiaffini, Mitglieder der *Berliner Capella*, Robert Ashley, "Blue" Gene Tyranny, Jan T. Schade, Werner Durand, Patrizia Nasini

Drawer (26,5 x 21,5 cm) with catalogue and 3 single records, ø 17cm, 45 RPM. Documentation of the activities of Carlo Tatò and Carlo Quartucci: *Rosenfest Berlin* 1984. Berliner Künstlerprogramm des DAAD / daadgalerie Berlin

Rosenquist, Jim
→ Record of Interviews ...

Rosz, Martin [C/S]

Title: George-Washinton-Hotel. Auszüge-Extracts von ihm selbst gelesenreading by himself. September 1978 in New York

ø 30cm, 33 RPM, 1980, part of the issue signed. Text und Ton Berlin in cooperation with Akademie der

Künste Berlin, Berliner Künstlerprogramm des DAAD, Künstlerhaus
Bethanien Berlin

Cover: multi-color print, design: Martin
Rosz

24 p. (n.pag.) text-booklet as supplement

Rotella, Mimmo [S]

Title: Poemi fonetici 1949-75. Plura Records

ø 30cm, 33 RPM, n.d., limited
edition of 1000, signed and numbered, Plura Edizioni, Milano

Cover: b/w, gatefold

Rotella, Mimmo
→ Revue OU

Roth, Björn
→ Dieter Roth
→ Hermann Nitsch

Roth & Rainer [C/S]

Title: Misch- und Trennkunst. Autonom -
Dialogische Thematik

ø 30cm, 33 RPM, 1978, limited
edition of 300, Edition Lebeer-
Hossmann, Brüssel/Hamburg with
Dieter Roth's Verlag, Zug

Cover: b/w, revised photos from the artists

Dieter Roth revised, signed and numbered part of the
edition by hand

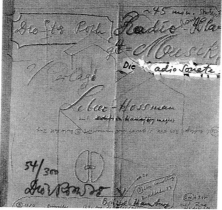

Roth, Dieter [C/S]

Title: Die Radio Sonate

ø 30cm, 33 RPM, 1978, limited
edition of 300, numbered and
signed, Edition Lebeer-Hossmann,
Brüssel/Hamburg with Edition
Hansjörg Mayer

Cover: two-color print, "adio Sonate" is
handwritten with red feltpen

Roth, Dieter / [C/S]
Karl Roth Karlsson

Title: Islenskra Fjalla. (Kalli live at
Danneckerstrasse)

Text/Music: Karl Roth Karlsson

Perf.: Dieter Roth (hammond organ, talk
+ applause), Karl Roth Karlsson (g,
voc, talk + applause)

ø 30cm, 33 RPM, 1975, limited
edition of 200, Dieter Roth's
Familienverlag, Zug

Cover: two-color print with reproduced
drawings and texts by Karl Roth
Karlsson

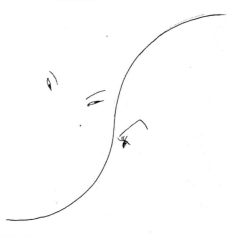

Roth, Dieter [C/S]

Title: Thy Quatsch est min Castello

ø 17cm, 45 RPM, 1979, limited
edition of 300, numbered, Dieter
Roth's Verlag, Stuttgart

Cover: b/w, according to a drawing by
Dieter Roth

Title, cover, and label refer to Num June Paiks record My
Jubilee ist unverhemmet

In 2 years I will be 50. No time for archeology of avantgarde, since I did not live in
Korea in the 40s, where only available informations were from Jap books printed before
the big war. So it was a great shock that
Paik used the name of Schönberg near the
word Quatsch, stepping on Schönberg's
head as well as Wagner's, knocking me
straight on my bleeding heart. Because he
was writing like the devil or the most
estreme anantgarde [!]. However there was
a record of Paik available in Germany in

1978, a pirate edition of Schönbergs opus 4, a string piece. It took no time, almost, to find it, released as it was by a close friend. I will never forget the exitement, as I put the tough 33LPM on the record player. never will i forget either the disappointment - this record was a pure sample of Paikian Quatsch.

Nothing happened for quite a while

1 year after this experience I took the record to a Schallplatten-Firma in a suburb of Hamburg. I played this record 4 times faster. My inner Little one seemed to smile and say: Schönberg revenged!

Mosfellssveit, March 29th 1979 Dieter Roth

P.S. I ask myself, why was i shocked by paik when he calls Schönberg's opus 4 "Wagnerian Quatsch"? Because I am an extreme Schönberg freak. On top of that Question goes an other one, why am I afraid of the word Quatsch combined with the name Schönberg? And then: Why do I feel the combination doing me harm? It is because I am myself a word, namely, a Quatsch. Hell, that hurts!

Quatsch means nothing so far. as far as i see - Quatsch, the incomparable

Covertext

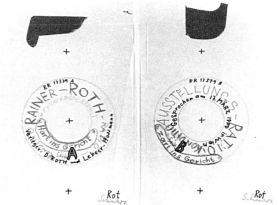

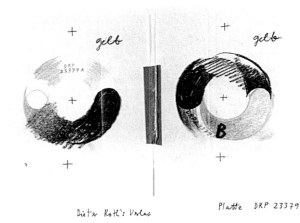

Dieter Roth
Drawings for record labels
1979. 21 x 29,7 cm

Roth, Dieter / Björn Roth [C/S]

Title: Autofahrt No 1 15-16h, 17. Apr. 79
Bilferd Nr 1 KD. 14-15, 17.Apr. 79

ø 30cm, 33 RPM, 1979, limited edition of 300, Dieter Roth's Verlag / Edition Hansjörg Mayer, Stuttgart

Cover: multi-color print of illuminated photos

Roth, Dieter

→   Richard Hamilton
→   das Kümmerling Trio
→   selten gehörte Musik
→   Sound Poetry

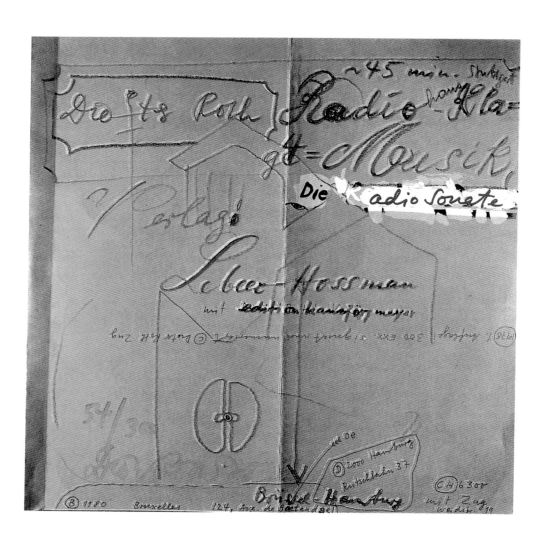

Roth Karlsson, Karl
→ Dieter Roth

Rothenberg, Jerome
→ Giorno Poetry Systems
→ Sound Poetry

Rowe, Vivien
→ Perfo 2

Ruch, Günther
→ Sound Poetry

Rühm, Gerhard [C/S]

Title: ICH KÜSSE HEISS DEN WAR-MEN SITZ gerhard rühm spielt und singt eigene chansons nach texten von rühm, bayer und wiener

Contents: ballade (rühm). marie, dein liebster wartet schon (bayer). moritat von der eisenbahn (bayer & rühm). dann bin ich gestorben (bayer). liebling, du hast mich heute ausgelacht (rühm). come again (rühm). darum spiel ich (rühm). marianne, deine kunst in ehren (rühm). ich habe zwei lieben (rühm). ich bin vermutlich wie die tiere (bayer & wiener) willst du, sprich (bayer & rühm). helene (rühm). mein stekkenpferd (rühm). hohle menschen (rühm & wiener). dar wein, dar wein, dar wein (rühm). die mutter hat das fleisch (rühm). schuppenlied (rühm). ich küsse heiß (rühm)

ø 30cm, 33 RPM, 1970, Da Camera Song, Heidelberg, SM 95022

Cover: b/w with a portrait photo and text by Gerhard Rühm, who also designed the cover

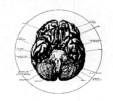

Rühm, Gerhard [P/S]

Title: Wahnsinn. Litaneien

Book, 21 x 18 cm, b/w, 92 p., included single, ø 17cm, 33 RPM. Gerhard Rühm liest aus Wahnsinn. Litaneien: Wahnsinn. Flüstergedicht. Sinngedicht. Nänie. Besäufnis. Lebenslauf. Carl Hanser Verlag, München, 1973

Rühm, Gerhard [C/S]

Title: das leben chopins und andere tondichtungen

Contents: das leben chopins. reime. reagans humor, klavierstück über einen witz des amerikanischen präsidenten. die amseln verstummen in den städten, ein kinderstück von heute. übersetzungen aus dem deutschen, vier gedichte für klavier. pornophonie. meditation über die letzten dinge

Perf.: Gerhard Rühm (p)

2 LPs, ø 30cm, 33 RPM, 1988, Edition Block, Berlin EB 115/6

Cover: two-color print, gatefold, frontcover: score drawing by Gerhard Rühm

tone-poems for piano

the method according to which my tone-poems are produced is fundamentally one and the same: a text is "set to music" in that each letter of the alphabet is ascribed to a note on the piano, whereby syllables - taken as units of speech - may be read as chords. in the order of succession and frequency of recurrence of individual notes, the music thus reflects the structural arrangement of the text. the present text cannot treat in detail the numerous possibilities for differentiation presented by this "method of transformation," which - like the row in serial music - serves as a vehicle for the selection and combination of material; still the disparate manifestations of sound in the pieces themselves would appear to give an adequate suggestion of such variants. the nature and content of a given text are however not without significance for its musical elaboration. although one is neither able nor intended to be able to decipher a piece merely by listening to it, the structural development together with the title will encourage the listener to make certain associations. in addition to its fundamental gesturally expressive character music is accordingly granted something of the semiotic qualitiy of verbal language. thus one can speak here of tone-poems in the most literal sense of the word.

Gerhard Rühm (Covertext)

Further records:
Foetus - Steirischer Herbst. Musikprotokoll 1976. ORF 0120184

Ophelia und die Wörter. Hörspiel Heute 1973. Deutsche Grammophon 2574 006

Rühm, Gerhard
→ Attersee und Rühm
→ Valie Export/Monsti Wiener
→ selten gehörte Musik
→ Sound Poetry

Russolo, Antonio
→ dada For Now
→ musica futurista

Russolo, Luigi
→ dada For Now
→ musica futurista

ø 30cm, 33 RPM, 1976, Art Super-market Records, Cambridge, Ma. USA

Cover: b/w

The Steel Instruments were inspired by a piece of sculpture by Connie Demby. A piece of stainless steel suspended from the ceiling, forming a natural curve. In the curve were suspended three objects which randomly struck the metal sheet.
The resonant quality of the sheet metal inspired me to experiment. The original instruments I built were crudely assembled and functioned mainly as sound sculptures. Over the years as part of a group called *Central Maine Power Music Company* I experimented with suspension systems to achieve the best resonant quality in the sheet metal. Both instruments can be tuned. I am developing playing a technique which is the foundation of a unique form of music evolving out of the instruments.

Covertext

RUTHENBECK

Ruthenbeck, Reiner   [P/S]

Title: Dachskulptur. 1972

Exhibition catalogue in the format of a box (20 x 16,5 cm); enclosed 1 record ø 17cm, 45 RPM, 1 leporello (120 x 17 cm), 3 double-sided printed cardboard pieces (19,5 x 15,8 cm) with title and texts by Johannes Cladders and Hans van der Grinten
Limited edition of 440, numbered, Städtisches Museum Mönchengladbach, 1972

Rutman, Robert   [S]

Title: U.S. Steel Cello Ensemble. Bitter Suites

Perf.:   David Zaig, Suzanne Bresler, Jim van Denakker, Rex Morril, Steve Baer, Robert Rutman with the Bow Chime and the Single String Steel Cello, which are instruments originated and designed by Robert Rutman

ø 30cm, 33 RPM, 1979, Rutdog Records, Cambridge/MA/USA 1009

Cover: b/w, frontside design: Robert Rutman, backside photos: Jack Weiseburg

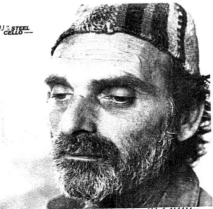

Rutman, Robert   [S]

Title: Sounds of Nothing

Contents: Sounds of Nothing. Gurjari Tori. Song of the Steel Cello

Rutkovsky, Paul
→ Voices Notes & Noise

Sacchi, Franca [S]

Title: ho sempre desiderato avere/ un cane, un gatto ed un cavallo/ ora ho un gatto ed un cavallo/ mi manca soltanto il cano

Contents: Concerto P. 2. Concerto P. 3

ø 30cm, 33 RPM, 1973, Edizioni Toselli, Milano

Cover: two-color print

Sahli
→ Sound Poetry

Salomé
→ Geile Tiere

Sanborn, John
→ Peter Gordon

Sanders, Ed
→ Giorno Poetry Systems
→ Sound Poetry

Sandoz, Claude
→ Perfo 2

Sanmark, Kurt
→ Sound Poetry

Santo S.A.
→ Sound Poetry

Santos, Carles [C/S]

Title: Perturbacion Inesperada

Contents: Perturbacion inesperada. Sauna. La boqueta amplificada. Marit reflexionant al despatx. Pertorbació inesperada

ø 30cm, 33 RPM, 1986, Linterna Musica, Madrid/Barcelona, No. A-586-013

Costume for Carles Santos designed by Mariaelena Roqué.

Pertorbació inesperada as flexidisc (ø 17cm, 33 RPM) together with the art magazine *Artics*.3, Barcelona, 1986

Sarenco / Franco Verdi [S]

Title: Sarenco / Franco Verdi

Music: Sarenco, Franco Verdi, L. Lotti, P. Guidolotti

Contents: Canta primavera. Paloma negra. Io bevo. Yvonne. Trieste mia-Tris-

tezze di Chopin. Troppo tardi. Madonna clara

Perf.: A.I.P.S Ensemble *San Remando*

ø 30cm, 33 RPM, 1979, Edizioni Factotum-Art, Verona No. 1-1979

Cover: b/w

Sarenco
→ Radiotaxi

Saret, Alan [C]

Title: Music in Similar Motion, 1969. Music In Fifths, 1969

Music: Philip Glass

ø 30cm, 33 RPM, 1973, Chatham Square Productions 1003

Cover: b/w, drawing by Alan Saret

**DE L'ENQUÊTE
SUR L'ARSENAL-ATELIER
DE LA RUE V.**

red characters *La Drama of the Tempest*. The backside of the cover contains signature and number.

Sarkis

→   La France à la Biennale

Sarkis   [C/S]

Title: De l'enquête sur l'arsenal-atelier de la rue V.

ø 30cm, 33 RPM, 1975, limited edition of 116, numbered and signed, Adelina Cüberyan, Genf

One side playable

Sarkis   [C/O]

Title: La Drama of the Tempest

ø 30cm, 33 RPM, 1979, limited edition of 30, numbered and signed, Edition La Salita

Both sides of the record *Les Brown's in Town!* and the cover are painted with the

p. 218, 219 **Sarkis**
Le Drap. A Propos de la Réunion. 1973
79 records (ø 30cm) with different covers

Sarkis. *La Drama Of The Tempest*
Installation. Galleria La Salita, Roma. 1974

SAVINIO, MUSICIEN 1914
Récital mi-scénique par Luigi Rognoni

Savinio, Alberto [C/S]

Title: Musicien, 1914. Récital miscénique par Luigi Rognoni

Contents: Il cuore di Guiseppe Verdi. Le général et la Sidonie. Je me sens mourir de néant. La passion des rotules. Matinée alphabétique. Le fanal d'épiderme. La mort de M. Sacerdote. Le doux fantôme. La solitude. Les chants de la mi-mort

Perf.: Antonio Ballista (pianoforte), Alide Maria Salvetta (soprano), Aleardo Corbetta (basso), Sergio Penazzi (fagotto), Alain Corot, Olga Durano (recitante)

2 LPs, ø 30cm, 33 RPM, 1978, Multipla records No. 3/4

Cover: gatefold, multi-color print incorporating a painting by Alberto Savinio (untitled), 1925/26

16 p.(n.pag.) supplement with texts and illustrations

Savinio, Alberto / [S]
George Antheil

Title: Futurismusik

Contents: Les chants de la mi-mort (Savinio). Death of the Machines. Venti preludi da: La femme 100 Têtes - after Max Ernst

Perf.: Daniele Lombardi (p)

ø 30cm, 33 RPM, n.d., Edi-Pan, Roma, Linea Obliqua 60003

Cover: three-color print

Enclosed booklet 24 p. with texts and photographs of Alberto Savinio and George Antheil

Albert Savinio had planned musical accompaniment for the *Chant de la mi-mort*.

"We cannot in silence overlook", writes the critic of *Soirées de Paris* with what incomparable, masterly skill and strength Savinio performs his works on the piano. Yes, it is a unique spectacle to see how this young composer, who detests jackets and sits shirt-sleeved at his instrument, behaves; to see how he raves and roars, how he kicks the pedals, swivels on his stool, and how in the storm of passion, despair, and unbounded joy, he hits the keyboard with his fists ... After each piece, the blood had to be wiped off the keys."
Two months later, the war broke out.

André Breton: *Alberto Savinio*. In: Alberto Savinio: *Menschengemüse zum Nachtisch*. München 1980

Scanga, Italo
→ Artsounds Collection

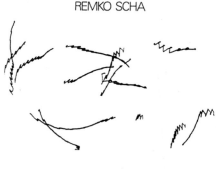

REMKO SCHA

MACHINE GUITARS

Scha, Remko [C/S]

Title: Machine Guitars

Contents: Shake. Throb. Thrash. Switch. Stroke. Sweep. Slam. Brush

ø 30cm, 33 RPM, n.d. (1982), Kremlin Products Eindhoven No. KR 006

Cover: b/w, three cover drawings (front and inside) made autonomously by the machines, design: Remko Scha

This record presents music emerging out of simple mechanical processes. All pieces are autonomously played by the machines, without human control or interference.

Scha, Remko
→ DUTCH "DIFFICULT" MUSIC

Scheffknecht, Romana
→ Fünfzehn Tonspuren

Scherstjanoi, Valeri
→ Sound Poetry

Schiaffini, Giancarlo
→ Rosenfest

Schlegel, Eva
→ Fünfzehn Tonspuren

Schlossberg, Edwin
→ Revolutions Per Minute

Werner Schmeiser / Fedo Ertl

Schmeiser, Werner / Fedo Ertl [O/S]

Title: Schmuck ist eine Sprache

ø 30cm, 1984, limited edition of 70, numbered, published by the artists

One-sided record with 14 grooves, title engraved, record cover riveted from untreated sheet iron, number punched

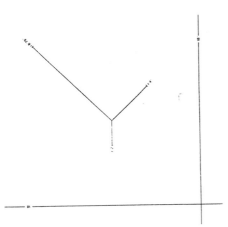

Schmidt, Thom [P]

Title: Weiche Ware (Software)

Contents: Modell 01/^{1} (87,35 Mhz UKW). Modell 01/^{2} (I can't get no) Satisfaction (Jagger-Richard)

Singlecover, included sheet, published by the artist 1982. Concept-work on the topic *Record*.

Schmidt, Walter

→ Voices Notes & Noise

Schmidt-Olsen, Carsten

→ Sound Poetry

Schmit, Tomas [O]

Title: tomas schmit's SCHALLPLATTE (99 cm). (fuer meinen freund broetz) (1970)

Wooden lath (5 x 99 x 1 cm), feltpen, hectographed label, numbered, signed, dated; 1970; approximately 10 copies

ne LATTE auf der "SCHALLP" steht. neues aus kaiserslautern. ich könnte auch sagen: schöne, seltene wort-sach-wort-sach-beziehung! tu ich aber nicht! wie bitte?

Tomas Schmit. In: *Tomas Schmit.* (cat.) Kölnischer Kunstverein, Köln 1978

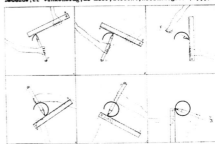

instant composers pool 010. han bennink:drums,dhung,rkangling,log drums,khène,vibra-pan,kaffir piano,dhung-dkar,oe-oe,elong,voice. misha mengelberg:piano&putney synthesizer. side a: and the great spotted woodpecker,......?"tajik,tajik,tajik" or "kik" and a very fast roll. (bennink). side b: where is the police? (mengelberg). recorded 23/3/71/stedelijk museum amsterdam by onno scholtze with 'steim' equipment. cover design tomas schmit. for mail orders, including postage in the common market f5, hfl., for other countries $5, to i.c.p. records, ff vinkumleg,de hoef,utrecht,holland.giro 789553.

Schmit, Tomas [C]

Title: Instant Composers Pool 010

Music: Han Bennink / Misha Mengelberg. Live recording of a concert in the Stedelijk Museum Amsterdam, March 23, 1971

ø 30cm, 33 RPM, 1971, I.C.P. Records Utrecht No. ICP 010

Cover: two-color print of a drawing by Tomas Schmit: Two new ways to draw a circle (1971)

saj-53, "chirps", steve lacy & evan parker. side 1: full scale/21'01''; side 2: relations/16'30'', twittering/4'10''. steve lacy (on right channel) & evan parker (on left channel), soprano saxophones. all music by steve lacy & evan parker. recorded live during "summer music", "haus am waldsee" berlin july 18th 1985. recorded & produced by jost gebers. cover by tomas schmit. free music production, behaimstr. 4, 1000 berlin 10 (west).

Schmit, Tomas [C]

Title: Chirps

Music: Steve Lacy / Evan Parker

ø 30cm, 33 RPM, 1985, Free Music Production Berlin No. SAJ-53

Three-color print of a drawing by Tomas Schmit with instructions: "a little game for a two-sided thing: fix your eyes upon the black dot in the drawing below for a minute or two (count to hundred or so). then turn over and, in same position, focus the black dot in the front drawing."

Schmit, Tomas
→   Peter Brötzmann

Schneider, Tommy
→   Fünfzehn Tonspuren

Schnitzler, Conrad   [S]

Title: Eruption 1. Eruption 2

ø 30cm, 33 RPM, n.d., Edition René Block Berlin No. KS 1001

Cover: black cardboard without information

Schnitzler, Conrad   [S]

Title: Meditation. Krautrock

ø 30cm, 33 RPM, n.d., Edition René Block Berlin No. KS 1002

Cover: red cardboard without information

Schnitzler, Conrad   [S]

Title: Die Rebellen haben sich in den Bergen versteckt. Jupiter

ø 30cm, 33 RPM, n.d., Edition René Block Berlin No. KS 1003

Cover: blue cardboard without information

Schnitzler, Conrad   [S]

Title: Gelb

Contents: 12 Stücke aus dem Jahr 1974

ø 30cm, 33 RPM, n.d. (1981), Edition Block Berlin, EB 110

Cover: yellow cardboard without information

Schnitzler, Conrad   [S]

Title: Der Riese und seine Frau (1976). Bis die blaue Blume blüht (1980)

ø 30cm, 33/45 RPM, n.d. (1981), Edition Block Berlin, EB 111

Cover: green cardboard without information

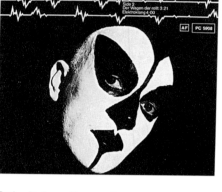

Schnitzler, Conrad   [C/S]

Title: Conrad Schnitzler

Contents: Auf dem schwarzen Kanal. Fabrik. Der Wagen rollt. Elektroklang

ø 30cm, 45 RPM, 1980, RCA Records Hamburg No. PC 5908

Cover: b/w

Schnitzler, Conrad   [S]

Title: Control

Contents: Control A. Control B

ø 30cm, 33 RPM, 1981, Dys, Ft. Collins, Colorado No. Dys 04

Cover: b/w, graphic design: Conrad and Richard Schnitzler according to a drawing by Tom Katsimpalis

Contains sheet with picture of a drawing by James Dixon

Schnitzler, Conrad   [S]

Title: Conal

Contents: N 1 - 21.45. N 2 - 21.50

ø 30cm, 33 RPM, 1981, Uniton Records Oslo No. UNITON 002

Cover: red with black print, design: Conrad and Richard Schnitzler

Schnitzler, Conrad   [S]

Title: Convex

Contents: Convex. Concav

ø 30cm, 33 RPM, 1982, No. GS 1-002

Cover: b/w, design: Conrad and Richard

Schnitzler, Conrad / Wolf Sequenza [S]

Title: Consequenz

Contents: Fata Morgana. Weiter. Tape 5. Bilgenratte. Afghanistan. Lügen haben kurze Beine. Nächte in Kreuzberg. Humpf. M5-477. Pendel. Wer geht da? Copacabana

ø 30cm, 33 RPM, n.d., No. KS 1004

Cover: white, with sticker, inscription with black felt pen, encirceled with red felt pen

Contains sheet with reproduced drawings and directions

Schnitzler, Conrad [S]

Title: CON 84

Contents: X 19... X 18... 28.6.84 Blasen. 16.4.84 (1+2). X 19. X 18#. X 18.. 16.4.84.. X 19.. X 18 (1+2). 16.4.84 Frei. X 18# (1+2). X 19...

ø 30cm, 33 RPM, 1984, limited edition of 222, numbered and signed, published by the artist

Cover: original hand-print, with stamp CON

Photostat of score included

Schnitzler, Conrad / Michael Otto [S]

Title: Micon in Italia

Contents: Sono Finite. Sage mir. Colore/ Suono. Espresso. Contanastro. Thompstone. Circus. Controllo. Poco Prima. Wa Höooa. Sul Nastro Con Fase. Collegato. Continua. Tradizionale Collegate. Rosso Rapido. Un Punto. Gino Ginelli. Hand-Clap

Perf.: Conrad Schnitzler (el), Michael Otto (bassoon)

ø 30cm, 33 RPM, 1986, Auf dem Nil, Milano DMM 03 R

Cover: b/w

Supplement (17 x 23,7 cm)

Schnitzler, Conrad

→ Das ist Schönheit

Schrom, Günther

→ Fünfzehn Tonspuren

Schwitters, Kurt [S]

Title: "An Anna Blume". (To Eve Blossom - A Anna Lafleur) "Die Sonate in Urlauten". (Sonata in Primeval Sounds - Sonate Présyllabique)

Contents: An Anna Blume (Kurt Schwitters). To Eve Blossom (Ernst Schwitters). A Anna Lafleur (Philip Granville). Die Sonate in Urlauten (Ernst Schwitters)

ø 30cm, 33 RPM, 1958, Limited edition of 100, numbered and signed by Ernst Schwitters, Lord's Gallery, London

Cover: two-color print, specification: signed by Ernst Schwitters

"An Anna Blume" (1919) was the most successful of his poems. It was the highlight of my father's traditional "Merz-evenings", lecture-recital evenings at his home in Hanover, regularly attended by the Hanover intelligentsia, and by artists and people interested in art from all over the world. Eventually in 1927 the Süd-deutsche Rundfunk got my father to recite this poem and his equally famous "Sonate in Urlauten". The present L/P record begins and ends with the original two recordings made at the time by my father. "An Anna Blume" is a conventional bourgeois declaration of love, interspersed with sarcastic nonsense, to force us to smile at our futility.

During those turbulent years of cultural development Kurt Schwitters met and collaborated with other leading Dadaists, Arp, Tzara, van Doesburg, Raoul Hausmann and others. During a lecture tour in Prague in 1921, Kurt Schwitters heard Raoul Hausmann's sound-poem "fmsbw". He immediately recognized the potentialities of this new form of expression, and he recited it constantly in his lectures calling it "Portrait of Raoul Hausmann". The time had come to rebuild after destruction and in more "constructivist" period, which in Kurt Schwitters' collages, paintings and sculpture extends from about 1923 to about 1928, he built up slowly, but with great logic and concentration, a totally abstract "sound-poem", the "Sonate in Urlauten ". Over the years the Sonata grew, both in size and variations, until it had little or no resemblance to Raoul Hausmann's original poem. The original "fmsbw" became "fümms böwötää zääuu-pögiff-kwiiee!" and was merely part of one of the many themes of the Sonata.

Ernst Schwitters (Excerpt from covertext)

Schwitters, Kurt [S]

Title:	Ursonate
Perf.:	Jaap Blonk
	ø 30cm, 33 RPM, 1986, BVHAAST, Amsterdam, No. 063
Cover:	multi-color print

Included booklet (8 p.) with printed text in faksimile. Shortly after its release this recording by order of the court had to be withdrawn.

selten gehörte Musik [S]

Title:	selten gehörte Musik von den 3. Berliner Dichterworkshop 12./13.7.73 an der Meinekestraße 6 in Berlin in der Wohnung des Rudolf Prinz zu Lippe
With:	Dieter Roth, Gerhard Rühm, Oswald Wiener
	ø 30cm, 33 RPM, 1973, edition of 1000, 100 copies are signed, numbered and with an original graphic by Roth, Rühm and Wiener, Edition Hansjörg Mayer, Stuttgart, London, Reykjavik
Cover:	three-color print

Dedicated to Kalli, Björssi, Una, David, Sarah, Vera, Adam as advice from their fathers

Schwitters, Kurt [S]

Title:	"An Anna Blume". (To Eve Blossom - A Anna Lafleur) "Die Sonate in Urlauten". (Sonata in Primeval Sounds - Sonate Présyllabique)
Contents:	Die Sonate in Urlauten (short version by Kurt Schwitters). Die Sonate in Urlauten (read by Ernst Schwitters). An Anna Blume (recited by Kurt Schwitters). To Eve Blossom (translated by Kurt Schwitters; adapted and read by Ernst Schwitters). A Anna Lafleur (translated and read by Philip Granville)
	ø 30cm, 33 RPM, not dated, limited edition of 100, numbered and signed by Philip Granville, Lord's Gallery, London
Cover:	b/w, specification: signed by Philip Granville

selten gehörte Musik

Also worth mentioning is the *selten gehörte Musik*, which emerged from the *Berliner Dichter-Workshop* in 1972, and which was the first literary meeting among Friedrich Achleitner, Günter Brus, Gerhard Rühm, and Oswald Wiener. The complete results without an intervening representative selection have been documented in one volume which contains all manuscripts that originated during the meeting. The contributors Dieter Roth, Rühm, and Wiener, began recording music at home; this resulted in concerts with enlarged or various casts in Munich, Berlin, Hamburg, Karlsruhe, and with extended participation again in Munich. Most of these concerts are documented on records.

Dieter Schwarz. Excerpt from: *Auf der Bogen Bahn.* Studien zum literarischen Werk von Dieter Roth. Zürich 1981

Schwitters, Kurt

→ dada For Now
→ Sound Poetry

selten gehörte Musik [S]

Title:	selten gehörte Musik. NOVEMBER-SYMPHONIE (Doppelsymphonie: 1.

dritter teil:

scherzo

(die themen sind karakteristisch verschieden vorzutragen)

Lanke trr gll *(munter)*	(M)	III
pe pe pe pe pe		8
Ooka ooka ooka ooka		

Lanke trr gll	III
pii pii pii pii pii	9
Züüka züüka züüka züüka	

Lanke trr gll	III
Rrmmp	4
Rrnnf	

Lanke trr gll	III
Ziiuu lenn trll?	3
Lümpff tümpff trll	10

Lanke trr gll	III
Rrumpff tilff too	4

Lanke trr gll	III
Ziiuu lenn trll?	3
Lümpff tümpff trll	10

Lanke trr gll	III
Pe pe pe pe pe	8
Ooka ooka ooka ooka	

Lanke trr gll	III
Pii pii pii pii pii	9
Züüka züüka züüka züüka	

Lanke trr gll	III
Rrmmp	4
Rrnnf	

Lanke trr gll

Kurt Schwitters. Facsimile of one page of *Die Sonate in Urlauten*. 1932

Symphonie. Symphonie 1A). 2. Berliner Musik-Workshop 15.-26. Nov. 1973

With: Dieter Roth, Gerhard Rühm, Oswald Wiener

2 LPs, ø 30cm, 33 RPM, 1974, edition of 1000, 100 copies with an additional single, Edition Hansjörg Mayer, Stuttgart

Cover: gatefold, multi-color print with numerous photos of the performing artists

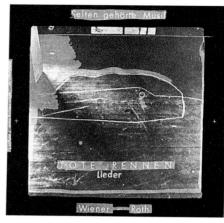

3 LPs, ø 30cm, 33 RPM, 1976, Edition Hansjörg Mayer, Stuttgart, London, Reykjavik

Cover: box, b/w, inside and outside with photos and drawings

selten gehörte Musik [S]

Title: selten gehörte Musik. TOTE RENNEN. Lieder

idea, text, music, vocals, piano, fluegelhorn, percussion, recording and cover design by Oswald Wiener and Dieter Roth, Iceland

ø 30cm, 33 RPM, 1977, Edition Hansjörg Mayer, Stuttgart/London, F 666.082

Cover: three-color print

selten gehörte Musik [S]

Title: selten gehörte Musik. Münchner Konzert Mai 1974

With: Günter Brus, Hermann Nitsch, Dieter Roth, Gerhard Rühm, Oswald Wiener

3 LPs, ø 30cm, 33 RPM, Edition Hansjörg Mayer Stuttgart, London, Reykjavik No. f 66 5508 - 10

Cover: box, b/w, with documentary photos by Karin Mack

selten gehörte Musik [S]

Title: selten gehörte Musik. Streich-quartett 558171 (Romenthal-quartett). Recorded in Diessen/-Ammersee, Villa Romenthal 12.11.1975. Plattenfüller Klavier zu 4 Händen (Roth, Nitsch). Recorded in Stuttgart, Nov. 1975

With: Günter Brus, Hermann Nitsch, Dieter Roth, Gerhard Rühm

selten gehörte Musik [S]

Title: selten gehörte Musik - Musica si ascolta raramente. Das Berliner Konzert. November 1974, Berlin, Kirche zum heiligen Kreuz

With: Attersee, Günter Brus, Hermann Nitsch, Arnulf Rainer, Dieter Roth, Gerhard Rühm, Dominik Steiger, Oswald Wiener

3 LPs, ø 30cm, 33 RPM, n.d. (1977), Pari e Dispari, Reggio Emilia; Edizioni Morra, Neapel; Edition Hansjörg Mayer, Stuttgart

Cover: box, one-color print, inside and outside with photos by Donatelli Sbarra

Also part of the edition Radiotaxi

selten gehörte musik [S]

Title: Abschöpfsymphonie

With: B. Roth, D. Roth, Renner, Hoss-mann, Cibulka, Attersee, Mayer, Nitsch, Rühm, Thomkins, Schwarz, Wiener

4 LPs in a box, ø 30cm, 33 RPM, Edition Hansjörg Mayer, Stuttgart, and Edition Lebeer-Hossmann, Bruxelles/Hamburg, 1979

Cover: one-color print inside, and outside with photo sequences of the concert, May 1979 in Munich, by Peter Frese

The fixed record labels are white without any information. A collection of additional labels with different titles is included.

Semah, Joseph
→ Perfo 2

Serra, Richard
→ Art By Telephone

Shabtay, Michal
→ Perfo 2

Shannon, Thomas
→ Revolutions Per Minute

Sherk, Bonnie
→ Sound Poetry

Sherman, Stuart
→ Perfo 2

Sherman, Stuart

"Liszten!", or Untitled. 1986

The first sonata in B-flat major by Franz Liszt (Dezsö Ranki, piano) half as record, half as musical score, mounted on cardboard, ø 30cm

The record is divided in 2.
The music is divided in 2.
The listening ("Lisztening") is divided by 1 into 1.
0 = 0.
Keep counting.
Stuart Sherman

See illustration below

p. 228, 229 **Stuart Sherman**
Drawings. 1987-88. 30,4 x 22,6 cm
Idea: Stuart Sherman. Renderings: Tom Zummer

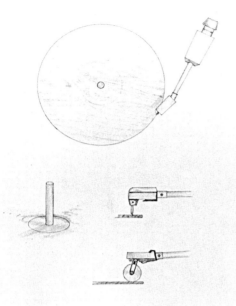

WOODEN RECORD, CIRCULAR SAW

THE NEEDLE GOES ROUND AND ROUND, BUT IT BEGINS HERE

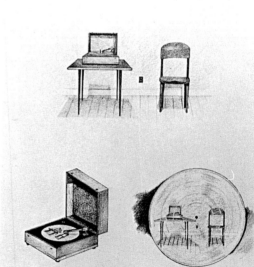

RECORD OF A PLACE

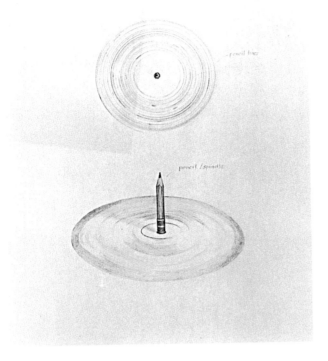

pencil lines

pencil /spindle

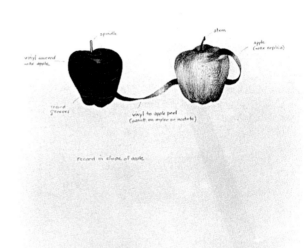

spindle

stem

Apple
(wax replica)

vinyl covered
wax apple

record
grooves

vinyl to apple peel
(paint on mylar or acetate)

record in shape of apple

Mozart Ebenbecri

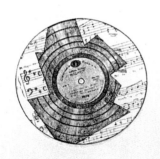

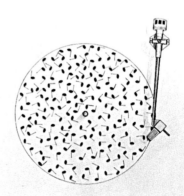

Actual record fragment completed by sheet music
of same Mozart composition.

Stuart Sherman

1987

Stuart Sherman

Siler, Todd
→ Revolutions Per Minute

da Silva, J.A.
→ Revue OU

Sinzinger, Ebba
→ Fünfzehn Tonspuren

Sirop A
→ Perfo 2

SITE
→ Revolutions Per Minute

Smithson, Robert
→ Art By Telephone

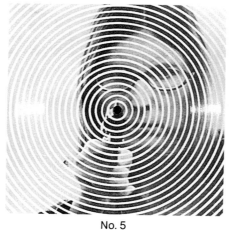

No. 5

S.M.S.   [P/S]

Title: S.M.S. The Letter Edged in Black Press

collection of 73 multiples in form of 6 portofolios, each 18 x 33 cm, published by William Copley, New York, 1968, limited edition of 2000

Among the 73 multiples are the records:

S.M.S. No. 2, April 1968. Marcel Duchamp, record, ø 17 cm, 33 RPM, one side playable, other side with glued on cardboard. On it the sentence in spiral form: *Esquivons les ecchymoses des Esquimaux aux mots exquis*

No. 2

S.M.S. No. 5, October 1968. Diane Wakoski: The Magellanic Clouds. Soundfoil on cardboard folding card (17,5 x 17,5 cm), 33 RPM

S.M.S. No. 6, 1968. Bernar Venet: The Infrared Polarization of the Infrared Star in Cygnus. Record, ø 17cm, 45 RPM

Smegma   [C/S]

Title: Pigs For Lepers

Contents: Antbone. ID-O-MATIC. In The Murder Room. Adena Arcives Presents. Dying Cows with Putrid Not Praiseworthy Predation. Madness Mombo. oh-ooh! DICKENS-MEGLEE Part 35. Mr. Potatoheads' Flotation Exercises

ø 30cm, 33 RPM, n.d., Pigface Records, Portland, USA, No. Pig 007

Cover: multi-color, original painting

Smegma
→ NON + Smegma

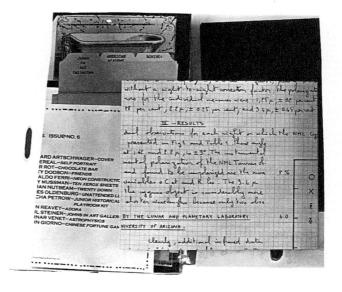

No. 6

STEREO LP 1009/10
CHATHAM SQUARE

MICHAEL SNOW

MUSICS FOR PIANO, WHISTLING MICROPHONE AND TAPE RECORDER

My first consideration in writing the text which you are now, I presume, reading ("presume": I guess that this text will still be here to read later even if you aren't reading it now) was to write something which when printed would cover all four faces of this album. Of several ideas for a design for this album cover or jacket this seemed at the time to be the best. Remains to be seen. Ruminations gradually clarified to this stage: I would write something that would fulfill several requirements, the basic one being that it function as a "design" or "image" that would be both decorative and "plastic". Another requirement that might better be approached now as an intention or ambition was the image quality and the reading quality be unified and that it be "literature" that could be read with aesthetic profit, at first, apart from the reader having any actual experience of the music which this will, in effect, enclose but consequently it should nevertheless have some connection, varying in strength, with the music, indeed, that some of it would be so written that it would be interesting to read while half-listening to the music. If you could give your undivided attention to both reading this and listening to the music I'd be very s surprised. However, I suppose its possible. Before I attempt to amplify that I ought to say that because of the design of this album you can read this without owning the album which I assume is enclosed in plastic. Perhaps it's not. Anyway the text continues on the two inside faces and concludes on the back. This is of course the beginning. It will get really interesting. Now I should return to a discussion of how, when and if you should simultaneously read this text and listen to the music. You can ignore my instructions but you will soon see that certain parts of this text might be read against or with certain parts of the music and I plan to make it evident when such parts occur. For the moment please don't put on one of the records. I don't want to give the impression that I intended the music contained herein to be mere background music for the reading of this text or any other activity. Obviously I have no control over that. If you want to put one of the records on right now, you can go right ahead, What can I do about it? Maybe one of them is playing right now. Which one? A guess: "Left Right" right? . . . Perhaps for some people it would be preferable to, at first, half-listen to the music and half-read this and later pay more attention separately to either. I hope that the music can be listened to often with or without this text. The music is more important than this. It occasioned it. However, I would really like this to be as good as the music . . . I've been making music since about 1945. I've been writing about ten years longer but not generally with the same intent as that behind the making of music, just casual writing, at first school stuff, some plays and skits at a summer camp, Camp Calumet. Later mostly letters, lots of letters, plus a couple of essays, one of which is somewhat close to this and most recently the script, largely dialogue, for a 4½ hour film. I'm self-taught on piano, trumpet and typewriter. Whistling is natural. I started out learning how to play blues-boogiewoogie piano because I liked it. No doubt there were other reasons too. I met some other problem children in high school who were playing other instruments, and gradually there were bands and then even gigs, especially after high school while I went to the Ontario College of Art. Subsequently for about 3 years I mostly made my living from music and played with many fine musicians such as Cootie Williams, Buck Clayton, Jimmy Rushing, George Lewis. In the summers of '48, '49, '50 for a week or two I and some of my Toronto jazz friends went to Chicago where we jammed here and there, once with the great Pee Wee Russell and went to some parties at the home of the equally great blues-boogie pianist Jimmy Yancey. He, Albert Ammons, Cripple Clarence Lofton, others and myself played at these parties and Yancey, very impressed proclaimed me his "pupil" and taught me some of his stuff. This may not impress you but it meant a lot to me then and now. Now back to the music sleeping on the discs between these sheets (unless it's already up and around the room) or rather back to this text which, to repeat, is more or less connected to the music. . . I should mention that since 1963 I have been especially interested in trying to compose, in my films, strong image and sound relationships. In 1964 I finished a film called "New York Eye and Ear Control". Shot and edited by myself, it has a sound track by a great (again!) group with Albert Ayler, Don Cherry, Roswell Rudd, Sonny Murray. This black and white film was an attempt to set up a simultaneity of separate but equal picture and sound . . . Sound-film aesthetics is a vast subject and perhaps this is not the time and place to discuss it. Perhaps it is. In my films I hope to modulate the spectator's consciousness by composing with varying emphasis on the nature of the sound in relation to various means of indicating the fictional source of the sound within the range of image possibilities (from abstract pure color-light to "realistic" representation). "Rameau's Nephew by Diderot (thanx to Dennis Young) by Wilma Schoen" made in '73-'74 is the most radical of these image-sound compositions and most closely related to this . . . Language, spoken or written, can certainly be categorized as representational. If you were now to play record #1, side #1 (don't) and read this (to yourself) while listening you'd be experiencing something related to the hearing/seeing/thinking experience of certain parts of certain of my films . . . The "image quality" of this text can be examined: Read this then look at it. Those are very different activities. When looked at it is meaningless. No jokes now. Something that can be read cannot be meaningless. Stressing the "look" may tend print towards "visual art" forms but when it arrives it has become "picture" not "sign". Nevertheless it is a peculiarity of language that it can claim that a picture can be "read". The reverse is difficult. A dictionary of picture-meanings would have to be in print not in pictures, an inter-language dictionary, a translation, finally a rendering not of meaning but of possible language equivalents . . . The first side of the first record is the beginning of a piece called "Falling Starts". It's a piano and tape recorder piece made in 1972 (first version 1970) and is dedicated to Baron Von Kayserling. It's arriving too late to help, he's been sleeping constantly for about 200 years. Lucky him, lucky Goldberg, lucky Bach and lucky us that this record wasn't available in 1792. Since we are lucky to have it hear and now lets finally hear it . . . It's on . . . Let's face the music and read! Those first groups of high sounds that you are hearing, have just heard of it you're just reading this and haven't as I suggested, put on the record, will hear when you do . . . do it now . . . are sped-up re-recordings of a piano phrase which at its "normal" speed should be heard soon, just has been heard, will be etc. This phrase was composed and played by myself for its use as a subject of tape recording compression and elongation. Tenses. Comprehension mention: Village Voice critic Tom Johnson wrote that this phrase (the musical phrase) is an "atonal" phrase. It's not. It's built on an F minor scale and harmonically there are some open major sevenths. Flatted fifths and seconds. Several phrases were tested out, this one seemed to have an internal fitness for its intended use. As you can hear, it starts very low, the right hand with slight acceleration rises and falls and rises and falls to the top of the keyboard while the accompanying bass figure revolves in the same low tonal area. The right hand phrase covers almost the entire range of the keyboard and the bass provides a reference for this aural space. The Chordal clusters and the requisite amount of resonance in performance generate new inner vibrations and re-reveal their original ones when slowed down as you may be hearing right now. If one has understood the subject phrase structurally then the subsequent variations may be more than sensation though that can be a lot. Bathyspheric bubbles under ping ping ping ping ping, "Falling Starts" continues its descant descent on Side 2 with the final and lowest version which is a fundamental experience of sound generation and reception as tactile. Membrane to membrane to brain. I recommend that you stop reading this for a few minutes and listen closely to the last few minutes of Side 1 and then go on with Side 2, listen to it for awhile and then resume reading this . . . The 2 sides obviously can be listened to separately but the first time you should hear the whole piece all the way through and don't read or talk. Now, this sentence is nothing very important, just something to read word by word while you're listening, a sentence that won't interfere much with your listening and since it doesn't say much (that's twice!), won't interpose other subjects between what you're doing (reading) and listening attentively . . . flutter flutter . . . putt putt putt putt putt . . . cars in the rain on a dark street . . . the helicopter arrives with the motorboat . . . Ultramarine whale dreams . . . a snore at the shore . . . pat pat pat pat pat pat . . . morning running shoes . . . The time-space between notes can now be cavernous. Days of mixed metaphors can seem to go by between a certain two bass notes . . . Boom! . . . sh sh sh sh sh sh sh s s s s s s s s s . . . Perhaps someone else could change the record so that you could go on reading this. Ask them to put on "W in the D". No, wait! Reading this between records may put more emphasis on its quality than perhaps it can take. The style so far has been quite plain hasn't it? It needs to be much more complex now. Là! L'Asie. Sol miré, phare d'haut, phalle ami docile à la femme, il l'adore, et dos ci dos là mille à mis! Phare effaré la femme y resolut d'odorer la cire et la fade eau. L'art est facile à dorer : fard raide aux mimis, domicile à lazzi. Dodo l'amie outreé! Surprise. That was less conversational, more musical but I didn't write it. I don't know who did. André Theberge gave it to me . . . OK, before "W in the D" gets started (wait a minute) the following is some information about it. It's a recording of me whistling and breathing. There are no electronic alterations in the sound. It's documentary, real time. I held the microphone in my hand and moved it into and out of the airstream of the whistled phrase (sometimes it's just air, no notes). The air intake preceding each phrase brackets them all. The length of each phrase was determined by how long I could whistle on the amount of air I'd stored. I tried to make each phrase a distinct event in itself although there are some repeats with slight variations of a dee dee dee dee dee dee dee dee repeated single air-note motif. Please don't read any of this aloud unless instructed to. You could however give notice to a request that the record be started now and you'll hear the just described phrase first. It begins the piece and you'll note later that it ends it although despite the fact that you've never heard it, if you trust this text you already know that that is how it ends. For my ear-mind the air blowing on the microphone produces an aural picture plane . . . A concert playing of this tape (made in 1970) occurred (N.Y.U. 1972). I had all the lights turned off and the tape whistled in the dark. This is very effective. It can enhance the associational, imagistic effect of some of the phrases and of course having seeing muted allows for a concentration on listening. If thinking doesn't take over one may perceive more of the subtleties that are in the music. If, as I suggested, you've already started the record you're probably at whooweedleyaduh whooweedleyaduh whooweedleyaduh whooweedleyaduh or if you are about to play the record why don't you leave off reading this for the duration of the piece, turn off the lights or just hold your hands over your eyes? . . . (I suppose that there are plenty of reasons why you might not want to do this and evidently you are still reading). Well, darkness isn't absolutely necessary, in fact it's not necessary at all . . . ruhrr tweet tweet tweet tweet tweet . . . The music is quite interesting with your eyes open looking at whatever you want to look at. Some people turn on their T.V. set with the sound off while listening to records. With the T.V. sound on as well can be interesting but please don't try it with this record. You could put every damn thing on and keep on reading this till the phone rings but if you do I hope you'll give your undivided attention to the music on some other occasion . . . By the way, marijuana and music, like Michael, microphone and my, both begin with M. M m m m m m m . . . Why don't you smoke some now while you're still listening to "W in the D" and reading this? "W in the D" is about 23 minutes long and you can breathe along with it . . . puff puff puff puff puff peep peep sweeahoh . . . here comes the ending now, sort of Beethovenesque in an airy way. The dee dee dee dee dee dee dee repeated note motif is repeated sans note, just air, and is followed by a long exhalation. That's it. Between records: One will perhaps note that the tapes used here date from '70-'72 and the record is being issued in '75. Perhaps you wondered why there aren't more recent pieces. No? Well, anyway for the last about three years apart from sound for my films, I have been very involved in playing freely improvised music with certain groups in Toronto (mostly The Artist's Jazz Band (A.J.B.) and apart from a couple of other solo tapes (one for trumpet), I have been a contributing member in these groups and the music is collective composition. I had been wanting to make these "personal" tapes publicly available for sometime and it finally became possible which made possible the idea of wrapping these solos in this solo. The original tapes are "home" tapes and not studio quality recordings. There is more s s s s s s s s s s s certainly. However, I felt that I could not re-make them in a studio. They partake of a certain time and place. They have been expertly assisted to this stage by Kurt Muncacsi of Basement Recording Studio and by Klaus Kertess . . . Now do you feel like hearing the last side? Hungry? Oh come on let's give it a spin . . . It's possible that you may not like my music or my prose or both together but I certainly hope not. That would certainly be a drag, spending the money and then not liking the music and then reading this crap to top it all off! Still, if you don't like the music and you do like this at least you've got this! If the album was recommended to you maybe you should discuss it later with whoever it was. All I can say is that I've done and am doing my best and that maybe you'll like the music more on re-hearing and you'll never have to read this again. Maybe this is better as "image" than as literature! I'll keep working on it. You do your best too. It's not just up to me . . . The following should be read aloud or sung: except for the occasional onomatapoeia, yes, the occasional onomatapoeia is excepted, please don't read aloud or sing any of this text along with any of the music. Why, oh why? Because, then the text is liable to become a song-lyric stimulus for your own, choose one now, choice of notes and the music an accompaniment. This is my text and my music and if you want something that can be "interpreted" please look elsewhere. Autre part. That sounds pretty autocratic I suppose and I realize that if you have bought this it could as accurately be said said to be "yours". Also if I'd never mentioned reading aloud or singing you might not have even thought of it and there'd be no problem. Still singing? Should have indicated a stop after "accompaniment" . . . Back to the music and on to the back of the album: the last side of the 2nd record is titled "Left Right," was taped in '71 and is also a tape-piano piece because it was recorded in a way that made a part of the recording process a part of the music. In other words it wasn't only a "documentary" recording of the piano being played. The preceding text was "documentary", it has been other "modes" and will meta-morphose again. If you would just put the record on now you would hear some qualities that are difficult for me to describe. (My limitations as a writer?). Maybe somebody else (maybe you) could describe them. "Distortion" has a moral tone, doesn't seem right but probably has to be used. The piano music was recorded by laying, lying the microphone on its side on the top of my old upright piano with the recording volume way past its proper maximum. This was done to a nice tape recorder, a Uher which seems to have survived the strain. The percussive playing of the chords smack-rattled the microphone against the piano top. Other sounds you will hear, are hearing or have heard (not that again!) are a metronone tick tick ticking and a telephone bell ringing. Rrrrreading matter. You can tell that I didn't answer the phone. I didn't answer it because I'd spent several hours getting the sound that I liked and the performance was going well and after my first dismay I hoped that the bell would sound well . . . rring, rrring, rring rring . . . it does, it fits, même famille. Who called? Later I coughed a bit, couldn't help it. Quite a slow tempo isn't it? Socialist and sinister. That tick tick tick tick tick tick sound which started the piece and continues throughout is the sound of the metropolitan gnome. Right now the music has just left being alternately a chord in the right hand and a single note on the left. It is essence of "oompah", a ragtime or "stride" left hand strain. I've played Jelly Roll Morton, Earl Hines, stride and ragtime influenced piano for many years so this piece comes out of that but also it is kin to a film I made in '68-'69 called ↔ wherein the camera pans back and forth at different tempi in sync with a percussive machine sound which emphasizes the arrival of the picture at each left or right extreme with a thump thump thump thump thump . . . To return to the music, now it's changed to a single note in the treble alternating with bass chords. I played this piece with alternating right and left hands, a backhanded compliment to Paul Wittgenstein. barm barm. Those are alternating chords in both hands brark breek brarch breekeek bracque back to top single note bottom chord crash ping crash ping crash ping crash ping. It certainly is a slow tempo. One of the reasons for that is that it enables one to have time to hear all the music that is emanating from the sounding of each note or chord. Hear what I mean? See what I mean? Left right, left right left right left right two hands two ears two loudspeakers all marking time not marching time. I'll type this just with my right hand and this with my left hand and this with my right now left then right then left then right then left then right then left . . . pause . . . electric typewriter. Typewriter and loudspeaker are interesting words, words that carry histories in their newness. A man in a bright blue windbreaker is running down the street. Words are inching across the page. . . . Your eyes are what? Me, I'm veering. Sex. One's mind rebounds. Mine did, I can't know whether another mind does or did. Turning off the music my mind rebounded from the coldness of this page to the heat of our bodies ensuite to a certain other body with my body in and on. A contributing member. Arrival at the station. Back to work. No, why don't you too think about fucking that someone who mutually. Deeper. Excuse me, I'll just get this out of your mind for a minute it's getting a bit too intimate in there . . . Sorry, but could you superimpose that warm wet picture on the sound? Now fade the picture out slowly till you're just listening. Now I'm just writing. You're listening and reading. Just one backward glance in the form of the reassurance that you'll very likely be able to think that over again just as you can play these records again or read this again. Perhaps this time you you you you're reading it it it it without the music but now this this this this time you're reading it with th th th th th the music on. Silent reading right? If so you'll note, perhaps, that the long slow tempo section is followed by a faster tempo coda . . . Mind keeps fading into her pants. Into mine too. Could it be that the way the jacket was open to be read suggested "opened" legs? "Jacket" like legs! The "Album" might be a better word there, with another letter . . . Let's try that fading out/fading in system again. "Mixing" or "dissolving" it's called . . . "Left Right" gets pretty fast, racing ahead of the metronone beat vers la fin. Lots of merging of the sustained "distortions" both there and here. Shaman. One presumes a lot if one presumes that one can direct another consciousness into varying states of attentiveness en face d'un construct made by one for that very purpose. Amplifying "varying states of attentiveness" I could say that I mean not only the intensity of the attention but its nature and focus. I do presume that I can do that and that I do it to myself. Impossible subject, I can never be objective. I tend to believe, because of occasional exterior manifestations, that many of the states of mind I experience in preceiving my work are frequently enough experienced by others. A passage can push you back into yourself so that its benevolent force reinforces your integrity and you momentarily become a core of concentrated yourself. Such a passage might modulate into an arrangement of elements that might draw your self out into an edifying dialogue of equals and then transform into a constellation that might invoke analysis or criticism of itself only to become that more familiar but often welcome Svengalism which provokes total identification sans corps with the "reality" of the observed/recorded/recounted and tilts one off the edge of the bed of regular mind-time into an ancient and honorable lunacy, surfacing with real tears or laughter which were fathered by the ghosts of the artist's gesture. This particular passage, will, no, does appear on the back face of this album jacket and so it is very possible that you who are reading this have not read what appears before on the 2 inner faces. You may have bought the album and for your own reasons or no evident reasons have decided to read the back first. I must admit I sometimes do that with books. Adopting the pose of assuming that I am writing for one solo reader at a time, I say to you (a group reading seems unlikely but possible, of course someone may be reading over your shoulder) (No not yours, yours. Or is it you who are looking over my shoulder?) that I feel that I can address you somewhat intimately but also somewhat abstractly. Consider the class of obscene phone calls. Good thing I didn't answer the 'phone . . . Hello, this text is being written, was written by the composer-performer of the music which is awaiting transmission on the discs enclosed by the cardboard bed on which what was written has been printed. The text and the record are records both. Both of the records could be transmitting right now. Write now a manifestation. You, singular or all embraceable you are perhaps reading these notes because you're considering the purchase of some recorded music. These notes may help you to decide to purchase those notes. There is a lot of information about the music, names, dates, lengths, theories, etc. on the two inside faces of the legs of this jacket. What?! Sorry, that's explained there, too. A jacket has sleeves not faces. I know. The faceless author of this is still also the composer-performer of the music which may be caused to emanate from the discs contained herein if united properly with the proper apparatus. Record player. So . . . let it suffice for me to say that I think highly of the mmmusic, a lot of living went into it and this and recommend it to you in the hopes of contributing to your life a rich source of aural stimuli for years to come and getting paid for it (I know that's illegal grammar). A negligible amount of money will buy this. I myself have sometimes been so influenced by the notes on an album to purchase same. That consideration just emerged, at the last minute as it were as one of the reasons for writing this text (other considerations are faced in the beginning of the text, front face that is) and others may reveal themselves in other parts of the text. As a matter of facet, let's face it, on the face of it, because of my typefacing these facetious faces you (you) haven't come face to face with the face of the composer-performer-author anywhere on the four thighds of this bed-jacket. How do I look? Blue eyed . . . Most of the requirements of this text smiling on the front face have been put to bed satisfied I think (I'll check with them in the morning). So . . . I can see the end approaching. In temporal works this kind of perception is rare excepting that écriture is a creature whose beginnings and endings are apprehendable reversed. This must be qualified by noting that the beginning of a work of literature is new and now the first time it is read and the meaning states that may be evoked by it can be said to be relatively few. In other words, most readers of the first page of a text would be in quite close agreement concerning it's nature, qualities and meaning. However, it can without doubt be stated that someone who read only the last passage or only the first and last passage of a work of literature would be apprehending an "object" which would seem in an almost infinite number of respects radically different from that passage apprehended by someone who had read the entire text from beginning to end. Such is the modifying power of the prior experience in a temporal work that the significance of the ending can only be truly apprehended against the record of the voyage towards it. In isolation it is not an ending is it?

Michael Snow, April 1975.

PRODUCED BY THE ISAACS GALLERY, 832 YONGE ST., TORONTO. MICHAEL SNOW AND CHATHAM SQUARE
PRINTED IN USA

Smyth, David
→ Revolutions Per Minute

Snow, Michael [C/S]

Title: 1016 NEW YORK EYE and EAR CONTROL

Contents: Dons Dawn. A Y. ITT

Perf.: Albert Ayler (ts), Don Cherry (tp), John Tchicai (as), Roswell Rudd (tb), Gary Peacock (b), Sonny Murray (dr)

ø 30cm, 33 RPM, 1966, ESP-DISK', New York ESP 1016

Cover: b/w, design: Michael Snow

This music was recorded on July, 1964 by New York artist Michael Snow for use as the soundtrack of his film entitled *New York Eye and Ear Control*. The music was recorded prior to the production of the film.

STEREO LP 1009/10
CHATHAM SQUARE

MICHAEL SNOW
MUSICS FOR PIANO, WHISTLING
MICROPHONE AND TAPE RECORDER

My first consideration in writing the text which you are now, I presume, reading ("presume": I guess that this text will still be here to read later even if you aren't reading it now) was to write something which when printed would cover all four faces of this album. Of several ideas for a design for this album cover or jacket this seemed at the time to be the best. Remains to be seen. Ruminations gradually clarified to this stage: I would write something that would fulfill several requirements, the basic one being that it function as a "design" or "image" that would be both decorative and "plastic". Another requirement that might better be approached now as an intention or ambition was the image

Snow, Michael [C/S]

Title: Musics For Piano, Whistling, Microphone and Tape Recorder

---

Contents: "Falling Starts" (Beginning). "Falling Starts" (Conclusion). "W in the D". "Left Right"

2 LPs, ø 30cm, 33 RPM, 1975, Chatham Square New York No. LP 1009/10

Cover: b/w, gatefold, with a text by Michael Snow

Snow, Michael [S]

Title: The Last LP. Unique Last Recordings of the Music of Ancient Cultures Assembled by Michael Snow

Contents: A: 1.Wu Ting Dee Lin Chao Cheu. 2.Si Nopo Da. 3.Ohwachira. 4.I Ching Dee Yen Tzen. 5.Póhl'nov-yessnikh. 6.Speech in Klögen.
B. 1.Mbowunsa Mpahiya. 2.Quuia-sukpu Quai Gami. 3.Amitābha Chenden Kālā. 4.Roiakuriluo. 5.Raga Lalat

ø 30cm, 33 RPM, Art Metropole, Canada No. 1001

Cover: multi-color print, gatefold

But recording itself has recently gone through some subtle and important changes which might – ought to – will alter the above-mentioned form of aural belief. From being an instrument of documentation, sound recording has become a musical instrument in itself. Recording has become as much a process of creation as of memorization.

Excerpt from covertext

Snow, Michael
→ The Artists' Jazz Band

Sobieralski
→ Piotr Nathan

AIR TO AIR
© GEMINI G.E.L.1975
EDITION: 1000
KEITH SONNIER

Sonnier, Keith [S]

Title: Air To Air

ø 30cm, 33 RPM, 1975, limited edition of 1000, Gemini G.E.L Los Angeles

Cover: b/w

Stereo LP of amplified space installation with transmission systems for communications by long distance audio connection between Los Angeles, California and New York City, New York

Sordide Sentimental [P/S]

Music: Throbbing Gristle

Contents: We hate you (Little girls). Five knuckle shuffle

6 pages folding sheet (29,6 x 62,7 cm) with glued on pocket for single, ø 17cm, 45 RPM, edition of 1560, numbered copies, design: Loulou Picasso, collage: Yves Von Bontee, text by Jean-Pierre Turmel, English translation included, Sordide Sentimental Rouen, 1979, No. SS 45001

S'Soreff, Stephen
→   Voices Notes & Noise

Sound   [S]

Title: Sound. An Exhibition of Sound Sculpture / Instrument Building and Acoustically Tuned Spaces. Los Angeles Institute of Contemporary Art, P.S.1. New York, 1979. Curated by Robert Smith and Bob Wilhite

Contents: Jim Hobart: Maraca Instrument. Bob Bates: Force Field. Richard Dunlap: The Rubber Band. Joan La Barbara: Excerpt from *q-uatre petites bêtes*. Ron George: improvisation. Ivor Darreg: Selection from *Composition for Turkish-Fretless Banjo*. Bob Wilhite: Two Spinners. Jim Gordon: Piece for Synthesizers, Computers and Other Instruments. Paul De Marinis: Pygmy Gamelan Goes to Art. Jim Pomeroy: Excerpt from *Back on the Ladder, The Beat Goes on*. Yoshi Wada: An Adapted Bag With Sympathy III. Christina Kubisch: Tempo Liquido. Gerald Oshita: Water Preludes. Tom Jenkins: One Man Band. Bill Fontana: Kirribilli Wharf. Doug Hollis: Aeolian Harp. Tom Marioni: Drop Brushing. Terry Fox: Labyrinth Scored for II Cats. Tom Recchion: Solos. Alex Bernstein: L.A. Proper. Karen Wolff/ William Kingsbury: Double cross-

ing. Bruce Fier: Score For Eleven Infinite Rainbows. Susan Rawcliffe: Trix Ocarinas. Will Parsons/Grace Bell: Road Runner/L.A. Dennis Evans: Location No. 2. John Duncan/ Michael le Donne-Bhennet: Koko Weef 6038

ø 30cm, 33 RPM, 1979, Los Angeles Institute of Contemporary Art

Sound < = > Sight   [P/S]

Three audio-visual projects by Ton Bruynèl, Dick Raaijmakers and Peter Struycken Catalogue 46 p.(n.pag) to homonymous exhibition in the Stedelijk Museum, Amsterdam, 1971, with 3 included flexidiscs, ø 17cm, 33 RPM

The Sounds of Sound Sculpture   [S]

Title: The Sounds of Sound Sculpture

With: Harry Bertoia, Francois and Bernard Baschet, Stephan von Huene, Reinhold Pieper Marxhausen, David Jacobs

ø 30cm, 33 RPM, 1975 realized by John Grayson and David Rosenboom, A.R.C. Publications, Vancouver A.R.C. 1001

Cover: b/w, supplement with texts and illustrations of sound-sculptures, 12 p.(n.pag.)

This A.R.C. record presents you with a re-presentation of the diverse Sounds of Sound Sulpture created over the last thirty years where the sounds are produced physically, without electronics, in real time.
With the advent of the mechanical age, in the late 19th century, the interest of many sculptors gradually came to be focused upon the object and its transformation through motion - *kinetic sculpture*. As an awareness of the inherent noise in kinetic sculpture developed, some artists formed a desire to sculpt the noise, as well as the moving visual object and thus, in the late 1940's, the field audio-kinetic or Sound Sulpture began its evolution. During the last decade a more complex interrelationship of the sound to the sculptural form has developed. This has evolved, for some artists, to the extent where the sound itself has become the sculptural form. This is exemplified by David Jacobs (Side II, Band 2) as he creates complex aural patterns and forms through his "Hanging Pieces".
The work of the artists presented on this record represents a good cross section of the possibilities which have been developed to date - the artists are, in a sense, the "founding fathers" of the art. All have been working in the field for twenty or thirty years.

Excerpt from included text

Sound Poetry

The discographic specifications for this kind of acoustic literature are not complete. We merely present a selection, especially since here we are dealing with a question of combining the arts - an issue which, in itself, is not clearly defined. Most authors of this poetry that speaks, sings, roars, whispers, stutters, and breathes, also work in the visual field. Their graphic and typograhic play on words, their letter-arrangements, their constellations, their textmontages and -collages are often scores at the same time. The translation of these scores by the author's voice makes a possible acoustic

interpretation of the visual text audible.
Many of the authors have already been registered individually in our compendium.
A nearly complete discography from its beginning to 1978 is found in Henri Chopin's volume: *Poesie Sonore Internationale* (cp. bibliography). Christian Scholz's treatise on Sound Poetry, to be published in 1989, will contain a complete discography (cp. bibliography).

U.B. / M.G.

Individual Authors

Amirkhanian, Charles: Lexical Music. LP (Arch Records, Berkeley. S-1779), 1979

Amirkhanian, Charles: Mental Radio. Nine Text-Sound Compositions. LP (Composers Recordings, New York. CRI SD 523), 1985

Bissett, Bill: Medicine My Mouth's On Fire. Book with record, ø 17cm, 33 RPM (Oberon Press, Toronto. T-57441), 1974

Chopin, Henri: LE DERNIER ROMAN DU MONDE histoire d'un Chef occidental ou oriental. Book with record, ø 17cm, 45 RPM (Ed. Cyanuur, Belgium), 1970

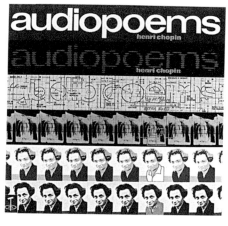

Chopin, Henri: audiopoems. LP (Tangent records, London. TGS 106), 1971

Chopin, Henri: POESIE SONORE. LP (IGLOO, Belgium. IGL 013), n.d.(1977)

Cobbing, Bob: Sound Poems. Jandl, Ernst: Sprechgedichte. LP (Writers Forum Records, London, WRF 1), n.d. (1965)

Four Horsemen: Canadada. LP (Griffin House, Toronto. IPS 1004), n.d.(1972)

Four Horsemen: Live in the West. LP (Starborne Productions, Toronto. STB 0177), n.d.

Helms, Hans G: Fa:m' Ahniesgwow. Book with record, ø 25cm, 33 RPM, in folder (M. DuMont Schauberg, Köln), 1960

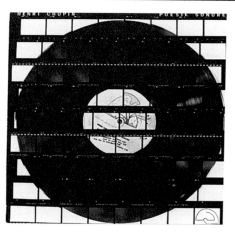

Hodell, Åke: verbal hjärntvätt. general bussig/igevär. Record, ø 17cm, 45 RPM (kerberos förlag, Stockholm), 1965

Hodell, Åke: lågsniff. Book with record, ø 17cm, 33 RPM (Rabén & Sjörgen, Stockholm. RM 5107), 1966

Hodell, Åke: MR. NIXON'S DREAMS. Book with record, ø 17cm, 33 RPM (Rabén & Sjörgen, Stockholm. RM 5264), 1970

Jandl, Ernst. Laut und Luise. Record, ø 17cm, 33 RPM (Verlag Klaus Wagenbach, Berlin. Wagenbachs Quartplatte 2), 1968

Jandl, Ernst / Mayröcker, Friederike: Fünf Mann Mensch. Record, ø 17cm, 33 RPM, as supplement to the book: Neues Hörspiel. Ed. by Klaus Schöning (Suhrkamp Verlag Frankfurt), 1969

Jandl, Ernst: Der künstliche Baum. Record, ø 17cm, 33 RPM (Luchterhand, Neuwied), n.d. (1970)

Jandl, Ernst: hosi + anna. Record, ø 17cm, 33 RPM (Verlag Klaus Wagenbach, Berlin. Wagenbachs Quartplatte 6), 1971

Jandl, Ernst: him hanflang war das wort. LP (Verlag Klaus Wagenbach, Berlin. Wagenbachs Quartplatte 20), 1980

Jandl, Ernst: Laut und Luise. Hosi + anna. LP (Verlag Klaus Wagenbach, Berlin. Wagenbachs Quartplatte 22), 1983

Jandl, Ernst: bist eulen? LP (Extraplatte, Wien. EX 316141), 1984

Johnson, Bengt Emil: Gubbdrunkning. Book with record, ø 17cm, 33 RPM (Bonniers, Stockholm. AB 5020), 1965

Ladik, Katalin: phonopoetics. phonetic interpretation of visual poetry. Record, ø 17cm, 33 RPM (Galerija Studentskog Kulturnog Centra, Beograd), 1976

Lemaître, Maurice: Poèmes et Musique Lettristes. Periodical with 2 records, ø 17cm, 45 RPM (LETTRISME, Paris. Nr. 24), 1971

MacLow, Jackson: MILAREPA GATHA. Record, ø 17cm, 45 RPM (Ediz. Pari & Dispari, Cavriago, Italy), 1976

Mon, Franz: Das Gras wies wächst. LP (Deutsche Grammophon, Luchterhand, Neuwied. 2574002), n.d. (1972)

Nannucci, Maurizio: Readings. Record, ø 17cm, 33 RPM (MN Records/Time, Firenze), 1969

Nannucci, Maurizio: parole/mots/words/wörter. Record, ø 17cm, 33 RPM (Recorthings e zona edizioni, Firenze), 1976

Reese, Williams: Sonance Project. LP (Line, Berkeley), 1977

Anthologies

Expressionistische Dichter des Sturm: August Stramm, Kurt Schwitters, Otto Nebel. Es liest aus ihren Werken Otto Nebel. LP (Amadeo, Wien. AVRS 2060), 1960

KONKRETE POESIE. SOUND POETRY. ARTIKULATIONEN. LP (Anastasia Bitzos, Bern), 1966. Works by Claus Bremer, Eugen Gomringer, Ernst Jandl, Paul de Vree, Franz Mon, Lily Greenham, Max Bense, Reinhard Döhl, Haroldo de Campos, Rolf Geissbühler

text und aktionsabend II. 2 records, ø 17cm, 33 RPM (edition anastasia bitzos, Bern), 1968. Works by Claus Bremer, Rolf Geissbühler, Jean-François Bory, Reinhard Döhl, Timm Ulrichs

Text-sound-compositions 1. A Stockholm Festival 1968. LP (Fylkingen Records, Stockholm. RELP 1049), 1968. Works by Åke Hodell, François Dufrêne, Bob Cobbing

Text-sound-compositions 2. A Stockholm Festival 1968. LP (Fylkingen Records,

Stockholm. RELP 1054), 1968. Works by Jarl and Sonja Hammarberg-Åkesson, Ilmar Laaban, Bengt af Klintberg, Sten Hanson, Bernard Heidsieck, Bengt Emil Johnson

Text-sound-compositions 3. LP (Fylkingen Records, Stockholm. RELP 1072), 1969. Works by Åke Hodell, Diter Rot, Emmett Williams, Sten Hanson, Svante Bodin

Text-sound-compositions 4. LP (Fylkingen Records, Stockholm. RELP 1073), 1969. Works by Lars-Gunnar Bodin, Bernard Heidsieck, Erik Thygesen, Ladislav Novák, Henri Chopin

Text-sound-compositions 5. LP (Fylkingen Records, Stockholm. RELP 1074), 1969. Works by Bengt Emil Johnson, Gust Gils, Bob Cobbing, Ilmar Laaban, Ladislav Novák, Christer Hennix Lille

Text-sound-compositions 6. LP (Fylkingen Records, Stockholm. RELP 1102), 1970. Works by Sandro Key-Åberg, Anna Lockwood, Harvey Matusow, Henri Chopin, Ladislav Novák, Svante Bodin

Text-sound-compositions 7. LP (Fylkingen Records, Stockholm. RELP 1103), 1970. Works by Franz Mon, Bob Cobbing, Arne Mallnäs, Ilmar Laaban, Bernard Heidsieck

International language experiments of the 50/60ies. LP (edition hoffmann, Friedberg), 1970. Lily Greenham speaks Lily Greenham, Peter Greenham, Helmut Heissenbüttel, Ernst Jandl, Neil Mills, Alain Arias-Misson, Herminio Molero, Edwin Morgan, Decio Pignatari, Gerhard Rühm, Kurt Sanmark, Vagn Steen, Elena Asins, Ronaldo Azeredo, Max Bense, Edgard Braga, Augusto de Campos, Haroldo de Campos, E.M. de Melo e Castro, Bob Cobbing, Ronald Draper, Pierre Garnier

sound texts. ? concrete poetry. visual texts. LP (Stedelijk Museum, Amsterdam), 1970. Works by Henri Chopin, Bernard Heidsieck, François Dufrêne, Paul de Vree, Bengt Emil Johnson, Sten Hanson, Bob Cobbing, Ladislav Novák, Ernst Jandl

Experiments in Disintegrating Language. Konkrete Canticle. LP (The Arts Council Of Great Britain, London), 1971. Works by Charles Verey, Neil Mills, Thomas A. Clark, Bob Cobbing, Paula Claire, Michael Chant

PHONETISCHE POESIE. Edited by Franz Mon (Luchterhand Schallplatte F 60 379), n.d. (1971). Works by Velemir Chlebnikov, Aleksej Kručënych, Kazimir Malevič, Raoul Hausmann, Kurt Schwitters, Maurice Lemaître, François Dufrêne, Henri Chopin, Bob Cobbing, Peter Greenham, Paul de Vree, Arrigo Lora-Totino, Ladislav Novák, Gerhard Rühm, Franz Mon, Ernst Jandl

TOUTE PREDICATION EST UN ATTENTAT A LA LIBERTE DE L'HOMME.- LA POESIE. COMME JE LA CONÇOIS, N'EST PLUS LA FEMME DE CHAMBRE DES PRINCES, PRELATS, POLITICIENS, PARTIS, OU ENCORE DU PEUPLE.-ELLE EST ENFIN ELLE-MEME UN PHENOMENE PHONETIQUE VOCAL EN SOI DE SOURCE PSYCHO PHYSIQUE ET OBJECTIVEMENT STRUCTURE A L'AIDE DE MOTS, DE SONS ET DE MOYENS MECHANIQUES ET GRAPHIQUES (ENREGISTREMENTS ET ECRITURES). LE VISUEL VERBAL PUR N'EXISTE PAS.- IL SUSCITE TOUJOURS LE SON OU LE BRUIT D'OU IL PROVIENT ET DONT IL EST LE SIGNE. LE POEME EST UNE EMISSION DE RESPIRATION AUDIBLE (AUDITION) OU SILENCIEUSE (LECTURE) CREATIVEMENT MODULEE, PROVOQUEE PAR LA NECESSITE DE DIRE, NE SE REFERANT A RIEN D'AUTRE QU'A LA SENSIBILITE DE L'ETRE (PRESENT ET PLANETAIRE). C'EST CE QUE JE COMPRENDS PAR L'INTENTION OBJECTIVE DES SONORITES VOCALES : UNE COMMUNICATION CONCERTEE DE VIBRATIONS CREATRICES SPONTANEES.- LA POESIE PHONETIQUE NE PEUT EXISTER SANS UNE REINVENTION DE LA RECITATION, C'EST-A-DIRE LA SONORISATION OU LA REGIE DU SON. TOUT DEPEND EN EFFET DES NOUVELLES POSSIBILITES D'EXPRESSION MECANIQUE POUR REALISER LA TRANSMISSION DE LA SENSIBILITE TOTALE DU POEME, LUI-MEME AU FOND UNE PARTIE DU SPECTACLE CINETIQUE TOTAL QU'HENRI CHOPIN PREVOIT PAR L'UTILISATION INEVITABLE DE LA MACHINE MUE PAR LES ONDES.- L'OEUVRE SONORE EST LE RESULTAT D'UN TRAVAIL D'EQUIPE SOUS LA REGIE DU POETE ET LA REPRODUCTION IDEALE EST CELLE REALISEE SUR DISQUE H.F.- LA ENCORE LA MACHINE EST INDISPENSABLE.- CELA VA DE SOI QUE LE RECITANT (SI CE N'EST PAS LE POETE) ET L'INGENIEUR DE SONS (EN CE QUI CONCERNE MES ENREGISTREMENTS) CONTRIBUENT PERSONNELLEMENT A L'ORIGINALITE DE LA REALISATION .- A L'AUBE DE L'ERE ELECTRONIQUE LA POESIE NE PEUT PLUS ETRE UN FABLIAU.-

Paul de Vree. In *Revue OU* 28/29 (1966)

EXPERIMENTS IN DISINTEGRATING LANGUAGE KONKRETE CANTICLE

PHONE TISCHE

Luchterhand Schallplatte herausgegeben von Franz Mon

Velemir Chlebnikov Aleksej Kručënych

Kazimir Malevič Raoul Hausmann Kurt Schwitters Maurice Lemaître François Dufrêne Henri Chopin Bob Cobbing

Peter Greenham Paul de Vree Arrigo Lora-Totino Ladislav Novák Gerhard Rühm Franz Mon Ernst Jandl

POESIE

POÈMES PHONÉTIQUES SUR SPATIALISME. Record, ø 17cm, 33 RPM (Columbia Records, Tokyo. PLP-7163), n.d.(1971). Works by Ilse and Pierre Garnier, Seiichi Niikuni

L'AUTONOMATOPEK I. Single, 33 RPM (opus International Disque, Paris), n.d. (1972). Works by Henri Chopin, Isidore Isou, Gil J. Wolman, Jacques Spacagna, Bob Cobbing, Anna Lockwood, Jean-Louis Brau, François Dufrêne

Gott schütze Österreich. Szenen, Dialektgedichte, Sprachübungen, Musiken, Urteile, Montagen. LP (Wagenbach Verlag, Berlin.

Wagenbachs Quartplatte 12), 1974. Works by Alexander, H.C. Artmann, Wolfgang Bauer, Jodik Blapik, Günter Brus, Ernst Jandl, Friederike Mayröcker, Hermann Nitsch, Gerhard Rühm, Aloisius Schnedel

10 + 2 : 12 American Text Sound Pieces. LP (Arch Records, San Francisco, LP 1752), 1974. Works by Charles Amirkhanian, Clark Coolidge, John Cage, John Giorno, Anthony Gnazzo, Charles Dodge, Robert Ashley, Beth Anderson, Brion Gysin, Liam O'Gallagher, Aram Saroyan

poesia sonora. Antalogia internazionale di ricerche fonetiche a cura di Maurizio Nannucci. LP (CBS 69145), 1975. Works by Bob Cobbing, Henri Chopin, Paul de Vree, François Dufrêne, Brion Gysin, Sten Hanson, Bernard Heidsieck, Ernst Jandl, Arrigo Lora-Totino, Franz Mon, Maurizio Nannucci, Arthur Pétronio

Text-Sound Festivals - 10 Years. LP (Fylkingen Records, Stockholm. FYLP 1010), n.d. (1977). Works by Lars-Gunnar Bodin, Sten Hanson, Åke Hodell, Bengt Emil Johnson, Ilmar Laaban, Charles Amirkhanian, Henri Chopin, Bob Cobbing, Bernard Heidsieck, Arrigo Lora-Totino

futura. POESIA SONORA. Critical historical anthology of sound poetry edited by Arrigo Lora-Totino. 7 LPs (Cramps Records, Milano. 5206 301-307), 1978. Works by Filippo Tommaso Marinetti, Francesco Cangiullo, Giacomo Balla, Fortunato Depero, Farfa, Vladimir Majakovskij, Velemir Chlebnikov, Vasilij Kamenskij, Aleksej Kručěnych, Il'ja Zdanevič, Pierre Albert-Birot, Arthur Pétronio, Christian Morgenstern, Paul Scheerbart, Hugo Ball, Tristan Tzara, Marcel Janco, Richard Huelsenbeck, Raoul Hausmann, Kurt Schwitters, Antonin Artaud, François Dufrêne, Henri Chopin, Bernard Heidsieck, Franz Mon, Gerhard Rühm, Nikolaus Einhorn, Ladislav Novák, Carlfriedrich Claus, Brion Gysin, Paul de Vree, Bob Cobbing, Isidore Isou, Maurice Lemaître, Altagor, Patrizia Vicinelli, Adriano Spatola, Maurizio Nannucci, Demetrio Stratos, Arrigo Lora-Totino, Il Concento Prosodico

POLYPHONIX 1. Première anthologie sonore. LP (Multipla Records, Milano. M 20138), 1982. Works with Tahar Ben Jelloun, Julien Blaine, Hugo Ball, (Eberhard Blum), Jean-François Bory, François Dufrêne, Jean-Pierre Faye, Lawrence Ferlinghetti, Allen Ginsberg, John Giorno, Michel Giroud, Brion Gysin, Joël Hubaut, Rhizotomes, Nanni Balestrini, Valeria Magli, Corrado Costa, Bernard Heidsieck, Dyali Karam, Jean-Jacques Lebel, Gherasim Luca, Andre Pieyre de Mandiargues, Taylor Mead, Michèle Métail, Angeline Neveu, Peter Orlovsky, Jerome Rothenberg, Maurice Roche, Sahli

One World Poetry. Live from Amsterdam. 2 LPs (Milkway Records, Amsterdam. BF-

211108-1 A/B), n.d.(1982). Works by Ed Sanders, Richard Murphy, Ad Zuiderent, Lizzy Sara May, Linton Kwesi Johnson, Miguel Algarin, Vincente Zito Lema, Barbara Barg, Avant Squares, John Giorno, Dick Higgins, Henri Chopin, Ton Lebbink, Mazisi Kunene, Michael Gibbs, Jim Carroll, Jerry Garcia & Bob Weir, Bernard Heidsieck, Simon Vinkenoog, H.H. ter Balkt, Hans Plomp, Mignon van Ingen, Remco Campert, Judith Herzberg, Leo van der Zalm, J. Bernlef, Elly de Waard, Hans van de Waarsenburg, Wiel Kusters, Frank M. Arion, Johnny van Doorn, William Burroughs, Lawrence Ferlinghetti, David Henderson, Franco Beltrametti, Diane di Prima, Michael McClure, Ken Kesey, Uli Becker, Alfred Miersch

REGIONAL ZEAL. Mouth Music from Olympia Washington. LP (Palace of Lights Records, Seattle. 04/1000), 1982. Works by Alex Stahl, Steve Peters, Steve Fisk, Harlan Mark Vale, Heidi Drucker, Customer Service, Cheri Knight, John Forster, Christopher David Kunkel, Robin James

Voooxing Poooêtre. International Record of Sound Poetry. LP (Amm.ne Comunale di Bondeno - Biblioteca Com.le Arci, Bondeno, Italy), 1982. Works by Bernard Heidsieck, Rod Summers, Klaus Groh, Enzo Minarelli, Giovanni Fontana, Agostino Contò, Richard Kostelanetz, Adriano Spatola, Vladan Radovanovic, Grupo Texto Poetico, Peter R. Meyer, Tibor Papp, Santo S.A., Giovanni A. Bignone, Jean-Jacques Lebel

MAIL MUSIC project by Nicola Frangione. LP (Armadio Officina Audio Editions, Italy. LP 001), 1983. Works by Maurizio Bianchi, Sergio Cena, Arrigo Lora-Totino, Ubaldo Giacomucci, Enzo Rosamilia, Vittore Baroni, Steen Moller Rasmussen, Tommy Rinnstein, Serse Luigetti, Masami Akita, Franco Ballabeni, Gerald Jupitter-Larsen, Richard Kostelanetz, Bellee Etienne Marge, Paulo Bruscky, Sergio-Emilio Morandi, Jesse Glass Jr., Sue Fishbein, Rod Summers, P I6.D 4, Jane Fay, Carlos Zerpa, Luca Miti, Guy

Bleus, Italo Mazza, Raffaele Cuomo, SWSW Thrght, Carsten Schmidt-Olsen, Lutz Niesporek, Giacomo Bergamini, Peter Paalvast, Günther Ruch, Emmett Walsh, Leif Brush, Piermario Ciani, Reservation-Henk-Jockec, Naif Orchestra, Hiroko Iwata, Giovanni Fontana, Jaroslav Pokorny, Ruggero Maggi, Peter R. Meyer, Guy Stuckens, Klaus Peter Dencker, José M. Pezuela Pintò, Peeter Sepp Rock Rat, Lon Spiegelman

3 vi tre 2. polipoetry issues directed by enzo minarelli. Record, ø 17cm, 45 RPM (3 vi tre, Alatri, Italy. EM 0283), 1983. Works by Giovanni Fontana, Enzo Minarelli

3 vi tre 3. polipoetry issues directed by enzo minarelli. Record, ø 17cm, 45 RPM (3 vi tre, Alatri, Italy. EM 00383), 1983. Works by Ernest Robson, Bliem Kern, Beth Anderson, Charles Amirkhanian

FESTIVAL d'IN(ter)VENTIONS 2. IN MEMORIAM GEORGES MACIUNAS. 2 LPs (Les Éditions INTERVENTION, Quebec), 1985. Works by Trio BI-Clan, Dick Higgins, Marie Lévesque, Clive Robertson, Jacques Doyon, Alison Knowles, Hervé Fischer, Pierre-André Arcand, Les Salopettes, The 4 Horsemen, Geneviève Letarte, Bonnie Sherk, Altman-Fournier, Alain-Martin Richard, Richard Martel, Jean-Claude Gagnon, Jean-Claude St-Hilaire, John Fekner, Monty Cantsin, Réjean Dugal, Jean-Yves Fréchette, Alexis Goufas

Lautpoesie. Eine Anthologie. Edited by Christian Scholz. LP (Gertraud Scholz Verlag, Obermichelbach. Nr. 01), 1987. Works by Jeremy Adler, Carlfriedrich Claus, Elke Erb, Bernard Heidsieck, Arrigo Lora-Totino, Franz Mon, Oskar Pastior, Josef Anton Riedl, Gerhard Rühm, Valeri Scherstjanoi, Larry Wendt

SOURCE [P/S]

Title: SOURCE music of the avant garde

published twice yearly by Composer/Performer Edition, Davis, California
Editor: Larry Austin

Music-Magazine with the following records:

Issue Number 4 (1968)
Source Record Number One. Record (ø 25cm, 33 RPM) with contributions by Robert Ashley, David Behrman
Source Record Number Two. Record (ø 25cm, 33 RPM) with contributions by Larry Austin, Allan Bryant
Issue Number 7 (1970)
Source Record Number Three. Record (ø 25cm, 33 RPM) with contributions by Alvin Lucier, Arthur Woodbury, Mark Riener
Issue Number 8 (1970)
Source Record Number Four. Record (ø 25cm, 33 RPM) with contributions by Larry Austin, Stanley Lunetta
Issue Number 9 (1971)
Source Record Number Five. Record (ø 25cm, 33 RPM) with contributions by Lowell Cross, Arrigo Lora-Totino
Source Record Number Six. Record (ø 25cm, 33 RPM) with contributions by Alvin Curran, Anna Lockwood

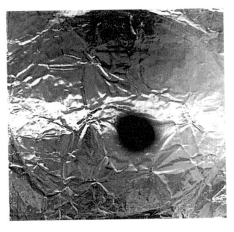

Cover: aluminium-foil, treated in colors

Three-colored cardboard, printed on both sides as graphic supplement

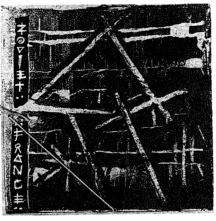

Soviet France [C/S]

Title: Hessian

ø 30cm, 45 RPM, 1982, Red Rhino Records (Screaming Red Music) No. Red 12

Cover: black printed motives on jute

Soviet France [C/S]

Title: Norsch

ø 30cm, 45 RPM, 1983, Red Rhino Records (Screaming Red Music), York, England, No. Red 23

Soviet France [C/S]

Title: Mohnomishe

2 LPs, ø 30cm, 33 RPM, 1983, Red Rhino Records (Screaming Red Music), York, England, No. Red 40

Cover: two-color print, on two fibre-boards, tied with red cord

Soviet France [C/S]

Title: Eostre

2 LPs, 33 RPM, 1984, Red Rhino Records, York, England, REDLP45

Cover: LPs between two white plastic sheets, folded in white silk-paper. Silk-paper and plastic-foil printed with black motives and red paint blots

Soviet France [C/S]

Title: Misfits. Loony Tunes and Squalid Criminals

ø 30cm, 33 RPM, 1986, Red Rhino Records, York, England, REDLP67

Cover: b/w, paper bag, LP between cardboard printed in color

Soviet France [C/S]

Title: A Flock of Rotations

ø 30cm, 33 RPM, 1987, Red Rhino Records, York, England, REDLP68

Cover: b/w, paper, LP between cardboard with two-color graphic

Spacagna, Jacques
→ Sound Poetry

Spatola, Adriano
→ Sound Poetry

Spiegelman, Lon
→ Sound Poetry

Stahl, Alex
→ Sound Poetry

Steen, Vagn
→ Sound Poetry

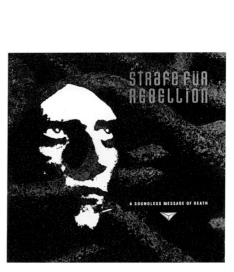

Steiger, Dominik [S]

Title: Wiener Lieder und Gemischte Weisen
erdacht, gesungen und gespielt von Dominik Steiger

Contents: Wiener Geschichten 1-6. Gemischte Weisen 1-9

ø 30cm, 33 RPM, 1979, limited edition of 300, Dieter Roth's Verlag Stuttgart

Cover: b/w, printed handwritten songtexts, stamped by Buchdienst Fesch-Wien

Steiger, Dominik
→ selten gehörte Musik

Steir, Pat
→ Word Of Mouth

Stenhouse, Andy J.
→ Voices Notes & Noise

Stevens, Leslie
→ Marko Pezzati

St-Hilaire, Jean-Claude
→ Sound Poetry

Stiletto
→ Voices Notes & Noise

Stitt, Andre
→ Perfo 2

Strafe für Rebellion [C/S]

Title: Strafe für Rebellion

Contents: Bum Bum. Siamang. Amüsierköpfe. Portugese People. Blaue Mig. Lo stato presente politico e morale. Irrsinniger Preis. Fliegen Fressen. Nie Haben. Argentinien. Mosche Bildt Njet. Abschied

Perf.: Bernd Kastner, Siegfried Syniuga (noise, instruments, voice, texts)

LP, ø 30cm, 33 RPM and Single, ø 17cm, 45 RPM, 1981/82, Pure

Freude Düsseldorf, No. PF 22 CK 11/Pf 24 CK 12

Cover: two-color print on protective cover with photo and songtexts

Strafe für Rebellion [C/S]

Title: A Soundless Message of Death

Contents: Thousand Heads Are Fond Of Rolling. Black Widow. A Soundless Message of Death. Hochofenballett. (Westen). Have You Ever Seen. (Liebe)

Perf.: Bernd Kastner, Siegfried Michail Syniuga (noise, instruments, voice and texts) and guest musicians

ø 30cm, 33 RPM, 1983/84, What's So Funny About..., Hamburg SF 02

Cover: two-color print, design: Feuer

Strafe für Rebellion [C/S]

Title: santa maria

Contents: For Mao, folk and religion. In Egypt in the month of May. Luna. Dien Bien Phu. Not for radio. Niet voor blanckes - Afrikaans. Santa Maria

Perf.: Bernd Kastner, Siegfried Michail Syniuga and guestmusicians

ø 30cm, 33 RPM, 1986, Touch TO6

Cover: two-color print, coverphotos: Paco, E. Weston

Strafe für Rebellion [C/S]

Title: Der Säemann

Perf.: Bernd Kastner, Siegfried Michail Syniuga, guests: Ka Marion Wedrich and M.M. Eckartz

ø 30cm, 33 RPM, 1987, UN Wien, No. 04

Cover: two-color print

Included folded page with texts and illustrations

Strafe für Rebellion [C/S]

Title: 5

Contents: Music Sister. Wiegenlied. Tory-ance. Mastino

Perf.: Bernd Kastner, Siegfried Michail Syniuga and guestmusicians

instruments: bronze-gong on a steel drum, screeching of a heavy object while being moved, singing sparrows, breathing gas-masks, E-guitar, small irish natural drum, cello, singing apes, grinding noises of a thin wire on a rotating record-player amplified by a small metal-box, grinding noises of several engines scratching on steel, screaming donkeys, nibbing cork-plates on a wet pane of glass, electric screw-driver, piano, boiling water in a water-heater, dogs, sea-gulls, several scratching fly-wheels, fly-wheel machines, hooting of sirens, a screeching piano, rubbing foam on a microphone

ø 30cm, 45 RPM, 1988, UN Records, Düsseldorf, and Touch, London

Cover: two-color print

Stramm, August
→ Sound Poetry

Stratos, Demetrio
→ Sound Poetry

Struycken, Peter
→ Sound <=> Sight

Stuckens, Guy
→ Sound Poetry

Subkultur Berlin [P/S]

Title: Subkultur Berlin. Selbstdarstellung Text-, Ton-Bilddokumente Esoterik der Kommunen Rocker subversiven Gruppen. (März liegt in Berlin)

Book (18,5 x 24 cm), 192 p., März Verlag, Darmstadt, 1969, published by Hartmut Sander and Ulrich Christians
White flexidisc (ø 17cm, 33 RPM) as supplement
The record contains: Dieter Kunzelmann, Hartmut Sander, Ulrich Christians, Benjamin Buchloh, Heike Proll, Peter Homann, Horst Tomeyer, Butscher and a selection of Berliner leftists (see telephone directory) on the occasion of a demonstration. It should not be difficult for any of them, to recognize themselves on this recording.

Süess, Dominik and Manuel [C]

Title: Klangklavier

Contents: John Cage: The perilous night. Giacinto Scelsi: Aitsi. Thomas Kessler: piano control. Karlheinz Stockhausen: Klavierstück VII. Henry Cowell: Aeolian harp. Werner Bärtschi: In Trauer und Prunk. Steve Ingham: Van horn boogie

ø 30cm, 33 RPM, n.d.(1984), Recommended Records Zürich, No. 004

Cover: two-color print, part of the issue with a silk-screen by Manuel Süess, numbered

Includes one-sided printed information sheet

WERNER BARTSCHI, Klavier

Summers, Rod
→   Sound Poetry

SWSW Thrght
→   Sound Poetry

Syniuga, Siegfried
→   Strafe für Rebellion

Szymanski, Fred
→   Views beside ...

Takis
→   Nam June Paik

Talen, Bill
→   High Performance

Tàpies, Antoni   [S]
Title: Comunicació sobre el mur.
         Communication sur le mur

         ø 30cm, 33 RPM, n.d., Erker-Ver-
         lag St. Gallen No. 30-776

Tàpies speaks about his work in Catalanian

Tarlo, Relly   [C/S]
Title: tracks 2

Tàpies
Comunicació sobre el mur
Communication sur le mur

Erker-Verlag St.Gallen

r   e   l   l   y   t   a   r   l   o

t r a c k s   2

Perf.:   Andries de Marez Oyens and
         Martijn Anhalt play the acoustic in-
         strument (consisting of 13 pipes)
         constructed by Relly Tarlo.

         ø 30cm, 33 RPM, n.d., Haags Ge-
         meentemuseum Den Haag, No.
         6818.345

Cover: b/w, design: Jacoba Bedaux

Tarlo, Relly
→   Perfo 2

Tas, Henk
→   Perfo 2

Tavener, John
→   Aspen Magazine

Texas, Gary
→   Fünfzehn Tonspuren

Thielsch, Walter
→   Das ist Schönheit
→   Holger Hiller

Thomkins, André   [C/S]
Title: Bösendorfer

Perf.:   André Thomkins (p, xyl, voc)

         ø 30cm, 33 RPM, 1981, limited
         edition of 300, Dieter Roth's Verlag
         Stuttgart, No. JST 258

Cover: multi-color print, designed by André
         Thomkins

Thygesen, Erik
→   Sound Poetry

Tinguely, Jean   [P/S]
Title: Tinguely. 3.20-4.6 1963

Music: Toshi Ichiyanagi

Exhibition catalogue in form of a leporello,
b/w, with single ø 17cm, 45 RPM, in a plastic bag, edition of 1000, numbered, Minami
Gallery, Tokyo, 1963

Tisa, Benedict
→   Voices Notes & Noise

Toebosch, Moniek [C/S]

Title: I Can Dance

Contents: Ja, Ja. Collages 1. Throatscratching. Collages 2. Collages 3. Love. Chattering Ladies. Duikflat. I can dance. Klap Klap. Klap Klap. Klap Klap

ø 30cm, 33 RPM, n.d.(1981), Claxon-Records Amsterdam No. 81-8

Cover: b/w, design: Moniek Toebosch

Toebosch, Moniek

→ DUTCH "DIFFICULT" MUSIC

Tödliche Doris

→ Die Tödliche Doris

Toniutti, Giancarlo [C/S]

Title: La Mutazione

Contents: part A - the tree. part B - Nekrose

ø 30cm, 33 RPM, 1985, BROKEN FLAG, Udine BFV 6

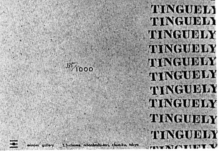

Cover: b/w, photos and design: Giancarlo Toniutti

In every event the tension to the disaster adds to itself new conscience. Before the disaster the environmental cauterization, as exposure of such an event's evolution. And in the cauterization the final event, the last mimesis, the last remaining still human act. (the mutation)

Giancarlo Toniutti (Covertext)

Topor, Roland [C/S]

Title: The Golden Years

Contents: Panic 1. Panic 2

         ø 30cm, 33 RPM, 1975, Stedelijk Museum, Amsterdam

Cover: multi-color print, gatefold

4 pages textsheet included. The record was published on the occasion of an exhibition of Roland Topor in the museum.

Toth, Gabor
→   Voices Notes & Noise

Tower, Jon   [S]

Title: Wrong Numbers. Compiled from telephone messages recorded between April 1985 and March, 1986

         ø 17cm, 45 RPM, 1986, Jon Tower

Cover: white protective cover, information sheet included

Traut, Christian   [C]

Title: Lousy days are here to stay

         ø 30cm, 33 RPM, n.d., Hurrah Records

Cover: b/w, design: Christian Traut according to a photo by Martin Kippenberger (showing Albert and Markus Oehlen)

Trio Bl-Clan
→   Sound Poetry

Tudor, David   [S]

Title: Rainforest IV. Berlin Version

         ø 30cm, 33 RPM, 1981, Edition Block, Berlin, GR-EB 1

Cover: gatefold, multi-color print, design and photos: René Block

Rainforest IV (1973) is an electroacoustic environment conceived by David Tudor and realized by the group *Composers Inside Electronics* (John Driscoll, Phil Edelstein, Ralph Jones, Martin Kalve, David Tudor and Bill Viola). Each composer has designed and constructed a set of sculptures which function as instrumental loudspeakers under his control, and each independently produces sound material to display his sculptures' resonant characteristics. The appreciation of "Rainforest IV" depends upon individual exploration, and the audience is invited to move freely among the sculptures.

Covertext

Tudor, David
→   Marcel Duchamp

Turner, Martin   [O/S]

Title: Ekliptischer Rhythmus. Konzert für planetarisches Schlagwerk. Uraufführung: 21. Juni 1954, 8:12 h, Rotenburg

         ø 30cm, various speed, 1982, original

Record made of plexiglass with one groove on which the constellation of the stars at the date of birth of a person is marked. In this case, the date of the artist. The record is accompanied by an etching (print of the record) which is signed.

The constellation of the star on the date of birth is applied into a circular groove on a plexiglass plate (ø 30cm) and by means of scratching or hatching marked as an acoustic event. When played on a record-player, a certain rhythm results which - in itself cyclic recurrent - varies with each person. Kepler's reflections on a harmony of the worlds, which is expressed in the regular polygons as the result of the division of a circle by the cardinal numbers (and to which - analogous to the mathematical - also musical intervals can be related), is here expanded by the rhythmic factor. It is important that not only the so-called main aspects are relevant but that each angular distance is part of the acoustic event, modified and in its sound characteristics differentiated only by the character of the planets and position and declination in the photogram. The print (etching) of the record shows these modifications optically.

Martin Turner

Tzara, Tristan
→   dada For Now
→   Sound Poetry

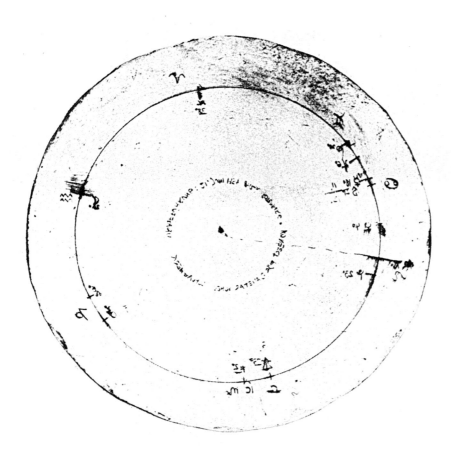

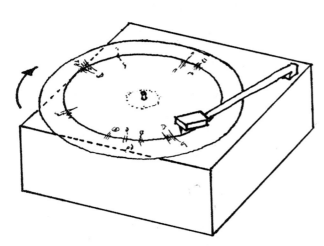

Martin Turner

Uecker, Günther
→   Art By Telephone

Ulay / Marina Abramovic
→   Word Of Mouth

Ulrichs, Timm   [O/S]

Title: schleifpapier-schallplatten. 1968

13 sandpaper discs of different grain and color, ø 17,3cm, glued on label without information

Timm Ulrichs in a 3-page hectographed program of his event "ICH HÖRE WAS, WAS DU NICHT SIEHST - demonstrationen totaler musik - " in the Freie Akademie der Künste, Hamburg (9.12.1972):

commercial sandpaper is displayed in a systematic demonstration whereby the different granulations (40, 50, 60, 80, 100, 120, 150, 180, 220, 240, 280, 320, 400,...) are transferred synesthetically into total music. (these mono-sandpaper records can be played with any modern lightweight pick-up. stylus and records should be kept dust-free!)

Ulrichs, Timm
→   Sound Poetry

VanDerBeek, Stan
→   Art By Telephone

Vale, Harlan Mark
→   Sound Poetry

Vautier, Ben [O/S]

Title: RÊVE D'AMOUR. 1986

Cloth-covered dummy on wooden base
(height 88 cm, width 38 cm). A small zinc-
pot is mounted as a head (height 8 cm, ø
14 cm), on which a single, RÊVE D'AMOUR
by Franz Liszt, serves as a top. Driven by
an electric motor, the pot and single and
about 30 glass-marbles (in the pot) turn.
Signature on the back of the dummy

Vautier, Ben [O/S]

Title: Music For La Monte Young. 1986

Small table on 3 legs. A record (ø 25cm,
Strawinsky *Ragtime. Serenade.*) is glued to
the table-top. A black functioning children's
humming-top is standing on the record.
Handpainted title in red *music for la monte
young* on the record. On the table in white,
musique fluxus / pour la monte young. Signature on table and label

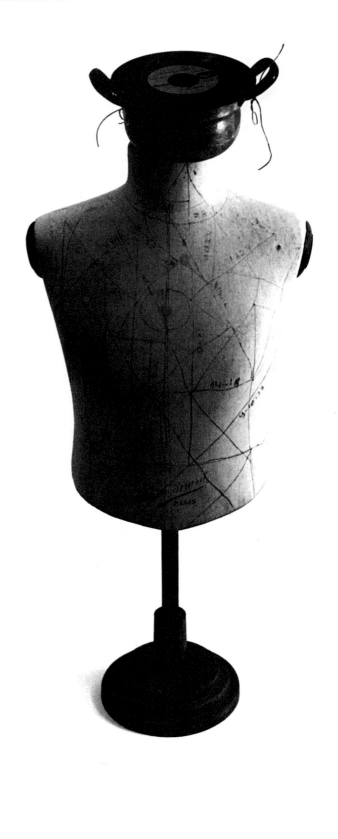

DISQUE DE MUSIQUE TOTAL

15 COMPOSITIONS MUSICALES POUR LA RECHERCHE ET L'ENSEIGNEMENT D'UNE MUSIQUE — TOTAL — en hommage à John CAGE

1. Posez le disque sur une table vide et regardez-le jusqu'à ce qu'il devienne intéressant (minimum quatre minutes).
2. Hésitez à l'écoute du disque (debout le disque à la main) 3 minutes.
3. Ecoutez sobrement et consciencieusement avec le plus d'attention possible le disque.
4. Eteignez le son et pendant toute la durée du disque écoutez attentivement, comme s'il s'agissait de la musique du disque, tous les bruits environnants (voitures, voix, bruits, etc.).
5. Faites le plus de bruit possible avec le disque (tappez des objets, etc.).
6. A la fin du disque enlevez l'arrêt automatique et écoutez le silence se repêter, si vous partez laissez l'appareil en marche 24 heures minimum.
7. Absence de musique et aussi musical que musique, faites l'expérience.
8. Recapitulez les circonstances qui ont amené le disque chez vous visualisez le plus de détails possibles.
9. Prenez le disque à la main et gardez-le jusqu'à ce qu'il devienne insupportable (minimum 7 heures).
10. Si vous aimez le disque, aimez-le. Si vous ne l'aimez pas, ne l'aimez pas. Comparez deux disques, un que vous aimez, et un que vous n'aimez pas.
11. Touchez le disque de toutes les façons possibles jusqu'à ce qu'il devienne intéressant (faites-le en public) 5 minutes.
12. Essuyez consciencieusement le disque, 3 minutes.
13. Ce disque en tant qu'œuvre d'art est une création de prétention, en réalité l'essence du disque est MOI, visualisez MOI, dites-vous que cela est musicale.
14. Faites n'importe quoi. n'importe comment avec ou sans le disque, mais faites-le en écoutant attentivement et consciencieusement.

CENTRE D'ART TOTAL - 32, rue Tondutti-de-l'Escarène - NICE

JE NE SIGNE PLUS

Ben Vautier

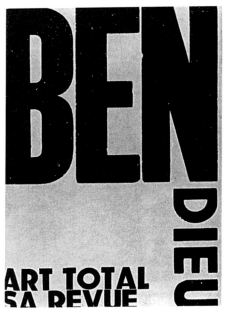

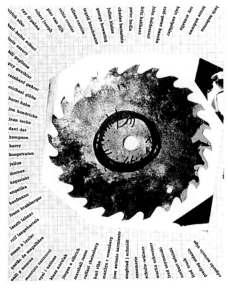

Views beside ... [P/S]

Anthology (33 x 25 cm), 332 p.(n.pag.) including single, ø 17cm, 45 RPM

Maurizio Nannucci: Finger's music. Thomas Kapielski: Ach du grüne 9ne. Fritz Balthaus: Sisyphos' knie, verbissen in tiegels hosenbein. Beth Anderson: Yés sir ree (Michael Blair perc.). Julius: I sing a song (Joan La Barbara voc.). Fred Szymanski: Analplasia for Italian and noise gate

Fritz Balthaus, ed. vogelsang Berlin, 1982, limited edition of 550

Part of the record issue without book. Cover made of book cover. Artists' name handwritten with feltpen

Vautier, Ben [C/S]

Title: TOTAL. Disque de musique. Je ne signe plus. 15 compositions musicales pour la recherche et l'enseignement d'une musique - total -. en hommage à John Cage

ø 17cm, 45 RPM, 1963, Centre d'Art Total, Nice

Cover: b/w

Ben Vautier supplies found records with his own labels.

Vautier, Ben [P/S]

Title: Ben-Dieu-Art Total-Sa Revue. (Moi, Ben je signe.)

Box (31 x 22 cm) contains publication 48 p. (n. pag.), including among many found objects a record:
CE DISQUE 45 TOURS - passé en 78 tours - est une création musicale.

Lebeer Hossmann Editeurs, Bruxelles / Hamburg, 1975

Venet, Bernar
→   Art By Telephone
→   S.M.S.

Verdi, Franco
→   Radiotaxi
→   Sarenco

Verey, Charles
→   Sound Poetry

Verheyen, Marieken
→   Perfo 2

Vicinelli, Patrizia
→   Sound Poetry

Vigo, Edgardo Antonio
→   Voices Notes & Noise

Viner, Frank Lincoln
→   Art By Telephone

Viola, Bill
→   David Tudor

Vivenza [S]

Title: Fondements Bruitistes

Contents: FONDEMENTS BRUITISTES (Dédiés à Vladimir Tatline). SERVOMÉCANISMES

ø 17cm, 45 RPM, 1984, Vivenza, Électro-Instiut, Grenoble

Cover: two-color print

Vivenza: One-man-*Électro-Institute* from Grenoble, continues the traditions of the Italian Futurism and the Russian Constructivism: Russolo, Balla, Tatlin, and Malewitsch are mentioned as ancestors. Vivenza sees himself - also politically - as the transmission-belt of an "objective materialism of sound", based on the idea, that the collective sound-space shapes the social consciousness. Rhythms, sounds, noise from machines are overlapped, added and subtracted - a harsh, unadorned acoustic industrialization. Vivenza choses for his recordings titles such as *Servo-mechanical realities* or *Bruitist foundation of action*.

Program notes of *Ars Electronica*, Linz, 1988

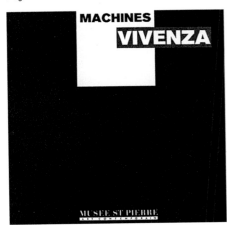

Vivenza [S]

Title: Machines

Contents: Machines. Éléments Mécaniques

ø 30cm, 45 RPM, 1985, Musée St. Pierre, Lyon / Vivenza Électro Institut, Grenoble

Cover: two-color print

Vivenza [S]

Title: Réalités Servomécaniques

Contents: Prolétariat & Industrie. Mécanismes du bruit. Automatismes concrets. Matérialité objective. Unité des machines. Réalités servoméchaniques

ø 30cm, 33 RPM, Vivenza, Électro Institut, Grenoble

Cover: two-color print

Voices Notes & Noise [C/S]

Title: Voices Notes & Noise. International Sound and Sight Compilation

Music: Martin Bisi, Viki Galvez Bisi, Un Departement, Veedtharm Morgan Fisher, Mixed Band Philanthropist, Let's Have Healthy Children, Victor Nubla, Officer!, Human Flesh, Zazou / Bongo, Ptôse, Goebbels / Harth / Stötzner, Hellebore, Doo Dooettes, Lichtenstein Lingery, Nurse With Wound, Madi-Diddi, Debile Menthol, Dissidents, Dressed Up Animals, The Lowest

Note On The Organ, DDAA, Christoph Wünsch, Malcolm, Reinhold Brunner

transparent record, ø 30cm, 33 RPM, 1984, Recommended Music, Würzburg

Cover: transparent plastic cover with one-color print of titles, loose sheet with color slides for "cut out - frame - project".

Slides by: Pierre-Alain Hubert, Tom Recchion, Hummel / Homeyer, Christophe Desforges, Ruggero Maggi, Harry C. Poole, Albrecht D., Walter Schmidt, Jürgen O. Olbrich, Benedict Tisa, Jupiter Larsen, Ryszard Wasko, Paul Rutkovsky, Reinhold Brunner, Pete Horobin, Edgardo Antonio Vigo, Leland Fletcher, Bakhchanyan, Vittore Baroni, Ubaldo Giacomucci, Pawel Petasz, Giovanni Fontana, B. George, Stiletto, Mario Borillo, Gabor Toth, Paul Hurst, Peter Weiss, Ilse Garnier, Baina Masquelier, Andy J. Stenhouse, Marilyn R. Rosenberg, Stephen S'Soreff

Vostell, Wolf [C/S]

Title: dé-coll/age Musik by Vostell

Contents: Radio-dé-coll/age. dé-coll/age manifesto. Sun in your head. El aeropuerto como sala de concierto. Elektronischer dé-coll/age happening Raum. Telemetre. MiM, 1969. Hodispannung. Fandango, 1975. Heuwagen, 1977. Giovanna La Pazza. San Diego Freeway. Garden of Delices

ø 30cm, 33 RPM, 1982, Muthipla Record Milano, No. M 20137

Cover: gatefold, multi-color print, documentary photos and text, design: Bruno Trombetti, art dir.: Gianni Sassi

Documentation of different soundwork by Wolf Vostell from 1959-1981

Vostell, Wolf [C/S]

Title: Garten der Lüste. Il giardino delle delizie. Text König Salomon aus dem Hohen Lied. (Hör Environment)

Perf.: Esperanza Abad, Nancy Bellow, Marie-Louise Gilles, Helga Hamm-Albrecht, Else Nabu, Paco Corales (Canto jondo), Capella St. Martini, Bremen-Lesum, Günter Koller (cond)

2 LPs, ø 30cm, 33 RPM, 1984, Multhipla Record Milano / Wewerka Edition Berlin, No. M 20138

Cover: mailing-box, multi-color print and original color-photo glued on, design: Wolf Vostell

Colored supplement (30,3 x 30,3 cm), 16 p.(n.pag.), partially out of pergamyn, documentary photos, scores, texts of performance on May 8, 1982 at the Weserburg in Bremen. Printed protective-covers with documentary photos revised by Vostell

Vostell, Wolf
→ Art By Telephone

de Vree, Paul
→ Radiotaxi
→ Revue OU
→ Sound Poetry

de Vries, Herman [C/S]

Title: Water. (the music of sound 1)

Contents: Thema 1: Bach. Thema 2: Ozean I. Thema 3: Ozean II. Thema 4: Regen. Thema 5: Quelle

ø 30cm, 33 RPM, 1977, limited edition of 100, signed, numbered and stamped, Edition Artists Press Bern, No. 30-549

Cover: cardboard with sticker, b/w, photos and text, inside cover, also cardboard with 2 color-photos glued on

Handwritten postcard (from Cape Cod, USA) by artist to Artists Press as supplement

Wackenhut
→ Perfo 2

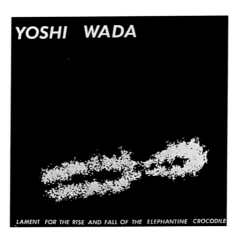

Wada, Yoshi [C/S]

Title: Lament For The Rise And Fall Of The Elephantine Crocodile

Perf.: Yoshi Wada (voc, adapted bagpipe with sympathy)

ø 30 cm, 33 RPM, 1982, India Navigation New York, No. IN 3025

Cover: b/w, design and photography by Marilyn Bogerd

Recorded in the *Dry Pool* (an empty swimming pool in the basement of Media Study, Buffalo, N.Y.)

Wada, Yoshi [S]

Title: Off The Wall

Perf.: Yoshi Wada (bagpipe), Wayne Hankin (bagpipe), Marilyn Bogerd (adapted org), Andreas Schmidt-Neri (perc)

ø 30cm, 33 RPM, 1985, Free Music Production Berlin, No. SAJ-49

Cover: gatefold, b/w with photos by Marilyn Bogerd and Dagmar Gebers, texts by Yoshi Wada and Tom Johnson; design: Manfred Kussatz

Recorded May 11/12, 1984, Künstlerhaus Bethanien, Berlin

Wada Yoshi
→ Sound

Waisvisz, Michel
→ DUTCH "DIFFICULT" MUSIC

Wakoski, Diane
→ S.M.S.

Waldman, Anne
→ Giorno Poetry Systems

Walsh, Emmett
→ Sound Poetry

Wolf Vostell

Warhol, Andy [C]

Title: The Velvet Underground & Nico

Music: The Velvet Underground & Nico

ø 30cm, 33 RPM, n.d.(1971), Verve Records, produced by Andy Warhol, No. 710 004

Cover: gatefold, multi-color print, with a banana as sticker

Warhol, Andy [C]

Title: The Academy In Peril

Music: John Cale

ø 30cm, 33 RPM, 1972, Reprise Records / Warner Bos. Records New York, No. MS 2079

Cover: gatefold, multi-color print, 25 pictures of Kodachrome-slide-frames, the area of the slide is punched out, the picture is on the inside

Warhol, Andy [P/S]

Title: Andy Warhol's Index (Book)

Book, 28 x 21,5 cm, 72 p.(n.pag.), Random House Inc., New York, 1967

In addition to various paper-objects, the book contains a glued on picture-disc mounted on cardboard. The picture shows a portrait of Lou Reed. The disc contains a conversation of Velvet Underground about the book with their first LP as background music.

Warhol, Andy

→ Aspen Magazine
→ Record of Interviews...

Wasko, Ryszard

→ Voices Notes & Noise

Warhol, Andy [C]

Title: Sticky Fingers

Music: The Rolling Stones

ø 30cm, 33 RPM, 1971, Rolling Stones Records, No. COC 59100

Cover: multi-color print, picture of jeans with real zipper

Supplement with list of titles and photo

Warhol, Andy [C]

Title: Love You Live

Music: The Rolling Stones

2 LPs, ø 30cm, 33 RPM, 1977, Rolling Stones Records, No. COC 89 101

Cover: gatefold, multi-color print with pictures of revised photos of the Rolling Stones

Watts, Robert [O]

Phono Records. 1970 - 72

The string record was made for an exhibition called *Rope & String* at the Janis Gallery, New York, in 1970.
Earlier, in 1960, I had used a red Beethoven record in a kinetic sculpture, and in 1964 I made a series of spray painted records for a Fluxus performance at the Flux Stone on Canal Street. These were played by the audience and as the paint wore off the music gradually was revealed.
During the period 1970-72 I began experiments with the manufacture of a series of records in different materials such as

Andy Warhol

Contents: Sex in der Stadt. Stromtod. Married Woman. Kokain Cowboy. Freiheitsfrau. Liebe ist ein Hospital. Was ist ein Hirn. Minimale Katastrophen. Alpha Rhythmen. Hör die Formen

Perf.: Peter Weibel (voc), Loys Egg (g), Paul Braunsteiner (g), Franz Machek (b), Wolfgang Steiner (dr)

ø 30cm, 33 RPM, 1982, Schallter, Wien, No. 204717

Cover: multi-color print, label and cover concept: Peter Weibl

Supplement with songtexts

Weibel, Peter / [C/S]
Loys Egg

Title: Dead In The Head

Music: Hotel Morphila Orchester

ø 17cm, 45 RPM, 1982, Extraplatte, Wien

metals, plastic, wood, clay, and latex. Most of these were made on a machine lathe at Rutgers University, and I thought of them as being sound portraits from this machine. The various bands on these records were varied in depth of cut, spacing and rpm. I was interested in variations in the sounds produced in this manner from the varied materials.

In: *Extended Play* (cat.) New York 1988

Watts, Robert
→ Record of Interviews...

Wegman, William
→ Art By Telephone

Weibel, Peter [C/S]

Title: Schwarze Energie

Music: Hotel Morphila Orchester

Cover: two-color print, concept: Peter Weibel

1 leaflet with songtexts included

Weibel, Peter / [C/S]
Loys Egg

Title: Liebe ist katastrofal

Music: Hotel Morphila Orchester

Contents: Liebe ist katastrofal. Sex in der Stadt

ø 17cm, 45 RPM, 1982, Ariola Schallplatten, Wien

Cover: two-color print

Weigand, Hans
→ Fünfzehn Tonspuren

7

Lawrence Weiner

Weiner, Lawrence [C/S]

Title: 7

Contents: Side I: A C Sharpened carried done again perhaps. A D Sharp-

252

Side I.

A C SHARPENED CARRIED DONE AGAIN PERHAPS
A C IN LINE WITH OTHERS OF ITS KIND
A LOW C SHARPENED CARRIED DONE AGAIN PERHAPS IN NOT THE SEQUENCE STATED
A C SHARPENED AND DESIGNATED AS A FLATTENED D
A MIDDLE C SHARPENED CARRIED DONE AGAIN PERHAPS AND THEN AGAIN
A C
A HIGH C SHARPENED CARRIED DONE AGAIN PERHAPS WITHIN THE CONTEXT THAT PRECEEDED
A C HIGH MIDDLE LOW
IF IN A CONTEXT A SHARPENED C CAN AS A FLATTENED D PASS
WHEN ALBEIT EVEN IN A CULTURAL CONTEXT DOES DESIGNATION
SLIP FROM CONVENIENCE INTO RELEGATION
WHEN IF IN A CONTEXT A SHARPENED C IS A FLATTENED D IS THIS
A RELEGATION OF NECESSITY
WHEN THEN AGAIN WITHIN A CONTEXT IS THIS A RECIPROCAL CONVENIENCE
A D SHARPENED FLATTENED CARRIED DONE AGAIN PERHAPS
A D IN LINE WITH OTHERS OF ITS KIND
A LOW D SHARPENED FLATTENED CARRIED DONE AGAIN PERHAPS IN NOT THE SEQUENCE STATED
A D SHARPENED AND DESIGNATED AS A FLATTENED E
A MIDDLE D SHARPENED CARRIED DONE AGAIN PERHAPS AND THEN AGAIN
A MIDDLE D SHARPENED FLATTENED CARRIED DONE AGAIN PERHAPS AND THEN AGAIN
A D
A HIGH D SHARPENED FLATTENED CARRIED DONE AGAIN PERHAPS WITHIN THE CONTEXT THAT PRECEEDED
A D HIGH MIDDLE LOW
IF IN A CONTEXT A SHARPENED D CAN AS A FLATTENED E PASS
WHEN ALBEIT EVEN IN A CULTURAL CONTEXT DOES DESIGNATION
SLIP FROM CONVENIENCE INTO RELEGATION
WHEN IF IN A CONTEXT A SHARPENED D IS A FLATTENED E IS THIS
A RELEGATION OF NECESSITY
WHEN THEN AGAIN WITHIN A CONTEXT IS THIS A RECIPROCAL CONVENIENCE
AND THEN IS THIS HIGH LOW JUSTIFICATION
AN E FLATTENED CARRIED DONE AGAIN PERHAPS
AN E IN LINE WITH OTHERS OF ITS KIND
A SLURRED E FLATTENED CARRIED DONE AGAIN PERHAPS IN NOT THE SEQUENCE STATED
AN E FLATTENED AND DESIGNATED AS A SHARPENED D
A MIDDLE E FLATTENED CARRIED DONE AGAIN PERHAPS AND THEN AGAIN
AN E
A HIGH E FLATTENED CARRIED DONE AGAIN PERHAPS WITHIN THE CONTEXT THAT PRECEEDED
AN E HIGH MIDDLE
IF IN A CONTEXT A FLATTENED E CAN AS A SHARPENED D PASS
WHEN ALBEIT EVEN IN A CULTURAL CONTEXT DOES DESIGNATION
SLIP FROM CONVENIENCE INTO RELEGATION
WHEN IF IN A CONTEXT A FLATTENED E IS A SHARPENED D IS THIS A RELEGATION OF NECESSITY
WHEN THEN AGAIN WITHIN A CONTEXT IS THIS A RECIPROCAL CONVENIENCE
AND THEN IS THIS HIGH LOW JUSTIFICATION
AN F SHARPENED CARRIED DONE AGAIN PERHAPS
AN F IN LINE WITH OTHERS OF ITS KIND
A SLURRED F SHARPENED CARRIED DONE AGAIN PERHAPS IN NOT THE SEQUENCE STATED
AN F SHARPENED AND DESIGNATED AS A FLATTENED G
A MIDDLE F SHARPENED CARRIED DONE AGAIN PERHAPS AND THEN AGAIN
AN F
A HIGH F SHARPENED CARRIED DONE AGAIN PERHAPS WITHIN THE CONTEXT THAT PRECEEDED
AN F HIGH MIDDLE
IF IN A CONTEXT A SHARPENED F CAN AS A FLATTENED G PASS
WHEN ALBEIT EVEN IN A CULTURAL CONTEXT DOES DESIGNATION SLIP
FROM CONVENIENCE INTO RELEGATION
WHEN IF IN A CONTEXT A SHARPENED F IS A FLATTENED G IS THIS
A RELEGATION OF NECESSITY
WHEN THEN AGAIN WITHIN A CONTEXT IS THIS A RECIPROCAL CONVENIENCE
AND THEN IS THIS HIGH LOW JUSTIFICATION
OR PERHAPS THE MIDDLE
A G SHARPENED FLATTENED CARRIED DONE AGAIN PERHAPS
A G IN LINE WITH OTHERS OF ITS KIND
A SLURRED G SHARPENED FLATTENED CARRIED DONE AGAIN
PERHAPS IN NOT THE SEQUENCE STATED
A G SHARPENED AND DESIGNATED AS A FLATTENED A
A MIDDLE G SHARPENED FLATTENED CARRIED DONE AGAIN PERHAPS AND THEN AGAIN
A G
A HIGH G SHARPENED FLATTENED CARRIED DONE AGAIN PERHAPS WITHIN THE CONTEXT THAT PRECEEDED
A G HIGH MIDDLE
IF IN A CONTEXT A SHARPENED G CAN AS A FLATTENED A PASS
WHEN ALBEIT EVEN IN A CULTURAL CONTEXT DOES DESIGNATION SLIP
FROM CONVENIENCE INTO RELEGATION
WHEN IF IN A CONTEXT A SHARPENED G IS A FLATTENED A IS THIS
A RELEGATION OF NECESSITY
WHEN THEN AGAIN WITHIN A CONTEXT IS THIS A RECIPROCAL CONVENIENCE
AND THEN IS THIS HIGH LOW JUSTIFICATION
OR PERHAPS THE MIDDLE
DONE AGAIN SLURRED IT FITS AND/OR SEEMS TO FIT
AN A SHARPENED FLATTENED CARRIED DONE AGAIN PERHAPS
AN A IN LINE WITH OTHERS OF ITS KIND
A SLURRED A SHARPENED FLATTENED CARRIED DONE AGAIN PERHAPS AND THEN AGAIN
AN A
A HIGH A SHARPENED FLATTENED CARRIED DONE AGAIN PERHAPS WITHIN THE CONTEXT THAT PRECEEDED
AN A HIGH MIDDLE
IF IN A CONTEXT A SHARPENED A CAN AS A FLATTENED B PASS
WHEN ALBEIT EVEN IN AN INACCULTURAL CONTEXT DOES DESIGNATION
SLIP FROM CONVENIENCE INTO RELEGATION
WHEN IF IN A CONTEXT A SHARPENED A IS A FLATTENED B IS THIS
A RELEGATION OF NECESSITY
WHEN THEN AGAIN WITHIN A CONTEXT IS THIS A RECIPOCAL CONVENIENCE
AND THEN IS THIS HIGH LOW JUSTIFICATION
OR PERHAPS THE MIDDLE
DONE AGAIN SLURRED IT FITS AND/OR SEEMS TO FIT
DONE AGAIN IT PLACES AND/OR IS PLACED
A B FLATTENED CARRIED DONE AGAIN PERHAPS
A B IN LINE WITH OTHERS OF ITS KIND
A SLURRED B FLATTENED CARRIED DONE AGAIN PERHAPS NOT IN THE SEQUENCE STATED
A B FLATTENED AND DESIGNATED AS A SHARPENED A
A MIDDLE B FLATTENED CARRIED DONE AGAIN PERHAPS AND THEN AGAIN
A B
A HIGH B FLATTENED CARRIED DONE AGAIN PERHAPS WITHIN THE CONTEXT THAT PRECEEDED
A B HIGH MIDDLE
IF IN A CONTEXT A FLATTENED B CAN AS A SHARPENED A PASS
WHEN ALBEIT EVEN IN A CULTURAL CONTEXT DOES DESIGNATION
SLIP FROM CONVENIENCE INTO RELEGATION
WHEN IF IN A CONTEXT A FLATTENED B IS A SHARPENED A IS THIS
A RELEGATION OF NECESSITY
WHEN THEN AGAIN WITHIN A CONTEXT IS THIS A RECIPROCAL CONVENIENCE
AND THEN IS THIS HIGH LOW JUSTIFICATION
OR PERHAPS THE MIDDLE
DONE AGAIN SLURRED IT FITS AND/OR SEEMS TO FIT
DONE AGAIN IT PLACES AND/OR IS PLACED
WITHIN THE JUSTTIFICATION SEEMS TO REST THE CONTEXT

Side I.

Spoken by Lawrence Weiner

Flute : Pierre-Yves Artaud

Produced by Yvon Lambert

Côté II.

UN DO DIÈSE REPORTÉ FAIT ENCORE PEUT-ÊTRE
UN DO EN RANG AVEC D'AUTRES DE SON GENRE
UN DO GRAVE DIÈSE REPORTÉ FAIT ENCORE PEUT-ÊTRE PAS DANS LA SÉQUENCE DÉCLARÉE
UN DO DIÈSE ET DÉSIGNÉ COMME UN RÉ BÉMOLISÉ
UN DO MOYEN DIÈSE REPORTÉ FAIT ENCORE PEUT-ÊTRE ET PUIS ENCORE
UN DO
UN DO AIGU DIÈSE REPORTÉ FAIT ENCORE PEUT-ÊTRE DANS LE CONTEXTE QUI A PRÉCÉDÉ
UN DO AIGU MOYEN GRAVE
SI DANS UN CONTEXTE UN DO DIÈSE PEUT PASSER POUR UN RÉ BÉMOLISÉ
LORSQUE MÊME DANS UN CONTEXTE CULTUREL LA DÉSIGNATION
PASSE-T-ELLE DE CONVENANCE A RELÉGATION
LORSQUE DANS UN CONTEXTE UN DO DIÈSE EST UN RÉ BÉMOLISÉ CECI
EST-IL UNE RELÉGATION DE NÉCESSITÉ
LORSQU'ENCORE DANS UN CONTEXTE CECI EST-IL UNE CONVENANCE RÉCIPROQUE
UN RÉ DIÈSE BÉMOLISÉ REPORTÉ FAIT ENCORE PEUT-ÊTRE
UN RÉ EN RANG AVEC D'AUTRES DE SON GENRE
UN RÉ GRAVE DIÈSE BÉMOLISÉ REPORTÉ FAIT ENCORE PEUT-ÊTRE PAS DANS LA SÉQUENCE DÉCLARÉE
UN RÉ DIÈSE ET DÉSIGNÉ COMME UN MI BÉMOLISÉ
UN RÉ MOYEN DIÈSE BÉMOLISÉ REPORTÉ FAIT ENCORE PEUT-ÊTRE ET PUIS ENCORE
UN RÉ
UN RÉ AIGU DIÈSE BÉMOLISÉ REPORTÉ FAIT ENCORE PEUT-ÊTRE DANS LE CONTEXTE QUI A PRÉCÉDÉ
UN RÉ AIGU MOYEN GRAVE
SI DANS UN CONTEXTE UN RÉ DIÈSE PEUT PASSER POUR UN MI BÉMOLISÉ
LORSQUE MÊME DANS UN CONTEXTE CULTUREL LA DÉSIGNATION
PASSE-T-ELLE DE CONVENANCE A RELÉGATION
LORSQUE DANS UN CONTEXTE UN RÉ DIÈSE EST UN MI BÉMOLISÉ CECI
EST-IL UNE RELÉGATION DE NÉCESSITÉ
LORSQU'ENCORE DANS UN CONTEXTE CECI EST-IL UNE CONVENANCE RÉCIPROQUE
ET PUIS CECI EST-IL UNE JUSTIFICATION AIGUE GRAVE
UN MI BÉMOLISÉ REPORTÉ FAIT ENCORE PEUT-ÊTRE
UN MI EN RANG AVEC D'AUTRES DE SON GENRE
UN MI BÉMOLISÉ REPORTÉ FAIT ENCORE PEUT-ÊTRE PAS DANS LA SÉQUENCE DÉCLARÉE
UN MI BÉMOLISÉ ET DÉSIGNÉ COMME UN RÉ DIÈSE
UN MI MOYEN BÉMOLISÉ REPORTÉ FAIT ENCORE PEUT-ÊTRE ET PUIS ENCORE
UN MI
UN MI AIGU BÉMOLISÉ REPORTÉ FAIT ENCORE PEUT-ÊTRE DANS LE CONTEXTE QUI A PRÉCÉDÉ
UN MI AIGU MOYEN
SI DANS UN CONTEXTE UN MI BÉMOLISÉ PEUT PASSER POUR UN RÉ DIÈSE
LORSQUE MÊME DANS UN CONTEXTE CULTUREL LA DÉSIGNATION
PASSE-T-ELLE DE CONVENANCE A RELÉGATION
LORSQUE DANS UN CONTEXTE UN MI BÉMOLISÉ EST UN RÉ DIÈSE CECI
EST-IL UNE RELÉGATION DE NÉCESSITÉ
LORSQU'ENCORE DANS UN CONTEXTE CECI EST-IL UNE CONVENANCE RÉCIPROQUE
ET PUIS CECI EST-IL UNE JUSTIFICATION AIGUE GRAVE
UN FA DIÈSE REPORTÉ FAIT ENCORE PEUT-ÊTRE
UN FA EN RANG AVEC D'AUTRES DE SON GENRE
UN FA DIÈSE LIÉ REPORTÉ FAIT ENCORE PEUT-ÊTRE PAS DANS LA SÉQUENCE DÉCLARÉE
UN FA DIÈSE ET DÉSIGNE COMME UN SOL BÉMOLISÉ
UN FA MOYEN DIÈSE REPORTÉ FAIT ENCORE PEUT-ÊTRE ET PUIS ENCORE
UN FA
UN FA AIGU DIÈSE REPORTÉ FAIT ENCORE PEUT-ÊTRE DANS LE CONTEXTE QUI A PRÉCÉDÉ
UN FA AIGU MOYEN
SI DANS UN CONTEXTE UN FA DIÈSE PEUT PASSER POUR UN SOL BÉMOLISÉ
LORSQUE MÊME DANS UN CONTEXTE CULTUREL LA DÉSIGNATION
PASSE-T-ELLE DE CONVENANCE A RELÉGATION
LORSQUE DANS UN CONTEXTE UN FA DIÈSE EST UN SOL BÉMOLISÉ CECI
EST-IL UNE RELÉGATION DE NÉCESSITÉ
LORSQU'ENCORE DANS UN CONTEXTE CECI EST-IL UNE CONVENANCE RÉCIPROQUE
ET PUIS CECI EST-IL UNE JUSTIFICATION AIGUE GRAVE
OU PEUT-ÊTRE LE MOYEN
UN SOL DIÈSE BÉMOLISÉ REPORTÉ FAIT ENCORE PEUT-ÊTRE
UN SOL EN RANG AVEC D'AUTRES DE SON GENRE
UN SOL DIÈSE BÉMOLISÉ LIÉ REPORTÉ FAIT ENCORE
PEUT-ÊTRE PAS DANS LA SÉQUENCE DÉCLARÉE
UN SOL DIÈSE ET DÉSIGNÉ COMME UN LA BÉMOLISÉ
UN SOL MOYEN DIÈSE BÉMOLISÉ REPORTÉ FAIT ENCORE PEUT-ÊTRE ET PUIS ENCORE
UN SOL
UN SOL AIGU DIÈSE BÉMOLISÉ REPORTÉ FAIT ENCORE PEUT-ÊTRE DANS LE CONTEXTE QUI A PRÉCÉDÉ
UN SOL AIGU MOYEN
SI DANS UN CONTEXTE UN SOL DIÈSE PEUT PASSER POUR UN LA BÉMOLISÉ
LORSQUE MÊME DANS UN CONTEXTE CULTUREL LA DÉSIGNATION
PASSE-T-ELLE DE CONVENANCE A RELÉGATION
LORSQUE DANS UN CONTEXTE UN SOL DIÈSE EST UN LA BÉMOLISÉ CECI
EST-IL UNE RELÉGATION DE NÉCESSITÉ
LORSQU'ENCORE DANS UN CONTEXTE CECI EST-IL UNE CONVENANCE RÉCIPROQUE
OU PEUT-ÊTRE LE MOYEN
FAIT ENCORE LIÉ IL S'AJUSTE ET/OU SEMBLE S'AJUSTER
UN LA DIÈSE BÉMOLISÉ FAIT ENCORE REPORTÉ PEUT-ÊTRE
UN LA EN RANG AVEC D'AUTRES DE SON GENRE
UN LA DIÈSE BÉMOLISÉ LIÉ REPORTÉ FAIT ENCORE PEUT-ÊTRE ET PUIS ENCORE
UN LA
UN LA AIGU DIÈSE BÉMOLISÉ REPORTÉ FAIT ENCORE PEUT-ÊTRE DANS LE CONTEXTE QUI A PRÉCÉDÉ
UN LA GRAVE MOYEN
SI DANS UN CONTEXTE UN LA DIÈSE PEUT PASSER POUR UN SI BÉMOLISÉ
LORSQUE MÊME DANS UN CONTEXTE CULTUREL LA DÉSIGNATION
PASSE-T-ELLE DE CONVENANCE A RELÉGATION
LORSQUE DANS UN CONTEXTE UN LA DIÈSE EST UN SI BÉMOLISÉ CECI
EST-IL UNE RELÉGATION DE NÉCESSITÉ
LORSQU'ENCORE DANS UN CONTEXTE CECI EST-IL UNE CONVENANCE RÉCIPROQUE
ET PUIS CECI EST-IL UNE JUSTIFICATION AIGUE GRAVE
OU PEUT-ÊTRE LE MOYEN
FAIT ENCORE LIÉ IL S'AJUSTE ET/OU SEMBLE S'AJUSTER
FAIT ENCORE IL SE PLACE ET/OU EST PLACÉ
UN SI BÉMOLISÉ REPORTÉ FAIT ENCORE PEUT-ÊTRE
UN SI EN RANG AVEC D'AUTRES DE SON GENRE
UN SI BÉMOLISÉ LIÉ REPORTÉ FAIT ENCORE PEUT-ÊTRE PAS DANS LA SÉQUENCE DÉCLARÉE
UN SI BÉMOLISÉ ET DÉSIGNÉ COMME UN LA DIÈSE
UN SI MOYEN BÉMOLISÉ REPORTÉ FAIT ENCORE PEUT-ÊTRE ET PUIS ENCORE
UN SI
UN SI AIGU BÉMOLISÉ REPORTÉ FAIT ENCORE PEUT-ÊTRE DANS LE CONTEXTE QUI A PRÉCÉDÉ
UN SI AIGU MOYEN
SI DANS UN CONTEXTE UN SI BÉMOLISÉ PEUT PASSER POUR UN LA DIÈSE
LORSQUE MÊME DANS UN CONTEXTE CULTUREL LA DÉSIGNATION
PASSE-T-ELLE DE CONVENANCE A RELÉGATION
LORSQUE DANS UN CONTEXTE UN SI BÉMOLISÉ EST UN LA DIÈSE CECI
EST-IL UNE RELÉGATION DE NÉCESSITÉ
LORSQU'ENCORE DANS UN CONTEXTE CECI EST-IL UNE CONVENANCE RÉCIPROQUE
ET PUIS CECI EST-IL UNE JUSTIFICATION AIGUE GRAVE
OU PEUT-ÊTRE LE MOYEN
FAIT ENCORE LIÉ IL S'AJUSTE ET/OU SEMBLE S'AJUSTER
FAIT ENCORE IL SE PLACE ET/OU EST PLACÉ
DANS LA JUSTIFICATION SEMBLE SE FONDER LE CONTEXTE

Côté II.

Dit par Béatrice Conrad-Eybesfeld (traductrice)

Flûte : Pierre-Yves Artaud

Édité par Yvon Lambert

Imp. SAINT-ROCH - Paris

Lawrence Weiner's record *7* of 1972 was produced by the Yvon Lambert Gallery who did *10 Works*, but that fact alone does not prevent its raising the question in a more acute form.

The front cover reads very much like the books, with short numbered verbal phrases specifying a musical structure within the limits of an empty parenthesis, an ellipsis, and the word 'perhaps' which takes the work out of the impositional mode which the artist considers fascistic. There is a translation into French, just like *10 Works*, and on the back a further elaboration in both languages. However, phrases like 'in not the sequence stated' still leave a good deal to the discretion of flautist Pierre-Yves Artaud, who provides musical exemplifications of the extended statements of the back of the cover as first spoken in 'Side I' by Lawrence Weiner and then on 'Coté II' by the translator Beatrice Conrad-Eybesfeld. The record has a certain kinship with *A translation from one language to another*. The performance of the flautist represents a translation of the spoken dialogue and the spoken words read in turn as a translation of their written equivalents on the back of the cover, but the contrast between the written English and the written French becomes more marked when it also involves the transposition from a male to a female voice.

The seven pieces deal with the seven notes of the musical scale and the basic concern of the record is that a single sound may be designated as a 'sharpened C' or a 'flattened D' according to its musical context (and may, as sound, function differently within that context), while the same verbal designation 'C' may refer to a note in high, low or middle register. It is centrally a matter of the operation of alternative systems of designation. The presentation is unusual in Lawrence Weiner's work, among other things, for the inclusion of editorial comments at the end of each piece which make the didactic point explicit. The key statement, repeated in each piece is:
'If in a context a flattened E can as a sharpened D pass
When albeit even in a cultural context does designation
Slip from convenience into relegation?'
The question is certainly apposite. It is consistent with the artist's general approach that the record should be, in format, just a standard record like any other record produced in France in 1972, but this would seem just one more reason to prefer the musical category. But would that be relegation? I'm not at all sure.

To most people, music implies a structure of pure sound, in a way that art, in spite of over fifty years of modernism, has not come to imply pure visibility - and perhaps never can because of the different nature of the sense of sight. I noticed in our class discussion that Lawrence Weiner said the flautist translated the spoken words into musical 'notation', and the alternation of spoken musical suggestions and the performance of the flautist does cause the musical sounds to take on the character of representations of their own verbal designations. If this implies much the sort of equivalence between actualized musical structure and verbal language as existed between the actualized material art structures and descriptive titles in the Seth Siegelaub catalogue, there is a difference in that the language of the titles readily evokes a material structure through a common understanding not only of the terms but also of the materials and processes involved. No such common understanding can be assumed in the case of music. The codification of music through the systems of its notation has long given to music a degree of clarity unknown in most phases of the visual arts, but even where that notation is further translated into the alphabetic designations of Lawrence Weiner's record, it requires expertise to conjure up a musical image on the basis of the description. A professional musician may come to a substantial appreciation of a musical composition through reading a score, but his reading is referred to an understanding in terms of sound. *7* makes language primary, but it would need a musicologist to give a detailed evaluation of the significance of that contribution.

One understands that the question whether vocal music preceded instrumental music is still in dispute, but even if the priority of vocal music were established, there is a distinction between the use of music as a formal adjunct to linguistic expression and the accommodation of that form to the possibility of linguistic designation. Lawrence Weiner's record is no more concerned with the literary aspects of songs than is his earlier art with the depictive possibilities of painting and sculpture. There might be an interesting comparison to be made with Wagner. He, too, made music more radically dependent on language than in previous periods, and his music too involves an exchange of meaning between different levels, dramatic, verbal and musical, but the transmuted meaning is emotion, the mode of transmutation 'symbolism' as opposed to the more rational process of 'signification' entailed in Lawrence Weiner's work. Might there perhaps emerge in the comparison of nineteenth-century music generally with that of the present the same contrast between literary and linguistic orientation which is so evident in the sphere of art?

Excerpt from Eric Cameron: *Lawrence Weiner: the books*. In: Studio International, Jan. 1974

ened flattened carried done again perhaps. An E Flattened carried done again perhaps. An F Sharpened carried done again perhaps. A G Sharpened flattened carried done again perhaps. An A Sharpened flattened carried done again perhaps. A B Flattened carried done again perhaps

Perf.: Lawrence Weiner (voc), Pierre-Yves Artaud (fl), Béatrice Conrad-Eybesfeld (voc)

ø 30cm, 33 RPM, n.d.(1972), Galerie Yvon Lambert, Paris

Cover: one-color print with text

Weiner, Lawrence [C/S]

Title: 4 CUTS PLACED IN. "A FIRST QUARTER", a Film by LAWRENCE WEINER

Music: Richard Landry

Contents: Requiem For Some. 4th Register. Piece For So. Vivace Duo

Perf.: Richard Landry (alto-fl, ts), Richard Peck (ts), Robert Prado (tp), Rusty Gilder (b), David Lee (dr)

ø 30cm, 33 RPM, 1972, Leo Castelli / chatham square productions, New York, No. 10028

Cover: b/w, with photos by Tina Girouard and Richard Landry

Weiner, Lawrence [C/S]

Title: HAVING BEEN DONE AT / HAVING BEEN DONE TO. ESSENDO STATO FATTO A

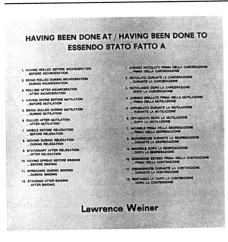

Perf.: English spoken by Lawrence Weiner, Italian spoken by Marina Girotto. Piano: Marina Girotto

ø 30cm, 33 RPM, 1973, Gian Enzo Sperone & Konrad Fischer, Roma

Cover: two-color print, back cover with photos of the participants by Elisabetta Catalano

Weiner, Lawrence [C/S]

Title: Niets aan verloren. Nothing To Loose

Perf.: Lawrence Weiner, Coosje van Bruggen (voc)

ø 30 cm, 33 RPM, 1976, Van Abbemuseum Eindhoven, No. RCS 352

Cover: b/w, photos and text

Weiner, Lawrence [C/S]

Title: Having Been Built On Sand. With Another Base (Basis) In Fact. Auf

---

HAVING BEEN BUILT ON SAND

WITH ANOTHER BASE (BASIS) IN FACT

AUF SAND GEBAUT

MIT EINER ANDERN BASIS TATSÄCHLICH

Sand gebaut. Mit einer andern Basis tatsächlich

Music: Richard Landry

Contents: 1. - 8. Song

Perf.: Britta Le Va, Tina Girouard, Lawrence Weiner, Richard Landry (voc), Instruments: ts, alto-fl, b-cl, voc, ss, fl

ø 30cm, 33 RPM, 1978, Rüdiger Schöttle München, No. 50316

Cover: two-color print

GENÈVE

LOVE OF LIFE ORCHESTRA

GENF

GENEVA

2·1·15·1980

GINEVRA

Weiner, Lawrence [C/S]

Title: Geneva

Music: Peter Gordon

Perf.: Love of Life Orchestra: Peter Gordon (keyboards and woodwind), David Van Tieghem (acoustic and electronic perc) and guest musicians

---

ø 30cm, 33 RPM, 1980, Lust/-Unlust Music, New York

Cover: two-color print, concept: Lawrence Weiner

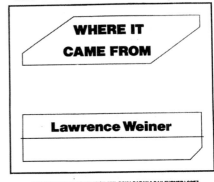

Weiner, Lawrence [C/S]

Title: Deutsche Angst. Where It Came From

Music: Peter Gordon

ø 17cm, 45 RPM, 1982, Les Disques du Crepuscule, Belgium, No. TWI 059

Cover: three-color print, design: Lawrence Weiner

Weiner, Lawrence
→ Rosenfest

Weiss, Peter
→ Voices Notes & Noise

Weisser, Stefan (Z'ev)   [S]

Title: Poextensions. Contexts

ø 17cm, 45 RPM, 1981, limited edition of 900, signed and numbered, Subterranean Records, Berkeley, CA

Cover: two-color print

Poextensions is the title of the acoustic contribution on the record. *Contexts* refers to the 6 double-sided printed sheets (17,8 x 17,8 cm), (visual poetry in cut-up-technique).
Stefan Weisser published all following records using the name Z'ev.

Wendt, Larry
→   Sound Poetry

Went, Johanna
→   High Performance

Wesley, John
→   Record of Interviews...

Wesselmann, Tom
→   Artsounds Collection
→   Record of Interviews...

Whitman, Robert   [S]

Title: Sounds for 4 Cinema Pieces

ø 17cm on red plastic (19 x 19 cm) 33 RPM, 1968, Museum of Contemporary Art, Chicago

Cover: two-color print

Wiener, Monsti
→   Valie Export

Wiener, Oswald
→   selten gehörte Musik

Wiley, William T.
→   Art By Telephone
→   Word Of Mouth

Wilhite, Bob
→   Sound

Stefan Wewerka. (Untitled).1967. 39,5x15,2 cm

Wilke, Hannah
→   Revolutions Per Minute

Williams, Emmett
→   Sound Poetry
→   das Kuemmerling Trio

Williams, Reese
→   Sound Poetry

Williamson, Philemona
→   Artsounds Collection

Wilp, Charles
→   Yves Klein

Wilson, Martha
→   High Performance

Wilson, Robert   [S]

Title: The Life and Times of Joseph Stalin

Contents: The. Beach. Life. Drawing Room. And. Cave. Times. An. Forest. Of. Temple. Joseph. Bedroom. Stalin. Planet. Opera

Perf.:   Byrd Hoffman School of Byrds

ø 30cm, 33 RPM, n.d.

Cover: white cover without information

Wilson, Robert
→   Giorno Poetry Systems
→   Philip Glass

Winters, Robin
→   Perfo 2

de Wit, Harry
→   DUTCH "DIFFICULT" MUSIC

Wölfl, VA   [O]

Title: Pferd. Horse. Elastic. 1984

Abrasive wheel, ø 30cm, with commercial label (dry grinding, max. 5100 RPM), sticker stamped and numbered by the artist, (100 copies). In protective record cover, stamped and numbered

Woelfli, Adolf   [S]

Title: Gelesen und vertont

Contents: Walzer 1913. 1. Antree! Ihr lieben Leutte! 2. Die Strafe. 3. Der Fluch. Marsch 1921. 4. Gedichte. Musik-stück 1914. 5. Städteverzeichnis Königreich Spanien. 6. Allgebrah. Walzer 1913. 7. Die-Gott-Vatter-Donnerinna-Fonttaine und der Tanz im Garten Eeden. 8. Trauermarsch-Lieder

Perf.:   Anton Bruhin, Fred Singeisen (voice); Trio Aarebögeler: Tinu Bauer (cl), Aschi Frei (acc), Kjell Keller (v); texts compiled and edited by Jürgen Glaesemer and Elka Spoerri

ø 30cm, 33 RPM, 1978, Bernische Kunstgesellschaft und Adolf Wölfli-Stiftung, Kunstmuseum Bern

Cover: gatefold, two-color print, picture on the cover *Liseli Bieri! Tood. - Der Engel des Herrn im Küchenschurz.* 1904, composition in two parts, each 75 x 100cm, pencil and blue pencil on paper

4 page supplement with texts included

Wolf, Ror   [O/S]

Title: Der Ball ist rund

Contents: Der Ball ist rund. Schwierigkeiten beim Umschalten

recorded by Hessischer Rundfunk 1978/1979
ø 30cm, 33 RPM, n.d.(1987), Edition RZ, Berlin, Ed.RZ -HS -1 Noch Musik

Cover: two-color print, transparent plastic cover

Picture disc of a football

Wolf, Winfried   [O]

Records treated with sandpaper, paint, and other materials. ø 30cm, 2 samples of a series from 1985

Wolff-William Kingsbury, Karen
→   Sound

Wolman, Gil J.
→   Poesie Physique
→   Revue OU
→   Sound Poetry

Word of Mouth   [P/S]

Title: Vision No. 4
Prepared Talks By 12 Artists Recorded On Ponape, An Island In The Pacific Ocean

With: Laurie Anderson. Chris Burden, Daniel Buren, John Cage, Bryan

Hunt, Joan Jonas, Robert Kushner, Brice Marden, Tom Marioni, Pat Steir, Marina Abramovic/Ulay, William T. Wiley

Box containing 3 white records, ø 30cm, 33 RPM, and a booklet 8 p. (n.pag) with photos and texts

Vision is an art journal edited and curated by Tom Marioni of the Museum of Conceptual Art (MOCA), published and produced by Kathan Brown of Crown Point Press, Oakland California.
For Vision No. 4 artists were given time on a phonograph record rather than pages in a magazine. Twelve artists from California, New York and Europe were each invited to prepare a twelve minute talk on any subject.

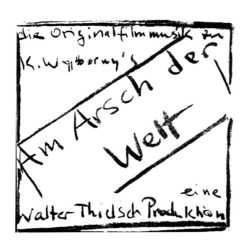

Wyborny, Klaus   [C/S]

Title: Am Arsch der Welt

Contents: Bete und Arbeite. Umsonst. Erstunken und Erlogen. Napoleon nach der Schlacht von Waterloo. Haben und Sein. Brustkrebs. Juli-

mond. Caprifischer. Gott ist tot. Der feuchte Wind des Frühlings. In der Wüste der Weisheit. Genauigkeit. Das Wunder unserer Zeit. Die Decke des Lebens. Am Arsch der Welt. Der Untergang des Abendlandes. Roll die Tränen. Wie ein Hauch

ø 17cm, 33 RPM, 1981, Walter Thielsch Produktion

Cover: b/w

Young, La Monte /   [C/S]
Marian Zazeela

Title: La Monte Young / Marian Zazeela

ø 30cm, 33 RPM, 1969, limited edition of 2800 numbered copies, numbers 1-98 are dated and signed, Edition X, München

Perf.:   La Monte Young, Marian Zazeela (voc, bowed gong)

Cover: two-color print, design: Marian Zazeela

Playback at 33 1/3 RPM, however this side (side 2) may also be played at any slower constant speed down to 8 1/3 RPM

Young, La Monte /   [C/S]
Marian Zazeela

Title: Dream House 78'17"

Perf.:   The Theatre of Eternal Music: La Monte Young (voc, sine waves), Marian Zazeela (voc), Jon Hassell (tp), Garrett List (tb)

ø 30cm, 33 RPM, 1973, Shandar, Paris, No. 83510

Cover: two-color print, gatefold, design: Marian Zazeela

The work presented within these model Dream Houses consists of a total environmental set of frequency structures in the media of sound and light. Two sources are

used to produce the frequencies in the sound medium: the sine wave oscillators generate a continuous live electronic sound environment, and *The Theatre of Eternal Music* performs additional frequencies at prescribed time intervals. Marian designed two sources to produce the frequencies in the light medium: an installation of floating sculptures and color sources is continuous, and during the live performances a series of slide projections entitled *Ornamental Lightyears Tracery* is also performed.

Excerpt from covertext

Young, La Monte /   [C/S]
Marian Zazeela

Title: The Well-Tuned Piano, 81 x 25

5 LPs, ø 30cm, 33 RPM, in a box

Cover: multi-color print, design: Marian Zazeela, design production: David Garland

Recorded live at the last 6 Harrison Street *Dream House* concert of the Well-Tuned Piano (La Monte Young, Piano), New York City 1981, presented by Dia Art Foundation. Gramavision, New York No. 188701-1

28 p. program booklet enclosed with photographs, timed score of theme titles, and notes by Terry Riley, David Farneth, Daniel Wolf, Marian Zazeela and La Monte Young

The Magenta Lights

The 6 Harrison Street *Dream House* Performance Space installation of *The Magenta Lights* was a site-specific environment created for the Trading Floor of the former New York Mercantile Exchange building under a longterm commission from the Dia Art Foundation. The work was on exhibition periodically from 1980 through 1985, and provided the setting for La Monte Young's performances of *The Well-Tuned Piano*.
The Magenta Lights is a realization of that aspect of my work, generically entitled *Light*, which uses the inherent properties of

colored light mixtures as a medium for the transfer of information concerning the position and relation of objects in space.

The work *Light* involves the installation of precisely positioned pairs of colored lights focused on symmetrically arrayed pairs of white aluminium mobile sculptures, causing the projection of colored shadows on the ceiling or walls of a room. Each mobile reflects the color of that portion of the spectrum represented by the light source focused directly on it, while the colors of the shadows cast by each mobile appear as the complement of the projected color mixed with the color of the paired light source focused on the adjacent mobile, all tempered by the eye's adaption to the overall color field. Light and scale are manipulated in such a way that the colored shadows, in their apparent corporeality, can become virtually indistinguishable from the mobile sculptural forms, enveloping the viewer in the continual interplay of reality and illusion.

The floating sculptures are suspended in different patterns created according to the structural properties of each environment. For this installation of *Light* I constructed a series of diagonals bisecting each of the four outer segments of the 29-foot ceiling of the Performance Space. Light sources were positioned at opposite corners to project the mobiles' shadows across the diagonals where they combined to create a radiant color field which permeated the entire space with its reflected hues. As the mobiles turn in space, reacting to movement and temperature changes in the environment, their shadows continuously display the resultant forms created by the angles and the distances of the light sources to the mobiles. The overall pattern of shadows gradually shifts through many transformations, including, rarely, the perfectly symmetrical alliance of all the component parts.

Since the earliest presentations of the 1964 tape version of *The Well-Tuned Piano* in concert, La Monte and I had concurred that a particular slide combination from *Ornamental Lightyears Tracery*, composed of colors in the range of magenta and blue only, provided the appropriate environment for

The Well-Tuned Piano. While each color combination has its own special properties, the colors of *The Magenta Lights* seem to most effectively charge the atmosphere with a perceptible aura of profound sensation. It is as though the soft reflected light of dusk were suspended in time.

Marian Zazeela (from the enclosed booklet)

Young, La Monte
→   Aspen Magazine

De Zaak
→   Perfo 2

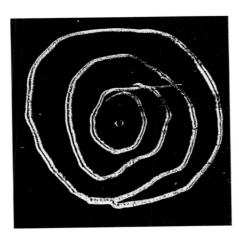

Zakarias, Yngve   [O]

Title: Holzfällerlied. 1986

Unlimited series of woodcuts, 25 x 25 cm, one side black, one side brown

Ingve Zakarias is a Norwegian artist living in Berlin whose medium is the wood cut. Recently Zakarias decided to sometimes hold back from painting the engraved wooden plates. The printing plate itself becomes an independent artistic manifestation, a wood relief with defined qualities. The type of wood, its grain, color, texture, size and thickness are added up to the figurative or abstract expression of the engravings.

Zakarias' records have their origin in this handling of the wood as a material. Zakarias reduces the records to its basic visual elements: the spiral, the hole, LP size, two sided. Only the outer round shape is ignored. For that reason the wood relief is only an image. The acoustic experience remains in the artist's studio, tied to the moment of the artistic process, when the hand armed with the gouge engraves the spiral into the wood. The ingeniously

perfectionated mechanics of the record player with its fine needle is replaced by the engraving hand of the artist.

Michael Glasmeier. In: *Extended Play.* (cat.) New York 1988

Zazeela, Marian
→   La Monte Young

Zdanevič, Il'ja
→   Sound Poetry

Zegveld, Peter
→   DUTCH "DIFFICULT" MUSIC

Zerpa, Carlos
→   Sound Poetry

Z'ev   [S]

Title: Salts of Heavy Metals

Contents: Brings. Brings. Cold Roll. Cries Dissolve as Sweet. The Number Seven. The Hand. The Palm. Skin on Thigh. Thorns. Yellow Arrow. Three Kinds of Game

ø 30cm, 45 RPM (105 db necessary volume), 1981, Lust/Unlust Music Inc., New York, Infidelity JMB 237

Cover: two-color print

Recorded 29.3.80 at Mabuhay Gardens

Regarding this "music": Acoustic research has determined that the primary external element responsible for an instruments' tone is reflection. This 1st referred to as "1st reflection".

Considering the static position of an instrument there is the only one "1st reflection".
Through the development of a "dynamic" (i.e moving through space) instrumental technique, this process of reflection is amplified.
There are now a multiplicity of "1st reflections" which continuously interreact with one another.
The control of this process, in conjunction with the materials involved, are my main (music) compositional elements.

Z'ev [S]

Title: The Invisible Man. The Old Sweat

ø 30cm, 33 RPM, Coercion, London, No. 001

Cover: two-color print

Z'ev

→ Stefan Weisser

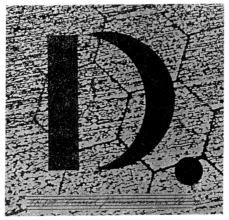

Z'ev [S]

Title: Open In Obscurity

Music: Mother Tongue

Perf.: Doro Franck (voice & texts), A.M. McKenzie (tapes, mixing & editing), Z'ev (perc & mixing)

ø 30cm, 33 RPM, 1988, Touch, London T 0:10

Cover: multi-color print

Zimmermann, Daniel [S]

Title: Alle Töne von Daniel Zimmermann

Contents: Louise Brown. Mückentanz. Ich habe alles in Schachteln verpackt.

ø 17cm, 45 RPM, 1986, limited edition of 300, numbered and signed, numbers 1-30 are part of the multiple *Jukebox*, Edition Marlene Frei, Zürich

Cover: one-color print

Ziranek, Sylvia
→ Perfo 2

Zoviet France
→ Soviet France

ZYX
→ Fünfzehn Tonspuren

Yngve Zakarias. *Holzfällerlied.* 1986

Chronology

1858

Léon Scott entwickelt den Phonoautograph, ein Gerät, das die Schwingungen des Schalls in ein Schriftbild umwandelt.

Léon Scott develops the Phonoautograph, an apparatus which transforms the vibrations of sound into type-face.

Léon Scott met au point le phonographe, un appareil capable de reproduire les oscillations du son.

1877

Der französische Dichter und Wissenschaftler Charles Cros hinterlegt bei der Pariser Académie des Sciences am 30. April seine Denkschrift über das "Paléophon", einen Apparat zur Schallwiedergabe, der aber aus finanziellen Gründen nicht realisiert werden konnte. Am 29. November zeichnet Thomas Alva Edison die ersten Skizzen zu seinem Phonographen und meldet ihn am 24. Dezember zum Patent an. Auf ihm rezitiert Edison den Anfang des Kinderlieds *Mary has a little lamb*.

The French poet and scientist Charles Cros deposits his memoir on the "Paléophon", an apparatus for the reproduction of sound, at the Parisian Academie des Sciences on April 30; the project could not be realized for financial reasons. On November 29, Thomas Alva Edison draws the first sketches of his Phonograph and applies for patent on December 24. Edison recites on it the beginning of the nursery-rhyme *Mary has a little lamb*.

le 30 avril le poète et scientifique français Charles Cros dépose à l'Academie des Sciences de Paris le mémoire dans lequel il décrit le "paléophone", un appareil ayant pour but la reproduction du son, mais qui pour des raisons financières ne sera pas réalisé. Le 29 novembre Thomas Alva Edison trace les premières esquisses de son phonographe et demande un brevet de 24 décembre. Edison y récite de début de la chanson enfantine *Mary has a little lamb*.

1878

Der Phonograph, der mittels einer Walze Stimmen aufnehmen und wiedergeben kann, löst ein großes Echo aus. Das "Wunder des 19. Jahrhunderts" erkundigt sich bei öffentlichen Auftritten nach dem Befinden der Zuhörer und teilt mit, daß es ihm selbst gut gehe.

The Phonograph, which can record and reproduce voices with a cylinder, arouses a great echo. The "Miracle of the 19th Century" inquires during public demonstrations about the well-being of the spectators and informs them that it himself is well.

Le phonographe, appareil qui moyennant un cylindre enregistre et reproduit les voix, fait sensation. Lors de représentations publiques le "miracle du dix-neuvième siècle" s'informe de l'état de santé du public et confirme qu'il se porte lui-même très bien.

Edison gründet die "Edison Speaking Phonograph Company" zur kommerziellen Ausnutzung des Apparates.

Edison founds the "Edison Speaking Phonography Company" for the commercial utilization of the apparatus.

Edison fonde la "Edison Speaking Phonograph Company" afin d'exploiter l'appareil commercialement.

In New York wird die erste Musikaufnahme vorgestellt. Jules Levy (Cornet) spielt den *Yankee Doodle*.

In New York, the first music recording is introduced. Jules Levy (cornet) plays the *Yankee Doodle*.

A New York on présente le premier enregistrement musical. Jules Levy (cornet) joue le *Yankee Doodle*.

Sprechende Puppen werden entwickelt.

Speaking dolls are developed.

On met au point des poupées parlantes.

1887

Emile Berliner meldet in Washington sein "Gramophone" zum Patent an. Damit beginnt der Siegeszug der Schallplatte, die die Walze ablöst.

Emile Berliner applies for patent in Washington for his "Gramophone". This marks the beginning of the triumphal march of the disc over the cylinder.

A Washington Emile Berliner demande un brevet pour son "gramophone". Ainsi s'annonce le triomphe du disque qui remplace le cylindre.

1888

In London wird Händels Oratorium *Israel in Ägypten* als erstes Konzert live aufgenommen. Johannes Brahms nimmt als erster Komponist eine Schallplatte auf: die *Ungarischen Tänze*.

In London, Händel's oratorio *Israel in Egypt* is the first concert which is recorded live. Johannes Brahms is the first composer to record: the *Hungarian Dances*.

A Londres on enregistre pour la première fois un concert en direct: l'oratorio de Haendel *Israel en Egypte*. Johannes Brahms est le premier compositeur à faire un enregistrement; il s'agit de ses *Danses hongroises*.

1889

Edison nimmt mit vier Phonographen in New York das Vorspiel zu Wagners *Meistersinger* auf. Dirigent: Hans von Bülow

Edison uses four phonographs to record in New York the prelude of Wagner's *Meistersinger*. Conductor: Hans von Bülow

A New York Edison enregistre avec quatre phonographes le prélude des *Maîtres chanteurs* de Wagner; chef d'orchestre: Hans von Bülow

around 1890

Münz-Phonographen werden aufgestellt.

Coin-phonographs are set up.

Production de phonographes fonctionnant avec de la monnaie.

1893

Emile Berliner gründet die "United States Gramophone Company" in Washington.

Emile Berliner founds the "United States Gramophone Company" in Washington.

Emile Berliner fonde à New York le "United States Gramophone Company".

1894

Die ersten Schallplattenspieler werden auf den Markt gebracht.

The first recordplayers appear on the market.

Les premiers tourne-disques font leur entrée sur le marché.

1895

Die Handkurbel des Grammophons wird durch einen Federmotor ersetzt.

The crank-handle of the gramophone is replaced by a spring action motor.

La manivelle du gramophone est remplacée par un moteur à ressort.

Die Brüder Pathé eröffnen in Paris ihr Aufnahmestudio. Unter dem Zeichen "Le Coq" bespielen sie Wachszylinder, u.a. mit der ersten Aufnahme von Caruso.

In Berlin findet die erste öffentliche Vorführung eines Tonfilms statt. Oskar Messter präsentiert einen Film gekoppelt mit einer Schallplatte von Emile Berliner.

Fred Gaisberg eröffnet sein Aufnahmestudio in Philadelphia, Emile Berliner den ersten Schallplattenladen ebenfalls dort.

In Hannover wird die "Deutsche Grammophon Gesellschaft" gegründet.

Gründung des Phonogramm-Archivs der Akademie der Wissenschaften in Wien

Nachdem die Firmennamen in die Schallplatten geritzt oder auf sie gestempelt wurden, erscheint die erste "Red-Label"-Schallplatte, besungen von Fedor Schaljapin.

Edison erfindet ein Verfahren zur Vervielfältigung der Walzen.

Die Schokoladenfabrik Stollwerk präsentiert ihren Kinderplattenspieler. In die Schokolade waren Schallrillen eingepreßt.

"Odeon" bringt beidseitig bespielte Schallplatten heraus.

Die Firma Lindström entwickelt den ersten Tonarm-Apparat.

In Paris wird im Postverkehr die sprechende Postkarte eingeführt.

Die Gramophone Company ersetzt ihr Firmenzeichen des "Recording Angel" durch "His Master's Voice" nach einem Gemälde von François Barraud, das den Hund Nipper und ursprünglich einen Phonographentrichter zeigt.

In New York wird die erste Jazz-Platte aufgenommen.

Entwicklung des elektrischen Schallplattenspielers

In Pittsburgh wird die erste Radiostation eingerichtet.

Lenin nimmt seine Rede *Was ist die Sowjetmacht* auf Platte auf. Sie wird vom Proletkult zur Aufklärung der Landbevölkerung eingesetzt.

1896

The Pathé brothers open their recording-studio in Paris. Under the trademark "Le Coq", they record on wax-cylinders, among others with the first recording of Caruso.

In Berlin, the first public presentation of a sound movie takes place. Oskar Messter presents a film linked together with a record by Berliner.

1897

Fred Gaisberg opens his recording-studio in Philadelphia, Emile Berliner opens the first record-store, also in Philadelphia.

1898

The "Deutsche Grammophon Gesellschaft" is founded in Hannover.

1899

Foundation of the Phonogram-Archive of the Akademie der Wissenschaften in Vienna

1901

After company-names have been etched or stamped onto the records, the first "Red-Label"-record appears, with Fedor Schaljapin singing.

1903

Edison invents a procedure for reproducing the cylinders.

The chocolate manufacturer Stollwerk presents its children's record player. The grooves were pressed into the chocolate.

1904

"Odeon" releases records which have been recorded on both sides.

1905

The company Lindström develops the first tone-arm device.

In Paris, the first talking postcard is introduced in the postal system.

1909

The Gramophone Company replaces the trademark "Recording Angel" with "His Master's Voice" according to a painting by François Barraud, which shows the dog Nipper and originally a phonograph-horn.

1917

The first Jazz-record is recorded in New York.

from 1918

Development of the electric recordplayer

1919

The first boadcasting station is established in Pittsburgh.

Lenin records his speech *What is the Soviet Power* on record. It is used by the proletarian cult to educate the rural population.

Les frères Pathé ouvrent à Paris un studio d'enregistrement. Sous l'étiquette "Le Coq" ils enregistrent des cylindres de cire, entre autres les premiers enregistrements de Caruso.

A Berlin a lieu la première projection d'un film parlant. Oskar Messter présente un film accompagné d'un disque d'Emile Berliner.

Fred Gaisberg ouvre son studio à Philadelphie et Emile Berliner le premier magasin de disques dans la même ville.

Fondation de la "Deutsche Grammophon Gesellschaft" à Hannovre.

Fondation des archives phonographiques de l'Académie des Sciences de Vienne

Après que les noms de compagnie aient été gravés sur les disques, apparaît le premier disque "Red-Label", chanté par Fedor Schaljapin.

Edison découvre un procédé pour la multiplication des cylindres.

La fabrique de chocolat Stollwerk présente ses tourne-disques pour enfants. Des sillons sont gravés dans le chocolat.

"Odeon" lance des disques enregistrés sur deux faces.

La compagnie Lindström met au point le premier appareil à bras.

Les postes parisiennes introduisent la carte postale parlante.

La Gramophone Company remplace l'étiquette du "recording Angel" par "His Master's Voice" suivant une peinture de François Barraud qui montre le chien Nipper et à l'origine un pavillon de phonographe.

A New York, premier enregistrement d'un disque de jazz.

Mise au point du tourne-disque électrique

Première station de radio à Pittsburgh.

Lénine enregistre sur disque son discours *Qu'est-ce que la puissance soviétique*. On l'utilise pour l'endoctrinement de la population rurale.

Die erste Flexidisc kommt auf den Markt.

Die abstrakten Filme *Studie I - V* von Oskar Fischinger werden synchron zur Schallplattenmusik vorgeführt.

Darius Milhaud experimentiert mit Stimmentransformationen durch Geschwindigkeitsveränderungen.

Laszlo Moholy-Nagy veröffentlicht in *Der Sturm* den Aufsatz *Neue Gestaltung in der Musik - Möglichkeiten des Grammophons*.

Gründung der "Electrola", um elektrische Platten herzustellen

Kurt Schwitters veröffentlicht seine Interpretation des Scherzos der *Ursonate* auf Schallplatte als Nummer 13 der Zeitschrift *Merz: Grammophonplatte*.

In Donaueschingen wird auf dem Kammermusikfest vorgeschlagen, Schallplatten als eigenschöpferisches Medium zu verwenden.

Christopher Stone wird bei der BBC in London der erste Disc-Jockey der Welt.

In Paris erscheint der Roman *Dan Yack* von Blaise Cendrars.

Columbia produziert die erste Sound-Effects-Schallplatte: *London Street Sounds*.

Die Deutsche Grammophon verkauft zum ersten Mal eine Schallplatte in einer Auflage von einer Million Exemplare: *Erzengel Gabriel verkündet den Hirten Christi Geburt.*

Paul Hindemith und Ernst Toch benutzen Schallplatten zu Musikmontagen.

Leopold Stokowski macht Versuche, die bislang übliche Drehzahl von 78 RPM auf 33 1/3 RPM zu verändern.

Die erste Picture-Disc erscheint bei RCA.

Unter dem Pseudonym Hektor Rottweiler erscheint in der Zeitschrift *23* Theodor W. Adornos Essay *Die Form der Schallplatte*.

In dem Film *L'Atalante* von Jean Vigo läßt der Schauspieler Michel Simon eine Schallplatte durch seinen Fingernagel erklingen.

Im Schallplattenladen, ein Film von und mit Karl Valentin und Liesl Karlstadt

1920
The first Flexidisc appears on the market.

1921-25
The abstract films *Study I-V* by Oskar Fischinger are shown synchronously with record-music.

1922-27
Darius Milhaud experiments with voice-transformations through speed-variation.

1923
Laszlo Moholy-Nagy publishes in *Der Sturm* his statement *New Plasticism in Music - Possibilities of the Gramophone*.

1925
Foundation of Electrola to produce electrical records

Kurt Schwitters publishes his interpretation of the scherzo of the *Ursonate* on record as No. 13 *Grammophonplatte* of the periodical *Merz*.

1926
In Donaueschingen, during the festival of chamber music, the suggestion is made to use records as a creative medium of its own.

1927
At BBC in London, Christopher Stone becomes the first disc jockey in the world.

1927/29
The novel *Dan Yack* by Blaise Cendrars is published in Paris.

1928
Columbia produces the first sound-effects-record: *London Street Sounds*.

The Deutsche Grammophon for the first time sells a million copies of a record: *Erzengel Gabriel verkündet den Hirten Christi Geburt*.

1930
Paul Hindemith and Ernst Toch use records for sound montages.

1931
Leopold Stokowski experiments to reduce the customary number of revolutions from 78 RPM to 33 1/3 RPM.

1933
The first Picture-Disc is issued by RCA.

1934
Theodor W. Adorno, using the pen name Hektor Rottweiler, publishes his essay *The Form of the Record* in the magazine *23*.

In the film *L'Atalante* by Jean Vigo, the actor Michel Simon plays a record with his fingernail.

Im Schallplattenladen, a film by and with Karl Valentin and Liesl Karlstadt

Le premier disque flexible arrive sur le marché.

Les films abstraits *Studie I-V* d'Oskar Fischinger sont projetés simultanément avec de la musique sur disques.

Darius Milhaud expérimente avec des transformations de la voie produites par des changements de vitesse.

Laszlo Moholy-Nagy publie dans *Der Sturm* l'article *La nouvelle création en musique - les possibilités du phonographe*.

Fondation de "Electrola" pour la fabrication de disques électriques

Kurt Schwitters publie sur disque son interprétation du Scherzo de la *Ursonate*; il s'agit du numéro 13 de la revue *Merz: Grammophonplatte*.

Lors du festival de musique de chambre de Donaueschingen on propose d'utiliser le disque comme moyen de création autonome.

Christopher Stone devient à la BBC de Londres le premier disc-jockey du monde.

Parution à Paris du roman *Dan Yack* de Blaise Cendrars.

Columbia produit le premier disque d'effets sonores: *London Street Sounds*.

Pour la première fois Deutsche Grammophon vend un disque à un million d'exemplaires: *Erzengel Gabriel verkündet den Hirten Christi Geburt*.

Paul Hindemith et Ernst Toch utilisent des disques pour des montages musicaux.

Leopold Stokowski fait des tentatives pour transformer la vitesse de rotation de 78 tours-minute en 33 tours-minute.

Parution chez RCA du premier picture-disc.

Theodor W. Adorno publie sous le pseudonyme d'Hector Rottweiler dans la revue *23* son article *Die Form der Schallplatte*.

Dans le film *L'Atalante* de Jean Vigo le comédien Michel Simon fait jouer un disque au moyen des ses ongles.

Im Schallplattenladen, un film de et avec Karl Valentin et Liesl Karlstadt

Marcel Duchamp: *Rotoreliefs. (Optical Discs)*

1935
Marcel Duchamp: *Rotoreliefs. (Optical Discs)*

Marcel Duchamp: *Rotoreliefs. (Optical Discs)*

An die Stelle der bisher schmucklosen, nur auf das Firmensignet beschränkten Schallplattenverpackung tritt die gestaltete Plattenhülle

from 1935
The plain record packaging which only carried the trademark is replaced by the designed cover.

Les pochettes de disque qui jusqu'alors se concentraient sur l'étiquette de la compagnie s'orientent vers le dessin de couverture

Edgard Varèse experimentiert mit Schallplatten, die rückwärts und mit verschiedenen Geschwindigkeiten abgespielt werden sollen.

1936
Edgard Varèse experiments with records, playing them backwards, using various speeds.

Edgard Varèse expérimente avec des disques qui doivent être joués à partir de la fin et avec différentes vitesses.

Die deutsche Firma AEG/Telefunken produziert das erste kommerzielle Tonbandgerät "Magnetophon".

1937
The German company AEG/Telefunken produces the first commercial taperecorder "Magnetophon".

La Compagnie allemande AEG/Telefunken produit le premier appareil à bandes magnétiques, le "magnétophone".

John Cage: *Imaginary Landscape No. 1*. Konzert für zwei Plattenspieler mit variabler Geschwindigkeit, Meßplatten zu Testzwecken, Klavier und Becken

1939
John Cage: *Imaginary Landscape No. 1*, concert for two recordplayers with variable speed, testrecords, piano and cymbal

John Cage: *Imaginary Landscape no. 1*. Concerto pour deux tourne-disques avec vitesse variable, disques-épreuves, piano et cymbales

John Cage: *Credo in Us*, Anweisung für den Plattenspieler: "if phonograph, use some classic: e.g. Dvořák, Beethoven, Sibelius or Shostakovich."

1942
John Cage: *Credo In Us*, directions for the recordplayer: "if Phonograph, use some classic: e.g. Dvořák, Beethoven, Sibelius or Shostakovich".

John Cage: *Credo in Us*, instructions pour le tourne-disque: "if phonograph, use some classic: e.g. Dvořák, Beethoven, Sibelius ou Shostakovich".

Die Schallplatte aus Vinylit-Kunststoff löst das Material Schellack ab. Die Firma Columbia veröffentlicht die erste Langspielplatte.

1948
The record made of vinyl-plastic replaces the material, shellack. Columbia publishes the first long playing record.

Les disques de gomme laque sont remplacés par ceux en vinylite. La compagnie Columbia publie le premier disque longue-durée.

Pierre Schaeffer experimentiert mit Schallplatten aus dem Schallarchiv des Rundfunks.

Pierre Schaeffer experiments with records from the sound archive of the radio station.

Pierre Schaeffer expérimente avec des disques issus des archives de la radio.

John Cage: *Imaginary Landscape No. 5*, Konzert für 42 Schallplatten

1952
John Cage: *Imaginary Landscape No.5*, concert for 42 records

John Cage: *Imaginary Landscape no. 5*, concerto pour 42 disques

Stereo wird propagiert.

1958
Stereo is propagated.

Le stéréo se propage.

Musik der Leere von Yves Klein auf Schallplatte

1959
Musik der Leere by Yves Klein on record

Yves Klein publie sur disque *Musik der Leere*

Jean Dubuffets *Expériences Musicales* erscheinen auf 6 Langspielplatten.

1961
Jean Dubuffet's *Expériences Musicales* are recorded on 6 longplaying records.

Les *Expériences musicales* de Jean Dubuffet paraissent sur 6 disques longue-durée.

Disque de Musique TOTAL von Ben Vautier

1963
Disque de Musique TOTAL by Ben Vautier

Disque de Musique TOTAL de Ben Vautier

Record Of Interviews mit Künstlern die an der Popular Image Exhibition in der Washington Gallery of Modern Art teilnehmen, hrsg. von Billy Klüver

Record Of Interviews with artists participating in the Popular Image Exhibition in the Washington Gallery of Modern Art, issued by Billy Klüver

Record of Interviews avec des artistes qui participent à la Popular Image Exhibition de la Washington Gallery of Modern Art, édt. Billy Klüver

Arthur Køpcke: *Music while you work*

Arthur Køpcke: *Music while you work*

Arthur Køpcke: *Music while you work*

Nam June Paik: *Random Access* (Schallplattenschaschlik)

Nam June Paik: *Random Access* (recordschaschlik)

Nam June Paik: *Random Access* (brochettes de disques)

Milan Knížák: *Broken Music*, Konzert in Prag

1965
Milan Knížák: *Broken Music*, concert in Prague

Milan Knížák: *Broken Music*, concert à Prague

1965

Aspen Magazine No. 1, Avantgarde Magazin mit regelmäßigen Schallplattenbeilagen	*Aspen Magazine No. 1*, Avantgarde Magazine with regular record-supplements	*Aspen Magazine No. 1*, revue d'avant-garde qui publie régulièrement des disques d'accompagnement.

1968/70

Mauricio Kagel: *Acustica*

Mauricio Kagel: *Acustica*

Mauricio Kagel: *Acustica*

1969

John Cage: *33 1/3*, Konzert für 12 Plattenspieler

John Cage: *33 1/3*, concert for 12 recordplayers

John Cage: *33 1/3*, concerto pour 12 tourne-disques

Katalog in Form einer Schallplatte zur Ausstellung *Art By Telephone* im Museum of Contemporary Art, Chicago, hrsg. von Jan van der Marck

Catalogue in form of a record of the exhibition *Art By Telephone* in the Museum of Contemporary Art, Chicago, issued by Jan van der Marck

Catalogue sous forme de disque pour l'exposition *Art by Telephone* au Museum of Contemporary Art de Chicago, édt. Jan van der Marck

1970

Mit der Schallplatte *Airconditioning* der Gruppe "Curved Air" wird das Phänomen der Picture-Disc wiederbelebt

The record *Airconditioning* by the group "Curved Air" marks the revival of the picture-disc

Avec le disque *Airconditioning* du groupe "Curved Air" le phénomène du picture-disc reprend vie

Isolation Unit, Aktion von Terry Fox mit Joseph Beuys in der Düsseldorfer Kunstakademie

Isolation Unit, action by Terry Fox with Joseph Beuys in the Kunstakademie, Düsseldorf

Isolation Unit, action de Terry Fox avec Joseph Beuys à la Kunstakademie de Düsseldorf

1973

selten gehörte Musik. von den 3. Berliner Dichterworkshop, erste Schallplatte dieser Reihe mit Dieter Roth, Gerhard Rühm und Oswald Wiener

selten gehörte Musik. von den 3. Berliner Dichterworkshop, first record of this series with Dieter Roth, Gerhard Rühm, and Oswald Wiener

selten gehörte Musik. von den 3. Berliner Dichterworkshop, premier disque de cette série avec Dieter Roth, Gerhard Rühm et Oswald Wiener

erscheint die Schallplatte *Schottische Symphonie. Requiem of Art* von Joseph Beuys und Henning Christiansen

appears the record *Schottische Symphonie. Requiem of Art* by Joseph Beuys and Henning Christiansen

Schottische Symphonie. Requiem of Art, disque de Joseph Beuys et Henning Christiansen

1975

The Sounds Of Sound Sculpture, Schallplatte herausgegeben von John Grayson und David Rosenboom anläßlich einer Ausstellung in der Vancouver Art Gallery

The Sounds of Sound Sculpture, record issued by John Grayson and David Rosenboom on the occasion of an exhibition in the Vancouver Art Gallery

The Sounds Of Sound Sculpture, disque édité par John Grayson et David Rosenboom à l'occasion d'une exposition à la Art Gallery de Vancouver

1976

The Entire Musical Work of Marcel Duchamp, vom S.E.M. Ensemble realisiert, erscheint auf Schallplatte

The Entire Musical Work of Marcel Duchamp performed by the S.E.M. Ensemble appears on record

Parution sur disque de *The Entire Musical Work of Marcel Duchamp*, réalisé par l'ensemble S.E.M.

1977

Airwaves, eine Anthologie akustischer Arbeiten von bildenden Künstlern auf zwei Schallplatten, hrsg. von Bob George

Airwaves, two record anthology of artist's aural work and music, produced by Bob George

Airwaves, une anthologie des travaux acoustiques d'artistes; deux disques, édt. Bob George

Im Fort Worth Art Museum in Texas wird die Wanderaustellung *The Record as Artwork* mit der Sammlung von Germano Celant eröffnet.

In the Fort Worth Art Museum in Texas, the touring exhibition *The Record as Artwork* is opened with the collection of Germano Celant.

Au Fort Worth Art Museum du Texas, ouverture de l'exposition itinérante *The Record as Artwork* avec la collection de Germano Celant.

1978

Ankündigung der Compact-Disc von Philips Industries

The Compact-Disc is advertised by Philips Industries

Les industries Philips annoncent le disque compact

1979

Sound, Schallplatte anläßlich einer Ausstellung mit Klangskulpturen, selbstgebauten Instrumenten und akustischen Räumen im Los Angeles Institute of Contemporary Art, organisiert von Robert Smith und Bob Wilhite

Sound, record on the occasion of an exhibition of sound sculpture, instrument building, and acoustically tuned spaces in the Los Angeles Institute of Contemporary Art, organized by Robert Smith and Bob Wilhite

Sound, disque à l'occasion d'une exposition de sculptures sonores, d'instruments de fabrication artisanale et d'espaces acoustiques à l'Institut of Contemporary Art de Los Angeles; organisateurs Robert Smith et Bob Wilhite

1980

musica futurista, eine Anthologie akustischer Arbeiten der italienischen Futuristen auf zwei Schallplatten, hrsg. von Daniele Lombardi unter Verwendung erhaltener Tonaufnahmen aus den 20er und 30er Jahren

musica futurista, an anthology of acoustic works by the Italian Futurists on two records, issued by Daniele Lombardi incorporating preserved recordings from the twenties and thirties

musica futurista, une anthologie des travaux acoustiques des futuristes italiens sur deux disques: l'éditeur Daniele Lombardi utilise des documents sonores des années 20 et 30

1981

Laurie Andersons *O Superman (for Massenet)* erreicht den zweiten Platz in der britischen (Rock-Single) Hitparade.

Laurie Anderson's *O Superman (for Massenet)* reaches second place on the British rock singles charts.

O Superman (for Massenet) de Laurie Anderson atteint la deuxième place du hit-parade anglais (rock-single).

Gründung der gelben Musik in Berlin, Galerie und Schallplattenhandlung für Künstlerschallplatten

Foundation of gelbe Musik in Berlin, a gallery and record-store for artists' records

Fondation de gelbe Musik à Berlin, galerie et magazin de disques spécialisé dans les disques d'artistes

1981/82

Revolutions Per Minute. (The Art Record), mit 21 Beiträgen verschiedener Künstler

Revolutions per Minute. (The Art Record) appears with 21 contributions by different artists

Revolutions per Minute (The Art Record) paraît avec 21 contributions de différents artistes

1982

Erste europäische Installation von John Cages *33 1/3* in der daadgalerie, Berlin

First European installation of John Cage's *33 1/3*, daadgalerie, Berlin

Première installation européenne de *33 1/3* de John Cage; daadgalerie de Berlin

Einrichtung einer Phonothek in der Hamburger Kunsthalle, die erste dieser Art in einem deutschen Ausstellungsinstitut

Installation of a *Phonothek* in the Kunsthalle Hamburg, the first one in a German museum

Installation de la phonothèque au Kunsthalle de Hambourg, la première du genre dans un lieu d'exposition allemand

1983

Die Tödliche Doris veröffentlicht *Chöre & Soli*, eine Box mit 6 Minischallplatten, einem Abspielgerät und einem Romanfragment

Die Tödliche Doris publishes *Chöre & Soli*, a box with 6 mini-records, a playing device and a fragment of a novel

La Tödliche Doris publie *Chöre & Soli*, une box avec 6 mini-disques, un tourne-disque et un fragment de roman

1985

La France à la Biennale, Schallplatte anläßlich der Biennale in Sao Paulo mit Beiträgen der französischen Teilnehmer: Pierre Bertrand, Sarkis, Christian Boltanski, Bertrand Lavier

La France à la Biennale, record on the occasion of the Biennale in Sao Paulo with contributions by the French participants: Pierre Bertrand, Sarkis, Christian Boltanski, Bertrand Lavier

La France à la Biennale, à l'occasion de la biennale de Sao Paulo, avec des contributions d'artistes français: Pierre Bertrand, Sarkis, Christian Boltanski, Bertrand Lavier

1986

Künstlerschallplatten, Ausstellung in der gelben Musik, Berlin

Künstlerschallplatten, exhibition at gelbe Musik, Berlin

Künstlerschallplatten, exposition à la gelbe Musik de Berlin

1987

Künstler.Schallplatten.gelbe MUSIK. Ausstellung in der Galerie Vorsetzen, Hamburg

Künstler.Schallplatten.gelbe MUSIK. Exhibition at Galerie Vorsetzen, Hamburg

Künstler.Schallplatten.gelbe MUSIK exposition à la galerie Vorsetzen de Hambourg

Patentnummer G 8704611.3: *Schallplatte als Geschenkartikel aus eßbarem Material*, eine Erfindung des Berliners Peter Lardong

Patent number G 8704611.3: *record as a gift out of edible material*, an invention by the Berliner Peter Lardong

Numéro de brevet G 8704611.3: *articles-cadeaux de matière comestible*, une invention du berlinois Peter Lardong

1988

Schallplatte *Abschiedssymphonie* opus 177 von Henning Christiansen. Die Symphonie basiert auf Tonmaterial der Eröffnungskonzerte zur *Biennale des Friedens* in Hamburg, 1985. Mitwirkende waren Henning Christiansen, Joseph Beuys (per Telefon) und Nam June Paik

Abschiedssymphonie, opus 177, record by Henning Christiansen. The symphony is based on sound-material of the opening concert of the *Biennale des Friedens* in Hamburg, 1985. Participants were Joseph Beuys (via telephone), Henning Christiansen and Nam June Paik

Disque *Abschiedsymphonie* opus 177 de Henning Christiansen. La symphonie utilise de matériau issu du concert d'ouverture de la *Biennale des Friedens* à Hambourg, 1985. Les participants étaient Henning Christiansen, Joseph Beuys (par téléphone) et Nam June Paik

Extended Play, Schallplattenausstellung von Christian Marclay und Ursula Block in der Emily Harvey Gallery, New York

Extended Play, exhibition curated by Christian Marclay and Ursula Block at Emily Harvey Gallery, New York

Extended Play, exposition de disques organisée par Christian Marclay et Ursula Block à la Emily Harvey Gallery de New York

Ausstellung *Broken Music* in der daadgalerie Berlin

Exhibition *Broken Music*, daadgalerie Berlin

Exposition *Broken Music* à la daadgalerie de Berlin

1989

Ausstellung *Broken Music* im Gemeentemuseum Den Haag und Magasin Grenoble

Exhibition *Broken Music*, Gemeentemuseum Den Haag and Magasin Grenoble

Exposition *Broken Music* au Gemeentemuseum de la Haye et au Magasin de Grenoble

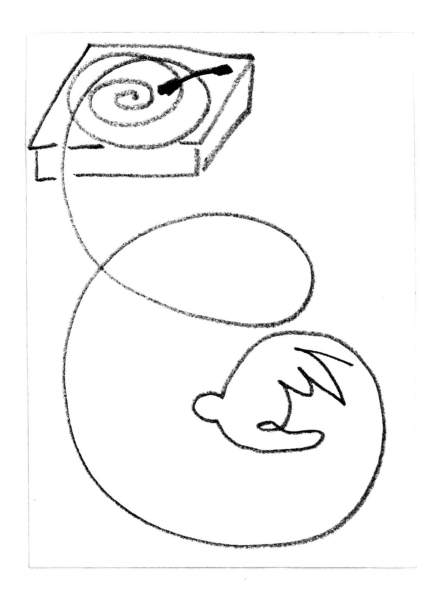

Nanne Meyer. Drawing. 1984

Christiane Seiffert

Wie macht das Holz Musik?

Der Erfinder ist Medium zwischen Gedanken und Gegenständen. Er nimmt die Kapriolen seiner Phantasie ernst und arbeitet daran, ihnen eine reale Form zu geben. Die Gedankenfülle führt zu überfülltem Raum.
Ein Brot und der surrende Kühlschrank sind bei Peter Lardong einzige Attribute der einstigen Küche. Immer schon ein Tüftler, stieg er vor drei Jahren mit zwei Zentnern Schokolade ins Plattengeschäft ein. Anlaß dazu war die Präsentation einer Phillips-Schallplatte im Fernsehen, die von innen nach außen abzuspielen ist. Eine solche hatte Lardong schon vor Jahren auf dem Trödel gefunden, von 1903. Von dieser machte er einen Gipsabdruck, den er an die Fernsehanstalt schickte.
Einmal von ihrem ureigenen Material befreit, eroberte die Schallplatte als ein rundes Ding mit hörbar zu machenden Rillen die Gedanken und die Freizeit des Gabelstaplerfahrers Lardong. Als richtiger Berliner wandte er sich von nun an mit jeder Neuheit an die verschiedenen Medien, die darauf eingingen. Seinen "Aprilscherz", eine Eisplatte, wollten sie aber lieber mit Geschmack haben. So wurde der Kühlschrank Umschlagplatz für Kakao-, Tee-, Cola-, Rührei-, und Wurstschallplatten. Er entwickelte ein Verfahren, Kohlensäure und Schaum als störende Schallträger aus den Getränken zu entfernen. Die Kurzlebigkeit der vereisten Leckereien ließ ihm keine Ruhe. Er ging die Schokolade an. Thomas Gottschalk und Jürgen von der Lippe hatten ihren Showkandidaten, der ihnen Freude machte, bis nach sechs Stunden die Schokolade vom Plattenteller rann. Das Problem bewältigte er auch. Haltbar, mit 10 knisterfreien Runden und Stereo, läuft seine Erfindung als "Geschenkartikel aus eßbarem Material" seit dem 27.3.87 unter der Patentnummer G 8704611.3. Prominente wie Nero Brandenburg, Dieter Thomas Heck oder Karl Dall ließen sich Singles bei ihm anfertigen, die Deutsche Grammophon das Lied *Safe me*.
Zwar versanken Filmkameras aus aller Welt in seiner süßen Erfindung, doch kein Angebot zur Verwertung erreichte ihn. Auch das Lebensmittelhygienegesetz macht Schwierigkeiten. Doch die sind seit kurzem ausgeräumt: Fein säuberlich verpackt der Erfinder die kleinen Platten, die zu Lachsackabspielgeräten gehören, in After Eight-Tütchen. Die After Eight-Schachtel wird zum Plattenspieler. Ein kleiner Motor dreht die Scheibe Schokolade, eine Schraube hält einen für jede Spielzeit zu erneuernden halben Zahnstocher fest. Lardong: "Da fragt man sich, wie macht das Holz Musik?" Er kann es erklären: Das Loch für den Zahnstocheranbau ist verbunden mit der Nadel eines Tonkopfes. Mit welcher unbekannten Größe ist Peter Lardongs Kopf verbunden?

How Does Wood Make Music?

The inventor is a medium between thoughts and things. He takes the caprioles of his fantasy seriously and works with the intent of giving them an actual form. The abundance of thoughts leads to an abundantly filled room.
For Peter Lardong a loaf of bread and a whirring refrigerator are the only attributes of the former kitchen. Always still the fiddler, he got involved three years ago in the record business with two hundred pounds of chocolate. The motivation for this was the television presentation of a Phillips' record which was playable from center to outside. Such a thing, from 1903, Lardong had already found years ago at a flea market. From this he made a plaster impression, which he then sent to the television station.
Once freed of its original material, the record, as a round thing with grooves to be sounded, conquered the thoughts and the free time of the forklift operator, Lardong. As a true Berliner, he wandered from now on with every novelty to the various media, which immediately gave an ear. His "April fool's trick" - an ice record; however they preferred to have this in flavors. Thus the refrigerator became a re-loading point for cocoa-, tea-, cola-, scrambled egg-, and sausage-records. He developed a process for removing carbonation and foam - as disturbing sound agents - out of drinks. The short life of the frozen goodies gave him no peace. He took on chocolate. Thomas Gottschalk and Jürgen von der Lippe had their game show candidate, who gave them a good time, until after six hours the chocolate ran from the turntable. This problem he also subdued. Long-lasting, with 10 scratch-free spins and in stereo, since 27 March 1987 his invention has gone as "a gift out of edible material" under the patent number G 8704611.3. VIP's like Nero Brandenburg, Dieter Thomas Heck, or Karl Dall gave him singles to complete; Deutsche Grammophon, the song *Safe me*.
Of course film crews from all over the world were completely engrossed by his sweet invention; yet he never got an offer for commercialization. Even the food preperation regulation created difficulties. But these have recently been brushed aside; in perfect cleanliness, the inventor packs the little records, which belong to a laughing jack-in-the-box, in After Eight wrappers. The After Eight carton becomes the record player. A little motor turns the chocolate slabs; a screw firmly holds half a toothpick, which has to be refurbished every play-time. Lardong: "Here one asks oneself, how does wood make music?" He explains it: the hole for the toothpick insertion is connected with the needle of a pickup head.
With what unknown dimensions is Peter Lardong's head connected?

Chocolate-record by **Peter Lardong.** 1987

Comment le bois peut-il produire de la musique?

L'inventeur est l'intermédiaire entre l'idée et l'objet. Il prend au sérieux les caprices de sa fantaisie et essaie de leur donner une forme réelle.

Chez Peter Lardong un pain et le ronflement du réfrigérateur sont les seuls accessoires de la cuisine d'autrefois. Voilà trois ans, à l'occasion de la présentation à la télévision d'un disque de Phillips, fonctionnant de l'intérieur vers l'extérieur, Lardong, toujours en quête de la dernière ingéniosité, fit son entrée sur le marché du disque avec un quintal de chocolat. Quelques années auparavant il en avait trouvé un exemplaire au marché aux puces, un disque datant de 1903. Il fit un moulage de plâtre qu'il envoya à la maison de télévision.

Une fois libérée de son matériau d'origine, cette chose ronde munie de sillons pouvant être rendus audibles, se mit à accaparer les pensées et les loisirs du conducteur d'élévateur à fourche Lardong. En bon berlinois ce dernier s'adressa dès lors avec sa nouveauté aux différents média qui tous acceptèrent. Mais ils auraient préféré que son "poisson d'avril", un disque de crème glacée, ait une essence de fraise ou de citron; et c'est ainsi que le réfrigérateur devint le lieu de transbordement de disques en cacao, thé, cola, oeufs brouillés ou saucisse. Lardong mit au point un procédé consistant à éliminer des boissons les parasites sonores que sont les acides carboniques et la mousse. La courte durée des friandises glacées ne lui laissait aucun répit; il se tourna donc vers le chocolat. Thomas Gottschalk et Jürgen von der Lippe se réjouissaient d'avoir trouvé le candidat pour leur show, jusqu'à ce que, au bout de six heures, le chocolat se mette à fondre sur le tourne-disque. Mais il résolut également ce problème et depuis le 27/03/87 son invention est accessible au consommateur sous le numéro de brevet G 8704511.3: un "article-cadeau de matière commestible", produit stéréo résistant à 10 tours garantis sans parasites. Des personnes célèbres telles que Nero Brandenburg, Dieter Thomas Heck ou Karl Dall se sont fait fabriquer un single chez lui et la Deutsche Grammophon lui a commandé la chanson *Safe me*.

Certes, de partout à travers le monde on envoya des caméras pour filmer son invention sucrée, mais jamais on ne lui offrit de l'exploiter, et ce sans compter les difficultés occasionnées par la loi sur l'hygiène alimentaire; mais depuis peu l'inventeur est parvenu à aplanir ces embûches: il emballe tout proprement le petit disque et son pick-up en forme de boîte à surprise dans des enveloppes d'After-Eight. La boîte d'After Eight se transforme en tourne-disque. Un petit moteur actionne la plaque de chocolat, une vis retient un demi-cure-dent qui doit être remplacé après chaque audition. Lardong: on se demande comment le bois peut produire de la musique? Son explication: le trou dans lequel on insère le cure-dent est relié à l'aiguille d'une tête de lecture. Et la tête de Lardong, avec quelle puissance inconnue est-elle en contact?

Fliegende Blätter. Supplement. 1904

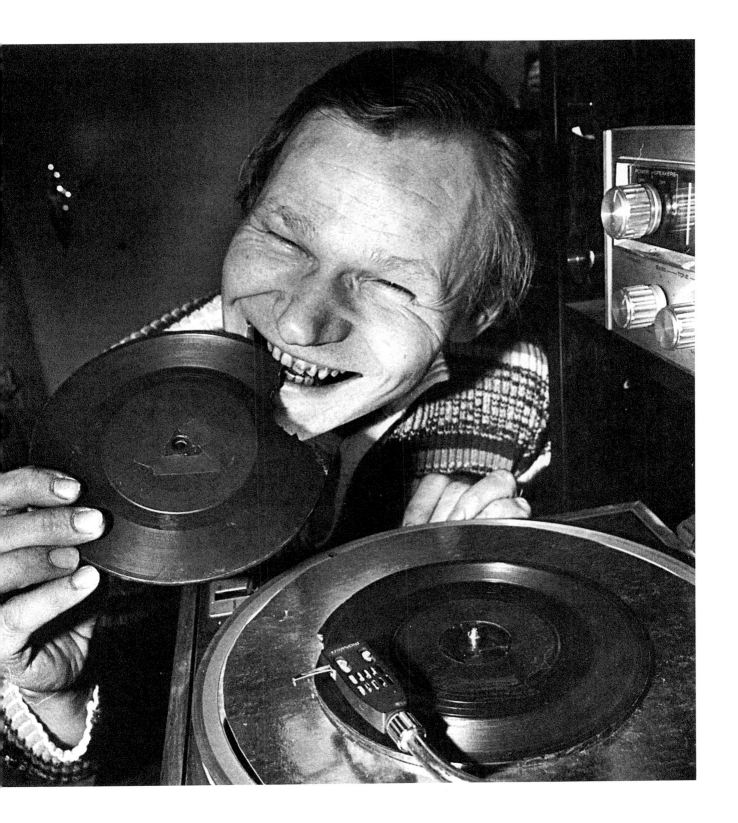

Peter Lardong

Bibliography

The following bibliography was created in Berlin and therefore mainly considers German publications dealing with the subject. In every case the titles are quoted in the original language. No special references to translations are made. Not taken into consideration are essays from record industry publications except when they are of cultural-historical interest. Critical reviews and essays from the daily and weekly press concerning specific artists and concerts are likewise not mentioned.   M.G.

Adorno, Theodor W.: *Die Form der Schallplatte*. In: Th. W. A.: *Musikalische Schriften VI*. Frankfurt a.M. 1984 (= Gesammelte Schriften 19)

Adorno, Theodor W.: *Nadelkurven*. In: Th.W.A.: *Musikalische Schriften VI*. Frankfurt a.M. 1984 (= Gesammelte Schriften 19)

Adorno, Theodor W.: *Oper und Langspielplatte*. In: Th.W.A.: *Musikalische Schriften VI*. Frankfurt a.M. 1984 (= Gesammelte Schriften 19)

Ästhetik der Compact Disc. Kassel, Basel, London 1985 (= Musikalische Zeitfragen 15)

Alsmann, Götz: *Nichts als Krach. Die unabhängigen Schallplattenfirmen und die Entwicklung der amerikanischen Musik 1943-1963*. Drensteinfurt 1985

Antheil, George: *Bad Boy of Music*. New York 1945

Artists & Sound. (cat.) Tate Gallery, London 1982

The Artists' Jazz Band À Montréal. (cat.) Musée d'art contemporain, Montréal 1974/75

The Artists' Jazz Band. (cat.) Centre Culturel Canadien, Paris 1978

Benamou, Michel / Caramello, Charles: *Performance in postmodern culture*. Madison, Wisconsin 1977

Berten, Walter Michael: *Musik und Mikrophon*. Düsseldorf 1951

Blaukopf, Kurt: *Hexenküche der Musik*. Teufen / St. Gallen, Wien (1957)

Blaukopf, Kurt (ed.): *IMZ Report: Records, Disques, Schallplatten*. Wien 1968

Blaukopf, Kurt: *Massenmedium Schallplatte*. Wiesbaden 1977

Blaukopf, Kurt (ed.): *The Phonogram in Cultural Communication*. Wien, New York 1982

Boileau, Pierre / Narcejac, Thomas: *A Cœur Perdu*. Paris 1959

Bornoff, Jack: *Music and the Twentieth Century Media*. Florence 1972

Bose, Fritz: *Die künstlerische Schallplatte. Hausmusik auf Schallplatten*. In: Allgemeine Musikzeitung 31/32 (1938)

Bose, Fritz: *Die Schallplatte als Musikinstrument*. In: Allgemeine Musikzeitung 10 (1935)

Bottone, Selimo R.: *Talking Machines and Records*. London 1904

Brauers, Jan: *Von der Äolsharfe zum Digitalspieler. 2000 Jahre mechanische Musik. 100 Jahre Schallplatte*. München 1984

Brennike, Helmut: *Der Weg zur Diskothek. Das Schallplattenbuch für den Musikfreund*. Zürich, Stuttgart 1959

Bruch, Walter: *Von der Tonwalze zur Bildplatte. 100 Jahre Ton- und Bildspeicherung*. München 1979 (= Sonderdruck Funkschau)

Bruer, Erna: *Die Schallplatte als Musiklehrer*. In: Skizzen 4 (1937)

Buchstäblich wörtlich wörtlich buchstäblich. Eine Sammlung konkreter und visueller Poesie der sechziger Jahre in der Nationalgalerie Berlin. (cat.) Staatliche Museen Preußischer Kulturbesitz, Berlin 1987

Burkhardt, Werner: *Schwarze Kunst...nur auf der schwarzen Scheibe*. In: Musik und Bildung 12 (1977)

Cage, John: *Empty Words. Writings '73-'78*. Middletown, Connecticut 1981

Cage, John: *Pour les oiseaux. Entretiens avec Daniel Charles*. Paris 1976

Cage, John: *Silence. Lectures and writings*. Middletown, Connecticut 1973

Cage, John: *M. Writings '67 - '72*. Middletown, Connecticut 1969

Cameron, Eric: *Lawrence Weiner: the books*. In: Studio International, Jan. 1974

Celant, Germano: *Off Media*. Bari 1977

Celant, Germano: *Record as Artwork 1959-73*. London 1973

Celant, Germano: *Record as Artwork*. In: Flash art 43 (1973/74)

Cendrars, Blaise: *Les confessions de Dan Yack*. Paris 1960

Chew, V.K.: *Talking Machines*. London 1981[2]

Chopin, Henri: *Poésie Sonore Internationale*. Paris 1979

Corner, Philip: *Popular Entertainments*. New York 1967

Cover. Pladeomslag 1950-81. (cat.) Aarhus, Stockholm 1981

Cros, Charles: *Œuvres complètes*. Paris 1954

Dannenberg, Hans: *Radio und Grammophon*. Köln 1928

Dean, Roger / Hipgnosis (ed.): *Album Cover Album I*. Zürich 1980

Dean, Roger / Howells, David (ed.): *Album Cover Album. The Second Volume*. Zürich 1983

Dean, Roger / Howells, David (ed.): *Album Cover Album 3*. Zürich 1986

Dearling, Robert & Celia: *The Guiness Book of Recorded Sound*. Enfield, Middlesex 1984

Dumesnil, René: *Le Livre du Disque*. Paris 1931

Echo. The Images of Sound. (cat.) Het Apollohuis, Eindhoven 1987

Écouter par les yeux. Objets et environnements sonores. (cat.) Musée d'Art Moderne de la Ville de Paris, 1980

Eisenberg, Evan: *The Recording Angel. Music, Records and Culture from Aristotle to Zappa*. New York 1987, London 1988

Electra. Electricity and electronics in the art of the XXth century. (cat.) MAM Musée d'Art Moderne de la Ville de Paris, 1983/84

Elste, Martin: *100 Jahre Schallaufzeichnung.* In: Fono forum 5 (1977)

Extended Play. (cat.) Emily Harvey Gallery, New York 1988

Faas, Hugo: *Der Preis der Scheibe. Zur Ökonomie der Schallplatte.* In: Der Rabe 14 (1986)

Facius, Walter (ed.): *Das Schallplattenbuch.* Düsseldorf 1956

Felton, Gary S.: *The record collector's international directory.* New York 1980

Fischer, Matthias / Holland, Dietmar / Rzehulka, Bernhard: *Gehörgänge. Zur Ästhetik der musikalischen Aufführung und ihrer technischen Reproduktion.* München 1986

Friedrich, Jörg: *Liebestod und Totenliebe. Aus der Welt der Schellackplatte.* In: Freibeuter 34 (1987)

Frow, Georges L.: *The Edison Disc Phonographs and the Diamond Discs.* Sevenoaks, Kent 1982

Frow, Georges L. / Sefl, Albert F.: *The Edison Cylinder Phonographs.* Sevenoaks, Kent 1978

50 Jahre Carl Lindström GmbH. Köln 1954

Für Augen und Ohren. Von der Spieluhr zum akustischen Environment. (cat.) Akademie der Künste, Berlin 1980

Für Augen und Ohren. (Magazin) Berliner Musiktage, Berlin 1980

Futurismo & Futurismi. (cat.) Palazzo Grassi, Venice 1986

Gaisberg, Fred W.: *The Music Goes Round.* New York 1942

Gaisberg, Fred W.: *Music on Record.* London 1947

Gammond, Peter / Horricks, Raymond (ed.): *The Music Goes Round and Round.* London 1980

Garlick, Lewis: *The graphic arts and the record industry.* In: Journal of the Audio Engineering Society 25 (1977)

Gelatt, Roland: *The Fabulous Phonograph. The Story of the Gramophone from Tin Foil to High Fidelity.* London 1956

Gilotaux, Pierre: *Les disques.* Paris 1971

Goldman, Frank / Hiltscher, Klaus: *The Gimmix Book of Records.* Zürich 1981

Gould, Glenn: *The Glenn Gould Reader.* New York 1984

Grayson, John (ed.): *Sound Sculpture. A collection of essays by artists surveying the techniques; applications; and future directions of sound sculpture.* Vancouver 1975

Greenfield, William: *For Singles only.* In: Print 5 (1981)

Griffiths, Paul: *Modern Music. The avantgarde since 1945.* New York 1981

Gronostay, Walter: *Die Schallplatte im kulturellen Leben unserer Zeit.* In: Kestenberg, Leo (ed.): *Kunst und Technik.* Berlin 1930

Große, Guenter: *Von der Edisonwalze zur Stereoplatte. Die Geschichte der Schallplatte.* Berlin 1981

Grundbacher, François: *Plattenhüllen - Die Kunst, Musik zu zeigen.* In: Du, Mai 1981

Günther, Marianne: *Rund um die Schallplatte.* Leipzig 1980

Haas, Walter: *Das Jahrhundert der Schallplatte.* Bielefeld 1977

Haas, Walter / Klever, Ulrich: *Schallplattenbrevier.* Frankfurt a.M. 1958

Haas, Walter / Klever, Ulrich: *Die Stimme seines Herrn. Eine Geschichte der Schallplatte.* Frankfurt a.M. 1959

Hast Du Töne. (cat.) Städtisches Museum Abteiberg, Mönchengladbach 1983

Heissenbüttel, Helmut: *Die Schallplatte als Mittel historisches Bewußtsein zu gewinnen.* In: Merkur 6 (1974)

Heißenbüttel, Helmut: *Der Tradition den Rücken kehren.* In: K-Kunstzeitschrift 1 (1985)

Herdeg, Walter (ed.): *Graphic record covers.* Zürich (1974)

High Fidelity und Stereophonie - ihr Platz und Rang im Musikleben. Symposion auf der "hifi 70" Düsseldorf. Karlsruhe 1971 (= Schriftenreihe "Musik und Gesellschaft" 10/11)

Hirsch, Hans: *Schallplatten zwischen Kunst und Kommerz.* Wilhelmshaven 1987

Hoffmann, Justin: *Maler als Musiker.* In: Wolkenkratzer Art Journal 11 (1986)

Images 33 tours. (cat.) Musée d'art et d'histoire, Genève 1981

Jüttemann, Herbert: *Phonographen und Grammophone.* Braunschweig 1979

Jungermann, Jimmy: *Schallplatten, mein Hobby.* Stuttgart 1958

Jungk, Klaus: *Musik im technischen Zeitalter. Von der Edison-Walze zur Bildplatte.* Berlin 1971

Kagel, Mauricio: *Theatrum Instrumentorum.* (cat.) Kölnischer Kunstverein, Köln 1975

Kagel, Mauricio: *Der Umweg zur Höheren Subfidelität.* In: Interfunktionen 4 (1970)

Kellein, Thomas: *"Fröhliche Wissenschaft". Das Archiv Sohm.* (cat.) Staatsgalerie Stuttgart, 1987

Kesting, Jürgen: *Die wiedergefundene Zeit.* In: Melos 2 (1977)

Kittler, Friedrich: *Grammophon, Film, Typewriter.* Berlin 1986

Klangmaschinen. (cat.) Dornbirn, Schaan 1984

Kluth, Heinrich: *Jeder sein eigener Schallplattenfabrikant.* Berlin 1932

Knížák, Milan: *Unvollständige Dokumentation. Some Documentary 1961 - 1979.* Berlin 1980

Køpcke, Arthur: *Bilder und Stücke.* (cat.) daadgalerie Berlin, Museum am Ostwall Dortmund, 1987/88

Kolleritsch, Otto (ed.): *Der musikalische Futurismus.* Graz 1976

Kostelanetz, Richard (ed.): *John Cage.* New York, Washington 1970

Kroll, Erwin: *Darf man die Schallplatte beliebig schnell laufen lassen?* In: Skizzen 1 (1938)

Leibowitz, Alan: *The record collector's handbook.* New York 1980

Lothar, Rudolph: *Die Sprechmaschine. Ein technisch-aesthetischer Versuch.* Leipzig 1924

Le Magasin du Phonographe. 100 ans de Phonographe. (cat.) Passage 44, Bruxelles 1978

Martin, George (ed.): *Making Music. The Guide to Writing, Performing & Recording.* London 1983

Marty, Daniel: *Grammophone. Geschichte in Bildern.* Karlsruhe 1981

Marvellous Music Machines. (cat.) Art Gallery, Cobourg, Ontario 1977

Mayer, Hugo: *Discjockey.* Frankfurt a.M. 1979

McLuhan, Marshall: *Understanding Media.* New York 1964

Meltzer, R.: *The Aesthetics of Rock.* New York 1970

Metzger, Heinz-Klaus: *Über Schallquellen.* In: H.-K.M.: *Musik wozu. Literatur zu Noten.* Frankfurt a.M. 1980

Moholy-Nagy, Laszlo: *Malerei Fotografie Film.* Mainz 1967 (= Neue Bauhausbücher)

Moholy-Nagy, Laszlo: *Neue Gestaltung in der Musik. Möglichkeiten des Grammophons.* In: Der Sturm 7 (1923)

Moholy-Nagy, Laszlo: *Produktion - Reproduktion.* In: De Stijl 7 (1922)

Molloy, Edward (ed.): *High fidelity sound reproduction.* London 1959

Moore, Jerrold Northrop: *A Voice in Time. The Gramophone of Fred Gaisberg 1873-1951.* London 1976

Multiples. Ein Versuch die Entwicklung des Auflagenobjektes darzustellen. An Attempt to present the Development of the Object Edition. (cat.) Neuer Berliner Kunstverein, Berlin 1974

Murrells, Joseph: *The Book of Golden Discs.* London 1974

m.u.(z.i.e.k.)². Zweitschrift 8 (1981)

Musik und Dichtung. 50 Jahre Deutsche Urheberrechtsgesellschaft. München 1953

Mynona (= Salomo Friedländer): *Goethe spricht in den Phonographen.* In: M.: *Rosa, die schöne Schutzmannsfrau und andere Grotesken.* Zürich 1965

Neal, Charles: *Tape Delay.* Harrow, Middx. 1987

Nesper, Eugen: *Nimm Schallplatten selber auf! Eine Anleitung zur Selbstherstellung von Schallplatten.* Stuttgart (1939)

Nesper, Eugen: *Die Schallplatte.* Berlin 1930

Nyman, Michael: *Experimental music. Cage and beyond.* New York 1974

O'Connell, Charles: *The other side of the record.* Westport, Conn. 1970

On the Wall / On the Air: Artists Make Noise. (cat.) Massachusetts 1985

Paik, Nam June: *Werke 1964 - 1976.* (cat.) Kölnischer Kunstverein, Köln 1976/77

Parzer-Mühlbacher, Alfred: *Die modernen Sprechmaschinen, deren Behandlung und Anwendung.* Wien, Pest, Leipzig 1902

Pauli, Hansjörg / Wünsche, Dagmar (ed.): *Hermann Scherchen. Musiker 1891-1966.* Berlin 1986

Peyser, Joan: *The New Music. The Sense Behind the Sound.* New York 1970

Phonographik. (cat.) Museum für Kunst und Gewerbe Hamburg, 1987

Phonographische Zeitschrift (ed.): *Die Sprechmaschinen.* Berlin 1908

Pickett, A.G. / Lemcoe, M.M.: *Preservation and Storage of Sound Recordings.* Washington 1959

Plattencover. Beiträge zur gesellschaftlichen Funktion von Rockmusik am Beispiel ihrer Verpackung. (cat.) Galerie 70, Berlin 1977

Prieberg, Fred K.: *Musica ex machina. Über das Verhältnis von Musik und Technik.* Berlin, Frankfurt a.M., Wien 1960

Proudfoot, Christopher: *Grammophone und Phonographen.* München 1981

Proudfoot, Christopher: *100 Years of Recorded Sound.* London 1977

Raum Zeit Stille. (cat.) Kölnischer Kunstverein, Köln 1985

Read, Oliver / Welch, Walter L.: *From Tin Foil to Stereo.* Indianapolis 1959

The Record as Artwork from Futurism to Conceptual Art. The Collection of Germano Celant. (cat.) The Fort Worth Art Museum, Fort Worth, Texas 1977/78

ReDEFINING THE OBJECT. (cat.) University Art Galleries, Wright State University Dayton, Ohio 1988

Reichardt, Robert: *Die Schallplatte als kulturelles und ökonomisches Phänomen.* Zürich 1962

Rhein, Eduard: *100 Jahre Schallplatte. Vom Phonographen über die Laser-Disc - wohin ?* Berlin 1987 (= Berliner Forum 2/87)

Riess, Curt: *Knaurs Weltgeschichte der Schallplatte.* Zürich 1966

Rilke, Rainer Maria: *Ur-Geräusch.* In: R.M.R.: *Von Kunst-Dingen. Kritische Schriften. Dichterische Bekenntnisse.* Leipzig, Weimar 1981

Rockwell, John: *All American Music. Composition in the Late Twentieth Century.* New York 1983

Roth, Dieter: *3 vorläufige Listen, zusammengestellt von Barbara Wien.* Basel 1987

Roth, Dieter: *Ladenhüter.* (cat.) Reinhard Onnasch Ausstellungen, Berlin 1983

Royal Scottish Museum, Edinburgh (ed.): *Phonographs & Gramophones.* Edinburgh 1977

Russolo: *Die Geräuschkunst 1913 - 1931.* (cat.) Museum Bochum, Kunstsammlung. Bochum 1985/86

Sacher, Reinhard Josef: *Musik als Theater. Tendenzen zur Grenzüberschreitung in der Musik von 1958 bis 1968.* Regensburg 1985

Schafer, Murray: *The Tuning of the World.* Toronto, New York 1977

Schallplattenhüllen. Funktion und Bildwelten. (cat.) Neuer Berliner Kunstverein, Berlin 1978

Schellmann, Jörg / Klüser, Bernd (ed.): *Joseph Beuys. Multiples.* München, New York 1985[6]

Scheugl, Hans / Schmidt jr., Ernst: *Eine Subgeschichte des Films. Lexikon des Avantgarde-, Experimental- und Undergroundfilms.* 2 vols. Frankfurt a.M. 1974

Schmitz, Martina: *Album Cover. Geschichte und Ästhetik einer Schallplattenverpackung in den USA nach 1940.* Köln 1985

Scholz, Christian: *Untersuchungen zur Geschichte und Typologie der Lautpoesie.* 3 vols. Obermichelbach 1989

Schulz-Köhn, Dietrich: *Die Schallplatte auf dem Weltmarkt.* Berlin 1940

Schwarz, Arturo: *The Complete Works of Marcel Duchamp.* London 1969

Section son. 13° Biennale de Paris. (cat.) Paris 1985

Sehen um zu Hören. Objekte & Konzerte zur visuellen Musik der 60er Jahre. (cat.) Städtische Kunsthalle Düsseldorf, 1975

Seymour, Henry: *The Reproduction of Sound.* London 1918

Sieber, Ernst et al.: *Schallplattenfibel.* Leipzig 1958

Sievers, Heinrich: *Kunst und Kitsch auf Schallplattenhüllen.* In: Neue Zeitschrift für Musik 5 (1959)

Sievers, Heinrich: *Musikgeschichtliche Aufgaben der Schallplatten.* In: Neue Zeitschrift für Musik 5 (1959)

Silbermann, Alphons: *Die Maschinen sprechen. Aphorismen über das Verhältnis von Schallplatte und Gesellschaft.* In: Fono forum 4 (1967)

Silbermann, Alphons: *Schallplatte und Gesellschaft.* Gütersloh 1963

Sonorità Prospettiche. Suono / Ambiente / Immagine. (cat.) Sala comunale d'arte contemporanea. Rimini 1982

Sound. An Exhibition of Sound Sculpture, Instrument-Building and Acoustically Tuned Spaces. (cat.) Institute of Contemporary Art, Los Angeles 1979

Sound / Art. (cat.) The Sculpture Center, New York; BACA/DCC Gallery Brooklyn, New York 1983

Sound / Vision. (cat.) Plymouth Arts Center, Spacex Gallery, Exeter 1985

Soundings. (cat.) Neuberger Museum, Purchase 1981

Speck, Reiner: *Beuys und Musik.* In: *Bücher Bilder Objekte aus der Sammlung Reiner Speck.* (cat.) Museum Haus Lange und Haus Esters, Krefeld 1983

Spieluhr - Schallplatte - Rundfunk, eine historische Entwicklung. (cat.) Historisches Museum, Hannover 1968

Strawinsky, Igor: *Meine Stellung zur Schallplatte.* In: Kultur und Schallplatte 9 (1930)

Streitobjekt Schallplatte. Ein Kulturträger im Spiegel der Meinungen - hundert Jahre nach Erfindung der Phonographie. Wiesbaden 1978 (= Schriftenreihe der Deutschen Phono-Akademie e.V. Hamburg)

Stuckenschmidt, Hans Heinz: *Die Mechanisierung der Musik.* In: H.H.St.: *Die Musik eines halben Jahrhunderts. 1925 - 1975. Essay und Kritik.* München, Zürich 1976

Stuckenschmidt, Hans Heinz: *Musik am Bauhaus.* Bauhaus-Archiv Berlin, 1978/79

Stuckenschmidt, Hans Heinz: *Stereophonie?* In: H.H.St.: *Die Musik eines halben Jahrhunderts. 1925-1975. Essay und Kritik.* München, Zürich 1976

Sumner, Melody / Burch, Kathleen / Sumner, Michael: *The guests go in to supper. John Cage, Robert Ashley, Yoko Ono, Laurie Anderson, Charles Amirkhanian, Michael Peppe, K. Atchley.* Oakland / San Francisco, California 1986

Sutaner, Hans: *Schallplatte und Tonband.* Leipzig 1954

Technik, Wirtschaft und Ästhetik der Schallplatte. Symposion auf der "hifi '68 Düsseldorf". Karlsruhe 1970 (= Musik und Gesellschaft 7/8)

Theweleit, Klaus: *buch der könige. orpheus ~~und~~ eurydike.* Basel, Frankfurt a.M. 1988

A Tour of the World's Records Markets. Hayes, Middlesex (1967)

Übrigens sterben immer die anderen. Marcel Duchamp und die Avantgarde seit 1950. (cat.) Museum Ludwig, Köln 1988

Valentin, Karl: *Im Schallplattenladen.* In: Schulte, Michael (ed.): *Alles von Karl Valentin.* München 1978

Vom Klang der Bilder. Die Musik in der Kunst des 20. Jahrhunderts. (cat.) Staatsgalerie Stuttgart, 1985

Waldinger, Karl-Georg: *Semiotische Analyse eines Popmusik-Covers.* Ratingen 1975

Weidemann, Kurt (ed.): *Book Jackets & Record Sleeves.* Stuttgart 1969

Zeller, Hans Rudolf: *Medienkompositionen nach Cage.* In: *John Cage.* Musik-Konzepte Sonderband, April 1978

Zeppenfeld, Werner: *Tonträger in der Bundesrepublik Deutschland. Anatomie eines medialen Massenmarktes.* Bochum 1979

Martin Kippenberger

Lenders

Fritz Balthaus, Berlin
Claus van Bebber, Kalkar
Eva Beuys-Wurmbach, Düsseldorf
René Block, Berlin
Claus Böhmler, Hamburg
Christian Boltanski, Paris
Christian Borngräber, Berlin
Monika Brehmer, Berlin
John Cage, New York
Henning Christiansen, Askeby
Hanne Darboven, Hamburg
Braco Dimitrijević, Paris
Werner Durand, Berlin
Karl-Heinz Eckert, Berlin
Ricarda Fischer, Berlin
M. und R. Fricke, Düsseldorf
gelbe Musik, Berlin
Christiane und Michael Glasmeier, Berlin
Alfred Greisinger, Augsburg
Benny KH Gutmann, Berlin
Dieter Hacker, Berlin
Konrad Heidkamp, Berlin
Klaus Höppner, Berlin
Sibylle Hofter, Oberhausen
Herbert Hossmannn, Hamburg
Thomas Kapielski, Berlin
Manfred Klauß, Berlin
Milan Knížák, Prag
Walther König, Köln
Nils Krüger, Berlin
Guto Lacaz, São Paulo
Peter Lardong, Berlin
Wittwulf Malik, Hamburg
Christian Marclay, New York
Margatow Archiv, Wahlershausen
Cildo Meireles, Rio de Janeiro
Merve Verlag, Berlin
Maurizio Nannucci, Firenze
Piotr Nathan, Berlin
Matthias Osterwold, Berlin
Jes Petersen, Berlin
Jochen Roemer, Berlin
Sarkis, Paris
Dieter Scheyhing, Berlin
Thom Schmidt, Berlin
Stuart Sherman, New York
Hanns Sohm, Markgröningen
Archiv Sohm, Staatsgalerie Stuttgart
Staatliche Museen Preußischer Kulturbesitz - Kunstbibliothek, Berlin
Eva Thomkins, Köln
Technische Universität, Berlin
Wolfgang Till, München
Martin Turner, Hamburg
Timm Ulrichs, Hannover
Ben Vautier, Nice
Barbara Wien, Berlin
Emmett Williams, Berlin
VA Wölfl, Essen
Winfried Wolf, Berlin
Ingve Zakarias, Berlin
Robert Zank, Berlin

Sources of photographs

Alma Art p.83
Anonymous p.85
Rainer Berson p.32
Eva Beuys-Wurmbach p.99(1), 102, 103
René Block p.74, 99
Anno Dittmer p.144(1)
Galleria La Salita, Roma p.217
Steve Gross p.178
Benny KH Gutmann p.143(2)
Emily Harvey p.252(2)
Manfred Montwé p.194
Maurizio Nannucci p.186(1)
Margret Nissen p.38, 39(2) and all other photographs in the compendium which are not mentioned in particular
Karl H. Paulmann p.59-69
Sarkis p.218/219
Gaby Sommer p.273
Stiftung Deutsche Kinemathek, Berlin p.36/37
Gerald Wesclowski p.148(1)
Werner Zellien all colour-photographs and p.11, 12, 13, 14/15, 16/17, 75, 100, 109, 124(1), 127 (1), 130(1), 161(5), 177(1), 179, 186(1), 187, 190(7), 191(3), 197(2), 227, 244(2)
Rikk Zimmerli p.134

Absolut modern sein. Culture technique in Frankreich 1889 - 1937. (cat.) Neue Gesellschaft für Bildende Kunst, Berlin 1986. p.29, 48
Walter Bruch. *Von der Tonwalze zur Bildplatte.* München 1979. p.19(2), 20(2), 21(2), 28, 30, 38, 272
Chaval. *Sie sollten weniger rauchen. Cartoons.* München 1972. p.52
Marcel Duchamp, Richard Hamilton. *The Bride Stripped Bare by Her Bachelors, Even.* London (1980). p.127(1)
Peter Fischli, David Weiss. *Plötzlich diese Übersicht.* Galerie & Edition Stähli, Zürich 1982. p.77
4 Taxis. 6/7 (1980). p.277
50 Jahre Bauhaus. (cat.) Württembergischer Kunstverein, Stuttgart 1968. p.58
50 Jahre Carl Lindström GmbH. Köln 1954. p.26, 28
Suzi Gablik. *Magritte.* München, Wien, Zürich 1971. p.41(1)
Interfunktionen. 4 (1970). p.153-156
Herbert Jüttemann. *Phonographen und Grammophone.* Braunschweig 1979. p.18, 20(1), 23, 27, 35
Klaus Jungk. *Musik im technischen Zeitalter.* Berlin 1971. p.50
G.F. Maffina. *Luigi Russolo e l'arte dei rumori.* Torino 1978. p.34
Laszlo Moholy-Nagy. *Malerei Fotografie Film.* Mainz, Berlin 1967. p.55
Mondrian. (cat.) Staatsgalerie Stuttgart, Haags Gemeentemuseum, The Baltimore Museum of Arts, 1981. p.42
Michael Schulte, Peter Syr (eds.). *Karl Valentins Filme.* München 1978. p.33
Arturo Schwarz. *The Complete Works of Marcel Duchamp.* London 1969. p.41(1)
Kurt Schwitters. *Das literarische Werk.* Friedhelm Lach (ed.). Vol. 1. Köln 1973. p.225

Translators

Carole Boudreault (German → French): Adorno, R. Block, U. Block, Glasmeier, Knížák, Seiffert, Zeller; Chronology
Ed Cantu (German → English): R. Block, U. Block, Moholy-Nagy, Zeller; Chronology, Captions, Compendium
Klaus Ebbeke (English → German): Knížák
John Epstein (German → English): Adorno, Glasmeier (together with Ed Cantu and Oona Smyth), Seiffert
Gina Kehayoff (French → German): Dubuffet
Marlene Kehayoff-Michel (German → French): Moholy-Nagy
Clio Mitchell (French → English): Dubuffet
Oona Smyth (German → English): Glasmeier (together with John Epstein and Ed Cantu)

Broken Music
© 2018 Ursula Block and Michael Glasmeier, Primary Information, DAAD, and gelbe Musik

ISBN: 978-0-9915585-9-9

All works by Jean Dubuffet are © 2018 Artists Rights Society (ARS), New York / ADAGP, Paris, and owned by Fondation Dubuffet, Paris.

Broken Music was originally published by gelbe Musik and Berliner Künstlerprogramm des DAAD in 1989 to accompany an exhibition of the same name.

Editors: Ursula Block and Michael Glasmeier
Editorial and Organizational Assistants: Inge Lindemann, Pauline Schneider, Ute Birk, and Werner Durand

This facsimile edition is published by Primary Information.

Second printing, 2019
Edition of 2,500

Managing Editor, facsimile edition: James Hoff
Managing Designer, facsimile edition: Rick Myers

Primary Information
155 Freeman Street, Ground Floor
Brooklyn, NY 11222
www.primaryinformation.org

Printed by Szaransky Print Company

Primary Information would like to thank Josh Bonati, Daniel Löwenbrück, Justin Luke, Ryan Martin, Fiona McGovern, and Printed Matter.

Primary Information is a 501(c)(3) non-profit organization that receives generous support through grants from the Michael Asher Foundation, the Robert D. Bielecki Foundation, the Greenwich Collection Ltd, the National Endowment for the Arts, the New York City Department of Cultural Affairs in partnership with the City Council, the New York State Council on the Arts with the support of Governor Andrew Cuomo and the New York State Legislature, the Orbit Fund, the Stichting Egress Foundation, The Andy Warhol Foundation for the Visual Arts, the Wilhelm Family Foundation, and individuals worldwide.

Cover: *Broken Music* (1963–79), Milan Knizak
Cover Photograph: Werner Zellien